the skillet

200+ SIMPLER WAYS TO MAKE JUST ABOUT ANYTHING, FROM PERFECT MEALS TO BREADS, DESSERTS, AND MORE

AMERICA'S TEST KITCHEN

Library of Congress Cataloging-in-Publication Data has been applied for.

ISBN 978-1-954210-91-2

AMERICA'S TEST KITCHEN

21 Drydock Avenue, Boston, MA 02210

Printed in Canada

10 9 8 7 6 5 4 3 2 1

Distributed by Penguin Random House Publisher Services

Tel: 800.733.3000

pictured on front cover: Lattice-Topped Chicken Pot Pie with Spring Vegetables (page 83)

pictured on back cover (clockwise from top left): Herbed Roast Pork Loin with Asparagus (page 147), Honey-Rosemary Roast Chicken and Root Vegetables (page 137), Cheesy Stuffed Shells (page 212), Loaded Beef Nachos (page 273), Strawberry-Rhubarb Crisp (page 323), Cast-Iron Pan Pizza (page 164)

Editorial Director, Books: Adam Kowit

Executive Food Editor: Dan Zuccarello

Deputy Food Editor: Stephanie Pixley

Executive Managing Editor: Debra Hudak

Project Editor: Elizabeth Carduff

Senior Editors: Joseph Gitter and Sara Mayer

Test Cooks: Olivia Counter, Carmen Dongo, Hannah Fenton, Laila Ibrahim, José Maldonado, and David Yu

Assistant Editor: Julia Arwine

Design Director: Lindsey Timko Chandler

Associate Art Director and Designer: Molly Gillespie

Associate Art Director: Kylie Alexander

Photography Director: Julie Bozzo Cote

Senior Photography Producer: Meredith Mulcahy

Senior Staff Photographers: Steve Klise and Daniel J. van Ackere

Staff Photographer: Kritsada Panichgul

Additional Photography: Joseph Keller and Carl Tremblay

Food Styling: Joy Howard, Sheila Jarnes, Catrine Kelty, Chantal Lambeth, Gina McCreadie, Kendra McNight, Ashley Moore, Christie Morrison, Marie Piraino, Elle Simone Scott, Kendra Smith, and Sally Staub

Project Manager, Books: Katie Kimmerer

Senior Print Production Specialist: Lauren Robbins

Production and Imaging Coordinator: Amanda Yong

Production and Imaging Specialist: Tricia Neumyer

Production and Imaging Assistant: Chloe Petraske

Copy Editor: Deri Reed

Proofreader: Vicki Rowland

Indexer: Elizabeth Parson

Chief Executive Officer: Dan Suratt

Chief Creative Officer: Jack Bishop

Executive Editorial Directors: Julia Collin Davison and Bridget Lancaster

Senior Director, Book Sales: Emily Logan

contents

Welcome to America's Test Kitchen

This book has been tested, written, and edited by the folks at America's Test Kitchen, where curious cooks become confident cooks. Located in Boston's Seaport District in the historic Innovation and Design Building, it features 15,000 square feet of kitchen space including multiple photography and video studios. It is the home of *Cook's Illustrated* magazine and *Cook's Country* magazine and is the workday destination for more than 60 test cooks, editors, and cookware specialists. Our mission is to empower and inspire confidence, community, and creativity in the kitchen.

We start the process of testing a recipe with a complete lack of preconceptions, which means that we accept no claim, no technique, and no recipe at face value. We simply assemble as many variations as possible, test a half-dozen of the most promising, and taste the results blind. We then construct our own recipe and continue to test it, varying ingredients, techniques, and cooking times until we reach a consensus. As we like to say in the test kitchen, "We make the mistakes so you don't have to." The result, we hope, is the best version of a particular recipe, but we realize that only you can be the final judge of our success (or failure). We use the same rigorous approach when we test equipment and taste ingredients.

All of this would not be possible without a belief that good cooking, much like good music, is based on a foundation of objective technique. Some people like spicy foods and others don't, but there is a right way to sauté, there is a best way to cook a pot roast, and there are measurable scientific principles involved in producing perfectly beaten, stable egg whites. Our ultimate goal is to investigate the fundamental principles of cooking to give you the techniques, tools, and ingredients you need to become a better cook. It is as simple as that.

To see what goes on behind the scenes at America's Test Kitchen, check out our social media channels for kitchen snapshots, exclusive content, video tips, and much more. You can watch us work (in our actual test kitchen) by tuning in to *America's Test Kitchen* or *Cook's Country* on public television or on our websites. Listen to *Proof* (AmericasTestKitchen.com/podcasts) to hear engaging, complex stories about people and food. Want to hone your cooking skills or finally learn how to bake—with an America's Test Kitchen test cook? Enroll in one of our online cooking classes.

However you choose to visit us, we welcome you into our kitchen, where you can stand by our side as we test our way to the best recipes in America.

- facebook.com/AmericasTestKitchen
- instagram.com/TestKitchen
- youtube.com/AmericasTestKitchen
- tiktok.com/@TestKitchen
- x.com/TestKitchen
- pinterest.com/TestKitchen

AmericasTestKitchen.com

CooksIllustrated.com

CooksCountry.com

OnlineCookingSchool.com

Join Our Community of Recipe Testers

Our recipe testers provide valuable feedback on recipes under development by ensuring that they are foolproof in home kitchens. Help the America's Test Kitchen book team investigate the how and why behind successful recipes from your home kitchen.

dive into the world of skillets

Crispy Gnocchi with Shredded Brussels Sprouts and Gorgonzola (page 211)

Introduction

The skillet is the unicorn of the kitchen, a pan that is often underestimated but should be highly valued. We believe that once you start cooking from this book you will look at skillets with new eyes and admiration for all they can do. Just for starters, a skillet can serve as a pasta pot, a Dutch oven, a casserole dish, a griddle, and a cake pan; plus, it does all the things you probably normally use it for masterfully, like making eggs of every sort, cooking pancakes, searing meat and chicken, stir-frying, sautéing, and more.

Well-made skillets are a valuable commodity in your kitchen, and the best ones, the brands and types we value most in the test kitchen, are beautiful, feel good in your hands, do what they are crafted to do, and many of them will last a lifetime. How far you go in the skillet world is up to you. Every recipe in this book includes a Sizing Up Your Skillet feature that highlights the skillets that will work with that particular recipe, indicates which skillet we prefer and why, and lists alternates we find acceptable along with anything you must do differently when using them.

Every recipe had to earn its place in this book, and many reveal surprising and innovative techniques. Like sautéed chicken breasts, where a few tricks ensure evenly cooked and moist chicken, and pan-seared steaks and thick-cut pork chops, which are among several recipes that use a cold sear method for perfectly cooked meat (and fish too). *The Skillet* is organized largely in chapters built around cooking techniques. In each chapter, core recipes, marked Technique 101, lay out visually how to pan-roast chicken, butter-braise steak, simmer pasta, and other skillet fundamentals. Oftentimes recipes that follow use the technique, so you can see how mastering it will make you a better cook. Vegetables get this treatment, too, and we suspect these recipes will change how you make some favorites, like our braised asparagus that delivers spears with more complex flavor than high-heat roasting. Also, consider sautéed mushrooms: Our recipe steams the mushrooms in water in a skillet first, a counter-intuitive method that yields an indulgent but easy side dish even on a weeknight.

There are many advantages to skillet cooking. It is often easier and more efficient because you use just one pan, sometimes rotating ingredients in and out of the pan, as with our simple stovetop macaroni and cheese (no béchamel, no custard, no boiling the pasta separately). And our steak Caesar salad takes the classic to a new level by using the skillet for both the croutons and the steak. Delicious! And if you need a quick back-pocket pasta recipe, check out our easy method for cooking pasta right in the skillet after building a simple sauce and adding water. The master recipe is for pasta with a simple tomato sauce and includes variations to jazz it up if you want. It's a pantry recipe and a great one to memorize. For a classic comfort food that usually requires a lot of work, see our two novel approaches to chicken pot pie: Both boast a creamy rich sauce infused with aromatics and herbs and packed with moist chunks of chicken; one has a topping made with torn store-bought croissants and the other a fancy, but easy-to-make, lattice top.

You can travel the world with recipes you make in your skillet, too, like India's beloved celebratory chicken biryani, simplified to be made in a skillet; Shanghai-style scallion oil noodles; and knafeh, a rich pastry popular in the Middle East (our version is modeled after one prevalent in Palestine). And then there is okonomiyaki, a savory filled pancake that is a sought-after griddled street food in Japan that we re-create using a skillet.

This book will also help you brush up on your cooking skills for many simple things. Take fried eggs. Do you just throw them in a skillet with some butter and call it a day? Our method includes preheating the pan, using two fats, covering the pan after adding the eggs, and finishing them off the heat. Now you can have diner-style eggs at home whenever you want.

Even breads and desserts can be easier when made in a skillet, as they take on burnished crusts and can often be brought warm to the table while still in the pan, whether it's cornbread, a fudgy cast-iron brownie, or fruit crisp.

In the pages that follow, we set the stage for all you need to understand about skillets to get started on your own skillet cooking adventures. Enjoy!

Skillet Cooking 101

You don't need a lot of skillets to cook successfully, but you do need more than just one. To cover your bases, you should have a stainless-steel skillet and a nonstick skillet (of which there are many choices). With these two skillets in hand, you'll be able to make just about any skillet recipe. That said, in the test kitchen, everyone has their favorites, and our testing gurus disagree about their favorites. One chooses stainless as her "desert island skillet" because it's never going to wear out or rust, it's roomy, and it heats evenly. Another chooses carbon steel because it sears beautifully but is lighter than cast iron and can go on the stove, on the grill, or in the oven.

In this book, the recipes use skillets made from a variety of materials, including stainless steel, carbon steel, nonstick coated, traditional cast iron, and enameled cast iron. Throughout the book we mostly use 12-inch skillets, but there are some times when a 10-inch skillet is needed, both to make one of our recipe variations that serve just two, or for a recipe that just works better in a smaller skillet, like Better Hash Browns (page 253). Just a few use an 8-inch skillet. In the pages that follow, you will find detailed information about each of these skillets and information on the test kitchen's picks for the best options and why.

What Ovensafe Means and Why You Should Care

It is important to have skillets that are ovensafe. Why? Because many recipes use the pan-roasting technique, which means that you start cooking on the stovetop and finish in the oven, like our Pan-Roasted Fish Fillets (page 148). If you have a flimsy skillet or one with a plastic handle, it is a nonstarter for such recipes because the handle may burn and the skillet itself may not be safe at higher oven temperatures. For instance, there are recipes where we are braising or baking in the oven, like Buffalo Chicken Dip with Spicy Monkey Bread (page 270) and Peach–Cornmeal Upside-Down Cake (page 317). Not to mention those like Cast-Iron Pan Pizza (page 164), where the skillet goes into a very hot oven, and Week-night Roast Chicken (page 134), where you preheat the skillet in the oven before adding a whole chicken. Being ovensafe is particularly important for traditional nonstick skillets, as the coating is the biggest limiting factor, followed by the material used to construct the handle. Seek out a nonstick skillet that is rated to at least 400 degrees. Note that nonstick skillets are not broiler safe.

What's the Difference Between a Skillet and a Sauté Pan?

Skillets and sauté pans have similar-size flat, broad cooking surfaces. But a sauté pan has straight high sides instead of the low sloped sides that are the hallmark of a skillet. They can be used for many of the same tasks, but there are specific times we reach for one or the other. We use a skillet when frying eggs, sautéing vegetables, searing meat, and making a pan sauce. A skillet's low walls encourage evaporation and make it easier to slide out delicate foods. The walls of sauté pans are high enough to make them useful for frying and help to corral splatters, contain food, and prevent spills, but low enough that it's easy to reach in with tongs. And their larger capacity makes them good when making larger braises.

Sauté Pan

Skillet

Wash by Hand

Straight talk: Don't put your good cookware in the dishwasher. Its high heat and harsh detergents can corrode metal and dry out the surface of your pans—even stainless-steel ones. Dishwasher detergent will also break down the seasoning on your cast-iron and carbon-steel pans. We know no one loves washing dishes by hand, but when it comes to the longevity and performance of your skillets, it really is worth it to roll up your sleeves and do it yourself.

To get burnt-on food off your pans, just fill the pan with water and set it to a simmer. Soon the hot water will rehydrate the burnt food and most of it will begin to lift right off. Any remaining residue should come off with a few passes of a soft sponge. For more specific information on cleaning cast iron, see page 11.

MANAGING HEAT LEVELS ON AN ELECTRIC STOVE

Electric stoves can be slow to respond to a cook's commands. This can pose a problem both with our cold-searing method, which requires an initial blast of high heat followed by a quick turndown to medium heat, as well as other recipes where the heat needs to be quickly lowered. If using an electric stovetop, preheat a second burner to medium heat while the food cooks on high heat. After the initial sear, transfer the pan to the medium-heat burner and continue cooking.

Skillet Accessories

There are a few items that will come in especially handy when using a skillet. First, there are spatulas to consider. A single spatula can cover all your turning and flipping needs, but it might not be the kind you think: It's a fish spatula. While the name makes it sound like it does only one thing, we think these spatulas are actually the best all-purpose turners out there and prefer them to conventional turners for many reasons. Their long, moderately flexible heads securely support large food items and can scoot under foods easily; and their narrow heads are easier to maneuver in tight spaces. Our favorite is the **Wüsthof Gourmet 7" Slotted Fish Spatula**. For non-stick surfaces, we like the **Matfer Bourgeat Exoglass Pelton Spatula**. We recommend that you buy two of each because there are many instances when you need two, such as for flipping salmon and other fish fillets. Tongs are also an essential tool, and we prefer the precision and control of tongs with uncoated metal pincers because coated pincers tend to be thicker and a little less precise. That said, coated pincers are safe to use with nonstick cookware, so if you often cook with nonstick pots and pans they might be the right choice for you. **OXO Good Grips** makes these tongs in both sizes, both with and without coated pincers.

A large spatula is one of the busiest tools in any kitchen and certainly comes in handy when skillet cooking, so we recommend that you have at least two, and we prefer silicone. Our winner is **Di Oro Living Seamless Silicone Spatula-Large**. It is firm enough to handle both scraping and scooping and fits neatly into tight corners.

A chain-mail scrubber can be used when cleaning a superdirty traditional cast-iron pan with stuck-on food. Its linked steel rings effortlessly lift away stuck-on bits without damaging the pan's finish. That said, it can be a bit too harsh for routine cleaning. We like the **Knapp Made Small Ring CM Scrubber**. Don't use this on enamel or stainless steel. Skillet handles come in handy for cast-iron skillets, whose handles can get very, very hot. Our winner is the **Nokona Leather Handle Mitt**. We do not advise using it—or any other handle cover—continuously while cooking, as it will become hot.

And finally, don't overlook the humble wooden spoon. This will be your ally when scraping up that valuable fond off the bottom of your skillet after searing meat or chicken and it has so many other uses as well, so stock up. The **Jonathan's Spoons Spootle** is our favorite.

MY SKILLET DIDN'T COME WITH A LID, NOW WHAT?

It still baffles us that so many skillets are sold without a matching lid. They come in handy for steaming, containing splatters, and keeping food warm. We recommend the **Lodge 12-inch Tempered Glass Cover** for all 12-inch skillets. For smaller skillets we recommend that you try using lids you already have at home to fit the skillets you have before spending money on a separate lid.

Skillet by Skillet
What You Need to Know

Stainless-Steel Skillets
THE CHAMPION OF FOND

Braised Chicken Thighs with Fennel,
Chickpeas, and Apricots (page 79)

Perfect searing, flavorful sauces, and stove-to-oven versatility make stainless-steel skillets essential to home kitchens. They are, without a doubt, the unflashy workhorses of the skillet world. If you want those flavorful browned bits to form on the bottom of your skillet to either be used to develop a pan sauce or to be stirred back into the dish, a stainless steel skillet is the one to use. For instance, we call for a 12-inch stainless-steel skillet when making Smothered Pork Chops (page 94), as it provides enough space for braising four bone-in pork chops and allows for good fond development, ensuring that the trademark sauce is flavorful. In fact, it is a go-to choice for many of the recipes in this book.

How to Clean Stainless Steel

When oil gets too hot, it breaks down into its components (glycerol and free fatty acids), which then scorch and form really sticky residues on a stainless skillet especially. The residue itself forms a barrier that prevents soap from getting to the surface of the skillet and dislodging the mess. As a result, dish soap is pretty much rendered powerless. **Bar Keepers Friend**, which contains surfactant, oxalic acid, and a mineral abrasive, can break down and physically scrape away grease and will render your skillet spotless with just a little effort.

Why Does My Food Always Stick?

Some sticking is actually desirable when you're cooking with stainless steel or copper. If you are cooking especially delicate foods, such as eggs or fish, opt for nonstick or well-seasoned standard cast iron or carbon steel. Otherwise, accept that a little bit of sticking is a normal part of the process, although you can minimize it by fully preheating the pan and using plenty of fat.

Once food has browned, it should release fairly easily.

If you preheat your pan and cook with fat and your food is still sticking more than you want, you may need just a little patience. When meat is first added to a pan, sulfur atoms in the protein react with metal atoms in the pan, forming a strong chemical bond that fuses the meat to the pan. Once the meat has formed a brown crispy crust, the links between the protein and metal loosen, allowing the protein to release much more cleanly than if you force it before it is ready.

The Anatomy of a Stainless-Steel Skillet

Cool, Grippy Metal Handle
Doesn't heat up when a skillet is in use; angled shape and/or brushed steel surface provides good grip; silicone-free, so skillet can move easily from stovetop to oven.

Broad Cooking Surface
Fits food without crowding, so it browns rather than steams.

Low, Flared Sides
Help moisture evaporate so that food can brown; make it easy to reach in with a spatula or tongs.

The Best Stainless-Steel Skillets

Our favorite stainless-steel skillet is the **All-Clad D3 Stainless 12" Fry Pan with Lid** and has been for several decades. Its fully clad construction helps it heat responsively and brown evenly. Its broad cooking surface provides ample room for searing and sautéing, and gently flaring sides allow moisture to evaporate quickly and let you pour from the pan easily. On the whole, the skillet is relatively lightweight and sturdy but well-balanced. It has a well-designed stay-cool handle, so it's especially easy to lift and maneuver. And while it's not cheap, it's durable—a worthy investment for home cooks.

If you'd like a smaller version of our favorite, we also recommend **All-Clad's 10-inch** and **8-inch** models. The 10-inch skillet comes in handy when cooking for two in scaled-down versions of our recipes as well as some full-scale recipes, and the 8-inch skillet can be used for toasting spices or a small quantity of nuts and more.

So what does fully clad really mean? In fully clad pans the entire body of the pan, rather than just the bottom, is composed of three or more layers of different metals bonded together. In the case of stainless-steel pans, aluminum is typically sandwiched between layers of stainless steel to give you the best of both metals: aluminum's relatively speedy heat conduction modulated by slower transmitting, heat-retaining steel for a pan that heats evenly and holds on to that heat. It's these layers that are known as "ply." We prefer pans with three layers (referred to as "tri-ply") over those with more layers. We've found that pans with more layers are heavier and, depending on the materials of the additional metal, can heat more slowly. And stay away from disk-bottom pans, which have layers of more conductive metal only on the bottom. These are prone to heating unevenly and scorching food near the edges.

COPPER SKILLETS

Copper pans are the bright and dazzling cousins of stainless-steel pans and, like them, excel at cooking evenly and responding quickly to changes in heat, making them a great choice for many everyday cooking tasks. Copper conducts heat 1.5 times faster than aluminum—another benefit of using them. But copper pans can cost a pretty penny and, honestly, their extra agility won't make that much difference in the quality of your cooking—and a good-quality stainless-steel skillet is almost as responsive and requires less care. But what should you know if you are set on having copper pans in your arsenal? They are made in one of two ways, either by sandwiching a highly conductive copper core between layers of nonreactive metal such as stainless steel, or by lining the interior of a solid copper pan with nonreactive stainless steel or tin. Tin-lined pans are easily damaged at temperatures above approximately 450 degrees Fahrenheit. Exposed copper will tarnish if not polished regularly. Our picks? The best 12-inch steel-lined: **Mauviel M'Heritage M'2000Ci Round Frying Pan**. The best 12-inch copper core: **All-Clad Copper Core 5-ply Bonded Fry Pan**.

Nonstick Skillets
RELIABLE OPTION FOR A CLEAN RELEASE

Rustic Bread Stuffing
(page 296)

Seventy percent of the skillets sold in the US are traditional nonstick skillets. There are multiple pans that qualify as nonstick because of their coatings, including seasoned carbon-steel skillets (see page 13), seasoned traditional cast-iron skillets (page 10), and ceramic skillets (opposite). For some recipes, there is just no other option other than a skillet with a nonstick coating. For instance, for the recipes where we use the cold-sear method (page 16), the key to the technique is to avoid using oil, so the nonstick surface is critical.

Traditional nonstick skillets have coatings made with PTFE. Best known by the brand name Teflon, PTFE (polytetrafluoroethylene) belongs to a larger category of chemical compounds called PFAS (per- and polyfluoroalkyl substances), which are responsible for making surfaces slippery and resistant to water and oils. When PTFE coatings are heated above 500 degrees, the coatings begin to break down and release fumes that can be harmful. All PTFE coatings will eventually wear out with use and stop being nonstick, so you will need to replace your nonstick skillet periodically. If you're looking for longevity, you may prefer to purchase a cast-iron or carbon-steel skillet instead.

That said, there are a few things you can and should do to use your nonstick cookware safely, minimizing the risk that the PFAS in their coatings will affect you.

Don't Use Metal Utensils on Them Metal spatulas and spoons can scratch the nonstick coating, potentially making it easier for PFAS to migrate out.

Don't Broil or Use Nonstick Skillets at Temperatures Above 500 Degrees Studies have shown that high temperatures can cause nonstick coatings to degrade and emit toxic fumes.

Don't Heat an Empty Skillet An empty skillet gets hotter than one with food in it, increasing your risk of toxic fumes. As a result, we always recommend heating any nonstick skillet with oil or butter in it, as these fats smoke at lower temperatures (usually around 350 or 400 degrees, depending on the type of fat), and provide a visual cue that the pan is getting too hot.

The Best Nonstick Skillets

Our best buy nonstick skillet is the **T-fal Professional Non-Stick Frypan**. This pan has a spacious and slippery surface, is lightweight and easy to handle, and induction compatible. It is ovensafe to 400 degrees. Our favorite high-end induction-compatible model is the **All-Clad Stainless 12" Nonstick Fry Pan**. It is more expensive because it is fully clad. It is heavier and a bit less comfortable to maneuver, but it is ovensafe to 500 degrees. Given that nonstick skillets have to be periodically replaced, you may want to really consider whether you should invest in an expensive one.

Ceramic Skillets
ECO-FRIENDLY ALTERNATIVE TO NONSTICK

Seared Scallops with Broccolini and Browned-Butter Pepper Relish (page 62)

A good ceramic nonstick skillet is an alternative to a traditional nonstick skillet, so whenever we call for nonstick in this book, you can always use a ceramic skillet. Slick and easy to clean, the best ceramic nonstick skillets are ideal for cooking delicate foods such as fish and eggs. And unlike traditional nonstick skillets, ceramic nonstick skillets don't rely on polytetrafluoroethylene (PTFE), commonly known as Teflon, to ensure that their surfaces are slippery—a plus for cooks who are concerned about the health and environmental consequences of this chemical.

There are some trade-offs, though. In general, we've found that ceramic nonstick isn't quite as nonstick or as durable as traditional nonstick and gets even less nonstick and durable over time. Ceramic surfaces are brittle by nature and thus more likely to develop microscopic surface cracks during everyday use than PTFE nonstick coatings are. It's a problem that quickly goes from bad to worse: The rougher a cooking surface becomes, the more likely food is to stick to it, and scrubbing off that stuck-on food can cause further degradation. Another thing to know is that ceramic nonstick skillets typically run hotter than traditional nonstick skillets, so they often brown foods faster. Food may stick slightly and the pan may take a little more effort to clean. For a fairly confident and experienced cook who wants to avoid PTFE, these aren't difficult adjustments to make.

The Best Ceramic Skillet

The winner of our testing was the **GreenPan Valencia Pro Ceramic Nonstick Frypan**, one of only three pans to pass our test of nonstick coating durability. It arrived slick and remained so throughout cooking and abuse tests. It also has a broad cooking surface, gently sloped walls and a comfortable handle. This brand also makes 10- and 8-inch skillets.

Traditional Cast-Iron Skillets
AN AMERICAN CLASSIC WITH UNPARALLELED HEAT RETENTION

Cast-Iron Oven-Fried Chicken
(page 189)

Traditional cast-iron pans are some of the most versatile pieces of cookware you can buy since they work on the stovetop, in the oven, and even on the grill. With plenty of use, a cast-iron skillet's surface becomes naturally nonstick, so even eggs will release easily (as long as you use a little butter or oil). We love cooking in these skillets; they're an essential part of our kitchen. Whether we're searing, frying, baking, braising, or roasting, these pans are incredibly sturdy; they're also naturally nonstick. For instance, we use a traditional cast-iron pan for making Sticky Buns (page 308). Its superior heat retention makes it the ideal vessel for achieving tall cinnamon buns that develop beautiful browning on the bottom, while its slick surface also ensures that the glaze sticks to the buns, not the pan. As you use this pan, its seasoning keeps improving because heated fat molecules link up to form a polymer (essentially a connected grid). This creates a hard, elastic film that bonds to the iron, protecting it from rust and forming a surface layer that easily releases food—and that is endlessly renewable. You can hand down these pans for generations.

Cast iron doesn't heat very evenly because its thermal conductivity, or ability to transfer heat from one part of the metal to another, is very low. What cast iron does do well is hold on to heat: Once a cast-iron pan is hot, it will stay that way much more effectively than a stainless steel (and nonstick) pan will. This makes it ideal for high-heat applications or when you want to get a good char.

Cast Iron and Acidic Ingredients

It is best to avoid cooking wine, tomatoes, and other acidic ingredients in a traditional cast-iron pan because if acidic ingredients are cooked for an extended period of time, trace amounts of molecules from the iron can loosen and leach into the food. Although these minute amounts are not harmful to consume, they may impart unwanted metallic flavors, and the pan's seasoning can be damaged as well.

Preheating Cast-Iron Skillets

In our testing, it became clear that cast iron is a poor conductor of heat and tends to heat unevenly on the stove (and more or less so depending upon the level of heat you use). We found the best way to get relatively even heat without too much work was to preheat the empty pan on the stovetop. For basic sautéing (oil heated until shimmering), you should plan to preheat your skillet over medium heat for 3 minutes. For searing proteins (oil heated until smoking), we recommend preheating the skillet for an additional 2 minutes.

Caring for Traditional Cast-Iron Skillets

These days, almost all traditional cast-iron skillets come preseasoned, and unless you have a skillet with significant damage, you'll almost never need to season one from scratch. Here is how to clean it after every use.

1 Wipe interior surface of still-warm skillet with paper towels to remove any excess food and oil. Rinse under hot running water, scrubbing with nonmetal brush or nonabrasive scrub pad to remove any traces of food. (Use small amount of soap if you like; rinse well.)

2 Dry skillet thoroughly (do not drip-dry), then heat over medium-low heat until all traces of moisture have evaporated. Add ¼ teaspoon oil to 12-inch pan and use paper towels to lightly coat interior surface with oil. Continue to wipe surface with paper towels until it looks dark and smooth and no oil residue remains. Let pan cool completely.

First Aid for a Rusty or Crusty Skillet

If you acquire an old skillet that's rusty and gunky, or maybe someone left yours to soak and you found it covered in rust—don't worry, it's easy to restore. Rust and gunk aren't harmful; just clean them off so you can reseason the pan. Start by scrubbing with steel wool and plenty of soap, just until its surface feels fairly smooth again (no need to be perfect!), then rinse, dry fully, and re-season. Here are two ways that work:

Stovetop Method Add about ½ teaspoon oil, spread with paper towels in very thin coat over pan, inside and out. Heat on medium about two minutes, wiping interior until oil seems gone (excess gets gunky). Traces of rust on towel are normal. Pan may smoke. Turn off heat, cool in place. Repeat if necessary.

Oven Method Heat oven to 500 degrees. Add about ½ teaspoon oil to pan, spread with paper towel, inside and out. Wipe off oil until it seems gone (excess gets gunky). Traces of rust on towel are normal. Invert skillet on oven rack; heat 1 hour. Turn off oven and leave pan to cool completely.

What Oil Should You Use for Seasoning?

You can actually use any oil when seasoning, but the more polyunsaturated the fat, the more readily it will oxidize and polymerize. We have found that flaxseed oil, which oxidizes and polymerizes faster than other vegetable oils, forms a particularly durable seasoning.

The Best Traditional Cast-Iron Skillets

We tested 12-inch preseasoned traditional cast-iron skillets, including artisan pans made by small American companies. While we were able to cook successfully in every skillet, our favorite pans shared certain traits: They were among the heaviest, at around 8 pounds, with sides measuring more than 2 inches tall. The **Smithey Ironware No. 12 Cast-Iron Skillet** is made by a small company in South Carolina. With a smooth, polished interior and a classic shape, it aced all our tests, searing, baking, and browning beautifully and releasing food like a nonstick pan would. But it's expensive, so we also chose a Best Buy: the **Lodge 12-Inch Cast Iron Skillet**, which offers equivalent performance at a bargain price. Its surface felt pebbly right out of the box and was a bit sticky in the beginning, but after a few rounds of cooking it released food like a champ. Both brands make skillets in multiple sizes.

Enameled Cast-Iron Skillets
A REAL LOOKER WITH GREAT HEAT RETENTION

Warm Marinated
Olives (page 258)

Colorful, sturdy, and virtually maintenance-free, enameled cast-iron skillets offer an inviting alternative to traditional cast iron.

They often get lumped in with traditional cast iron. We've been guilty of that ourselves. Sure, both are cast iron, but enameled versions offer a different range of features and cooking options. Like traditional cast iron, these pans have excellent heat retention, so they sear, fry, and braise well, maintaining the heat you want without undesirable temperature dips as food is added or flipped. But unlike traditional cast iron, the enamel coating makes them virtually maintenance-free. You never have to season them, and you can soak, use soap, and scrub as much as you like. Best of all, you can cook almost anything—even acidic foods that need to simmer for a long time—because the enamel seals the cast iron, making the pan rust-proof and nonreactive (unlike traditional cast iron). While both traditional and enameled cast-iron pans are induction-compatible, the smoother enameled bottoms can be a little gentler on glass cooktops (though you should still lift and place heavy pans carefully, rather than dropping or dragging). Finally, their colorful appearance is pretty enough to bring to the table for serving.

The downside? Don't expect enameled cast-iron skillets to be—or become—nonstick. Enamel is a glasslike coating heated to very high temperatures and bonded to the pan's surface. It will not become seasoned as you use it, the way plain cast iron does. While some manufacturers claim their pans will become nonstick with use, in our hands-on testing experience, we have found it not to be the case. Seasoning is oil that has been heated until it polymerizes, meaning that its molecules link, bonding together and to the metal cooking surface of a pan to create a natural, renewable nonstick coating. Enamel prevents the oil from bonding to the surface as successfully as it does to plain metal. As a result, food sticks, and this won't change over time as it does with traditional cast iron.

The Best Enameled Cast-Iron Skillets

Our ATK recommended favorite is **Le Creuset Signature Skillet, 11¾"**. With low, flaring sides; an oversize helper handle; wide pour spouts; a broad, satiny interior; and balanced, moderate weight, this expensive but beautifully made skillet (available in a variety of colors), is a pleasure to cook in. At half its price, the **Viking Enameled Cast Iron 12-Inch Fry Pan** is our Best Buy. Shaped like a traditional cast-iron skillet with straighter, less flared sides, it has small but adequate pour spouts, a broad cooking surface, and a heavier weight—well balanced by large main and helper handles. Unlike most enameled cast iron, it has a glossy enamel finish inside, making it a bit easier to clean, and a matte finish outside, which adds welcome grippiness to its handles. A sturdy, handsome pan, it comes in only charcoal gray.

Carbon-Steel Skillets
THE DARLING OF PROFESSIONAL CHEFS

Pork Potstickers
(page 262)

A carbon-steel skillet is truly a jack of all trades and master of many. And assuming it's well seasoned, it's as slick as nonstick—but naturally so—boasting a supersmooth patina that improves with use. The price is right too. Throughout this book you will see it as an alternate for other skillets, and sometimes the first choice, as with our recipe for Singapore Noodles (page 223), where it stands in for a wok because its relative light weight allows for ease while tossing, and its superior heat retention provides for rapid high-heat cooking.

Carbon steel is an alloy made up of about 1 percent carbon and 99 percent iron. Despite its name, it actually contains a bit less carbon than cast iron. This slightly lower carbon content makes carbon steel less brittle than cast iron. So pans made with it can be thinner and more lightweight. The smooth surface of carbon steel makes it easy to acquire a slick patina of polymerized oil during seasoning. All of this adds up to a pan that is maneuverable, is excellent at searing (like stainless steel), and becomes naturally nonstick over time (like cast iron). Carbon-steel skillets are reactive, so it is best not to use them when wine, tomatoes, or other acidic ingredients are involved.

Seasoning Carbon-Steel Skillets

Carbon-steel skillets often arrive unseasoned. Because they have such a smooth surface, it takes just a single application of oil for a new pan to be slick enough for cooking, but be aware that a new carbon-steel pan may look brown, blotchy, and streaky for months before it builds up a solid patina. The method below is by far the easiest route to proper seasoning. After this, you can start cooking. Further cooking will build on this seasoning. Repeat these steps once if your food sticks the first time you try to cook in the pan.

1 Remove the pan's wax or grease coating, if any, using very hot water, dish soap, and vigorous scrubbing with a bristly brush. Dry the pan, then put it over low heat to finish drying. Add ⅓ cup oil, ⅔ cup salt, and peels from two potatoes (or substitute one sliced onion).

2 Cook over medium heat, occasionally moving peels around pan and up sides to rim, for 8 to 10 minutes. (If using onion, cook for 15 minutes or until onion turns very dark brown and almost burnt.) Discard contents, allow pan to cool, and rinse thoroughly. Dry pan and return it to medium heat to finish drying.

The Best Carbon-Steel Skillets

The best carbon-steel skillets have thick, solid construction and smooth interiors; minimal handle rivets (or none) to trap food; sides that are neither too high or too low; and an ergonomically angled handle. We recommend Mauviel pans as well as pricier options made by Northwest, Smithey, and Blu.

The Maillard Reaction and Fond Power

The process by which browning or caramelizing food produces flavor is known as the Maillard reaction. Just think about tucking into a nicely browned steak, a piece of poultry with deep-mahogany skin, or bread with a honey-brown exterior; here you are reaping the benefits of this chemical reaction, technically a complex series of reactions responsible for not only changing the color of the food but also adding a vast amount of flavor.

This reaction occurs almost daily in the kitchen when you cook food that contains protein—which is practically every food. Proteins and natural sugars in a food are transformed by heat to create new complex flavor compounds. The fond, or browned bits, left behind in a cooking vessel, often a skillet, is a gold mine of flavor. The classic way to harvest fond is to add liquid (usually water, wine, or broth) to the pan and scrape. This is true whether your intent is to ultimately make a pan sauce or to simply add more flavor to a braise or stew. The moisture and scraping motion release the stuck-on bits, which then dissolve into the liquid; this process is called deglazing. The darker the fond, the more pronounced that caramelized flavor will be. But your sauce or final dish will taste bitter if the fond has blackened. Fond should be caramel-colored to dark brown; if the fond is getting too dark, add a little water to the pan and reduce the heat slowly. (For more information on building a pan sauce, plus recipes, see pages 32 and 33.)

Fond Visuals

To get a visual, skillet-by-skillet picture of the level of fond development with different skillets, we made sautéed chicken breasts in two skillets—a stainless-steel and a ceramic (nonstick) skillet—and compared the results. The images clearly show that a stainless-steel skillet is the powerhouse of fond development.

Stainless-Steel Skillet

Ceramic (Nonstick) Skillet

Skillet Basics That Make a Difference

Preheat Properly

One mistake many home cooks make is not preheating their skillet and oil properly before adding food. Browning builds flavor—but only when your skillet and oil are good and hot. While developing our skillet recipes, we kept a close eye on the oil; monitoring its appearance as the skillet heats up is the best way to gauge when it's time to start cooking. Hot oil that creates faint waves in web-like patterns (we call it shimmering) is perfect for sautéing onions and vegetables that would burn at higher temperatures. Just-smoking oil (with small wisps of smoke escaping from the surface) is best for creating well-crusted meat, chicken, and other foods that need more heat to develop browning.

Shimmering Oil

Just-Smoking Oil

Don't Crowd the Pan

Allowing space between the food will keep it from steaming. Four chicken breasts or pork chops fit perfectly into a 12-inch skillet with room to spare, but jam more into the same pan and the chicken or pork will steam, not brown. Another strategy is to cook ingredients such as cut-up meat and chicken in batches, which also enhances browning and avoids steaming.

Pay Attention to Hot Spots

If a recipe does not specify how to arrange the food in the pan, keep in mind that generally the inner circle of the skillet will get hotter and the edges will stay cooler, but this will depend on your stove's burner and the size of the pan. If certain parts of your skillet develop brown spots sooner than others, know to rotate the food so that it is evenly taking advantage of hot and cool spots.

Bloom Spices

Blooming spices in a skillet releases their aromatic oils that can suffuse an entire dish. By simply heating spices in oil, butter, or the juices rendered from browned meat or chicken, you can immediately (and effortlessly) elevate their flavors.

Build Flavor in Layers

Working in stages is key to building and preserving flavor and cooking each component to its ideal state. A good example of cooking in stages and rotating ingredients in and out of the skillet to build flavor is Chicken Biryani (page 87), which features layers of spiced chicken, rice, and aromatics lavished with butter and studded with dried fruit. Another example is Tinga de Pollo (page 88), where we first cook the chicken in two batches and then add the onion and cook until softened, followed by the aromatics until fragrant and then the tomatoes, broth, and other ingredients, thereby building a rich base for this appealing dish.

Techniques That Make the Most of Your Skillet

These seven techniques highlight how the skillet can be used as a multi-purpose tool. A skillet can take the place of a traditional Dutch oven used for braising and poaching; it can easily move from stovetop to oven; it can be a roasting pan; it can be used in place of a plancha or griddle; and it can even serve as an alternative to a cake pan or casserole dish.

Pan Roast

This restaurant technique is a terrific way to cook meat and fish. For our **Herbed Roast Pork Loin with Asparagus** (page 147), we sear the spice-rubbed pork in a skillet and then transfer it to the oven to roast in the oven's even heat. Then we use the empty skillet to cook the asparagus while the pork rests.

Poach

Poaching often doesn't live up to its promise to deliver perfectly cooked moist fish, chicken, or vegetables, perhaps because you really need a precise technique. We found the skillet to be a great vehicle for this because you can use a lot less liquid since we employ a modified poach/steam technique, as in our **Perfect Poached Fish** (page 100). Elevating the fish fillets on lemon slices in a stainless-steel skillet keeps the undersides from overcooking while a poaching liquid that includes enough wine lowers its boiling point and produces more steam, surprisingly, even at a low temperature.

Griddle and Fry

If you crave double-stacked **Smashed Burgers** and wonder if you can make them at home, the answer is yes! Our recipe (page 174) uses a traditional cast-iron skillet, which allows for supercrispy browning of the thin burgers without overcooking them. We heat the empty skillet over medium-low heat for 5 minutes to get it hot and ensure even heat before adding the patties. And for crispy fried chicken without all the oil? Our **Cast-Iron Oven-Fried Chicken** (page 189) really delivers. The first step is to preheat a traditional cast-iron skillet in a hot oven until the skillet gets superhot and then add the oil and breaded chicken and return it to the oven to "fry" the chicken. The high sides of a cast-iron skillet also accommodate the frying of our **Crispy Vegetable Fritters** (page 265), a terrific appetizer. For our **Roast Beef Panini with Tangy Coleslaw** (page 170), we place the sandwiches in a cold stainless-steel skillet and weight them with a Dutch oven to re-create a panini press—no need to go to the deli to enjoy this comfort-food classic!

Sear

Searing involves cooking meat at a high temperature to create a browned crust. In this book you will find a few twists on searing; for **Butter-Based Rib-Eye Steak** (page 34), we combine searing, basting, and lots of flipping in a smoking-hot skillet to promote even cooking and prevent a gray band of meat.

We also discovered a cold-searing technique. We start **Pan-Seared Steaks** (page 30) in a cold (unpreheated) skillet over high heat to burn off moisture and prevent the steaks from steaming, quickly lower the heat to keep the steaks sizzling but cooking evenly, and flip the steaks every 2 minutes. This revolutionary technique is used throughout the book with a few twists on the method.

Sauté

Sautéing is used to cook smaller pieces of food or thinner cuts of meat all the way through, whereas searing is used to produce a brown crust on thicker cuts of protein as well as on vegetables. Sautéing also involves regular movement of food in the pan versus searing, during which we leave the food in place to brown. See **Lemon-Thyme Chicken with Garlicky Greens and White Beans** (page 24).

Bake

Most people don't think of using a skillet for baking breads or desserts, but there are actually many advantages to doing so. Take our **Fluffy Dinner Rolls** (page 305). Their soft, tender crumb and reflective buttery sheen are enough to make the rolls unique, but on top of these qualities, they're baked in a cast-iron skillet for a chewy, beautifully burnished crust without additional effort. You can also use a skillet to bake our rustic **Peach–Cornmeal Upside-Down Cake** (page 317). And it is the perfect pan in which to make a **Hasselback Potato Casserole** (page 295).

Braise

Braising is a terrific method to render meat or chicken incredibly tender in the oven while incorporating a variety of rich sauce flavorings—indeed developing layers of flavors. Think braised chicken or braised beef. While this is often done in a Dutch oven, a skillet is actually a great pan for braising. For **Braised Steaks with Root Vegetables** (page 90), the skillet is used in multiple ways: first browning and braising the steak and vegetables and then creating a luscious sauce after transferring the fork-tender meat and vegetables to a serving platter.

Pushing the Limits of What a Skillet Can Do

We left no trick unexplored as we developed these skillet recipes, from appetizers to desserts. And we discovered some unique ways a skillet can deliver superior results and even company-worthy meals. Here are some examples:

Creating Fantastic Pasta Dishes Is Easy in Just One Skillet

Spaghetti all'Assassina (page 203) is one of many dishes in this book where the pasta cooks right in the sauce, but with a twist: The hallmarks of this classic dish are strands of spaghetti that range from soft to al dente to crisp and a spicy, supercomplex sauce that clings to the pasta. A lot of flipping ensures that the pasta makes contact with the pan and then we let it cook without moving until the underside is deeply browned and some strands are charred.

Browning Chicken Before Braising Creates a Reduced Sauce for Crispy, Not Flabby, Skin

For our Braised Chicken Thighs with Lemon, Spices, and Torn Basil (page 74), we eliminate flabby skin by first browning the chicken skin side down in a stainless-steel skillet for a full 8 minutes before flipping. We then build a savory sauce in stages in the empty skillet before adding back the chicken and transferring the skillet to the oven. By using a reduced sauce rather than one that totally covers the chicken, the chicken skin keeps its appealing crispness.

Achieving Tall Sticky Buns Is Even Easier in a Skillet

Sticky Buns, the ultimate morning treat, can be made in a skillet—from the butterscotch glaze through proofing and baking. Our recipe (page 308) uses a cooked flour-and-water paste (known as tangzhong) that traps water so that the dough is not sticky, and the increased hydration converts to steam during baking, ensuring that the buns are fluffy and light.

Preheating Your Skillet in the Oven Ensures the Most Evenly Cooked Roast Chicken Ever

The problem plaguing most roast chicken is that by the time the chicken thighs are cooked through, the tender breast meat, which takes less time to reach the desired doneness temperature, is overcooked and dry. We discovered an unusual solution to this problem when developing Weeknight Roast Chicken (page 134). First we place a 12-inch stainless-steel skillet in the oven as it preheats. Then we place the chicken, breast side up, in the skillet. Because the thighs have contact with hot skillet pan right away, they get a jump-start on cooking. When the breasts register 120 degrees and the thighs 135 degrees, we turn off the heat and let carryover cooking do the rest.

Making Stuffed Shells in a Skillet Beats a Casserole Dish in Every Way

Cheesy Stuffed Shells (page 212) are usually a big project involving several pots and a casserole dish. Here we streamline it, first building a bright sauce in the skillet and setting aside some of it for topping, then filling the shells and placing them right in the skillet topped with the reserved sauce. The skillet goes in the oven to bake until cohesive and delightfully cheesy. No pot of boiling water required.

Turning Out a Gorgeous Soufflé Takes Mere Minutes of Baking Time

Yes, you can make a Lemon Soufflé (page 318) while your guests wait after dinner is over because it is really that simple. A 10-inch stainless-steel skillet is key so that the soufflé rises up the sides of the skillet—which it would not do in a nonstick skillet. And a few minutes on the stovetop followed by 7 minutes in the oven is all it takes for it to rise dramatically before you bring it right to the table.

Ditching Your Baking Stone Actually Leads to a Supercrispy Cast-Iron Pan Pizza

Serious pizza makers may find our Cast-Iron Pan Pizza recipe (page 164) a heresy, but the cast-iron skillet proves to be the perfect pan for making an easy, crispy pizza; and a generously oiled skillet essentially "fries" the cheese around all the edges of the pizza. After it finishes baking, a quick turn on the stovetop ensures that the bottom crust is crispy.

sauté, sear & stir-fry

Sautéed Chicken Breasts

Serves 4

Total Time 30 minutes

½ cup all-purpose flour

4 (6- to 8-ounce) boneless, skinless chicken breasts, trimmed

½ teaspoon table salt

¼ teaspoon pepper

2 tablespoons vegetable oil

VARIATIONS

Sautéed Chicken Thighs

Substitute 8 (3- to 4-ounce) boneless, skinless thighs for breasts. Cook chicken until well browned and registers 175 degrees, increasing cook time range to 5 to 7 minutes per side.

Sautéed Chicken Breasts for Two

Halve all ingredients. Proceed with recipe in 10- or 12-inch stainless-steel skillet.

Why This Recipe Works Master these easy techniques for perfectly sautéed chicken breasts and it will offer you a lifetime of versatile, easy dinners. First, pound the chicken to an even thickness so that all the pieces cook at the same rate. This also helps them lie flat, so they develop an enticing brown crust with lots of flavor picked up from the skillet. For chicken breasts that are well browned yet moist and tender, the key is both a light coating of flour and using plenty of heat: Since it is all too easy to overcook a boneless, skinless chicken breast, the dusting of flour helps protect the chicken from drying out—a win-win from many angles. As for the heat level, which is always important when cooking in a skillet, heating the oil over medium-high heat until it is smoking before adding the chicken is essential, as low or moderate heat draws the meat's moisture to the surface, which interferes with browning. We like using a stainless-steel skillet here because it is the best option for making a pan sauce using the fond left behind. And while these are simple techniques, simple doesn't need to mean snooze-worthy. These satisfying (and versatile!) sautéed chicken breasts should be in every cook's repertoire—they can be paired with a variety of sauces for a quick weeknight dinner or shredded, sliced, or chopped for salads, tacos, sandwiches, or bowls. If your chicken breasts are larger than 6 to 8 ounces each, use fewer of them to maintain a total weight of 1½ to 2 pounds. You can use the fond left in the pan to create a pan sauce (pages 32–33) or serve the chicken with an herb sauce, relish, or chutney (pages 150–151).

1 Spread flour in shallow dish. Place chicken breasts on cutting board and cover with plastic wrap. Using meat pounder, gently pound chicken to even thickness. Pat chicken dry with paper towels and sprinkle with salt and pepper. Working with 1 breast at a time, dredge in flour, shaking off excess.

2 Heat oil in 12-inch stainless-steel skillet over medium-high heat until just smoking. Cook chicken until well browned and registers 160 degrees, about 5 minutes per side. Serve.

Sizing Up Your Skillet

stainless steel • **enameled cast iron** • **nonstick** • **traditional cast iron** • **carbon steel**

A 12-inch stainless-steel skillet provides enough space for browning four chicken breasts and develops valuable fond for building a pan sauce. An enameled cast-iron skillet also will work for these reasons. A nonstick, traditional cast-iron, or carbon-steel skillet can also be used; however, they will not develop as much fond. If using a cast-iron skillet, you will need to preheat the empty skillet over medium heat for 5 minutes before proceeding with step 2.

perfecting
SAUTÉED CHICKEN BREASTS

To create chicken breasts of even thickness, simply pound the thicker ends of the breasts until they are all of uniform thickness. Though some breasts will still be larger in size, they will cook at the same rate. A little flour helps keep the chicken from drying out.

1   Pound Breasts to Uniform Thickness.

2   Pat Chicken Dry and Season.

3   Dredge in Flour.

4   Heat Oil in Skillet Until Smoking, Then Add Chicken.

Lemon-Thyme Chicken with Garlicky Greens and White Beans

Serves 4

Total Time 45 minutes

2 teaspoons minced fresh thyme or ¾ teaspoon dried

1 teaspoon grated lemon zest, plus lemon wedges for serving

¾ teaspoon table salt, divided

½ teaspoon pepper, divided

½ cup all-purpose flour

4 (6- to 8-ounce) boneless, skinless chicken breasts, trimmed

¼ cup extra-virgin olive oil, divided

2 ounces pancetta or bacon, cut into ¼-inch pieces

1 pound Swiss chard, stems chopped, leaves cut into 1-inch pieces

4 garlic cloves, sliced thin

¼ teaspoon red pepper flakes

1 (15-ounce) can cannellini or Great Northern beans

Why This Recipe Works It's no secret that lemon and thyme pair perfectly with chicken. Here we dust boneless chicken breasts with piquant lemon zest and minced thyme before coating the chicken with flour. This keeps the zest and thyme from burning when sautéing the chicken. To make this a full meal, after cooking the chicken we keep it warm in a low oven while we build both a hearty side dish and a sauce on the stovetop, utilizing the fond left behind in the skillet. To add a hit of flavor, we first sauté a bit of pancetta, then add Swiss chard stems, which need a head start on the leaves. Slivered garlic and red pepper flakes add pungency and meld beautifully with the beans and Swiss chard. The starchy liquid from the canned beans helps create a full-bodied sauce in the time it takes the Swiss chard to wilt. If your chicken breasts are larger than 6 to 8 ounces each, use fewer of them to maintain a total weight of 1½ to 2 pounds. You will need a 12-inch skillet with a tight-fitting lid for this recipe.

1 Adjust oven rack to middle position and heat oven to 200 degrees. Combine thyme, lemon zest, ½ teaspoon salt, and ¼ teaspoon pepper in bowl. Spread flour in shallow dish. Place chicken breasts on cutting board and cover with plastic wrap. Using meat pounder, gently pound chicken to even thickness. Pat chicken dry with paper towels and sprinkle with thyme mixture. Working with 1 breast at a time, dredge in flour, shaking off excess.

2 Heat 2 tablespoons oil in 12-inch stainless-steel skillet over medium-high heat until just smoking. Cook chicken until well browned and registers 160 degrees, about 5 minutes per side. Transfer to plate and keep warm in oven.

3 Cook pancetta in remaining 2 tablespoons oil in now-empty skillet over medium heat until rendered and crisp, about 3 minutes. Add chard stems and cook until softened, 3 to 5 minutes. Stir in garlic, pepper flakes, remaining ¼ teaspoon salt, and remaining ¼ teaspoon pepper and cook until fragrant, about 30 seconds. Stir in beans and their liquid and any accumulated chicken juices, scraping up any browned bits, then stir in chard leaves. Cover and cook, stirring occasionally, until chard is tender, about 4 minutes. Slice chicken and serve with chard mixture, passing lemon wedges separately.

VARIATION

Lemon-Thyme Chicken with Garlicky Greens and White Beans for Two

Reduce salt to ¼ teaspoon, red pepper flakes to pinch, and cannellini beans to ¾ cup plus ¼ cup canning liquid; halve remaining ingredients. Proceed with recipe using 10- or 12-inch skillet. Use ⅛ teaspoon salt and ⅛ teaspoon pepper in steps 1 and 3.

Sizing Up Your Skillet

stainless steel • **enameled cast iron** • **nonstick** • **traditional cast iron** • **carbon steel**

A 12-inch stainless-steel skillet provides enough space for browning four chicken breasts and develops valuable fond that adds flavor to the Swiss chard and bean mixture. An enameled cast-iron skillet will work for these reasons. A nonstick, traditional cast-iron, or carbon-steel skillet can also be used; however, they will not develop as much fond. If using a cast-iron skillet, you will need to preheat the empty skillet over medium heat for 5 minutes before proceeding with step 2.

Chicken and Couscous with Fennel, Apricots, and Orange

Serves 4

Total Time 1 hour

½ cup all-purpose flour

4 (6- to 8-ounce) boneless, skinless chicken breasts, trimmed

1 teaspoon table salt, divided

¼ teaspoon pepper

½ cup extra-virgin olive oil, divided

1 red onion, sliced thin

1 fennel bulb, stalks discarded, bulb halved, cored, and sliced thin

1 cup couscous

3 garlic cloves, minced

⅛ teaspoon cayenne pepper, divided

1 cup orange juice, divided

¾ cup chicken broth

½ cup coarsely chopped dried apricots

¼ cup minced fresh cilantro, divided

Why This Recipe Works For a change of pace from the usual chicken and rice, couscous offers the perfect option for a quick supper, and this recipe streamlines the process because you can cook both elements in one skillet. As with our other seared boneless chicken breasts, we dredge them in flour before browning to guard against dryness and give them a nice crust. The fond left in the pan provides a flavor base for our vegetables, aromatic fennel and sharp red onion, which we sauté to soften slightly before adding the couscous and toasting it briefly to release its nutty flavor and prevent clumping. While couscous is often hydrated in water or chicken broth, for even more flavor we supplement chicken broth with orange juice. Orange and apricots are a marvelous complement to fennel—their acidic sweetness brings out more of the fennel's flavor. Stirring in fresh cilantro and then drizzling the final dish with a mix of more orange juice, olive oil, and cayenne offers a fragrant flavor boost that elevates everything. If your chicken breasts are larger than 6 to 8 ounces each, use fewer of them to maintain a total weight of 1½ to 2 pounds.

1 Adjust oven rack to middle position and heat oven to 200 degrees. Spread flour in shallow dish. Place chicken breasts on cutting board and cover with plastic wrap. Using meat pounder, gently pound chicken to even thickness. Pat chicken dry with paper towels and sprinkle with ½ teaspoon salt and pepper. Working with 1 breast at a time, dredge in flour, shaking off excess.

2 Heat 2 tablespoons oil in 12-inch nonstick skillet over medium-high heat until shimmering. Cook chicken until well browned and registers 160 degrees, about 5 minutes per side. Transfer chicken to plate and keep warm in oven.

3 Heat 1 tablespoon oil in now-empty skillet over medium heat until shimmering. Add onion, fennel, and remaining ½ teaspoon salt and cook until vegetables are softened, 5 to 7 minutes. Stir in couscous, garlic, and pinch cayenne and cook until fragrant, about 30 seconds. Stir in ¾ cup orange juice, broth, and apricots and bring to simmer. Off heat, cover and let sit until liquid is absorbed, about 5 minutes.

4 Whisk 2 tablespoons cilantro, remaining 5 tablespoons oil, remaining pinch cayenne, remaining ¼ cup orange juice together in bowl. Add remaining 2 tablespoons cilantro to couscous and gently fluff with fork to combine. Season with salt and pepper to taste. Drizzle oil–orange juice mixture over chicken and couscous before serving.

Sizing Up Your Skillet

nonstick • traditional cast iron • carbon steel

A 12-inch nonstick skillet provides enough space for browning four chicken breasts, and its slick surface allows you to create a flavorful couscous side dish without concern for sticking. A traditional cast-iron or carbon-steel skillet is also appropriate to use for these reasons. If using a traditional cast-iron skillet, you will need to preheat the empty skillet over medium heat for 3 minutes before proceeding with step 2.

Turkey Meatballs with Charred Zucchini and Yogurt Sauce

Serves 4

Total Time 1 hour

½ cup panko bread crumbs

1 large egg

½ cup chopped fresh parsley, divided

2 garlic cloves, minced, divided

1½ teaspoons grated lemon zest, plus 1 tablespoon juice

1 teaspoon table salt, divided

¼ teaspoon ground cumin

¼ teaspoon pepper

1½ pounds 93 percent lean ground turkey

1 cup plain Greek yogurt

3 tablespoons extra-virgin olive oil, divided

3 zucchini (8 ounces each), halved lengthwise and sliced on bias 2 inches thick

Why This Recipe Works This simple weeknight dinner uses a nonstick skillet to cook lemony turkey meatballs with garlic, an abundance of parsley, and a hit of cumin. We chill the meatballs to firm them up, which helps them cook without falling apart in the skillet; you can just give the skillet a gentle shake a few times during the 10-minute cook time so that they brown on all sides. After removing the meatballs from the skillet, we turn our attention to a somewhat unusual side dish: planks of zucchini that cook through quickly in the skillet and develop a lovely char. To take this dish to the next level, we make a quick lemon-parsley sauce with Greek yogurt. Paired with the tender meatballs and charred zucchini, the sauce makes the meal feel special, although it is nearly effortless to make.

1 Combine panko, egg, ¼ cup parsley, half of garlic, lemon zest, ¾ teaspoon salt, cumin, and pepper in large bowl. Add turkey and, using your hands, gently knead mixture until combined. Using lightly moistened hands, pinch off and roll 2-tablespoon portions of the mixture into balls and transfer to plate (you should have about 24 meatballs). Cover and refrigerate for at least 15 minutes or up to 24 hours.

2 Combine yogurt with lemon juice, ⅛ teaspoon salt, remaining ¼ cup parsley, and remaining garlic in small bowl. Season with salt and pepper to taste; set aside for serving.

3 Heat 2 tablespoons oil in 12-inch nonstick skillet over medium-high heat until shimmering. Add meatballs and cook, gently shaking skillet and turning meatballs as needed, until browned on all sides and meat registers 160 degrees, 10 to 12 minutes. (Reduce heat as needed to prevent scorching.) Transfer meatballs to serving platter and tent with aluminum foil. Wipe skillet clean with paper towels.

4 Add remaining 1 tablespoon oil and zucchini cut side down to now-empty skillet and cook over medium-high heat until well browned on first side, 3 to 5 minutes. Flip zucchini, reduce heat to medium, and sprinkle with remaining ⅛ teaspoon salt. Cook, turning as needed, until tender and deep golden brown, 3 to 5 minutes. Serve meatballs with zucchini and yogurt sauce.

Sizing Up Your Skillet

nonstick • **traditional cast iron** • **carbon steel**

A 12-inch nonstick skillet provides enough space for browning all of the delicate meatballs at once without concern for sticking. It can then be easily wiped clean and used again for browning the zucchini. A traditional cast-iron or carbon-steel skillet will also work well for these reasons. If using a traditional cast-iron skillet, you will need to preheat the empty skillet over medium heat for 3 minutes before proceeding with step 3.

Pan-Seared Steaks

Serves 4 to 6

Total Time 20 minutes

2 (12- to 16-ounce) boneless strip or rib-eye steaks, 1½ inches thick, trimmed

1 teaspoon coarsely ground pepper

   Coarse or flake sea salt

VARIATIONS

Spice-Crusted Pan-Seared Steaks

Combine 2 tablespoons chopped fresh rosemary, 2 teaspoons ground coriander, 2 teaspoons grated lemon zest, 1½ teaspoons dry mustard, and 1 teaspoon red pepper flakes with pepper in bowl and sprinkle onto steaks before cooking.

Pan-Seared Thick-Cut Steak for Two

Halve all ingredients. Proceed with recipe in 10- or 12-inch nonstick skillet.

Why This Recipe Works Pan-searing strip or rib-eye steaks usually leads to a smoky, grease-splattered kitchen—but it doesn't have to. To devise a fast, mess-free method for achieving deeply seared, rosy meat, we start the steaks in a "cold" (not preheated) nonstick skillet over high heat and flip them every 2 minutes. That way, the meat's temperature increases gradually, allowing a crust to build up on the outside without overcooking the interior. Because we are cooking in a nonstick skillet, it isn't necessary to lubricate the skillet with oil; plus, the well-marbled meat exudes enough fat to achieve a good sear (adding more simply encourages splatter). We start cooking over high heat to burn off moisture and prevent the steaks from steaming but quickly lower the heat to medium. At the more moderate temperature, the meat keeps sizzling, but there is no risk of the fat smoking. If you have time, salt the steaks for at least 1 hour or up to 24 hours before cooking: Sprinkle each steak with 1 teaspoon of Diamond Crystal Kosher Salt (if using Morton Kosher Salt, which is denser, use only ¾ teaspoon), refrigerate, and then pat dry with paper towels before cooking. Electric stoves can be slow to respond to a cook's commands, which can pose a problem with this method; see page 4 for workaround strategies. You can use the fond left in the pan to create a pan sauce (see pages 32–33) or serve the steaks with an herb sauce, relish, or chutney (pages 150–151). Before serving, slice the steaks and sprinkle them with coarse sea salt so that every bite is well seasoned.

1 Pat steaks dry with paper towels and sprinkle with pepper, pressing to adhere. Place steaks 1 inch apart in cold 12-inch nonstick skillet. Place skillet over high heat and cook steaks for 2 minutes. Flip steaks and cook on second side for 2 minutes. (Neither side of steaks will be browned at this point.)

2 Flip steaks, reduce heat to medium, and continue to cook, flipping steaks every 2 minutes, until browned and meat registers 120 to 125 degrees (for medium-rare), 4 to 10 minutes; for more information on meat doneness temperatures, see page 339. (Steaks should be sizzling gently; if not, increase heat slightly. Reduce heat if skillet starts to smoke.) Transfer steaks to cutting board and let rest for 5 minutes. Slice steaks ½ inch thick against grain, season with coarse or flake sea salt to taste, and serve.

Sizing Up Your Skillet

nonstick • traditional cast iron • carbon steel

The slick surface of a 12-inch nonstick skillet prevents the steaks from sticking without oil and allows more savory browning to stick to the meat, not the pan. A traditional cast-iron or carbon-steel skillet will also work well for these reasons.

perfecting
PAN-SEARED STEAKS

We start the steaks in a cold skillet and flip them every 2 minutes, allowing a crust to build up without overcooking the interior. Cooking first over high heat eliminates moisture and helps with browning. Quickly lowering the heat ensures even cooking.

1 Start Steaks in a Cold Nonstick Skillet.

2 Don't Add Oil.

3 Start High; Then Go Low(er).

4 Flip Steaks Every 2 Minutes.

PAN SAUCES

An easy-to-make pan sauce can take a simple, perfectly seared steak, pork chop, chicken breast, or fish fillet to the next level. The beauty of pan sauces is that while the meat or fish rests off the heat, you can take advantage of any flavorful browned bits, or fond, left in your skillet. First, we usually sauté aromatics in the fat left behind and then add a liquid or two (wine, vermouth, brandy, broth, etc.) to deglaze the pan and capture the essence of the flavorful fond from the skillet. The recipes below provide lots of options for making a pan sauce.

Vermouth-Herb Pan Sauce

Makes about ¾ cup; enough for 4 servings

This sauce pairs best with poultry, pork, and fish.

1	shallot, minced
¾	cup chicken broth
½	cup dry vermouth or white wine
3	tablespoons unsalted butter, cut into 3 pieces and chilled
2	teaspoons minced fresh parsley, basil, dill, tarragon, or thyme

Pour off all but 1 tablespoon fat from skillet. (If necessary, supplement with oil.) Add shallot and cook over medium heat until softened, about 1 minute. Stir in broth and vermouth, scraping up any browned bits, and simmer until reduced and slightly syrupy, 5 to 7 minutes. Off heat, whisk in butter, 1 piece at a time, until melted and sauce is thickened and glossy. Stir in herb and any accumulated meat juices. Season with salt and pepper to taste.

Lemon-Caper Pan Sauce

Makes about ¾ cup; enough for 4 servings

This sauce pairs best with poultry, pork, and fish.

1	small shallot, minced
1	cup chicken broth
¼	cup lemon juice (2 lemons)
2	tablespoons capers, rinsed
3	tablespoons unsalted butter, cut into 3 pieces and chilled
2	tablespoons minced fresh parsley

Pour off all but 1 tablespoon fat from skillet. (If necessary, supplement with oil.) Add shallot and cook over medium heat until softened, about 1 minute. Stir in broth, scraping up any browned bits. Bring to simmer and cook until liquid is reduced to ⅓ cup, about 4 minutes. Stir in lemon juice and capers and simmer until liquid is reduced to ⅓ cup, about 1 minute. Off heat, whisk in butter, 1 piece at a time, until melted and sauce is thickened and glossy. Stir in parsley and any accumulated meat juices. Season with salt and pepper to taste.

Mustard-Cream Pan Sauce

Makes about ½ cup; enough for 4 servings

This sauce pairs well with beef, pork, and poultry.

1	shallot, minced
½	cup chicken broth
2	tablespoons brandy
2	tablespoons heavy cream
1½	tablespoons Dijon mustard
2	tablespoons unsalted butter, cut into 2 pieces and chilled

Pour off all but 1 tablespoon fat from skillet. (If necessary, supplement with oil.) Add shallot and cook over medium heat until softened, about 1 minute. Stir in broth, brandy, heavy cream, and mustard, scraping up any browned bits. Bring to simmer and cook until liquid is reduced to ½ cup, about 6 minutes. Off heat, whisk in butter, 1 piece at a time, until melted and sauce is thickened and glossy. Whisk in any accumulated meat juices and season with salt and pepper to taste.

Porcini-Marsala Pan Sauce

Makes about ½ cup; enough for 4 servings

This earthy sauce pairs well with poultry, beef, and pork. It is worth spending a little extra for a moderately priced dry Marsala ($10 to $12 per bottle).

¾ cup chicken broth, divided

¼ ounce dried porcini mushrooms, rinsed

1 shallot, minced

½ cup dry Marsala

2 tablespoons unsalted butter, cut into 2 pieces and chilled

1 tablespoon minced fresh parsley

1 Microwave ½ cup broth and mushrooms in covered bowl until steaming, about 1 minute. Let sit until softened, about 5 minutes. Drain mushrooms through fine-mesh strainer lined with coffee filter, reserving soaking liquid, and chop mushrooms.

2 Pour off all but 1 tablespoon fat from skillet. (If necessary, supplement with oil.) Add shallot and cook over medium heat until softened, about 1 minute. Off heat, stir in Marsala, scraping up any browned bits. Return skillet to medium heat and simmer until Marsala is reduced to glaze, about 3 minutes. Stir in remaining ¼ cup broth, reserved soaking liquid, and mushrooms. Bring to simmer and cook until liquid is reduced to ⅓ cup, 4 to 6 minutes. Off heat, whisk in butter, 1 piece at a time, until melted and sauce is thickened and glossy. Whisk in parsley and any accumulated meat juices. Season with salt and pepper to taste.

Red Wine–Peppercorn Pan Sauce

Makes about ½ cup; enough for 4 servings

This sauce pairs well with beef and pork. Use a good-quality medium-bodied wine, such as a Côtes du Rhône or Pinot Noir, for this sauce.

1 large shallot, minced

½ cup dry red wine

¾ cup chicken broth

2 teaspoons packed brown sugar

3 tablespoons unsalted butter, cut into 3 pieces and chilled

1 teaspoon coarsely ground pepper

¼ teaspoon balsamic vinegar

Pour off all but 1 tablespoon fat from skillet. (If necessary, supplement with oil.) Add shallot and cook over medium heat until softened, about 1 minute. Stir in wine, scraping up any browned bits. Bring to simmer and cook until wine is reduced to glaze, about 3 minutes. Stir in broth and sugar and simmer until reduced to ⅓ cup, 4 to 6 minutes. Off heat, whisk in butter, 1 piece at a time, until melted and sauce is thickened and glossy. Whisk in pepper, vinegar, and any accumulated meat juices. Season with salt and pepper to taste.

Cilantro-Coconut Pan Sauce

Makes about ½ cup; enough for 4 servings

This sauce pairs well with poultry, pork, and fish. Regular or low-fat coconut milk can be used in this pan sauce.

1 large shallot, minced

1 tablespoon grated fresh ginger

2 garlic cloves, minced

¾ cup canned coconut milk

¼ cup chicken broth

1 teaspoon sugar

¼ cup chopped fresh cilantro

2 teaspoons lime juice

1 tablespoon unsalted butter, chilled

Pour off all but 1 tablespoon fat from skillet. (If necessary, supplement with oil.) Add shallot, ginger, and garlic and cook over medium heat until shallot is softened, about 1 minute. Stir in coconut milk, broth, and sugar, scraping up any browned bits. Bring to simmer and cook until reduced to ½ cup, about 6 minutes. Off heat, stir in cilantro and lime juice, then whisk in butter until melted. Season with salt and pepper to taste.

Sizing Up Your Skillet

nonstick • stainless steel • carbon steel • traditional cast iron

Some of the recipes in this chapter (Pan-Seared Steaks, Thick-Cut Pork Chops, Salmon, and Shrimp) use the cold-sear method, which necessitates using a nonstick skillet. You can still make a fine pan sauce in a nonstick skillet despite the fact that it does not develop as much fond as when using a stainless-steel skillet.

Butter-Basted Rib-Eye Steak with Shallot and Thyme

Serves 2

Total Time 30 minutes, plus 1 hour salting

1 (1¼- to 1½-pound) bone-in rib-eye steak, 1½ inches thick, trimmed

2 teaspoons kosher salt

½ teaspoon pepper

2 tablespoons vegetable oil

4 tablespoons unsalted butter

1 shallot, peeled and quartered through root end

2 garlic cloves, lightly crushed and peeled

5 sprigs fresh thyme

VARIATIONS

Butter-Basted Rib-Eye Steak with Rosemary-Orange Butter

Substitute 8 (2-inch) strips orange zest for garlic and 1 sprig fresh rosemary for thyme.

Butter-Basted Sirloin Steaks for Four

Substitute 2 boneless sirloin steaks of a similar thickness. Increase salt to 4 teaspoons, pepper to 1 teaspoon, and butter to 6 tablespoons.

Why This Recipe Works There's steak, and then there's pan-seared, butter-basted rib-eye steak. The two processes serve different purposes, and the second isn't just for flavor. Searing involves cooking the surface of meat at a high temperature to create a browned crust. Basting requires continuously spooning hot fat over the steak to continue cooking it evenly. To prevent a gray band from forming under the crust (an indicator of overcooked, dried-out meat), we also flip the steak every 30 seconds as it sears. Why? A hot skillet cooks food from the bottom up. When a protein is flipped, some heat from the seared side dissipates into the air, but lingering residual heat continues to cook the protein from the top down. The more a protein is flipped, the more it cooks from both sides. Basting with hot butter infused with shallot, garlic, and thyme also helps the steak to cook on both sides and boosts its rich flavor. This recipe also works with a boneless sirloin steak of a similar thickness. This recipe was developed with Diamond Crystal Kosher Salt. (If using Morton Kosher Salt, which is denser, decrease the amount to 1½ teaspoons.)

1 Sprinkle steak evenly on both sides with salt and place on wire rack set in rimmed baking sheet. Refrigerate uncovered for at least 1 hour, or up to 24 hours.

2 Pat steak dry with paper towels and sprinkle with pepper. Heat oil in 12-inch stainless-steel skillet over high heat until just smoking. Place steak in skillet and cook for 30 seconds. Flip steak and continue to cook for 30 seconds. Continue flipping steak every 30 seconds for 3 more minutes.

3 Slide steak to back of skillet, opposite handle, and add butter to front of skillet. Once butter has melted and begun to foam, add shallot, garlic, and thyme sprigs. Holding skillet handle, tilt skillet so butter pools near base of handle. Use metal spoon to continuously spoon butter and aromatics over steak, concentrating on areas where crust is less browned. Baste steak, flipping every 30 seconds, until steak registers 120 to 125 degrees (for medium-rare), 1 to 4 minutes; for more information on meat doneness temperatures, see page 339.

4 Remove skillet from heat and transfer steak to cutting board; tent with aluminum foil and let rest for 10 minutes. Discard aromatics from pan and transfer butter mixture to small bowl. Carve meat from bone and slice steak crosswise ½ inch thick against grain. Serve with butter mixture.

perfecting
BUTTER-BASTED RIB-EYE STEAK

Searing in a smoking-hot skillet creates a gorgeous mahogany crust. Frequent flipping promotes even cooking and prevents a gray band of meat. Basting with butter and aromatics cooks the steak from the top down.

1 Salt Steak and Refrigerate for 1 Hour.

2 Flip Every 30 Seconds for 3 Minutes.

3 Baste with Hot Butter and Aromatics.

Sizing Up Your Skillet

stainless steel • traditional cast iron • enameled cast iron • carbon steel

A 12-inch stainless-steel skillet provides enough space to properly brown the large steak and scoop up the flavorful butter for basting. A traditional cast-iron, enameled cast-iron, or carbon-steel skillet will also work well for these reasons. If using a cast-iron skillet, you will need to preheat the empty skillet over medium heat for 5 minutes before proceeding with step 2.

Seared Bistro-Style Steak with Crispy Potatoes and Salsa Verde

Serves 4 to 6

Total Time 40 minutes

1½ pounds yellow waxy potatoes, unpeeled, cut into 1-inch wedges

1 teaspoon table salt, divided

1 (2-pound) flank steak, trimmed

½ teaspoon pepper

3 tablespoon vegetable oil, divided

½ cup Salsa Verde (page 150)

Why This Recipe Works Searing a steak in a skillet is not a revolutionary idea, but we love this recipe because you can sear the steaks, then use the skillet again to make crispy potatoes that take on incredible flavor from the steak juices and fond left behind. The piéce de rèsistance is a bright salsa verde with pungent anchovy, lemon, capers, garlic, and parsley; it coats everything and comes together in seconds in a food processor. To get juicy, bistro-style steaks without breaking the bank or hunting down obscure cuts of meat, we turned to common, affordable flank steak. By cutting a 2-pound piece of meat into four portions, we create thick steaks ideal for pan searing. For the perfectly crisp side of potatoes that uses the same pan, we cut yellow potatoes into wedges and jump-start their cooking in the microwave. These potato wedges are so crispy and so imbued with the flavor of the flank steak that your family or guests will swoon over them. Feel free to substitute another herb sauce or relish (pages 150–151) in place of the Salsa Verde.

1 Toss potatoes with ½ teaspoon salt in bowl. Cover and microwave, tossing occasionally, until potatoes begin to soften, 5 to 7 minutes. Drain off any accumulated liquid and set potatoes aside.

2 Cut steak in half lengthwise, then cut each piece in half crosswise to create 4 steaks. Pat steaks dry with paper towels and sprinkle with remaining ½ teaspoon salt and pepper. Heat 1 tablespoon oil in 12-inch nonstick skillet over medium-high heat until just smoking. Cook steaks until well browned and meat registers 120 to 125 degrees (for medium-rare), 5 to 7 minutes per side; for more information on meat doneness temperatures, see page 339. Transfer steaks to cutting board, tent with aluminum foil, and let rest while finishing potatoes.

3 Heat remaining 2 tablespoons oil in now-empty skillet over medium heat until shimmering. Add potatoes and cook, turning occasionally, until well browned, about 10 minutes. Slice steaks thin against grain and serve with potatoes, passing Salsa Verde separately.

VARIATION

Seared Bistro-Style Steak with Crispy Potatoes and Salsa Verde for Two

Halve all ingredients. Proceed with recipe in 10- or 12-inch nonstick skillet.

Sizing Up Your Skillet

nonstick • **traditional cast iron** • **carbon steel**

A 12-inch nonstick skillet provides enough space to properly sear the steaks, then brown the potatoes without concern for sticking. A traditional cast-iron or carbon-steel skillet will also work well for these reasons. If using a traditional cast-iron skillet, preheat the empty skillet over medium heat for 5 minutes before proceeding with step 2.

Stir-Fried Cumin Beef

Serves 4

Total Time 45 minutes

1 tablespoon water

¼ teaspoon baking soda

1 pound flank steak, trimmed, cut with grain into 2- to 2½-inch-wide strips, each strip sliced against grain ¼ inch thick

4 garlic cloves, minced

1 tablespoon grated fresh ginger

1 tablespoon cumin seeds, ground

2 teaspoons Sichuan chili flakes

1¼ teaspoons Sichuan peppercorns, ground

½ teaspoon sugar

4 teaspoons dark soy sauce

1 tablespoon Shaoxing wine

½ teaspoon cornstarch

¼ teaspoon table salt

¼ cup vegetable oil, divided

½ small onion, sliced thin

2 tablespoons coarsely chopped fresh cilantro

Why This Recipe Works If you have a carbon-steel skillet in your arsenal of pans, it is a great choice for stir-frying because, much like a wok, its surface gets hot enough (and stays hot) to brown proteins rapidly and cook vegetables so they retain their color and crunch. Plus, this lighter skillet makes it easy to toss the food as it cooks. Cumin beef has roots in Hunan cuisine, and typically features tender pieces of meat stir-fried with onions (and/or peppers) and aromatics (garlic and ginger) that are lightly glossed in a soy sauce–based glaze, seasoned with spices (cumin, Sichuan peppercorns, and dried chiles or chili powder), and finished with cilantro. Before cooking, we briefly treat slices of beefy flank steak with baking soda, which raises the meat's pH so that it stays moist and tender during cooking. To prevent the meat from overcooking before it browns, we stir-fry it in two batches until the juices reduce to a sticky fond that coats each slice. Quickly stir-frying sliced onion allows it to soften but retain a hint of its raw bite and crunch. Grinding whole cumin seeds and Sichuan peppercorns releases vibrant aromatic compounds that give the dish plenty of fragrance, while Sichuan chili flakes add moderate heat. You can substitute 1 tablespoon ground cumin for the cumin seeds. If you can't find Sichuan chili flakes, gochugaru (Korean red pepper flakes) are a good substitute.

1 Combine water and baking soda in medium bowl. Add beef and toss to coat. Let sit at room temperature for 5 minutes.

2 While beef rests, combine garlic and ginger in small bowl. Combine cumin, chili flakes, Sichuan pepper, and sugar in second small bowl. Add soy sauce, Shaoxing wine, cornstarch, and salt to beef mixture. Toss until well combined.

3 Heat 1 tablespoon oil in 12-inch carbon-steel skillet over medium-high heat until just smoking. Add half of beef mixture and increase heat to high. Using tongs, toss beef slowly but constantly until exuded juices have evaporated and meat begins to sizzle, 2 to 6 minutes. Transfer to clean bowl. Repeat with 1 tablespoon oil and remaining beef mixture.

4 Heat remaining 2 tablespoons oil in now-empty skillet over medium heat until shimmering. Add garlic mixture (oil will splatter) and cook, stirring constantly, until fragrant, 15 to 30 seconds. Add onion and cook, tossing slowly but constantly with tongs, until onion begins to soften, 1 to 2 minutes. Return beef to skillet and toss to combine. Sprinkle cumin mixture over beef and toss until onion takes on pale orange color. Transfer to serving platter, sprinkle with cilantro, and serve immediately with rice.

VARIATION

Stir-Fried Cumin Beef for Two

Reduce Sichuan peppercorns to ½ teaspoon; halve remaining ingredients. Proceed with recipe using 10- or 12-inch carbon-steel skillet, cooking beef in single batch with 1 tablespoon oil in step 3.

Sizing Up Your Skillet

carbon steel ● **nonstick**

A well-seasoned 12-inch carbon-steel skillet is a good alternative to the traditional 14-inch flat-bottomed wok used for stir-frying because its relative light weight allows for ease while tossing, and its superior heat retention provides for rapid high-heat cooking. While a 12-inch nonstick skillet does not have the same heat retention, it can also be used.

Steak Caesar Salad

Serves 4 to 6

Total Time 40 minutes

1½ pounds sirloin steak tips, trimmed and cut into 2-inch pieces

3 tablespoons Worcestershire sauce, divided

2¾ teaspoons pepper, divided

1½ teaspoons table salt, divided

4 ounces ciabatta, cut into ½-inch cubes (4 cups)

2 tablespoons water

½ cup extra-virgin olive oil, divided

1 tablespoon minced garlic, divided

1 ounce Parmesan cheese, grated (½ cup), plus extra for serving

⅓ cup mayonnaise

2 tablespoons lemon juice

3 romaine lettuce hearts (18 ounces), cut into 1-inch pieces

Why This Recipe Works Perfectly seared steak takes a simple Caesar salad to a whole new level of indulgence. Because we wanted to make the croutons and steak in the same skillet, we chose a nonstick skillet to keep the croutons from sticking, but we made sure to get the skillet smoking hot in order to get a good sear on the steak. We use beefy sirloin steak tips for the steak for their flavor and because they are easy to cut into pieces. Tossing the steak tips with Worcestershire sauce adds pungency, and we of course season them with a plentiful amount of pepper and salt. While the steak marinates, we make garlicky croutons, first softening the bread cubes with a splash of water and squeezing them until the water is absorbed. Cooking them in olive oil along with the garlic delivers crispy, browned croutons in under 10 minutes. Then we sear the steak in the empty skillet. While the steak rests, we whisk together an extra-lemony Caesar dressing to help cut the richness of the marinated steak tips. Sirloin steak tips, also known as flap meat, can be sold as whole steaks, cubes, and strips. To ensure uniform pieces, we prefer to purchase whole steaks and cut them ourselves.

1 Toss steak with 2 tablespoons Worcestershire, 2 teaspoons pepper, and ¾ teaspoon salt in bowl; set aside. Toss bread and water together in large bowl, squeezing bread gently until water is absorbed. Add ¼ cup oil, 2 teaspoons garlic, ¼ teaspoon pepper, and ¼ teaspoon salt and toss to combine. Transfer mixture to 12-inch nonstick skillet and cook over medium-high heat, stirring often, until bread is browned and crisp, 7 to 10 minutes. Transfer to a large plate.

2 Heat 1 tablespoon oil in now-empty skillet over medium-high heat until just smoking. Add steak and cook until browned on all sides and meat registers 120 to 125 degrees (for medium-rare), about 7 minutes; for more information on meat doneness temperatures, see page 339. Transfer steak to separate plate and tent with aluminum foil.

3 Whisk Parmesan, mayonnaise, lemon juice, remaining 1 tablespoon Worcestershire, remaining ½ teaspoon pepper, remaining ½ teaspoon salt, remaining 3 tablespoons oil, and remaining 1 teaspoon garlic together in large bowl. Add lettuce and croutons and toss to combine. Season with salt and pepper to taste. Slice steak thin against grain and serve with salad, passing extra Parmesan separately.

Sizing Up Your Skillet

nonstick • **traditional cast iron** • **carbon steel**

A 12-inch nonstick skillet provides enough space to spread the croutons into an even layer and crisp them without concern for sticking; it can then be used to properly sear the steak. A traditional cast-iron or carbon-steel skillet will also work well for these reasons.

Pan-Seared Thick-Cut Pork Chops

Serves 4

Total Time 30 minutes

2 (14- to 16-ounce) bone-in pork rib chops, 1½ inches thick, trimmed

½ teaspoon pepper

Coarse or flake sea salt

VARIATIONS

Pan-Seared Thick-Cut Pork Chops with Maple Agrodolce

While pork rests, pour off all fat from skillet. Add ¼ cup balsamic vinegar, 2 tablespoons maple syrup, 2 tablespoons minced shallot, 2 tablespoons chopped golden raisins, pinch red pepper flakes, and pinch table salt and bring to boil over medium heat. Reduce heat to low and simmer until reduced and slightly thickened, 8 to 10 minutes (sauce will continue to thicken as it cools). Serve.

Pan-Seared Thick-Cut Pork Chop for Two

Halve all ingredients. Proceed with recipe in 10- or 12-inch nonstick skillet.

Why This Recipe Works The precursor to the cold-sear method used here (as well as with the pan-seared steaks on page 30) is the reverse-sear method where the meat is cooked most of the way in a low oven so that the stovetop cooking can be brief. But that approach takes the better part of an hour and doesn't avoid the smoke and the splatter. The cold-sear method (placing the meat in a cold pan and turning up the heat) has many advantages: It's quick, it's mess-free, and it allows for a deep crust to build up gradually without overcooking the meat. It is critical to use 1½-inch-thick rib chops, because they are thick enough to build up a mahogany exterior and burnished crust before cooking through. Regular flipping (every 2 minutes) is the key to this technique: It evenly heats both sides of the chops at almost the same time, cooking the chops faster and more evenly than an uninterrupted sear over high heat, which invariably encourages a gray band of overcooked meat to form just below the surface. Using a nonstick pan means that no oil is necessary. Starting over high heat drives off moisture and prevents the chops from steaming; then, lowering the heat to medium encourages browning without smoking. This recipe also works with boneless pork chops of a similar thickness. If you have time, salt the chops for at least 1 hour or up to 24 hours before cooking: Sprinkle each chop with 1½ teaspoons of Diamond Crystal Kosher Salt (if using Morton Kosher Salt, which is denser, use 1⅛ teaspoons), refrigerate them, then pat dry with paper towels before cooking. If the pork is enhanced (injected with a salt solution), do not salt the chops ahead. Electric stoves can be slow to respond to a cook's commands, which can pose a problem with this method; see page 4 for workaround strategies. You can use the fond left in the pan to create a pan sauce (see pages 32–33) or serve the chops with an herb sauce, relish, or chutney (pages 150–151).

1 Pat chops dry with paper towels and sprinkle with pepper. Place chops 1 inch apart in cold 12-inch nonstick skillet, arranging so narrow part of one chop is opposite wider part of second. Place skillet over high heat and cook chops for 2 minutes. Flip chops and cook on second side for 2 minutes. (Neither side of chops will be browned at this point.)

2 Flip chops, reduce heat to medium, and continue to cook, flipping chops every 2 minutes, until exterior is well browned and meat registers 140 to 145 degrees, 10 to 15 minutes. (While cooking, chops should sizzle; if not, increase heat slightly. Reduce heat if skillet starts to smoke.)

3 Transfer chops to carving board and let rest for 5 minutes. Carve meat from bone and slice ½ inch thick. (When carving, note that meat at tapered end near bone may retain slightly pink hue despite being cooked.) Season meat with coarse or flake sea salt to taste, and serve.

perfecting
PAN-SEARED THICK-CUT PORK CHOPS

A cold-sear method allows a deep crust to form without any overcooking. Starting on high heat drives off moisture and prevents steaming, then switching to low leads to browning.

1 Start Chops in a Cold Nonstick Skillet.

2 Don't Add Oil.

3 Start High; Then Go Low(er).

4 Flip Chops Every 2 Minutes.

Sizing Up Your Skillet

nonstick • **traditional cast iron** • **carbon steel**

The slick surface of a 12-inch nonstick skillet prevents the chops from sticking without oil and allows more savory browning to stick to the meat, not the pan. A traditional cast-iron or carbon-steel skillet will also work well for these reasons.

Pan-Seared Thick-Cut Boneless Pork Chops with Apples and Spinach

Serves 4

Total Time 45 minutes

2   teaspoons ground coriander

¾   teaspoon table salt, divided

¼   teaspoon pepper

1   (1½- to 2-pound) boneless center-cut pork loin roast, trimmed

2   tablespoons vegetable oil, divided

2   apples, cored and cut into 1-inch wedges

1   red onion, chopped

12   ounces (12 cups) baby spinach

1   tablespoon minced fresh tarragon

Why This Recipe Works Thick-cut boneless pork chops benefit from the cold-sear method (with lots of flipping) just like our pan-seared thick-cut bone-in chops (page 42). And because they lend themselves well to a weeknight meal, we wanted to use a skillet to both sear the chops and make an appealing side dish. To ensure chops of equal size, we cut a boneless center-cut pork loin roast into 2-inch-thick chops ourselves. After seasoning them with salt, pepper, and citrusy coriander, we arrange them in a cold nonstick skillet, place over high heat, and sear each side for 2 minutes. We then reduce the heat and flip them every 2 minutes to help them cook through evenly. While the pork rests, we make our side in the same pan. Look for a pork loin that is 6 to 7 inches long and about 1½ inches thick. We prefer natural pork in this recipe. If the pork is enhanced (injected with a salt solution), do not include salt in the spice mixture. Electric stoves can be slow to respond to a cook's commands, which can pose a problem with this method; see page 4 for workaround strategies.

1 Combine coriander, ½ teaspoon salt, and pepper in bowl. Cut pork loin crosswise into 4 chops of equal thickness. Pat chops dry with paper towels and sprinkle with spice mixture. Place chops 1 inch apart in cold 12-inch nonstick skillet. Place skillet over high heat and cook chops for 2 minutes. Flip chops and cook on second side for 2 minutes. (Neither side of chops will be browned at this point.)

2 Flip chops, reduce heat to medium, and continue to cook, flipping chops every 2 minutes, until exterior is well browned and meat registers 140 to 145 degrees, 10 to 15 minutes. (While cooking, chops should sizzle; if not, increase heat slightly. Reduce heat if skillet starts to smoke.) Transfer chops to cutting board, tent with aluminum foil, and let rest while preparing apples and spinach.

3 Wipe skillet clean with paper towels. Heat 1 tablespoon oil in now-empty skillet and heat over medium-low heat until shimmering. Add apples cut side down and cook until caramelized on first side, about 2 minutes. Flip and continue to cook until caramelized on second side and tender, about 2 minutes; transfer to serving bowl.

4 Add remaining tablespoon oil to now-empty skillet and heat over medium heat until shimmering. Add onion and remaining ¼ teaspoon salt and cook until softened and lightly browned, about 5 minutes. Add spinach to skillet 1 handful at a time and cook until wilted and tender, about 2 minutes. Off heat, season with salt and pepper to taste. Sprinkle apples with tarragon and serve alongside pork and spinach.

Sizing Up Your Skillet

nonstick • **traditional cast iron** • **carbon steel**

The slick surface of a 12-inch nonstick skillet prevents the chops from sticking without oil and allows more savory browning to stick to the meat, not the pan. It can then be easily wiped clean and used again for browning the apples and sautéing the spinach. A traditional cast-iron or carbon-steel skillet will also work well for these reasons.

Bacon-Wrapped Pork Tenderloin Medallions with Sweet Potatoes

Serves 4 to 6

Total Time 1 hour

3	tablespoons unsweetened applesauce
3	tablespoons whole-grain mustard
2	tablespoons Dijon mustard
4	teaspoons cider vinegar
1	tablespoon honey
1	tablespoon minced fresh chives
12–14	slices bacon
1½	pounds sweet potatoes, unpeeled, halved lengthwise and sliced crosswise ¾ inch thick
½	teaspoon table salt
2	(12- to 16-ounce) pork tenderloins, trimmed
¼	teaspoon pepper
2	tablespoons vegetable oil, plus extra as needed

Why This Recipe Works These beautiful bacon-wrapped pork medallions, served with a pungent but honey-sweetened mustard-apple sauce, are easy enough to pull off on a weeknight but fancy enough to serve at a dinner party. Cutting the pork tenderloins into medallions solves one of the issues of cooking them: their oblong shape. To preserve their tidy cylindrical shape and add a big hit of flavor, we wrap a blanched bacon strip around each, fastening it with toothpicks. Searing the medallions produces plenty of fond in which we then cook the sweet potatoes (after microwaving them briefly) so that they absorb some of the remaining bacon fat. And pouring the pork juices left on the plate into the sauce adds even more rich flavor.

1 Whisk applesauce, whole-grain mustard, Dijon mustard, vinegar, honey, and chives in bowl until combined; set aside.

2 Arrange bacon slices, slightly overlapping, on paper towel–lined plate and microwave until fat begins to render but bacon is still pliable, 3 to 5 minutes; let cool slightly.

3 Toss sweet potatoes with salt in bowl. Cover and microwave until tender, 5 to 10 minutes, stirring halfway through microwaving. Drain off accumulated liquid and set potatoes aside.

4 Slice pork crosswise into 1½-inch-thick medallions and arrange cut side down on cutting board. Pat dry with paper towels and sprinkle with pepper. Working with 1 piece at a time, wrap 1 slice bacon around circumference, stretching as needed, and secure overlapping ends with toothpick. (Two smaller pieces from tapered ends of tenderloins can be arranged side to side before wrapping to create larger single piece.)

5 Heat oil in 12-inch nonstick skillet over medium-high heat until just smoking. Add pork cut side down and cook until well browned on first side, about 4 minutes. Flip pork and continue to cook until browned on second side, about 4 minutes, adjusting heat as needed to prevent scorching. Reduce heat to medium. Using tongs, stand each piece on its side and cook, turning pieces as necessary, until sides are well browned and pork registers 135 to 140 degrees, 5 to 10 minutes. Transfer pork to serving platter, tent with aluminum foil, and let rest while finishing potatoes.

6 Pour off all but 2 tablespoons fat from skillet. (If necessary, supplement with extra oil.) Heat fat left in skillet over medium-high heat until shimmering. Add sweet potatoes and cook, turning as needed, until well browned, 5 to 7 minutes. Stir accumulated pork juices into mustard sauce. Serve pork with sweet potatoes and sauce.

VARIATION

Bacon-Wrapped Pork Tenderloin Medallions with Sweet Potatoes for Two

Reduce salt to ⅛ teaspoon; halve remaining ingredients. Proceed with recipe in 10- or 12-inch nonstick skillet. Pour off all but 1 tablespoon fat from skillet in step 6.

Sizing Up Your Skillet

nonstick • traditional cast iron • carbon steel

A 12-inch nonstick skillet provides enough space to properly sear the pork medallions, then brown the potatoes without concern for sticking. A traditional cast-iron or carbon-steel skillet will also work well for these reasons. If using a traditional cast-iron skillet, you will need to preheat the empty skillet over medium heat for 5 minutes before proceeding with step 5.

Cast-Iron Pork Fajitas

Serves 4 to 6

Total Time 1 hour

2 teaspoons kosher salt, divided

1½ teaspoons pepper, divided

1 teaspoon ground cumin

1 teaspoon chili powder

1 teaspoon garlic powder

1 teaspoon dried oregano

⅛ teaspoon ground allspice

2 (12- to 16-ounce) pork tenderloins, trimmed

3 tablespoons vegetable oil, divided

2 yellow, red, orange, or green bell peppers, stemmed, seeded, and cut into ¼-inch-wide strips

1 onion, halved and sliced ¼ inch thick

2 garlic cloves, minced

¼ cup chopped fresh cilantro

1 tablespoon lime juice

12 (6-inch) flour tortillas, warmed

VARIATION
Cast-Iron Pork Fajitas for Two

Halve all ingredients. Proceed with recipe in 10- or 12-inch cast-iron skillet.

Why This Recipe Works Restaurants have an advantage when making multipart dishes such as fajitas—a team of cooks as well as special oval cast-iron skillets to cook the fajitas and vegetables in so they go to the table in full sizzle. With a cast-iron skillet in hand you can easily create the same results, including bringing the skillet to the table for serving. To start, we wanted to veer away from the usual chicken, steak, and shrimp and branch out with another popular quick-cooking, tender cut: pork tenderloin. Seasoned properly with a generous amount of a complex, boldly flavored spice mixture, we knew it would be a hit. To fit two tenderloins in a 12-inch cast-iron skillet, we cut the tenderloins in half crosswise. Pounding the cylindrical tenderloins into ¾-inch-thick steaks increases their surface area and helps ensure even browning. The first step is to heat up the cast-iron skillet while empty so that it is plenty hot when the steaks hit the skillet. When the pork is done, we crank up the heat to allow the peppers and onion to get that delicious blistering and soften and brown quickly. And in a happy twist, the bits of delicious spice rub left behind after removing the meat adhere easily to the vegetables, distributing more flavor throughout the dish. This recipe was developed with Diamond Crystal Kosher Salt. (If using Morton Kosher Salt, which is denser, decrease the amount for the spice rub to 1½ teaspoons and the amount added with the onion to ¼ teaspoon.) We prefer natural pork in this recipe. If using enhanced pork (injected with a salt solution), reduce the salt in step 1 to 1 teaspoon. Serve the fajitas with pico de gallo, avocado or guacamole, sour cream, your favorite hot sauce, and lime wedges.

1 Combine 1½ teaspoons salt, 1 teaspoon pepper, cumin, chili powder, garlic powder, oregano, and allspice in bowl. Cut tenderloins in half crosswise. Working with 1 piece at a time, cover pork with plastic wrap and, using meat pounder, pound to even ¾-inch thickness. Pat pork dry with paper towels and sprinkle with spice mixture.

2 Heat 12-inch traditional cast-iron skillet over medium heat for 3 minutes. Add 2 tablespoons oil to skillet and swirl to coat. Place pork in skillet and cook until meat is well browned and registers 135 to 140 degrees, 5 to 7 minutes per side. Transfer pork to cutting board, tent with aluminum foil, and let rest while preparing pepper mixture.

3 Add remaining tablespoon oil and bell peppers to now-empty skillet and cook over medium-high heat for 3 minutes. Stir in onion, remaining ½ teaspoon salt, and remaining ½ teaspoon pepper and cook until vegetables are just softened, 3 to 5 minutes. Stir in minced garlic and cook until fragrant, about 30 seconds. Off heat, stir in cilantro and lime juice.

4 Slice pork thin crosswise. Stir any accumulated pork juices from cutting board into vegetables. Push vegetables to 1 side of skillet and place pork on empty side. Serve pork and vegetables with tortillas.

Sizing Up Your Skillet

traditional cast iron • **stainless steel** • **nonstick** • **enameled cast iron**

A 12-inch traditional cast-iron skillet provides enough space to brown the pork and vegetables. It makes an attractive serving vessel, and its superior heat retention keeps the pork and vegetables warm at the table. An enameled cast-iron skillet can also be used for these reasons. A stainless-steel or nonstick skillet can also be used; you will need to add the 2 tablespoons of oil to the skillet and heat over medium-high heat until just smoking before proceeding with step 2.

Khua Kling

Serves 6 to 8

Total Time 50 minutes

Curry Paste

10 dried arbol chiles, stemmed, halved lengthwise, and seeds removed

2 large shallots, chopped coarse

2 lemongrass stalks, trimmed to bottom 6 inches, halved length-wise, and sliced thin

4 garlic cloves, chopped coarse

4 Thai red chiles, stemmed and chopped coarse

4 makrut lime leaves, middle vein removed and sliced thin crosswise

1 (2-inch) piece fresh galangal, chopped coarse

1 (2-inch) piece fresh turmeric, chopped coarse

2 teaspoons kapi

¾ teaspoon table salt

Pork

1 tablespoon vegetable oil

1 pound ground pork, broken into 1-inch chunks

2 teaspoons fish sauce

2 teaspoons packed brown sugar

1 teaspoon pepper

4 Thai red chiles, stemmed and sliced ¼ inch thick on bias (optional)

3 makrut lime leaves, middle vein removed and sliced thin crosswise

6 cups cooled steamed jasmine rice

1 English cucumber, peeled if desired, sliced into ¼-inch rounds and chilled

Why This Recipe Works Famed for its fiery burn, this southern Thai pork curry is also fragrant, floral, and complex considering how quickly it comes together in a carbon-steel skillet. For a curry paste, dried and fresh chiles bring plenty of heat, but their fire is balanced by the citrusy-floral flavors of lemongrass, galangal, and makrut lime leaves and grounded by umami-rich Thai shrimp paste (kapi) and earthy turmeric. After grinding all the paste ingredients with an immersion blender, the recipe moves very quickly. We mash the spicy curry paste into a hot skillet until it starts to stick, then add ground pork and mash and chop until the meat and paste combine. A small amount of sugar and fish sauce smooths out the flavors at the end and some black pepper adds a subtle but lingering burn. For a fragrant finish, we simply stir in some more sliced lime leaves and chiles. Tossing the fiery khua kling with plenty of steamed jasmine rice and alternating bites of the mixture with chilled cucumber slices makes for a literally sensational meal. You'll need an immersion blender (or a mortar and pestle) for this recipe. Lemongrass, galangal, turmeric, kapi, and makrut lime leaves can be found at well-stocked supermarkets and Asian markets that carry Thai ingredients; they freeze well. You can substitute 1½ teaspoons dried turmeric for the fresh turmeric. To avoid inhaling spicy fumes while stir-frying, use an exhaust fan or open a window. This dish is meant to be intensely spicy and should be eaten with rice in a ratio of 1 part pork to 2 parts rice. The sliced chiles enable diners to customize the spice level, but they can be omitted if desired. Chilled cucumber slices make a complementary, cooling accompaniment.

1 For the curry paste Place arbols in small bowl and cover with 1 cup boiling water. Let sit for 20 minutes. Drain, reserving liquid. Combine arbols, shallots, lemongrass, garlic, Thai chiles, lime leaves, galangal, turmeric, kapi, and salt in 2-cup liquid measure. Use immersion blender in a mashing, up-and-down motion to blend to coarse paste, about 2 minutes, stirring and scraping down sides halfway through blending. (Paste can be refrigerated for 4 days or frozen for up to 4 months.)

2 For the pork Heat oil in 12-inch carbon-steel skillet over medium heat until shimmering. Add curry paste and cook, stirring constantly with wooden spoon, until paste just begins to stick, about 2 minutes. Add pork and mash and chop until meat and paste are mostly combined. Increase heat to medium-high and continue to cook, stirring and chopping constantly, until pork breaks into small pieces and is mostly cooked but some pink bits remain, about 3 minutes (if mixture starts to stick, deglaze with reserved arbol liquid, using 1 tablespoon at a time).

3 Add fish sauce, sugar, and pepper and cook, stirring constantly, until pork is fully cooked and no moisture remains. Off heat, stir in sliced chiles, if using, and lime leaves. Transfer to serving bowl. Serve with rice and cucumber slices.

Sizing Up Your Skillet

carbon steel • nonstick

We like a well-seasoned 12-inch carbon-steel skillet here as a good alternative to the traditional 14-inch flat-bottomed wok used for stir-frying because its relative light weight allows for ease while tossing, and its superior heat retention provides for rapid high-heat cooking. While a 12-inch nonstick skillet does not have the same heat retention, it can also be used.

Pan-Seared Salmon

Serves 4

Total Time 40 minutes

½ cup kosher salt for brining

4 (6- to 8-ounce) skin-on salmon fillets, 1 inch thick

1 teaspoon kosher salt, divided

¾ teaspoon pepper, divided

VARIATIONS

Pan-Seared Blackened Salmon

Combine 2 teaspoons paprika, ¾ teaspoon garlic powder, ¾ teaspoon onion powder, ½ teaspoon dried oregano, ½ teaspoon dried thyme, ½ teaspoon ground white pepper, and ½ teaspoon cayenne pepper with ¼ teaspoon salt and ¼ teaspoon pepper in small bowl. After patting salmon dry in step 1, brush all over with 2 tablespoons melted unsalted butter and sprinkle all over with spice mixture.

Pan-Seared Salmon for Two

Halve all ingredients. Proceed with recipe in 10- or 12-inch nonstick skillet. Dissolve ¼ cup Diamond Crystal Kosher Salt (if using Morton Kosher Salt, which is denser, use only 3 tablespoons) in 1 quart cold water in step 1.

Sizing Up Your Skillet

nonstick • traditional cast iron • carbon steel

The slick surface of a 12-inch nonstick skillet prevents the fillets from sticking without oil and allows more savory browning to stick to the fish, not the pan. A traditional cast-iron or carbon-steel skillet will also work well for these reasons.

Why This Recipe Works To achieve perfectly cooked salmon, we wanted to take advantage of the intense heat of the skillet and produce a golden-brown, ultracrisp crust on the fillets while keeping their interiors moist. The first step is to brine the fish to season it and keep it moist. Instead of adding the fish to a hot skillet, we season it and also sprinkle salt and pepper in a cold, dry skillet (to create a buffer between the salmon and pan). We then add the salmon to the skillet, skin side down, and only then turn on the heat. To ensure uniform cooking, buy a 1½- to 2-pound center-cut salmon fillet and cut it into four pieces. Using skin-on salmon is important here, as we rely on the fat underneath the skin as the cooking medium (as opposed to adding extra oil). Arctic char can also be used in place of the salmon. If using arctic char or wild salmon, cook it until it registers 120 degrees. This recipe was developed with Diamond Crystal Kosher Salt. (If using Morton Kosher Salt, which is denser, decrease the amount for the brine to 6 tablespoons.) If you don't want to serve the fish with the skin, we recommend peeling it off the fish after it is cooked. Serve the salmon with a creamy sauce (pages 102–103) or an herb sauce, relish, or chutney (pages 150–151).

1 Dissolve ½ cup salt in 2 quarts cold water in large container. Submerge salmon in brine and let sit at room temperature for 15 minutes. Remove salmon from brine and pat dry with paper towels.

2 Sprinkle bottom of 12-inch nonstick skillet evenly with ½ teaspoon salt and ½ teaspoon pepper. Place fillets skin side down in cold skillet and sprinkle tops of fillets with ¼ teaspoon salt and ¼ teaspoon pepper. Heat skillet over medium-high heat and cook fillets without moving them until fat begins to render, skin begins to brown, and bottom ¼ inch of fillets turns opaque, 6 to 8 minutes.

3 Using tongs, flip fillets and continue to cook without moving them until centers are still translucent when checked with tip of paring knife and register 125 degrees, 6 to 8 minutes. Transfer fillets skin side down to serving platter and let rest for 5 minutes before serving.

Brining seasons the fish and keeps it moist. The fat from the skin serves as a cooking medium since we start with a cold skillet and no oil. Salting the fish encourages browning and leads to moister fish.

1 Start with a Brine.

2 Leave the Skin On.

3 Season the Pan and the Salmon.

4 Start the Salmon in a Cold Nonstick Skillet.

5 Don't Add Oil.

Sizing Up Your Skillet

nonstick • **traditional cast iron** • **carbon steel**

The slick surface of a 12-inch nonstick skillet ensures that the savory browning sticks to the fish, not the pan. A traditional cast-iron or carbon-steel skillet will also work well for this reason. If using a traditional cast-iron skillet, you will need to preheat the empty skillet over medium heat for 5 minutes before proceeding with step 3.

Crispy Pan-Seared Black Sea Bass with Green Olive, Almond, and Orange Relish

Serves 4

Total Time 30 minutes, plus 45 minutes salting

Relish

½   cup slivered almonds, toasted

½   cup brine-cured green olives, pitted and chopped coarse

1   garlic clove, minced

1   teaspoon grated orange zest plus ¼ cup juice

¼   cup extra-virgin olive oil

¼   cup minced fresh mint

2   teaspoons white wine vinegar

    Cayenne pepper

Fish

1¾ teaspoons kosher salt, divided

¾   teaspoon sugar

4   (6- to 8-ounce) skin-on black sea bass fillets, 1 inch thick

2   tablespoons vegetable oil

VARIATION

Crispy Pan-Seared Black Sea Bass with Green Olive, Almond, and Orange Relish for Two

Halve all ingredients. Proceed with recipe in 10- or 12-inch nonstick skillet.

Why This Recipe Works Serving fish skin-on is a way to instantly elevate it, creating succulence and textural contrast as well as an elegant presentation. If you're going to do it, you want crisp, potato-chip-thin skin covering ultramoist fish. For a restaurant-quality dish, we salt the fillets before we cook them. Why? First, the salt seasons the flesh deeply by diffusion. Second, salt actually dissolves some of the proteins in the fish and forms a gel that can hold on to more moisture so that the flesh near the outside doesn't overcook in the pan. The second secret is going low and slow: Start the fish in a hot pan, but immediately drop the flame to maintain an even, steady sear. Cooking the fish most of the way on the skin side—an old-school, fancy French technique dubbed "unilateral" cooking—ensures that the skin gets incredibly crispy while the flesh stays moist. This recipe was developed with Diamond Crystal Kosher Salt; if using Morton Kosher Salt, which is denser, decrease the amount for the salt-sugar mixture to 1⅛ teaspoons. This recipe works well with 1-inch-thick fish fillets that have skin that is pleasant to eat; red snapper and bluefish are good options. Do not use fillets thicker than 1 inch, as they are difficult to cook through without scorching the skin or overcooking the bottom layer of flesh. If using arctic char, cook the fillets to 120 degrees (for medium-rare). If using bluefish, cook the fillets to 130 degrees (for medium-rare). Electric stoves can be slow to respond to a cook's commands, which can pose a problem with this method; see page 4 for workaround strategies.

1 For the relish Pulse almonds, olives, garlic, and orange zest in food processor until nuts and olives are finely chopped, 10 to 12 pulses, scraping down sides of bowl as needed. Transfer to bowl and stir in orange juice, oil, mint, and vinegar. Season with salt and cayenne to taste; set aside for serving.

2 For the fish Combine 1½ teaspoons salt and sugar in bowl. Using sharp knife, make 3 or 4 shallow slashes, about ½ inch apart, in skin side of each fillet, being careful not to cut into flesh and leaving ½ inch of skin at the edges intact. Sprinkle flesh side of fillets evenly with salt mixture and place, skin side up, on wire rack set in rimmed baking sheet. Sprinkle skin side with remaining ¼ teaspoon salt. Refrigerate for at least 45 minutes or up to 1½ hours.

3 Pat fillets dry with paper towels. Heat oil in 12-inch nonstick skillet over high heat until just smoking. Place fillets skin side down in skillet. Immediately reduce heat to medium-low and, using fish spatula, firmly press fillets for 20 to 30 seconds to ensure even contact between skin and skillet. Continue to cook until skin is well browned and flesh is opaque except for top ¼ inch, 6 to 12 minutes. (If at any time during searing, oil starts to smoke, or sides of fish start to brown, reduce heat so that oil is sizzling but not smoking.)

4 Off heat, flip fillets with 2 spatulas and continue to cook using residual heat of skillet until bass registers 135 degrees, 30 seconds to 1 minute. Transfer bass skin side up to serving platter and serve with relish.

Sautéed Tilapia

Serves 4

Total Time 40 minutes

4   (5- to 6-ounce) skinless tilapia fillets

1   teaspoon kosher salt

2   tablespoons vegetable oil

Lemon wedges

VARIATION

Sautéed Tilapia with Chive Lemon-Miso Butter

Combine 2 tablespoons white miso, 1 teaspoon grated lemon zest plus 2 teaspoons juice, and ⅛ teaspoon pepper in small bowl. Add 4 tablespoons softened unsalted butter and stir until fully incorporated. Stir in 2 tablespoons minced fresh chives. After transferring thick halves of tilapia to platter, dollop with two-thirds of miso butter. Dollop thin halves of tilapia with remaining miso butter.

Sautéed Tilapia for Two

Halve all ingredients. Proceed with recipe in 10-or 12-inch nonstick skillet.

Why This Recipe Works The beauty of thin white fish fillets is that they cook quickly in a smoking hot skillet and can be served simply with a squeeze of lemon or dressed up with a compound butter or simple herb sauce, relish, or chutney (see pages 150–151). But if you simply toss a fillet like the widely available and inexpensive tilapia into a skillet without a precise method (or don't use the right skillet), you are courting disaster: fish that sticks to the pan, uneven cooking, and no flavorful browning. So what is the best technique? First, we salt the fish and let it sit for 15 minutes. This draws moisture out of the fish, which we simply wipe away with a paper towel, a step that encourages browning; it also makes the fish moister and better seasoned. Equally important is dividing each fillet into a thick and a thin portion and sautéing them separately, which allows for more precise cooking and even browning. Tilapia is firm and resilient enough to cook in a nonstick skillet over aggressive heat without falling apart. The result, in just minutes, is top-notch fish. You can use fresh or frozen tilapia in this recipe (if frozen, thaw before cooking). Flounder, sole, or catfish fillets of a similar size can be substituted. This recipe was developed with Diamond Crystal Kosher Salt. (If using Morton Kosher Salt, which is denser, decrease the amount to ¾ teaspoon.)

1 Place tilapia on cutting board and sprinkle both sides with salt. Let sit at room temperature for 15 minutes. Pat tilapia dry with paper towels. Using seam that runs down middle of fillet as guide, cut each fillet in half lengthwise to create 1 thick half and 1 thin half.

2 Heat oil in 12-inch nonstick skillet over high heat until just smoking. Add thick fillet halves to skillet. Cook, tilting and gently shaking skillet occasionally to distribute oil, until undersides are golden brown, 2 to 3 minutes. Using thin spatula, flip fillets. Cook until second sides are golden brown and tilapia registers 130 to 135 degrees, 2 to 3 minutes. Transfer tilapia to serving platter.

3 Return skillet to high heat. When oil is just smoking, add thin fillet halves and cook until undersides are golden brown, about 1 minute. Flip and cook until second sides are golden brown, about 1 minute. Serve with lemon wedges.

Sizing Up Your Skillet

nonstick • **traditional cast iron** • **carbon steel**

The slick surface of a 12-inch nonstick skillet ensures that the savory browning sticks to the fish, not the pan. A traditional cast-iron or carbon-steel skillet will also work well for this reason. If using a traditional cast-iron skillet, you will need to preheat the empty skillet over medium heat for 5 minutes before proceeding with step 2.

perfecting
SAUTÉED TILAPIA

Cutting the fillets into thick and thin portions and cooking in batches delivers even cooking and perfect browning. Salting encourages browning and leads to moister fish.

1 Salt for 15 Minutes at Room Temperature.

2 Divide Fillets into Thick and Thin Portions.

3 Start Hot and Cook Fast.

Pan-Seared Tuna Steaks with Cucumber-Peanut Salad

Serves 4

Total Time 25 minutes

1   English cucumber, halved lengthwise and sliced thin

⅓   cup unsalted dry-roasted peanuts, chopped coarse

¼   cup fresh cilantro leaves

¼   cup fresh mint leaves

2   tablespoons vegetable oil, divided

1   tablespoon lime juice

1   tablespoon fish sauce

1   teaspoon chili-garlic sauce

1⅛   teaspoons table salt, divided

4   (6- to 8-ounce) tuna steaks, 1 inch thick

2   teaspoons pepper

½   teaspoon sugar

Why This Recipe Works   Seared tuna, with a nice browned crust and a ruby-red interior, is a quick way to a fresh weeknight dinner. Pair it with a no-cook side salad and you've got a special summer supper almost too snappy to be true. To cook the tuna steaks to perfection, we first pat them dry, season with salt and pepper, and then sprinkle sugar on each side. The sugar helps them brown in short order, and cooking them in a ripping-hot nonstick skillet keeps them from sticking. The cucumber salad brings the rosy-centered tuna to life. Peanuts are a crunchy (and rich) contrast to the refreshing sliced cucumbers and mint and cilantro leaves. The fish sauce and lime juice in the dressing complement the tuna, and a hint of chili-garlic sauce kicks it up. The salad serves as a base for the tuna and a side dish for a complete, healthful meal.

1   Toss cucumber, peanuts, cilantro, mint, 1 tablespoon oil, lime juice, fish sauce, chili-garlic sauce, and ⅛ teaspoon salt together in bowl; set aside until ready to serve.

2   Pat tuna dry with paper towels. Sprinkle with remaining 1 teaspoon salt and pepper. Sprinkle sugar evenly over 1 side of each steak. Heat remaining 1 tablespoon oil in 12-inch nonstick skillet over medium-high heat until just smoking. Place steaks sugared side down in skillet and cook, flipping every 1 to 2 minutes, until well browned and center is translucent red when checked with tip of paring knife and registers 110 degrees (for rare), 2 to 4 minutes. Transfer steaks to cutting board and slice ½ inch thick. Serve with cucumber salad.

Sizing Up Your Skillet

nonstick ● **traditional cast iron** ● **carbon steel**

The slick surface of a 12-inch nonstick skillet ensures that the savory browning sticks to the fish, not the pan. A traditional cast-iron or carbon-steel skillet will also work well for this reason. If using a traditional cast-iron skillet, you will need to preheat the empty skillet over medium heat for 5 minutes before proceeding with step 2.

Pan-Seared Shrimp with Pistachios, Cumin, and Parsley

Serves 4

Total Time 45 minutes

1½ pounds extra-large shrimp (21 to 25 per pound), peeled, deveined, and tails removed

½ teaspoon table salt, divided

1 garlic clove, minced

1 teaspoon ground cumin

1 teaspoon paprika

⅛ teaspoon cayenne pepper

2 tablespoons extra-virgin olive oil, divided

⅛ teaspoon sugar

¼ cup fresh cilantro leaves and tender stems, chopped

¼ cup fresh parsley leaves and tender stems, chopped

1 tablespoon lemon juice

¼ cup shelled pistachios, toasted and chopped coarse

VARIATION

Pan-Seared Shrimp with Peanuts, Black Pepper, and Lime

Substitute 2 teaspoons coarsely ground coriander seeds for cumin and red pepper flakes for cayenne; add 1 teaspoon coarsely ground peppercorns and 1 teaspoon sugar to spice mixture. Increase cilantro to ½ cup and omit parsley. Substitute lime juice for lemon juice and 3 tablespoons chopped dry-roasted peanuts for pistachios.

Why This Recipe Works When it comes to achieving deep, flavorful browning on the outside and snappy, succulent meat on the inside, shrimp aren't so simple. For one thing, they're tiny, so it's almost impossible to get any color on them before they dry out. We start by briefly salting them so that they retain moisture even as they're seared over high heat. Tossing a little sugar with the shrimp (patted dry after salting) boosts browning and underscores the shrimp's sweetness. To cook them, we arrange the shrimp in a single layer in a cold nonstick skillet so that they make even contact with the surface. They heat up gradually with the skillet, so they don't buckle and thus brown uniformly; slower searing also creates a wider window for ensuring that they don't overcook. Once the shrimp are spotty brown and pink at the edges on the first side, we remove them from the heat, turn each one, and let the pan's residual heat cook them the rest of the way. A flavorful spice mixture for seasoning the shrimp comes together in the same skillet. We prefer untreated shrimp, but if your shrimp are treated with sodium or preservatives like sodium tripolyphosphate, skip the salting in step 1. You can substitute jumbo shrimp (16 to 20 per pound) for the extra-large shrimp; if substituting, increase the cooking time by 1 to 2 minutes.

1 Toss shrimp and ¼ teaspoon salt together in bowl; set aside for 15 to 30 minutes. Meanwhile, combine garlic, cumin, paprika, cayenne, and remaining ¼ teaspoon salt in small bowl.

2 Pat shrimp dry with paper towels. Add 1 tablespoon oil and sugar to bowl with shrimp and toss to coat. Add shrimp to cold 12-inch nonstick skillet in single layer and cook over high heat until undersides of shrimp are spotty brown and edges turn pink, 3 to 4 minutes. Remove skillet from heat. Working quickly, use tongs to flip each shrimp; let sit until second side is opaque, about 2 minutes. Transfer shrimp to large plate.

3 Add remaining 1 tablespoon oil to now-empty skillet. Add spice mixture and cook over medium heat until fragrant, about 30 seconds. Off heat, return shrimp to skillet. Add cilantro, parsley, and lemon juice and toss to combine; sprinkle with pistachios and serve.

VARIATION

Pan-Seared Shrimp with Pistachios, Cumin, and Parsley for Two

Reduce sugar to pinch; halve remaining ingredients. Proceed with recipe in 10- or 12-inch nonstick skillet.

perfecting
PAN-SEARED SHRIMP

Salting delicate shrimp helps them retain moisture, while sugar enhances browning. A cold skillet allows them to heat up gradually without overcooking.

1   Salt Briefly, Then Add Sugar.

2   Start in a Cold Nonstick Skillet.

3   Finish off the Heat.

Sizing Up Your Skillet

nonstick • **traditional cast iron** • **carbon steel**

The slick surface of a 12-inch nonstick skillet ensures that the savory browning sticks to the shrimp, not the pan. A traditional cast-iron or carbon-steel skillet will also work well for this reason.

Seared Scallops with Broccolini and Browned Butter–Pepper Relish

Serves 4

Total Time 50 minutes

1½ pounds large sea scallops, tendons removed

1 pound broccolini, trimmed and rinsed

1 tablespoon vegetable oil

½ teaspoon table salt

¼ teaspoon pepper

4 tablespoons unsalted butter

3 tablespoons pine nuts

1 cup jarred mild or hot peppadew peppers, quartered, plus 2 table-spoons brine

1 shallot, sliced thin

Why This Recipe Works There is really no margin of error when cooking scallops, but the techniques for getting them right are simple. First, make sure to remove excess moisture by gently blotting the scallops with a dish towel and letting them sit briefly draped with the towel. A large nonstick skillet keeps the delicate scallops from sticking and provides enough space to allow for browning instead of steaming. You really want to get a good sear and appealing crust on the scallops, so high heat and quick cooking are imperative; be vigilant and watch your timing. For this recipe, we use the skillet multiple ways to create a fast-moving but elegant meal. First, we use a steam/sauté method for cooking broccolini. In the empty skillet, we then cook the scallops over high heat using vegetable oil, not butter (which will burn before the scallops are done). Then, for the crowning touch, we cook pine nuts in butter in the empty skillet and then add shallots, zingy peppadew peppers, and a little of their brine off the heat. The buttery relish pairs beautifully with the scallops and the peppers add brightness. Be sure to purchase "dry" scallops and remove the tough tendon attached to the side. If peppadew peppers are unavailable, you can substitute stemmed and seeded sweet cherry peppers; whisk ¼ teaspoon sugar into brine before adding to skillet. You will need a 12-inch nonstick skillet with a tight-fitting lid for this recipe; if your skillet lid does not fit securely and allows too much steam to escape, add a bit more water in step 3 to keep the skillet from drying out.

1 Place scallops on clean dish towel and place second clean dish towel on top. Gently press to blot liquid. Keeping towel on top, let scallops sit at room temperature for 10 minutes while towels absorb moisture.

2 Cut broccolini stalks measuring more than ½ inch in diameter at base in half lengthwise. Cut stalks measuring ¼ to ½ inch in diameter at base in half lengthwise, starting below where florets begin and keeping florets intact. Leave whole stalks measuring less than ¼ inch in diameter at base.

3 Bring ⅓ cup water to boil in 12-inch nonstick skillet over high heat. Add broccolini, cover, reduce heat to medium-low, and cook for 3 minutes. Uncover broccolini and toss gently with tongs. Cover and continue to cook until broccolini is bright green and crisp-tender, 3 to 5 minutes. Transfer broccolini to platter and cover to keep warm. Wipe skillet clean with paper towels.

4 Heat oil in now-empty skillet over high heat until just smoking. Sprinkle scallops with salt and pepper. Arrange scallops flat side down, spaced evenly apart, in skillet. Cook until well browned, about 2 minutes per side. Transfer scallops to platter with broccolini.

5 Cook butter and pine nuts in again-empty skillet over medium heat until nuts are toasted and butter is lightly browned, about 2 minutes. Off heat, stir in peppers and shallot and cook using residual heat until softened and heated through, about 2 minutes. Stir in pepper brine and season with pepper to taste. Add broccolini and toss to coat with sauce. Nestle scallops into skillet and serve.

Sizing Up Your Skillet

nonstick • **traditional cast iron** • **carbon steel**

The slick surface of a 12-inch nonstick skillet ensures that the savory browning sticks to the scallops, not the pan. A traditional cast-iron or carbon-steel skillet will also work well for this reason.

Kimchi Bokkeumbap

Serves 4 to 6

Total Time 45 minutes

1   (8-inch square) sheet gim

2   tablespoons vegetable oil, divided

2   (¼-inch-thick) slices deli ham, cut into ¼-inch pieces (about 4 ounces)

1   large onion, chopped

6   scallions, white and green parts separated and sliced thin on bias

1¼   cups cabbage kimchi, drained with ¼ cup juice reserved, cut into ¼-inch strips

¼   cup water

4   teaspoons soy sauce

4   teaspoons gochujang paste

½   teaspoon pepper

3   cups cooked short-grain white rice

4   teaspoons toasted sesame oil

1   tablespoon sesame seeds, toasted

VARIATION

Kimchi Bokkeumbap for Two

Reduce vegetable oil to 4 teaspoons and cabbage kimchi to ⅔ cup with 2 tablespoons juice reserved; halve remaining ingredients. Proceed with recipe in 12-inch carbon-steel skillet. Use 2 teaspoons vegetable oil in steps 2 and 3.

Why This Recipe Works This punchy, radiant fried rice is comfort food on the fly in many Korean households, and like all fried rice dishes, it starts with leftover cooked rice (and in this case, well-fermented kimchi as well). Using classic stir-frying techniques, we prepare this version in a carbon-steel skillet; its relative light weight and sloped sides make it possible to rapidly cook, toss, and fold effectively. In addition to the rice and the kimchi, the seasonings and additions to bulk it up vary widely from cook to cook. We start by stir-frying some aromatics (chopped onion and sliced scallions) with chopped ham—a popular addition that we like for its smoky flavor and pleasantly springy texture. Then we add lots of chopped cabbage kimchi along with some of its savory, punchy juice and a little water and season it with soy sauce, toasted sesame oil, and gochujang to add savoriness, rich nuttiness, and a little more heat. We simmer the cabbage leaves so that they soften a bit, stir in the rice, and cook the mixture until the liquid is absorbed. Finally, we top the rice with small strips of gim (seaweed paper), sesame seeds, and scallion greens. This recipe works best with day-old rice; alternatively, cook your rice 2 hours ahead, spread it on a rimmed baking sheet, and let it cool completely before chilling for 30 minutes. Plain pretoasted seaweed snacks can be substituted for the gim; omit the toasting in step 1. You'll need at least a 16-ounce jar of kimchi; if it doesn't yield ¼ cup juice, make up the difference with water. If using soft, well-aged kimchi, omit the water and reduce the cooking time at the end of step 2 to 2 minutes.

1 Grip gim with tongs and hold 2 inches above low flame on gas burner. Toast gim, turning every 3 to 5 seconds, until gim is aromatic and shrinks slightly, about 20 seconds. (If you do not have a gas stove, toast gim on rimmed baking sheet in 275-degree oven until gim is aromatic and shrinks slightly, 20 to 25 minutes, flipping gim halfway through toasting.) Using kitchen shears, cut gim into four 2-inch-wide strips. Stack strips and cut crosswise into thin strips.

2 Heat 1 tablespoon vegetable oil in 12-inch carbon-steel skillet over medium-high heat until just smoking. Add ham, onion, and scallion whites and cook, tossing slowly but constantly, until onion is softened and ham is beginning to brown at edges, 6 to 8 minutes. Stir in kimchi and reserved juice, water, soy sauce, gochujang, and pepper. Cook, stirring occasionally, until kimchi turns soft and translucent, 4 to 6 minutes.

3 Sprinkle rice over top, reduce heat to medium-low, and cook, stirring and folding constantly until mixture is evenly coated, about 3 minutes. Stir in sesame oil and remaining 1 tablespoon vegetable oil. Increase heat to medium-high and cook, stirring occasionally, until mixture begins to stick to skillet, about 4 minutes. Transfer to serving bowl. Sprinkle with sesame seeds, scallion greens, and gim and serve.

Sizing Up Your Skillet

carbon steel   •   **nonstick**

A well-seasoned 12-inch carbon-steel skillet is a good alternative to the traditional 14-inch flat-bottomed wok used for stir-frying because its relative light weight allows for ease while tossing, and its superior heat retention provides for rapid high-heat cooking. While a 12-inch nonstick skillet does not have the same heat retention, it can also be used.

Charred Broccoli Salad with Avocado, Grapefruit, and Ginger-Lime Dressing

Serves 4

Total Time 1 hour

1¼ pounds broccoli crowns

1 tablespoon tamarind juice concentrate

1 tablespoon grated fresh ginger

1 tablespoon honey

1 teaspoon grated lime zest plus 3 tablespoons juice (2 limes)

1 red Thai chile, stemmed and sliced thin

¾ teaspoon salt, divided

3 shallots, sliced thin

6 tablespoons vegetable oil

2 grapefruits

2 avocados, halved, pitted, and cut into 1-inch wedges

1½ cups fresh Thai basil, cilantro, and/or mint leaves, divided

3 tablespoons roasted salted peanuts, chopped

Why This Recipe Works This charred broccoli salad is a stunner, and the combination of broccoli wedges and a pungent Thai-inspired dressing, plus chunks of avocado and grapefruit, make it all the more appealing. So how does the skillet figure into the equation? We use it to crisp up sliced shallots in a hefty amount of oil, first over high heat and then lower heat so they become brown and sweet instead of turning bitter; then we strain out the flavorful oil and let the shallots become even crispier as they drain on paper towels. Meanwhile, we return the reserved shallot oil to the skillet along with the broccoli wedges and a little water, cover the skillet, and let the broccoli steam and soften until the water evaporates. Now the broccoli is ready for charring, which simply involves pressing each side of the wedges flat against the skillet until beautifully smoky brown. With the cooking done, all that is left is to combine the broccoli with a zesty dressing of tamarind, lime, and ginger and add avocado, grapefruit, basil, and the crispy shallots. For a beautiful finishing touch, we top this colorful salad with chopped peanuts, plus more grapefruit, basil, and shallots. Tamarind juice concentrate is sometimes labeled tamarind concentrate; do not substitute tamarind juice, tamarind nectar, or tamarind paste. If you cannot find tamarind juice concentrate, omit it and increase the lime juice to ¼ cup. You will need a 12-inch skillet with a tight-fitting lid for this recipe.

1 Cut broccoli crowns into 4 wedges if 3 to 4 inches in diameter, or 6 wedges if 4 to 5 inches in diameter. Whisk tamarind concentrate, ginger, honey, lime zest and juice, Thai chile, and ½ teaspoon salt together in large bowl; set dressing aside.

2 Set fine-mesh strainer over medium bowl and line a plate with paper towels. Cook shallots and oil in 12-inch nonstick skillet over medium-high heat, stirring constantly, until shallot edges just begin to brown, 5 to 7 minutes. Reduce heat to medium-low and continue to cook until golden brown, 5 to 7 minutes. Drain shallots through prepared strainer, reserving oil, and season with salt to taste. Transfer shallots to lined plate and set aside to drain and turn crisp.

3 Wipe skillet clean with paper towels. Add reserved oil to skillet. Add broccoli, cut side down (pieces will fit snugly; if a few pieces don't fit in bottom layer, place on top) and drizzle with 2 tablespoons water. Cover and cook over medium-high heat, without moving broccoli, until it is bright green, about 4 minutes.

4 Sprinkle broccoli with remaining ¼ teaspoon salt and press gently into skillet with back of spatula. Cover and cook until undersides of broccoli are deeply charred and stems are crisp-tender, 4 to 6 minutes. Uncover and turn broccoli so second cut side is touching skillet. Move any pieces that were on top so that they are flush with skillet surface. Continue to cook, uncovered, pressing gently on broccoli with back of spatula, until second cut side is deeply browned, 3 to 5 minutes. Transfer broccoli to bowl with dressing.

5 Cut away peel and pith from grapefruits. Quarter grapefruits, then slice crosswise into 1-inch-thick pieces. Add three-quarters grapefruit, avocados, 1 cup herbs, and half of shallots to bowl with broccoli and toss gently to coat. Arrange broccoli mixture attractively on serving platter and top with peanuts, remaining grapefruit, remaining ½ cup herbs, and remaining shallots. Serve.

Sizing Up Your Skillet

nonstick • **traditional cast iron** • **carbon steel**

A 12-inch nonstick skillet provides enough space for arranging the large broccoli pieces in an even layer. Its slick surface also ensures that the savory browning sticks to the broccoli, not the pan. A traditional cast-iron or carbon-steel skillet will also work well for these reasons.

Seared Halloumi and Vegetable Salad Bowls

Serves 4

Total Time 45 minutes

¼ cup extra-virgin olive oil, divided

1 pound eggplant, cut into ½-inch pieces

1 head radicchio (10 ounces), cored and cut into 1-inch pieces

1 red bell pepper, stemmed, seeded, and cut into ½-inch pieces

1 zucchini, trimmed and sliced lengthwise into ribbons

6 ounces halloumi cheese, sliced into ½-inch-thick slabs

2 tablespoons honey

1 teaspoon minced fresh thyme

1 garlic clove, minced

½ teaspoon grated lemon zest plus 2 tablespoons juice

¼ teaspoon table salt

⅛ teaspoon pepper

1 cup jarred whole artichoke hearts packed in water, halved, rinsed, and patted dry

Why This Recipe Works A mix of cooked and raw ingredients, this beautiful salad incorporates flavors and ingredients you might find in a Greek meze spread into a filling bowl meal. And it gives the skillet a workout. That said, it all moves along very quickly, especially if you've prepped all your ingredients ahead. First, we use the skillet to sauté chunks of eggplant until browned. After removing the eggplant, we heat more oil until shimmering, and add radicchio and bell pepper, cooking them until they just begin to get that tasty and appealing char. The star of this dish, slabs of rich halloumi, get a turn in the skillet for mere minutes, only until the cheese is just warmed through and beginning to brown. After searing the halloumi slabs, we cut them into ½-inch pieces, so its flavor is distributed throughout our bowl. An herbaceous honey-thyme vinaigrette contrasts with the salty cheese and bitter radicchio. To slice the zucchini, use a vegetable peeler to shave the length of the squash, rotating the squash 90 degrees after each slice.

1 Heat 1 tablespoon oil in 12-inch nonstick skillet over medium-high heat until shimmering. Add eggplant and cook, stirring frequently, until tender and browned, 8 to 10 minutes; transfer to large bowl. Heat 1 tablespoon oil in now-empty skillet over medium-high heat until shimmering. Add radicchio and bell pepper and cook until wilted and beginning to char, 4 to 6 minutes. Transfer to bowl with eggplant; stir in zucchini and set aside.

2 Heat 1 tablespoon oil in again-empty skillet over medium heat until shimmering. Add halloumi in single layer and cook until golden brown, 2 to 4 minutes per side. Transfer cheese to cutting board and cut into ½-inch pieces.

3 Whisk honey, thyme, garlic, lemon zest and juice, salt, and pepper together in bowl. While whisking constantly, slowly drizzle in remaining 1 tablespoon oil until combined. Toss vegetable mixture with half of vinaigrette to coat, then season with salt and pepper to taste. Divide among individual serving bowls, then top each with halloumi and artichokes. Drizzle with remaining vinaigrette and serve.

VARIATION

Seared Halloumi and Vegetable Salad Bowls for Two

Reduce oil to 8 teaspoons; halve remaining ingredients. Proceed with recipe in 10- or 12-inch nonstick skillet. Use 2 teaspoons oil to cook eggplant, radicchio, bell pepper, and halloumi. Whisk 2 teaspoons oil into dressing.

Sizing Up Your Skillet

nonstick • **traditional cast iron** • **carbon steel**

A 12-inch nonstick skillet provides enough space for browning the vegetables and searing the halloumi. Its slick surface also ensures the savory browning sticks to the vegetables and cheese, not the pan. A traditional cast-iron or carbon-steel skillet will also work well for these reasons. If using a cast-iron skillet, you will need to preheat the empty skillet over medium heat for 3 minutes before proceeding with step 1.

Seared Tofu with Panch Phoron, Green Beans, and Pickled Shallots

Serves 4

Total Time 1¼ hours

⅓ cup red wine vinegar

2 tablespoons sugar

1⅛ teaspoons table salt, divided

1 large shallot, sliced thin

28 ounces extra-firm or firm tofu, drained

1 cup plain whole-milk yogurt

¾ cup minced fresh cilantro

1 teaspoon grated lime zest plus 1 tablespoon juice

2 garlic cloves, minced

¾ teaspoon ground turmeric

1 pound green beans, trimmed and halved

2 tablespoons water

¼ cup vegetable oil, divided

4 teaspoons panch phoron

Panch Phoron

Makes about ¼ cup

1 tablespoon cumin seeds

1 tablespoon fennel seeds

1 tablespoon mustard seeds

1 tablespoon nigella seeds

1½ teaspoons fenugreek

Combine all ingredients in bowl. (Panch phoron can be stored in airtight container for up to 1 month.)

Why This Recipe Works A wonderful thing about tofu is that it absorbs the flavors of whatever it is paired with, plus there are many methods for cooking it, from stir-frying and searing to roasting and broiling. This adventurous dish features torn pieces of tofu (which absorb even more flavor than sliced tofu) seared in a nonstick skillet and accompanied by green beans and panch phoron, a highly aromatic whole-seed spice blend of equal amounts of mustard, cumin, fennel, and nigella seeds as well as some fenugreek. The method for blooming the whole seeds in oil before adding them to a recipe is called tadka, and is used often in Indian cooking. But before any cooking happens, we quick-pickle shallot slices (using the microwave) to add piquancy to the final dish. While the shallots are pickling and the tofu is draining, we add the green beans to the skillet with a little water, oil, and salt, and cover it so that the beans steam-cook; when the water evaporates, we give them a good sear in the skillet, so they turn appealingly brown. Tearing the tofu into rough pieces and allowing them plenty of time to drain ensures that the craggy edges turn golden brown and crisp in the skillet. Once the beans and tofu are cooked, we add more oil and the panch phoron and toast until the seeds pop and become fragrant. Tossed right in the skillet with the beans and tofu, the fragrant spices and oil infuse the dish with unmistakable aroma and flavor. For a beautiful finished dish, we spread a serving plate with a layer of cilantro- and lime-spiked yogurt, then top with the seasoned tofu and beans, leaving a border of the yogurt visible. And finally, a sprinkle of the quick pickled shallots adds an extra pop of acidity and another unique layer of flavor. You will need a 12-inch skillet with a tight-fitting lid for this recipe.

1 Microwave vinegar, sugar, and ⅛ teaspoon salt in medium bowl until steaming, about 2 minutes. Add shallot and stir until submerged. Let sit for 10 minutes, stirring occasionally.

2 Line rimmed baking sheet with triple layer of paper towels. Gently tear tofu into rough 1½-inch pieces and transfer to lined baking sheet. Top tofu with second layer of paper towels and let drain for 10 minutes.

3 Combine yogurt, cilantro, lime zest and juice, and garlic in separate bowl and season with salt to taste; set sauce aside for serving. Drain shallots and set aside for serving.

4 Combine green beans, 2 tablespoons water, 1 tablespoon oil, and ¼ teaspoon salt in 12-inch nonstick skillet. Cover and cook over medium-high heat, tossing occasionally, until beans are nearly tender, 6 to 8 minutes. Uncover and continue to cook until water has evaporated and beans are just beginning to brown in spots, 2 to 4 minutes; transfer to large bowl.

5 Sprinkle tofu with remaining ¾ teaspoon salt and turmeric. Heat 1 tablespoon oil in now-empty skillet over medium-high heat until shimmering. Add tofu and cook until golden brown, 8 to 10 minutes, turning as needed and adding 1 tablespoon oil halfway through cooking. Transfer tofu to bowl with green beans.

6 Add panch phoron and remaining 1 tablespoon oil to again-empty skillet and cook over medium-high heat until fragrant and seeds start to pop, about 1 minute. Off heat, immediately add green beans and tofu and toss gently to combine.

7 Spread yogurt sauce over surface of serving platter. Arrange tofu and green bean mixture attractively on top, sprinkle with pickled shallots, and serve.

Sizing Up Your Skillet

nonstick • **traditional cast iron**

A 12-inch nonstick skillet provides enough space for browning the tofu. Its slick surface also ensures that the savory browning sticks to the tofu, not the pan. A traditional cast-iron skillet will also work well for these reasons; add the panch phoron and oil to skillet off heat in step 6 and let cook using the pan's residual heat.

CHAPTER TWO

simmer, braise & poach

Braised Chicken Thighs with Lemon, Spices, and Torn Basil

Serves 4 to 6

Total Time 1½ hours

- 8 (5- to 7-ounce) bone-in chicken thighs, trimmed
- 1 teaspoon table salt
- ½ teaspoon pepper
- 1 tablespoon vegetable oil
- 1 shallot, minced
- 2 garlic cloves, minced
- 1 teaspoon ground cumin
- ½ teaspoon ground coriander
- 1½ cups chicken broth
- ½ teaspoon grated lemon zest plus ½ cup juice (3 lemons)
- 2 teaspoons water
- 1½ teaspoons cornstarch
- 1 teaspoon coriander seeds, lightly crushed
- 2 tablespoons unsalted butter, cut into 2 pieces
- 10 large basil leaves, torn into pieces

VARIATION

Braised Chicken Thighs with Lemon, Spices, and Torn Basil for Two

Halve all ingredients. Proceed with recipe in 10-inch ovensafe stainless-steel skillet. In step 2, pour off all but 1 tablespoon fat from skillet; in step 3, reduce sauce to ¾ cup, 3 to 5 minutes.

Why This Recipe Works There are endless ways to cook chicken thighs, but braising them is a terrific method for rendering them meltingly tender in the oven and then incorporating a variety of rich sauce flavorings. One key to this technique is to crisp up the skin in a skillet first, as there is nothing worse than flabby chicken thigh skin. This also develops a delicious fond on the bottom of the skillet that infuses the whole dish with deep flavor. So we start by searing bone-in, skin-on thighs to crisp the skin, then brown the undersides for a few more minutes. After going into the oven, they simmer skin side up in a flavorful mix of chicken broth, cumin, and coriander, essentially overcooking until they reach 195 degrees, which melts the collagen in the meat and turns it succulent, tender, and juicy. Finally, we reduce the sauce to concentrate its flavors before whisking in a cornstarch slurry to thicken it into a luxurious, velvety consistency. Last-minute additions of butter, lemon zest, and large pieces of torn basil make a fragrant finish. If your chicken thighs are larger than 5 to 7 ounces each, use fewer of them to maintain a total weight of 2½ to 3½ pounds; adjust cooking time as needed. You will need a 12-inch ovensafe skillet for this recipe.

1 Adjust oven rack to middle position and heat oven to 325 degrees. Pat chicken dry with paper towels and sprinkle with salt and pepper. Heat oil in 12-inch stainless-steel skillet over medium heat until shimmering. Add chicken thighs skin side down and cook, without moving them, until well browned, about 8 minutes. Flip chicken and brown on second side, about 3 minutes. Transfer chicken to large plate.

2 Pour off all but 2 tablespoons fat from skillet. Add shallot and garlic to fat left in skillet and cook over medium heat, stirring frequently, until garlic is golden brown, about 1½ minutes. Add cumin and ground coriander and cook, stirring constantly, for 1 minute. Add broth and lemon juice and bring to simmer, scraping up any browned bits. Nestle chicken skin side up into skillet and add any accumulated juices. Transfer skillet to oven and cook until chicken registers at least 195 degrees, 35 to 40 minutes. Whisk water and cornstarch together in small bowl; set aside.

3 Using potholders, remove skillet from oven. Being careful of hot skillet handle, transfer chicken to serving platter and tent with aluminum foil. Place skillet over high heat. Stir coriander seeds into liquid and bring to boil. Cook, occasionally scraping bottom and side of skillet to incorporate fond, until sauce is thickened and reduced to 1½ cups, 8 to 10 minutes. Reduce heat to medium-low. Whisk cornstarch mixture to recombine, then whisk into sauce and simmer until thickened, about 1 minute. Off heat, whisk in lemon zest and butter until fully incorporated. Season with salt and pepper to taste. Return chicken to skillet and spoon sauce around chicken. Top with basil and serve.

Browning chicken thighs and then braising them in the oven renders them tender and succulent. We overcook them until fall-apart tender in a mixture of broth and spices, which we then reduce into a luxurious sauce.

1 Brown before Braise.

2 Place Thighs Skin-Side Up.

3 Simmer in Oven.

4 "Overcook" Your Thighs.

Sizing Up Your Skillet

stainless steel • enameled cast iron • nonstick

A 12-inch stainless-steel skillet provides enough space for browning and braising eight chicken thighs and develops valuable fond for building a flavorful sauce. An enameled cast-iron skillet will also work for these reasons. If using enameled cast iron, you will need to preheat the empty skillet over medium heat for 3 minutes before proceeding with step 1. An ovensafe nonstick skillet can also be used; however, it will not develop as much fond. Due to the acidic cooking liquid, we do not recommend using a traditional cast-iron or carbon-steel skillet.

Sherry-Braised Chicken Thighs with Chorizo and Potatoes

Serves 4 to 6

Total Time 1½ hours

8   (5- to 7-ounce) bone-in chicken thighs, trimmed

1   tablespoon smoked paprika, divided

1½   teaspoons table salt, divided

4   ounces Spanish chorizo, cut into ¼-inch pieces

6   garlic cloves, sliced thin

2   tablespoons extra-virgin olive oil

1   pound small red potatoes, unpeeled, halved

1   onion, halved and sliced ¼ inch thick

1   red bell pepper, stemmed, seeded, and cut into ½-inch pieces

1   tablespoon all-purpose flour

1   cup plus 1 tablespoon dry sherry, divided

1   cup chicken broth

½   teaspoon red pepper flakes

¼   cup heavy cream

2   teaspoons fresh thyme leaves

Why This Recipe Works We wanted a memorable chicken dinner that took advantage of all the complex, complementary flavors of Spanish chorizo and sherry, and we wanted it to come together in one skillet. Following the technique for browning chicken thighs in a skillet on the stovetop and then braising them in the oven, we first build impactful flavor by slowly heating chopped chorizo and sliced garlic in the pan, creating an oil infused with deep flavor, and then set the chorizo and garlic aside. Browning the chicken thighs in that oil seasons them thoroughly with the smoky spice and punchy garlic. After setting aside the browned chicken, we cook the potatoes in the empty skillet with the onions and peppers until softened. To give the braising liquid the full flavor of warm, savory, nutty sherry, we deglaze the skillet with a full cup of the fortified wine. The chorizo and garlic are returned to the skillet and everything is thickened with a roux. Once the chicken is united with the flavorful braising mixture, it all goes into the oven for a quick braise. At the end, we remove the chicken and make a sauce right in the skillet, adding richness with a little cream and brightness with a jolt of more sherry. If your chicken thighs are larger than 5 to 7 ounces each, use fewer of them to maintain a total weight of 2½ to 3½ pounds; adjust cooking time as needed. You can substitute Portuguese linguica for the dry-cured Spanish chorizo; do not use fresh Mexican chorizo. We recommend using an affordable sherry that you enjoy drinking on its own. Use small red potatoes measuring 1 to 2 inches in diameter; if using larger potatoes, cut them into 1-inch pieces. Serve with crusty bread. You will need a 12-inch ovensafe skillet for this recipe.

1 Adjust oven rack to middle position and heat oven to 325 degrees. Pat chicken dry with paper towels and sprinkle with 1 teaspoon paprika and 1 teaspoon salt.

2 Cook chorizo, garlic, and oil in 12-inch stainless-steel skillet over medium heat until oil is bright red and garlic is just beginning to brown, about 6 minutes, reducing heat if pan begins to smoke. Using slotted spoon, transfer chorizo and garlic to bowl; set aside.

3 Add chicken skin side down to fat left in skillet and cook, without moving it, until well browned, about 8 minutes. Flip chicken and brown on second side, about 3 minutes. Transfer chicken to large plate.

4 Pour off all but 2 tablespoons fat from skillet. Add potatoes, onion, bell pepper, and remaining ½ teaspoon salt and cook over medium-high heat, stirring occasionally, until onion is just softened, about 5 minutes. Stir in flour and cook for 1 minute. Stir in 1 cup sherry, broth, pepper flakes, chorizo and garlic, and remaining 2 teaspoons paprika and bring to boil. Nestle chicken skin side up in skillet and add any accumulated juices. Transfer skillet to oven and cook until chicken registers at least 195 degrees, 35 to 40 minutes.

5 Using pot holders, remove skillet from oven. Being careful of hot skillet handle, transfer chicken to serving platter. Stir cream into vegetable and chorizo mixture and cook over medium-high heat until sauce is slightly thickened, 3 to 5 minutes. Off heat, stir in remaining 1 tablespoon sherry. Season with salt and red pepper flakes to taste. Sprinkle vegetable mixture with thyme and serve with chicken.

Sizing Up Your Skillet

stainless steel ● **enameled cast iron** ● **traditional cast iron** ● **nonstick**

A 12-inch stainless-steel skillet provides enough space for browning and braising eight chicken thighs and develops valuable fond for building a flavorful sauce. An enameled cast-iron skillet will also work for these reasons. A traditional cast-iron or ovensafe nonstick skillet can also be used; however, they will not develop as much fond.

Sizing Up Your Skillet

stainless steel • enameled cast iron • traditional cast iron • nonstick

A 12-inch stainless-steel skillet provides enough space for browning and braising eight chicken thighs and develops valuable fond for building a flavorful sauce. An enameled cast-iron skillet will also work for these reasons. A traditional cast-iron or ovensafe nonstick skillet can also be used; however, they will not develop as much fond. If using a cast-iron skillet, you will need to preheat the empty skillet over medium heat for 3 minutes before proceeding with step 2.

Braised Chicken Thighs with Fennel, Chickpeas, and Apricots

Serves 4 to 6

Total Time 1½ hours

2 tablespoons extra-virgin olive oil, divided

4 garlic cloves, minced

1½ teaspoons paprika

½ teaspoon ground turmeric

½ teaspoon ground cumin

¼ teaspoon ground ginger

¼ teaspoon cayenne pepper

2 (15-ounce) cans chickpeas, rinsed, divided

8 (5- to 7-ounce) bone-in chicken thighs, trimmed

½ teaspoon table salt

¼ teaspoon pepper

1 large fennel bulb, stalks discarded, bulb halved and cut into ½-inch-thick wedges through core

4 (2-inch) strips lemon zest, plus lemon wedges for serving

1 cinnamon stick

½ cup dry white wine

1 cup chicken broth

1 cup pitted large brine-cured green or black olives, halved

½ cup dried apricots, halved

2 tablespoons chopped fresh parsley

Why This Recipe Works The combo of stovetop browning and oven braising delivers a simple skillet tagine infused with warm spices and rounded out with the addition of fennel, chickpeas, and apricots. We use skin-on chicken thighs and brown the meat to crisp up the skin; then we brown fennel in the rendered fat and bloom a blend of spicy, earthy, ground spices (mashing them into the skillet) and a whole cinnamon stick, which cook with the chicken and infuse the whole dish with flavor. A few broad ribbons of lemon zest give the tagine its citrus back note. Brine-cured olives provide meatiness and piquant flavor, and some dried apricots, which plump among the chickpeas in the broth, create well-rounded sweetness for this well-spiced and earthy braise. Chopped parsley, stirred in right before serving, is the perfect finishing touch to freshen the flavors. If your chicken thighs are larger than 5 to 7 ounces each, use fewer of them to maintain a total weight of 2½ to 3½ pounds; adjust cooking time as needed. You will need a 12-inch ovensafe skillet with a tight-fitting lid for this recipe.

1 Adjust oven rack to middle position and heat oven to 325 degrees. Combine 1 tablespoon oil, garlic, paprika, turmeric, cumin, ginger, and cayenne in bowl; set aside. Place ½ cup chickpeas in second bowl and mash to coarse paste with potato masher.

2 Pat chicken dry with paper towels and sprinkle with salt and pepper. Heat remaining 1 tablespoon oil in 12-inch stainless-steel skillet over medium heat until shimmering. Add chicken skin side down and cook, without moving it, until well browned, about 8 minutes. Flip chicken and brown on second side, about 3 minutes. Transfer chicken to large plate.

3 Pour off all but 2 tablespoons fat from skillet. Arrange fennel cut side down in fat left in skillet. Cover and cook over medium heat until lightly browned, 3 to 5 minutes per side. Push fennel to sides of skillet. Add spice mixture, lemon zest, and cinnamon stick to center and cook, mashing spice mixture into skillet, until fragrant, about 30 seconds. Stir spice mixture into fennel. Stir in wine, scraping up any browned bits, and cook until almost evaporated, about 2 minutes.

4 Stir in mashed chickpeas, whole chickpeas, broth, olives, and apricots and bring to simmer. Nestle chicken skin side up into skillet and add any accumulated juices. Transfer skillet to oven and cook until chicken registers at least 195 degrees, 45 to 50 minutes.

5 Using pot holders, remove skillet from oven. Being careful of hot skillet handle, discard lemon zest and cinnamon stick. Season with salt and pepper to taste. Sprinkle with parsley and serve with lemon wedges.

VARIATION

Braised Chicken Thighs with Fennel, Chickpeas, and Apricots for Two

Halve all ingredients. Proceed with recipe in 10-inch ovensafe skillet.

Chicken Pot Pie with Leeks, Carrots, and Croissant Topping

Serves 4 to 6

Total Time 1 hour

1½ pounds boneless, skinless chicken thighs, trimmed and cut into 1-inch pieces

1 teaspoon table salt, divided

¼ cup extra-virgin olive oil, divided

12 ounces mushrooms

1 pound leeks, white and light green parts only, halved lengthwise, sliced ¼ inch thick, and washed thoroughly

2 carrots, peeled and cut into ¼-inch pieces

4 garlic cloves, minced

4 teaspoons fresh thyme leaves, divided

6 tablespoons all-purpose flour

2 cups chicken broth

½ cup heavy cream

¼ teaspoon pepper

1 teaspoon sherry vinegar

3 large baked croissants, torn into rough 1-inch pieces (5 cups)

VARIATION

Chicken Pot Pie with Leeks, Carrots, and Croissant Topping for Two

Reduce croissants to 2 cups torn pieces; halve remaining ingredients. Proceed with recipe in 10-inch skillet.

Why This Recipe Works In this one-pan chicken pot pie, the skillet does it all, from cooking the vegetables to building the flavorful gravy for simmering the chicken and building the final dish. Many recipes start with poaching or searing chicken. We simply salt some hard-to-overcook chicken thigh pieces and then cook them directly in our flavorful gravy after sautéing the vegetables. Mushrooms and leeks are a classic pairing with chicken, so we start first by browning the mushrooms in the skillet. Then we add the leeks and carrots to the empty skillet and cook until the leeks become soft and fragrant and the carrots are just starting to soften. A roux is built on top of the vegetables so that the casserole will thicken properly after we deglaze the pan with broth and cream before adding the chicken and cooking it through. Many quick pot pies turn to store-bought pie dough for the topping. We found that we could never get our topping truly crisp, and it tended to get soggy sitting on the pie's base. Instead, we use convenient, fully-baked croissants to give us that buttery, flaky crust we associate with a really satisfying pie. What's more, the croissants require just a couple of minutes under the broiler to become crisp, making this a truly weeknight-friendly meal. You can use one variety of mushroom or a combination. Stem and halve portobello mushrooms and cut each half crosswise into ½-inch pieces. Trim white or cremini mushrooms; quarter them if large or medium or halve them if small. Tear trimmed oyster mushrooms into 1- to 1½-inch pieces. Stem shiitake mushrooms; quarter large caps and halve small caps. Cut trimmed maitake (hen-of-the-woods) mushrooms into 1- to 1½-inch pieces. Slices of rustic Italian or French bread torn into 1-inch pieces can be substituted for the croissants. You will need a 12-inch broiler-safe skillet with a tight-fitting lid for this recipe.

1 Toss chicken with ½ teaspoon salt in medium bowl; set aside.

2 Heat 2 tablespoons oil in 12-inch stainless-steel skillet over medium-high heat until shimmering. Add mushrooms, cover, and cook until liquid is released, about 3 minutes. Uncover and continue to cook until liquid has evaporated and mushrooms are lightly browned, 3 to 5 minutes. Transfer mushrooms to bowl with chicken.

3 Adjust oven rack 10 inches from heating element and heat broiler. Heat remaining 2 tablespoons oil in now-empty skillet over medium heat until shimmering. Add leeks and carrots and cook until beginning to soften, 3 to 5 minutes. Stir in garlic and 2 teaspoons thyme and cook until fragrant, about 1 minute. Stir in flour and cook for 1 minute.

4 Slowly stir in broth and cream, scraping up any browned bits and smoothing out any lumps. Stir in chicken, mushrooms, remaining ½ teaspoon salt, and pepper and bring to simmer. Reduce heat to low, cover, and cook, stirring occasionally, until chicken is cooked through, 10 to 15 minutes. (Filling will thicken considerably at first and then thin out.)

5 Stir in vinegar and season with salt and pepper to taste. Arrange croissant pieces on top of filling and sprinkle with remaining 2 teaspoons thyme. Broil until top is light golden brown, 1 to 4 minutes. Let cool for 5 minutes before serving.

Sizing Up Your Skillet

stainless steel • **traditional cast iron** • **enameled cast iron**

A 12-inch stainless-steel skillet provides enough space for assembling the casserole. A traditional cast-iron or enameled cast-iron skillet will also work well for this reason. If using a cast-iron skillet, you will need to preheat the empty skillet over medium heat for 3 minutes before proceeding with step 2.

Sizing Up Your Skillet

stainless steel ● **nonstick** ● **traditional cast iron** ● **enameled cast iron**

A 12-inch stainless-steel skillet provides enough space for assembling the pot pie. An ovensafe nonstick, traditional cast-iron, or enameled cast-iron skillet will also work well for this reason. If using a cast-iron skillet, you will need to preheat the empty skillet over medium heat for 3 minutes before proceeding with step 4.

Lattice-Topped Chicken Pot Pie with Spring Vegetables

Serves 4 to 6

Total Time 1¼ hours, plus 15 minutes chilling

1 (9½ by 9-inch) sheet puff pastry, thawed

1½ pounds boneless, skinless chicken thighs, trimmed and cut into 1-inch pieces

1 teaspoon table salt, divided

1 tablespoon extra-virgin olive oil

1 leek, white and light green parts only, halved lengthwise, sliced ¼ inch thick, and washed thoroughly

4 teaspoons fresh thyme leaves, divided

6 tablespoons all-purpose flour

2 cups chicken broth, plus extra as needed

½ cup heavy cream

¼ teaspoon pepper

1 large egg, lightly beaten

1 teaspoon coarse sea salt (optional)

1 pound asparagus, trimmed and cut on bias into 1-inch lengths

½ cup frozen peas

1½ tablespoons chopped fresh tarragon or parsley

1 tablespoon grated lemon zest plus 2 teaspoons juice

VARIATIONS

Lattice-Topped Chicken Pot Pie with Spring Vegetables for Two

Reduce salt to ¼ teaspoon. Halve remaining ingredients except for puff pastry. Proceed with recipe in 10-inch skillet, trimming pastry to 10-inch circle in step 2.

Why This Recipe Works The preparations required for chicken pot pie have largely relegated it to a Sunday treat, but moving this dish to a skillet speeds up the process and also improves the results. For an elegant and crisp crust, we parbake the crust separately, which keeps it from becoming soggy and ensures that it is done at the same time as the filling. Rather than start from scratch, we use store-bought puff pastry and weave it into a simple but stunning lattice top. Boneless, skinless chicken thighs are easy to prep and stay moist through cooking. To give our pot pie fresh spring flavor, we swap in a leek for the usual onion and stir in fresh asparagus, peas, and tarragon toward the end of cooking the filling. To thaw frozen puff pastry, let it sit either in the refrigerator for 24 hours or on the counter for 30 minutes to 1 hour. We prefer to place the baked pastry on top of the filling in the skillet just before serving for an impressive presentation; however, you can also cut the pastry into wedges and place them over individual portions of the filling. You will need a 12-inch ovensafe skillet with a tight-fitting lid for this recipe.

1 Roll puff pastry sheet into 12½ by 12-inch rectangle on lightly floured counter with long side facing counter edge. Using pizza cutter or sharp knife, cut pastry widthwise into ten 1¼-inch-wide strips.

2 Arrange 5 parallel pastry strips across sheet of parchment paper, spaced 1¼ inches apart. Fold back first, third, and fifth strips almost completely. Lay additional pastry strip perpendicular to second and fourth strips, keeping it snug to folded edges of pastry, then unfold strips. Repeat laying remaining 4 pastry strips, spaced 1¼ inches apart, across parchment, alternating between folding back second and fourth strips and first, third, and fifth strips to create lattice pattern. Using pizza cutter, trim edges of pastry to form 12-inch circle. Transfer dough, still on parchment, to baking sheet and refrigerate until firm, about 15 minutes.

3 Adjust oven rack to middle position and heat oven to 400 degrees. Toss chicken with ½ teaspoon table salt in medium bowl; set aside.

4 Heat oil in 12-inch stainless-steel skillet over medium heat until shimmering. Add leek and cook until beginning to soften, 3 to 5 minutes. Stir in 2 teaspoons thyme and cook until fragrant, about 1 minute. Stir in flour and cook for 1 minute.

5 Slowly stir in broth and cream, scraping up any browned bits and smoothing out any lumps. Stir in chicken, remaining ½ teaspoon table salt, and pepper and bring to simmer. Reduce heat to low, cover, and cook, stirring occasionally, until chicken is cooked through, 10 to 15 minutes. (Filling will thicken considerably at first and then thin out.)

6 Meanwhile, brush dough with beaten egg and sprinkle with remaining 2 teaspoons thyme and sea salt, if using. Bake until golden brown, 12 to 15 minutes, rotating sheet halfway through baking. Transfer crust, still on sheet, to wire rack and let cool.

7 Stir asparagus into filling and cook over medium heat until crisp-tender, 3 to 5 minutes. Off heat, stir in peas and let sit until heated through, about 5 minutes. Stir in tarragon and lemon zest and juice. Season with salt and pepper to taste. Set pastry on top of filling and serve.

Arroz con Pollo

Serves 4 to 6
Total Time 1½ hours

Chicken and Rice

6   (5- to 7-ounce) bone-in chicken thighs, trimmed

1¾ teaspoons table salt, divided

1   teaspoon pepper, divided

3   tablespoons vegetable oil, divided

1   red onion, halved and sliced ½ inch thick

1   red bell pepper, stemmed, seeded, and cut into ½-inch-wide strips, divided

3   garlic cloves, smashed and peeled

1   tablespoon ají amarillo paste

1   teaspoon ground cumin

1   teaspoon dried oregano

1   cup beer

1½ cups fresh cilantro leaves and tender stems

1   cup (1 ounce) baby spinach

¾   cup chicken broth, plus extra as needed

1½ cups long-grain white rice, rinsed

2   carrots, peeled, halved lengthwise, and sliced ½ inch thick

½   cup frozen peas

Sarza Criolla

1   red onion, halved and sliced thin

¼   cup chopped fresh cilantro

2   tablespoons lime juice

½   teaspoon table salt

¼   teaspoon pepper

Why This Recipe Works This Peruvian version of arroz con pollo features moist, tender chicken nestled in a richly flavored green rice and topped with sarza criolla, a piquant condiment of sliced red onion, cilantro, lime juice, salt, and pepper. Although most recipes build layers of flavors in a Dutch oven, we found that a large nonstick skillet works beautifully. We use the rendered fat from browned chicken thighs to cook our aderezo, or aromatic base, and then deglaze it with beer. Blending this aderezo with flavorful cilantro and verdant spinach creates a green cooking liquid for the rice, infusing it with flavor. We toast the rice in the skillet for an extra layer of flavor before we add the aromatic cooking liquid and browned chicken pieces. Much like the socarrat in paella, any crispy browning at the base of the rice adds to the overall experience of the dish, so be sure to include it when serving. Ají amarillo paste (ground fresh ají amarillo chiles) can be found in jars in supermarkets and online. A brown ale or mild lager works best here. If your chicken thighs are larger than 5 to 7 ounces each, use fewer of them to maintain a total weight of 2 to 2½ pounds; adjust cooking time as needed. You will need a 12-inch skillet with a tight-fitting lid for this recipe.

1 For the chicken and rice Pat chicken dry with paper towels and sprinkle with 1½ teaspoons salt and ¾ teaspoon pepper. Heat 2 tablespoons oil in 12-inch nonstick skillet over medium-high heat until shimmering. Brown chicken, 3 to 4 minutes per side; transfer to plate.

2 Add onion, half of bell pepper, and remaining ¼ teaspoon salt to fat left in skillet and cook over medium heat until softened, about 5 minutes. Stir in garlic, ají amarillo paste, cumin, oregano, and remaining ¼ teaspoon pepper and cook until fragrant, about 30 seconds. Stir in beer, scraping up any browned bits, and cook until liquid has reduced slightly, about 3 minutes. Remove skillet from heat and let mixture cool slightly.

3 Transfer cooled vegetable mixture to blender. Add cilantro, spinach, and broth and process until smooth, about 1 minute, scraping down sides of blender jar as needed. Transfer mixture to 4-cup liquid measuring cup. (You should have 3½ cups; if necessary, spoon off excess or add extra broth so that volume equals 3½ cups.)

4 Heat remaining 1 tablespoon oil in now-empty skillet over medium-high heat until shimmering. Add rice and carrots and cook until rice is lightly toasted and fragrant, about 2 minutes. Stir in pureed vegetable mixture and bring to simmer. Nestle chicken skin side up into rice and add any accumulated juices. Arrange remaining bell pepper strips attractively over top. Reduce the heat to medium-low, cover, and cook until chicken registers at least 185 degrees and rice is tender, 25 to 30 minutes. Off heat, scatter peas over top, cover, and let sit until heated through, about 10 minutes.

5 For the sarza criolla Meanwhile, soak onion in ice water for 10 minutes. Drain well and pat dry with paper towels. Combine onion, cilantro, lime juice, salt, and pepper in bowl. Serve chicken and rice with sarza criolla.

VARIATION

Arroz con Pollo for Two

Reduce salt for the Chicken and Rice to 1 teaspoon. Sprinkle chicken with ¾ teaspoon salt in step 1 and add remaining ¼ teaspoon salt with vegetables in step 2. Halve remaining ingredients and proceed with recipe in 10-inch nonstick skillet.

Sizing Up Your Skillet

nonstick • **traditional cast iron**

A 12-inch nonstick skillet provides enough space for browning six chicken thighs and simmering them with a generous amount of rice. Its slick surface also ensures that the dish can be easily scooped out for serving without sticking. A traditional cast-iron skillet will also work for these reasons; you will need to preheat the empty skillet over medium heat for 3 minutes before proceeding with step 1.

Chicken Biryani

Serves 6

Total Time 1 hour

2¼ cups water, plus 3 tablespoons warm water

2 cups basmati rice

1 cinnamon stick

2 teaspoons cumin seeds

1¾ teaspoons table salt, divided

½ teaspoon saffron threads, crumbled

6 tablespoons ghee

2 cups thinly sliced onions

⅓ cup dried currants

2 pounds boneless, skinless chicken thighs, trimmed and cut into 1½-inch pieces

½ teaspoon pepper

1 jalapeño chile, stemmed, seeded, and minced

3 garlic cloves, minced

1 tablespoon grated fresh ginger

1 tablespoon garam masala

½ cup plain whole-milk yogurt

¼ cup chopped fresh cilantro and/or mint

1 recipe Herb-Yogurt Sauce (page 102)

Why This Recipe Works One of India's beloved celebratory dishes, chicken biryani features layers of spiced chicken, rice, and aromatics. In a traditional chicken biryani, richly spiced and perfectly fluffy saffron basmati rice, lavished with ghee and studded with dried fruit, is layered with sauced chicken, and the two are cooked together before being topped with fried onions and chopped herbs. However, it can be time-consuming to develop deep flavor by steeping whole spices and cooking the components in stages. So we simplified the dish: Instead of a Dutch oven, we use a 12-inch nonstick skillet and chunks of boneless chicken thighs and skip the usual lengthy marinating time. It was easy to sauté the onions, rather than deep-frying them, and then brown the chicken in the same large skillet, saving a pan. Finally, rather than partially cooking the rice in spice-infused water—which sometimes results in either under- or overcooked rice—we cook the rice through in the microwave, flavor it with currants and saffron water, and then steam it briefly with the chicken. With garnishes of deeply browned onions, fresh cilantro, and an easy, herby yogurt sauce, this streamlined biryani is as flavorful as more traditional versions. To make the biryani spicier, reserve some of the jalapeño seeds and add them along with the minced jalapeño. You will need a 12-inch skillet with a tight-fitting lid for this recipe.

1 Microwave 2¼ cups water, rice, cinnamon stick, cumin, and ¾ teaspoon salt in large covered bowl for 5 minutes. Continue to microwave on 50 percent power for 15 minutes. Carefully remove bowl from microwave and let sit covered for 5 minutes.

2 Combine saffron and 3 tablespoons warm water in small bowl and set aside. Set fine-mesh strainer over medium bowl. Melt ghee in 12-inch nonstick skillet over medium heat. Add onions and cook, stirring often, until dark brown, 11 to 14 minutes. Transfer onions to prepared strainer and press with spatula to squeeze out excess ghee (reserve ghee). Spread onions on small plate, sprinkle with ¼ teaspoon salt, and set aside for serving.

3 Add currants and ¼ cup reserved ghee to rice and gently fluff with fork to combine. Combine chicken, pepper, remaining reserved ghee, and remaining ¾ teaspoon salt in now-empty skillet and cook over medium-high heat until browned and cooked through, about 10 minutes. Stir in jalapeño, garlic, ginger, and garam masala and cook until fragrant, about 1 minute. Off heat, stir in yogurt until combined.

4 Spoon rice over chicken mixture and spread into even layer. Drizzle saffron water evenly over rice, spiraling in from edge of skillet to center. Cover skillet, return to medium heat, and cook until heated through and steam escapes from under lid, about 5 minutes. Off heat, sprinkle biryani with reserved fried onions and cilantro. Serve with herb-yogurt sauce.

Sizing Up Your Skillet

nonstick • **traditional cast iron**

A 12-inch nonstick skillet provides enough space for browning the chicken and layering on the seasoned rice to heat through. Its slick surface also ensures that the dish can be easily scooped out for serving without sticking. A traditional cast-iron skillet will also work for these reasons; you will need to preheat the empty skillet over medium heat for 3 minutes before proceeding with step 2.

Tinga de Pollo

Serves 4 to 6

Total Time 1½ hours

2 pounds boneless, skinless chicken thighs, trimmed

½ teaspoon table salt

¼ teaspoon pepper

2 tablespoons vegetable oil, divided

1 onion, halved and sliced thin

2 garlic cloves, minced

1 teaspoon ground cumin

¼ teaspoon ground cinnamon

1 (14.5-ounce) can fire-roasted diced tomatoes

½ cup chicken broth

2 tablespoons minced canned chipotle chile in adobo sauce plus 2 teaspoons adobo sauce

½ teaspoon brown sugar

1 teaspoon grated lime zest plus 2 tablespoons juice, plus lime wedges for serving

12 (6-inch) corn tortillas, warmed

1 avocado, halved, pitted, and cut into ½-inch pieces

2 ounces cotija cheese, crumbled (½ cup)

6 scallions, minced

Why This Recipe Works Tinga de pollo is a traditional taco filling that typically combines shredded chicken with a flavorful tomato-chipotle sauce. Using our brown-and-braise technique and a large skillet, we brown meaty boneless chicken thighs in batches, and then start to build our sauce with the fond left behind. By sautéing sliced onions and aromatics and then adding the liquid components (fire-roasted tomatoes, broth, and chipotle chiles and adobo sauce), we build a flavorful sauce in which to continue cooking the chicken until it reaches 195 degrees, which allows lots of collagen to break down and deliver supertender meat. We shred the chicken and whirl the sauce in a blender; then, both chicken and sauce go back into the skillet so that the flavors can meld and everything can warm through before serving. A little brown sugar, lime juice, and lime zest further create balanced complexity. You will need a 12-inch skillet with a tight-fitting lid for this recipe.

1 Pat chicken dry with paper towels and sprinkle with salt and pepper. Heat 1 tablespoon oil in 12-inch stainless-steel skillet over medium-high heat until shimmering. Brown half of chicken, 3 to 4 minutes per side. Transfer to large plate and repeat with remaining chicken; transfer to plate.

2 Add onion and remaining 1 tablespoon oil to now-empty skillet and cook over medium heat until softened, about 5 minutes. Add garlic, cumin, and cinnamon and cook until fragrant, about 1 minute. Stir in tomatoes and their juice, broth, chipotle and adobo sauce, and sugar, scraping up any browned bits, and bring to simmer.

3 Return chicken and any accumulated juices to skillet. Reduce heat to medium-low, cover, and simmer until chicken registers at least 195 degrees, 15 to 20 minutes, flipping chicken after 5 minutes. Transfer chicken to cutting board, let cool slightly, then shred into bite-size pieces using 2 forks.

4 Transfer cooking liquid to blender and process until smooth, 15 to 30 seconds. Return sauce and shredded chicken to now-empty skillet. Cook over medium heat, stirring frequently, until sauce is thickened and clings to chicken, 5 to 10 minutes. Stir in lime zest and juice and season with salt and pepper to taste. Serve with tortillas, passing avocado, cotija, scallions, and lime wedges separately.

VARIATION
Tinga de Pollo for Two

Reduce tomatoes to ¾ cup plus 2 tablespoons juice; halve remaining ingredients. Proceed with recipe in 10- or 12-inch skillet.

Sizing Up Your Skillet

stainless steel ● **nonstick** ● **enameled cast iron**

A 12-inch stainless-steel skillet provides enough space for simmering the chicken and its wide surface provides for a quick reduction of the sauce before serving. A nonstick or enameled cast-iron skillet will also work for these reasons. If using an enameled cast-iron skillet, you will need to preheat the empty skillet over medium heat for 3 minutes before proceeding with step 1. Due to the acidic cooking liquid, we do not recommend using a traditional cast-iron or carbon-steel skillet.

Braised Steaks with Root Vegetables

Serves 4

Total Time 2½ hours

- 4 (6-to 8-ounce) beef blade steaks, ¾ to 1 inch thick, trimmed
- ½ teaspoon table salt
- ⅛ teaspoon pepper
- 2 tablespoons vegetable oil, divided
- 1 onion, halved and sliced thin
- 3 garlic cloves, minced
- 1 tablespoon minced fresh thyme or 1 teaspoon dried
- 1 tablespoon all-purpose flour
- 1½ cups beef broth
- 1 cup water
- ½ cup dry red wine
- 12 ounces red or yellow waxy potatoes, unpeeled, cut into 1-inch pieces
- 12 ounces carrots, celery root, turnips, and/or radishes, peeled and cut into 1-inch pieces
- 1 cup frozen peas
- 1 tablespoon minced fresh parsley

Why This Recipe Works This technique for oven-braised steaks and vegetables starts with browning the meat, which adds flavor, before braising it all until the steaks are deliciously fork-tender. This is key because the fond that we scrape up when deglazing the skillet forms the building blocks of flavor that infuse every aspect of the dish. We use the skillet in four ways: to brown the meat; to sauté the aromatics and build a sauce; to braise everything together in a low oven; and finally, to finish the sauce (and add the peas). For the steak, we use blade steaks; we then combine them with a medley of root vegetables and turn it all into a one-dish skillet dinner perfect for a cold winter's night: It's a tender, hearty, and boldly meaty dish that also feels both humble and luxurious. Using one skillet for the entire process is effective, as it allows the vegetables to take on great beefy flavor. Reducing the leftover braising liquid into a rich and savory spoonable sauce is the crowning touch. Make sure to buy steaks that are about the same size to ensure even cooking. This recipe also works with boneless beef short ribs, chuck steaks, and flat-iron steaks of similar thickness. You will need a 12-inch ovensafe skillet with a tight-fitting lid for this recipe.

1 Adjust oven rack to lower-middle position and heat oven to 325 degrees. Pat steaks dry with paper towels and sprinkle with salt and pepper. Heat 1 tablespoon oil in 12-inch stainless-steel skillet over medium-high heat until just smoking. Brown steaks, 3 to 5 minutes per side. Transfer steaks to plate.

2 Heat remaining 1 tablespoon oil in now-empty skillet over medium heat until shimmering. Add onion and cook until softened, about 5 minutes. Stir in garlic, thyme, and flour and cook until fragrant, about 1 minute. Stir in broth, water, and wine, scraping up any browned bits and smoothing out any lumps, and bring to simmer.

3 Place steaks in skillet and add any accumulated juices. Nestle potatoes and carrots around steaks. Cover, transfer skillet to oven, and cook until steaks are tender and paring knife can be slipped in and out of meat with very little resistance, about 1½ hours.

4 Using potholders, remove skillet from oven. Being careful of hot skillet handle, transfer steaks and vegetables to serving platter, tent with aluminum foil, and let rest while finishing sauce. Bring sauce to simmer over medium-high heat and cook until thickened and reduced to about ¾ cup, 10 to 15 minutes. Stir in peas and cook until heated through, about 2 minutes. Season with salt and pepper to taste. Return steaks and vegetables to skillet and spoon portion of sauce over top. Sprinkle with parsley and serve.

perfecting BRAISED STEAKS

The skillet is used in four different ways: to brown the meat, sauté the vegetables, braise the steak (and the vegetables) in the oven, and create a luscious sauce.

1   Brown Before Braise.

2   Deglaze and Scrape Up the Fond.

3   Simmer in the Oven.

4   Reduce the Braising Liquid.

Sizing Up Your Skillet

stainless steel • **enameled cast iron** • **nonstick** • **traditional cast iron**

A 12-inch stainless-steel skillet provides enough space for browning and braising the steaks and creates the valuable fond for building a flavorful sauce. An enameled cast-iron skillet will also work for these reasons. An ovensafe nonstick or traditional cast-iron skillet can also be used; however, they will not develop as much fond. If using a cast-iron skillet, you will need to preheat the empty skillet over medium heat for 5 minutes before proceeding with step 1.

Keema Aloo

Serves 4 to 6

Total Time 1¼ hours

2	tablespoons vegetable oil
6	black peppercorns
4	green cardamom pods
2	black cardamom pods
1	cinnamon stick
1	red onion, halved and sliced thin crosswise
1	teaspoon grated garlic
1	teaspoon grated fresh ginger
1	pound 90 percent lean ground beef
¾	teaspoon table salt
2	teaspoons ground coriander
2	teaspoons Kashmiri chile powder
½	teaspoon ground turmeric
½	teaspoon ground cumin
2	(6-ounce) vine-ripened tomatoes, cored and chopped
1	(8-ounce) Yukon Gold potato, peeled and cut into ½-inch pieces
¼	cup plain whole-milk yogurt
2	tablespoons water
1	long green chile, halved lengthwise (optional)
¼	cup chopped fresh cilantro, plus extra for garnish

Why This Recipe Works Keema is a rich and savory spiced ground meat dish that's been a staple of South Asian cuisine for centuries, even gracing the tables of Turkic sultans and Mughal emperors of the 15th and 16th centuries. Whether it's made with ground goat, lamb, beef, or poultry, the meat is broken into small bits, coated with a complexly spiced, velvety sauce that's rich and savory, and then simmered in a large skillet. Our version features garam masala, a warming spice mix of whole cinnamon and black and green cardamom as well as ground coriander, cumin, turmeric, and Kashmiri chile powder. We bloom the whole spices early in the skillet to coax out their oil-soluble compounds. Then we carefully brown red onion to deepen its flavor before spiking the mixture with grated garlic and ginger. Next we add lean ground beef and, when it sizzles and browns, stir the ground spices into the masala. As soon as the spices are fragrant, we add tomatoes, whole-milk yogurt, and ½-inch pieces of potato. The tomatoes break down as the keema simmers, and the yogurt adds subtle richness. Together, they create a clingy sauce that flavors every bite of beef and seeps into the potato. Have your ingredients in place before you begin to cook. Look for black and green cardamom pods, Kashmiri chile powder, and 4- to 5-inch long green chiles at Indian or Pakistani markets. If you cannot find Kashmiri chile powder, toast and grind one large guajillo chile and use 2 teaspoons; if a long green chile is unavailable, substitute a serrano or omit. For a milder keema, omit the fresh chile or use only half of it. A rasp-style grater makes quick work of turning the garlic and ginger into pastes. Serve with roti, Pan-Grilled Flatbreads (page 299), or basmati rice. You will need a 12-inch skillet with a tight-fitting lid for this recipe.

1 Heat oil in 12-inch stainless-steel skillet over medium heat until shimmering. Add peppercorns, green and black cardamom pods, and cinnamon stick and cook, stirring occasionally, until fragrant, about 30 seconds. Add onion and cook, stirring occasionally, until browned, 7 to 10 minutes.

2 Add garlic and ginger and cook, stirring constantly, until fragrant, about 30 seconds. Add beef and salt. Increase heat to medium-high and cook, stirring to break up meat into very small pieces and scraping up any browned bits. Continue to cook, stirring occasionally, until mixture sizzles and bottom of skillet appears dry, 7 to 12 minutes.

3 Add coriander, chile powder, turmeric, and cumin and cook, stirring constantly, until spices are well distributed and fragrant, about 1 minute. Add tomatoes; potato; yogurt; water; and chile, if using, and cook, stirring frequently, until tomatoes release their juice and mixture begins to simmer, about 2 minutes. Adjust heat to maintain gentle simmer. Cover and cook, stirring occasionally, until tomatoes have broken down, potatoes are tender, and wooden spoon scraped across bottom of skillet leaves clear trail, 12 to 18 minutes. Stir in cilantro and season with salt and pepper to taste. If desired, remove cinnamon stick and cardamom pods. Transfer to serving bowl, sprinkle with extra cilantro, and serve.

VARIATION

Keema Aloo for Two

Halve all ingredients. Proceed with recipe in 10-inch skillet.

Sizing Up Your Skillet

stainless-steel • **nonstick** • **traditional cast iron** • **enameled cast iron**

A 12-inch stainless-steel skillet provides enough space for simmering the keema. A nonstick, traditional cast-iron, or enameled cast-iron skillet will also work for this reason. If using a cast-iron skillet, you will need to preheat the empty skillet over medium heat for 3 minutes before proceeding with step 1.

Smothered Pork Chops

Serves 4

Total Time 1½ hours

- 4 (6- to 8-ounce) bone-in pork rib or blade-cut chops, ½ to ¾ inch thick, trimmed
- ½ teaspoon pepper
- 4 slices bacon, cut into ¼-inch pieces
- 2 onions, halved and sliced thin
- 2 tablespoons water
- ¼ teaspoon table salt
- 2 garlic cloves, minced
- 1 teaspoon minced fresh thyme or ¼ teaspoon dried
- 2 tablespoons all-purpose flour
- 2 cups chicken broth
- 2 bay leaves

VARIATIONS

Smothered Pork Chops with Cider and Apples

Substitute apple cider for chicken broth and 1 large Granny Smith apple, peeled, cored, and cut into ½-inch wedges, for 1 onion. Increase salt to ½ teaspoon.

Smothered Pork Chops for Two

Halve all ingredients except water, but do not reduce the amount of fat used to cook the onions. Proceed with recipe in 10- or 12-inch skillet.

Why This Recipe Works Smothered pork chops are true comfort food, especially when seared in a skillet in bacon fat and then braised in the oven with a rich gravy until tender and succulent. The skillet is the true hero of this mouthwatering recipe because it allows us to create layers of flavors in stages before braising. Bone-in, rib-end pork chops are the most juicy and flavorful pork chop; we found that thin, ½- to ¾-inch chops pick up more flavor than thick chops and don't overwhelm the gravy. Cooking bacon in the skillet to start develops fat and flavorful fond, upon which we quickly brown the chops on each side; this develops even more fond in our trusty skillet. Adding the onion and water is next, at which point we can scrape up the fond and begin to build the sauce, the "smothering" aspect of the dish. You will need a 12-inch ovensafe skillet with a tight-fitting lid for this recipe.

1 Adjust oven rack to middle position and heat oven to 325 degrees. Using sharp knife, cut 2 slits, about 2 inches apart, through outer layer of fat and silver skin on edge of each chop. Pat chops dry with paper towels and sprinkle with pepper.

2 Cook bacon in 12-inch stainless-steel skillet over medium heat until rendered and crispy, 5 to 7 minutes. Using slotted spoon, transfer bacon to paper towel-lined bowl; set aside. Pour off all but 2 tablespoons fat (if necessary, supplement with oil). Heat fat left in skillet over medium-high heat until just smoking. Brown 2 chops, 3 to 4 minutes per side. Transfer to large plate and repeat with remaining chops; transfer to plate.

3 Pour off all but 1 tablespoon fat from skillet. Add onions, water, and salt to fat left in skillet. Cook over medium heat, scraping bottom of skillet with wooden spoon to loosen any browned bits, until onions are softened and browned around edges, about 5 minutes. Stir in garlic and thyme and cook until fragrant, about 30 seconds. Reduce heat to medium-low, add flour, and cook, stirring often, until well browned, about 5 minutes.

4 Slowly whisk in broth, scraping up any browned bits and smoothing out any lumps, and bring to simmer. Add bay leaves. Nestle chops into skillet in pinwheel pattern, with ribs pointing toward center. (Ribs may overlap slightly.) Add any accumulated juices, cover, and transfer skillet to oven. Cook until pork is tender and paring knife can be slipped in and out with very little resistance, about 30 minutes.

5 Using potholders, remove skillet from oven. Being careful of hot skillet handle, transfer chops to serving platter and tent with aluminum foil. Bring sauce to simmer over medium-high heat and cook uncovered, stirring frequently, until thickened, 5 to 7 minutes. Discard bay leaves and season sauce with salt and pepper to taste. Spoon sauce over chops, sprinkle with reserved bacon, and serve.

perfecting
SMOTHERED PORK CHOPS

We brown the chops in bacon fat and then build an aromatic base in the skillet, making the most of the fond left behind when adding broth. We then thicken it with a roux before oven-braising the chops. Arranging them in a pinwheel fashion in the skillet helps them cook through evenly.

1 Choose the Right Chop.

2 Prevent the Curl.

3 Arrange Chops in Pinwheel Fashion in the Skillet.

4 Oven-Braise 'Em.

Sizing Up Your Skillet

stainless steel ● **enameled cast iron** ● **nonstick** ● **traditional cast iron**

A 12-inch stainless-steel skillet provides enough space for braising four bone-in pork chops and develops valuable fond for building a flavorful sauce. An enameled cast-iron skillet will also work for these reasons. An ovensafe nonstick or traditional cast-iron skillet can also be used; however, they will not develop as much fond.

Mapo Tofu

Serves 4 to 6

Total Time 1 hour

28 ounces soft tofu, cut into ½-inch cubes

1 cup chicken broth

6 scallions, sliced thin

8 ounces ground pork

1 teaspoon vegetable oil, plus extra as needed

9 garlic cloves, minced

⅓ cup doubanjiang (broad bean chile paste)

1 tablespoon grated fresh ginger

1 tablespoon douchi (fermented black beans)

1 tablespoon Sichuan chili flakes

1 tablespoon Sichuan peppercorns, toasted and coarsely ground

2 tablespoons hoisin sauce

2 teaspoons toasted sesame oil

2 tablespoons water

1 tablespoon cornstarch

Why This Recipe Works If you think tofu is boring, this thrilling braise of custardy curds cloaked in a garlicky, spicy meat sauce—the signature dish of the Sichuan province of China—will change your mind. Beloved by die-hard chili fans, mapo tofu features soft cubes of tofu and a modest amount of pork or beef swimming in a glossy red sauce with loads of garlic and ginger, multiple fermented bean seasonings, numbing Sichuan peppercorns, and fiery Sichuan chili flakes. Cooks from Japan to Peru have since adapted mapo tofu to local tastes, but this original Sichuan version is hard to beat, continuing to break sweats, race heartbeats, and produce sniffs of spicy satisfaction. We start our version by poaching cubed tofu along with scallions in chicken broth in the microwave, which helps the cubes stay intact. Then we get out a large nonstick skillet to first cook the meat and then make the sauce. Meat is a flavoring here, not the main event, so only a small amount of ground pork complements the other components. In addition to hefty amounts of ginger and garlic, we use four Sichuan pantry powerhouses: doubanjiang (broad bean chili paste), douchi (fermented black beans), Sichuan chili flakes, and Sichuan peppercorns. The chili flakes pack some heat and the peppercorns, which are nutty, floral, and citrusy, deliver a mild tingling sensation. This dish moves along very quickly with the skillet accommodating the rotation of different ingredients until we pour in the tofu and broth and then add hoisin, sesame oil, and the cooked pork. A mixture of cornstarch and water thickens the sauce into a perfect silky consistency. If you can't find Sichuan chili flakes, substitute an equal amount of gochugaru (Korean red pepper flakes). If you can't find fermented black beans, you can use an equal amount of fermented black bean paste or sauce or 2 additional teaspoons broad bean chili paste.

1 Place tofu, broth, and scallions in large bowl and microwave, covered, until steaming, 5 to 7 minutes. Let stand while preparing remaining ingredients.

2 Cook pork and vegetable oil in 12-inch nonstick skillet over medium heat, breaking up meat with wooden spoon, until meat just begins to brown, 5 to 7 minutes. Using slotted spoon, transfer pork to separate bowl. Pour off all but ¼ cup fat from skillet. (If necessary, supplement with vegetable oil.)

3 Add garlic, doubanjiang, ginger, douchi, chili flakes, and peppercorns to fat left in skillet and cook over medium heat until spices darken and oil begins to separate from paste, 2 to 3 minutes.

4 Gently pour tofu with broth into skillet, followed by hoisin, sesame oil, and cooked pork. Cook, stirring gently and frequently, until simmering, 2 to 3 minutes. Whisk water and cornstarch together in small bowl. Add cornstarch mixture to skillet and continue to cook, stirring frequently, until sauce has thickened, about 3 minutes. Serve.

Sizing Up Your Skillet

nonstick • stainless steel • traditional cast iron • enameled cast iron • carbon steel

A 12-inch nonstick skillet provides enough space for simmering the mapo tofu. A stainless-steel, traditional cast-iron, enameled cast-iron, or carbon-steel skillet will also work for this reason.

Italian-Style Sausage and Pepper Subs

Serves 4

Total Time 40 minutes

1 tablespoon vegetable oil

1½ pounds hot or sweet Italian sausage (8 sausages)

3 red or green bell peppers, stemmed, seeded, and cut into ¼-inch-wide strips

1 large onion, halved and sliced thin

1 tablespoon tomato paste

1 tablespoon Worcestershire sauce

1 tablespoon minced fresh oregano or 1 teaspoon dried

2 garlic cloves, minced

4 (8-inch) Italian sub rolls, split lengthwise

Why This Recipe Works A submarine sandwich filled with sausages and peppers is most familiar as the stuff of street festivals and ball games, but it also makes a perfect quick weeknight meal at the dinner table or a gathering around the TV on game day, no grill or griddle required. We start by browning the sausages in the skillet, which leads to a great sear and plenty of flavor. We then add the peppers, onions, and a little water, cover the pan, and cook the sausages through. Next, we pull the sausages out and brown our peppers and onions in all the delicious bits the sausages left behind in the skillet. For even more complex flavor, we add some tomato paste, Worcestershire sauce, oregano, and garlic. This savory combination coats the peppers and onions and gives each bite a burst of flavor. You will need a 12-inch skillet with a tight-fitting lid for this recipe.

1 Heat oil in 12-inch stainless-steel skillet over medium-high heat until just smoking. Brown sausages on all sides, about 5 minutes. Distribute bell peppers and onion around sausages. Add ⅓ cup water, cover, and cook until sausages register 160 to 165 degrees and vegetables are softened, 7 to 9 minutes, flipping sausages halfway through cooking.

2 Transfer sausages to cutting board, tent with aluminum foil, and let rest while finishing vegetables. Increase heat to medium-high and cook without stirring until liquid has evaporated and vegetables are lightly browned, 5 to 7 minutes. Stir in tomato paste, Worcestershire, oregano, and garlic and cook until fragrant, about 1 minute. Halve sausages crosswise and serve with rolls and pepper-onion mixture.

VARIATION

Italian-Style Sausage and Pepper Subs for Two

Reduce bell pepper to 1 large; halve remaining ingredients. Proceed with recipe in 10- or 12-inch skillet.

Sizing Up Your Skillet

stainless steel ● **enameled cast iron** ● **nonstick** ● **traditional cast iron**

A 12-inch stainless-steel skillet provides enough space for browning and simmering the sausage and vegetable mixture and develops valuable fond for building a flavorful sauce to coat the vegetables. An enameled cast-iron skillet will also work for these reasons. A nonstick or traditional cast-iron skillet can also be used; however, they will not develop as much fond. If using a cast-iron skillet, you will need to preheat the empty skillet over medium heat for 3 minutes before proceeding with step 1.

Perfect Poached Fish

Serves 4

Total Time 30 minutes

- 1   lemon, sliced into thin rounds
- 4   sprigs fresh parsley
- 1   shallot, sliced thin
- ½   cup dry white wine
- 4   (6- to 8-ounce) skinless salmon fillets, 1 inch thick
- ½   teaspoon table salt
- ¼   teaspoon pepper

VARIATIONS

Perfect Poached Salmon with Bourbon and Maple

Omit parsley. Whisk 2 tablespoons bourbon, 3 tablespoons maple syrup, 2 tablespoons whole-grain mustard, 1 tablespoon cider vinegar, and shallot together in bowl. Substitute bourbon mixture for wine. After removing salmon and lemon slices from skillet, return skillet to high heat and simmer cooking liquid until slightly thickened and reduced to 2 tablespoons, 4 to 5 minutes. Off heat, whisk in 1 tablespoon unsalted butter and 1 tablespoon minced fresh chives. Spoon sauce over salmon before serving.

Perfect Poached Fish for Two

Halve all ingredients. Proceed with recipe in 10-inch skillet.

Why This Recipe Works Poaching rarely lives up to its promise to produce silken, delicately flavored fish, but this technique, where the poaching is done in a skillet, is reliable, foolproof, and dead-simple. Best of all, it makes each fish taste distinctly like itself. Cooking fish with liquid produces steam that delicately cooks the fish—if done right. A low temperature prevents overcooking, but it doesn't create enough steam to evenly cook the fish. High heat, on the other hand, overcooks the fish. To find a technique that would really work, we first increased the ratio of wine to water in our poaching liquid. The additional alcohol lowers the liquid's boiling point, producing more vapor at a lower temperature; this allows the portion of fish that is not submerged to cook through properly. For better flavor, we do not fully submerge the fillets, and we rest them on some lemon slices to avoid overcooking on the bottom. This recipe will work with a variety of fish. If using arctic char or wild salmon, cook the fillets to 120 degrees (for medium-rare) and start checking for doneness after 8 minutes. If using black sea bass, cod, haddock, hake, or pollock, cook the fish to 135 degrees. If using halibut, mahi-mahi, red snapper, or swordfish, cook the fish to 130 degrees and let rest, tented with foil, for 10 minutes before serving. We recommend serving the fish with a creamy or herb sauce from pages 102–103 or 150–151. You will need a 12-inch skillet with a tight-fitting lid for this recipe.

1 Arrange lemon slices in single layer across bottom of 12-inch stainless-steel skillet. Top with parsley sprigs and shallot, then add wine and enough water (about ½ cup) to just cover lemon slices. Pat salmon dry with paper towels, sprinkle with salt and pepper, and place, skinned side down, on top of lemon slices in skillet. Bring to simmer over medium-high heat. Reduce heat to low, cover, and cook, adjusting heat as needed to maintain gentle simmer, until salmon registers 125 degrees (for medium-rare), 11 to 16 minutes.

2 Remove skillet from heat and, using spatula, carefully transfer salmon and lemon slices to paper towel-lined plate to drain. (Discard poaching liquid.) Carefully lift and tilt fillets to remove lemon slices and transfer to serving platter. Serve.

perfecting
POACHED FISH

A poaching liquid that includes enough wine lowers its boiling point and produces steam even at a low temperature. Elevating the fish on lemon slices keeps it from overcooking on the bottom.

1 Elevate Your Fish.

2 Add Alcohol to Get Steamy.

3 Cover the Skillet.

Sizing Up Your Skillet

stainless steel • **nonstick** • **enameled cast iron**

A 12-inch stainless-steel skillet provides enough space for poaching four fish fillets. A nonstick or enameled cast-iron will also work for this reason.

QUICK CREAMY SAUCES

Refreshing and light, a dairy- or mayonnaise-based sauce can bring a dish to life with a few simple ingredients and is an incredibly versatile way to add creaminess and tang to just about anything. All the sauces here (save the Tzatziki and Spicy Avocado–Sour Cream Sauce) can be refrigerated for up to 4 days.

Herb-Yogurt Sauce

Makes about 1 cup

This sauce pairs well with poultry, fish, and vegetables. It is also nice swirled into creamy soups. Do not substitute low-fat or nonfat yogurt here.

1   cup plain whole-milk yogurt

¼   cup minced fresh chives, cilantro, dill, parsley, mint, and/or tarragon

1   garlic clove, minced

¼   teaspoon table salt

¼   teaspoon pepper

Whisk all ingredients together in bowl and season with salt and pepper to taste. Cover and refrigerate for at least 30 minutes to allow flavors to meld.

Yogurt-Tahini Sauce

Makes about 1 cup

This rich and creamy sauce is especially good with roasted or grilled vegetables, as well as poultry, lamb, and fish. It also makes a nice topping for grains and salads. Do not substitute low-fat or nonfat yogurt here.

⅔   cup plain whole-milk yogurt

⅓   cup tahini

2   tablespoons water

1   garlic clove, minced

Whisk all ingredients together in bowl and season with salt and pepper to taste. Cover and refrigerate for at least 30 minutes to allow flavors to meld.

Tzatziki

Makes about 1 cup

This tangy Mediterranean sauce pairs well with poultry, meat, fish, and vegetables. It is also great as a dip for crudités and pita bread. Using Greek yogurt here is key; do not substitute regular plain yogurt or the sauce will be very watery.

½   cucumber, peeled, halved lengthwise, seeded, and shredded

¼   teaspoon table salt

½   cup plain whole Greek yogurt

1   tablespoon extra-virgin olive oil

1   tablespoon minced fresh mint and/or dill

1   small garlic clove, minced

Toss cucumber with salt in colander and let drain for 15 minutes. Whisk yogurt, oil, mint, and garlic together in bowl, then stir in cucumber. Cover and refrigerate for at least 30 minutes to allow flavors to meld. Season with salt and pepper to taste. (Tzatziki can be refrigerated for up to 2 days.)

Spicy Avocado–Sour Cream Sauce

Makes about 1 cup

This sauce pairs well with poultry, meat, fish, and vegetables. It is also great dolloped on spicy chili or drizzled over tacos.

1   cup sour cream

½   avocado, cut into 1-inch pieces

1   jalapeño chile, stemmed, seeded, and chopped

1   teaspoon lime juice

Process all ingredients in food processor until smooth, scraping down sides of bowl as needed, and season with salt and pepper to taste. (Sauce can be refrigerated for up to 2 days.)

Horseradish–Sour Cream Sauce

Makes about 1 cup

This sauce pairs well with meat and vegetables and is a nice accompaniment to poached salmon. Buy refrigerated prepared horseradish, not the shelf-stable kind, which contains preservatives and additives.

½   cup sour cream

½   cup prepared horseradish, drained

¾   teaspoon table salt

⅛   teaspoon pepper

Whisk all ingredients together in bowl. Cover and refrigerate for at least 30 minutes to allow flavors to meld. Season with salt and pepper to taste.

Rémoulade

Makes about 1 cup

This sauce is especially good with seafood, vegetables, and fried foods.

⅔   cup mayonnaise

4   teaspoons lemon juice

1   teaspoon Dijon mustard

1   small garlic clove, minced

1   tablespoon capers, rinsed

1   tablespoon minced fresh parsley

1   tablespoon sweet pickle relish

Whisk all ingredients together in bowl. Cover and refrigerate for at least 30 minutes to allow flavors to meld. Season with salt and pepper to taste.

Braised Halibut with Leeks and Mustard

Serves 4

Total Time 35 minutes

- 4   (6- to 8-ounce) skinless halibut fillets, ¾ to 1 inch thick
- 1   teaspoon table salt, divided
- 6   tablespoons unsalted butter
- 1   pound leeks, white and light green parts only, halved lengthwise, sliced thin, and washed thoroughly
- 1   teaspoon Dijon mustard
- ¾   cup dry white wine
- 1   teaspoon lemon juice, plus lemon wedges for serving
- 2   tablespoons minced fresh parsley, basil, dill, or tarragon

VARIATION

Braised Halibut with Leeks and Mustard for Two

Halve all ingredients. Proceed with recipe in 10- or 12-inch skillet.

Why This Recipe Works Skillet braising, much like poaching, is a great method for cooking fish. It entails cooking the fish in a small amount of liquid that simmers and steams, and since it is moist-heat cooking, it is gentle and thus forgiving, all but guaranteeing tender fish. Plus, it allows for a great one-pan meal: It's easy to add vegetables to the skillet to cook at the same time and then turn the cooking liquid into a sauce. We use halibut here for its sweet, delicate flavor and firm texture, which makes for easier handling, and pair it with classic French flavors of leeks, white wine, and Dijon mustard. Because the portion of the fillets submerged in liquid cooks more quickly than the upper half that cooks in the steam, we cook the fillets for a few minutes in the pan in butter on just one side. We then remove them from the skillet so we can sauté the leeks and build a cooking liquid with the wine and Dijon. Then the fish is returned to the pan (parcooked side up to even out the cooking) and braised to tender perfection. The wine and mustard cooking liquid, supplemented by the juices released by the fish and leeks during cooking, reduces to a fantastic sauce infused with the unmistakable earthy flavor of the leeks. A final squeeze of lemon juice brightens the entire dish. Striped bass and swordfish are good substitutes for the halibut. You will need a 12-inch skillet with a tight-fitting lid for this recipe.

1 Pat halibut dry with paper towels and sprinkle with ½ teaspoon salt. Melt butter in 12-inch stainless-steel skillet over low heat. Place halibut skinned side up in skillet, increase heat to medium, and cook, shaking skillet occasionally, until butter begins to brown (fish should not brown), 3 to 4 minutes. Using spatula, carefully transfer halibut to plate, raw side down.

2 Add leeks, mustard, and remaining ½ teaspoon salt to fat left in skillet and cook, stirring frequently, until leeks begin to soften, 2 to 4 minutes. Stir in wine and bring to gentle simmer. Place halibut raw side down on top of leeks. Cover skillet and cook, adjusting heat to maintain gentle simmer, until halibut flakes apart when gently prodded with paring knife and registers 130 degrees, 10 to 14 minutes. Remove skillet from heat and, using 2 spatulas, transfer halibut and leeks to serving platter or individual plates. Tent with aluminum foil.

3 Return skillet to high heat and simmer briskly until sauce is thickened, 2 to 3 minutes. Off heat, stir in lemon juice and season with salt and pepper to taste. Spoon sauce over halibut and sprinkle with parsley. Serve immediately with lemon wedges.

Sizing Up Your Skillet

stainless steel • **nonstick** • **enameled cast iron**

A 12-inch stainless-steel skillet provides enough space for braising four fish fillets. A nonstick or enameled cast-iron skillet will also work for this reason. If using an enameled cast-iron skillet, you will need to preheat the empty skillet over medium heat for 3 minutes before proceeding with step 1. Due to the slightly acidic cooking liquid, we do not recommend using a traditional cast-iron skillet.

Chraime

Serves 4

Total Time 1 hour

3 tablespoons extra virgin olive oil, plus extra for drizzling

1 onion, chopped fine

1 red bell pepper, stemmed, seeded, and chopped

1 jalapeño chile, stemmed, seeded, and minced

¾ teaspoon table salt

¼ cup tomato paste

6 garlic cloves, minced

1 tablespoon tabil

1 tablespoon ground dried Aleppo pepper

2 teaspoons paprika

¼ teaspoon pepper

1½ cups water

1½ pounds skinless cod, ½ to ¾ inch thick, cut into 3-inch pieces

10 ounces cherry tomatoes

½ cup chopped fresh cilantro

Lemon wedges

Why This Recipe Works Chraime is a traditional fish stew brought to Israel by Libyan and Moroccan Jewish immigrants that commonly appears on Shabbat, Rosh Hashanah, and Passover tables. Essentially, it is fish simmered in a skillet in a spicy, garlicky, tomatoey sauce. Our take pays homage to both Libyan and Moroccan versions: grassy fresh jalapeños and bright Aleppo pepper bring varied heat, while tomato paste and bell pepper provide balancing sweetness. To easily bring in the varied spices, we turn to the Tunisian spice blend tabil, which adds a range of flavors, from earthy muskiness to bright citrus notes. To build the aromatic sauce in the skillet, we sauté the aromatics, bloom the spices along with tomato paste, and deglaze with water to scrape up the fond left in the skillet. A 15-minute simmer creates a deeply resonant sauce for nestling in our pieces of cod to simmer along with cherry tomatoes that add fresh pops of sweet acidity. A finishing handful of cilantro and a squeeze of lemon balance all the flavors. You can make your own tabil by combining 3 tablespoons cracked coriander seeds, 2 tablespoons caraway seeds, and 1 tablespoon cumin. Leftover tabil can be stored in airtight container for up to 1 month; use as a garnish for other stews, soups, salads, and/or dips. Black sea bass, haddock, hake, or pollock can be substituted for the cod. This dish is typically spicy; for a milder dish reduce the amount of Aleppo pepper to 1 or 2 teaspoons. Serve with challah. You will need a 12-inch skillet with a tight-fitting lid for this recipe.

1 Heat oil in 12-inch stainless-steel skillet over medium heat until shimmering. Add onion, bell pepper, jalapeño, and salt and cook until vegetables are softened, 5 to 7 minutes. Stir in tomato paste, garlic, tabil, Aleppo pepper, paprika, and pepper and cook until fragrant, about 30 seconds. Stir in water, scraping up any browned bits, and bring to simmer. Reduce heat to low, cover, and cook until flavors meld, about 15 minutes.

2 Nestle cod into sauce and spoon some of sauce over fish. Sprinkle tomatoes around cod and return to simmer. Reduce heat to low, cover, and cook until fish flakes apart when gently prodded with paring knife and registers 135 degrees, 5 to 7 minutes. Season with salt and pepper to taste. Sprinkle with cilantro and drizzle with extra oil. Serve with lemon wedges.

Sizing Up Your Skillet

stainless steel • nonstick • enameled cast iron

A 12-inch stainless-steel skillet provides enough space for simmering the fish stew. A nonstick or enameled cast-iron skillet will also work for this reason. If using an enameled cast-iron skillet, you will need to preheat the empty skillet over medium heat for 3 minutes before proceeding with step 1. Due to the acidic cooking liquid, we do not recommend using a traditional cast-iron skillet.

Sizing Up Your Skillet

stainless steel • **nonstick** • **traditional cast iron** • **enameled cast iron**

A 12-inch stainless-steel skillet provides enough space for sautéing the shrimp topping and simmering the grits. An ovensafe nonstick, traditional cast-iron, or enameled cast-iron skillet will also work for these reasons. If using a cast-iron skillet, you will need to preheat the empty skillet over medium heat for 3 minutes before proceeding with step 2.

Shrimp and Grits with Andouille

Serves 4

Total Time 1¼ hours

1 pound extra-large shrimp (21 to 25 per pound), peeled, deveined, tails removed, shells reserved

½ teaspoon pepper, divided

¼ teaspoon dried oregano

¼ teaspoon paprika

2 garlic cloves, minced

3 tablespoons unsalted butter, divided

4 scallions, white and green parts separated and sliced thin

2 tablespoons tomato paste

4½ cups water, plus extra as needed

6 ounces andouille sausage, cut into ¼-inch pieces

2 cups whole milk

1½ teaspoons table salt

1 cup old-fashioned grits

2 ounces extra-sharp cheddar cheese, shredded (½ cup)

VARIATION

Shrimp and Grits with Andouille for Two

Halve all ingredients. Proceed with recipe in 10-inch ovensafe skillet. You should have 2 cups stock after straining; add 2 tablespoons stock with shrimp in step 3 and remaining 1¾ cups plus 2 tablespoons stock with milk in step 4.

Why This Recipe Works Shrimp and grits is one of those classic dishes found in homes throughout the Southern United States in many appealing variations. Recently, it has become such a restaurant darling that you'll find it on menus all across the country. In our version, we borrow a little inspiration from Cajun country by incorporating andouille sausage and its smoky and spicy kick to amp up the heat and flavor. The skillet gets a workout with this dish as so many ingredients rotate in and out of it until finally it goes into the oven in all its glory to meld all the ingredients together and fully melt the cheese into the grits. People often discard shrimp shells, but here we sauté them with scallion whites and tomato paste and simply add water to deglaze the pan to make a savory shrimp stock that we incorporate in stages, infusing our grits with deep shrimp flavor. For the shrimp-andouille topping, the sausage is cut into tiny pieces so that it will render its smoky, salty juices as it browns. We then cook the shrimp right in the skillet with the sausage and a little stock (to prevent burning) and some butter for richness. We use more shrimp stock combined with milk to cook our grits for a creamy, rich texture and then we stir in the cheese off heat to bind everything together. We top the grits with our irresistible shrimp-andouille mixture and place in the oven to cook briefly. A final sprinkle of scallion greens completes the dish. If you use fresh-milled grits such as Anson Mills Colonial Coarse Pencil Cob Grits, you will need to increase the simmering time by 25 minutes and may need to add more water during simmering in step 4.

1 Adjust oven rack to middle position and heat oven to 450 degrees. Cut shrimp into ½-inch pieces and toss with ¼ teaspoon pepper, oregano, paprika, and garlic in bowl; set aside.

2 Melt 2 tablespoons butter in 12-inch ovensafe stainless-steel skillet over medium heat. Add shrimp shells and scallion whites and cook, stirring occasionally, until shells are bright pink, about 5 minutes. Stir in tomato paste and cook for 30 seconds. Stir in water, scraping up any browned bits. Bring to simmer and cook for 5 minutes. Strain shrimp stock through fine-mesh strainer set over bowl, pressing on solids to extract as much liquid as possible; discard solids. You should have 4 cups stock (If necessary, supplement with extra water). Wipe skillet clean with paper towels.

3 Cook sausage in now-empty skillet over medium-high heat until browned, 3 to 5 minutes. Add shrimp, ¼ cup shrimp stock, and remaining 1 tablespoon butter and cook until shrimp are just opaque, about 2 minutes. Transfer shrimp and sausage mixture to bowl; set aside.

4 Add remaining 3¾ cups shrimp stock, milk, and salt to again-empty skillet and bring to boil over medium-high heat. Slowly whisk in grits, making sure no lumps form. Reduce heat to medium-low and cook, whisking frequently and scraping sides and bottom of skillet to make sure grits do not stick, until grits are thick and creamy, 15 to 25 minutes. (Add extra water, 1 tablespoon at a time, if grits become too stiff while cooking.)

5 Off heat, whisk in cheddar and remaining ¼ teaspoon pepper until fully combined. Top grits with shrimp-andouille mixture. Transfer skillet to oven and bake until shrimp and sausage mixture is heated through, about 5 minutes. Sprinkle with scallion greens and serve.

Kousa Mihshi

Serves 4

Total Time 2¼ hours

Hashweh

½ cup long-grain white rice

8 ounces ground lamb

2 tablespoons extra-virgin olive oil, divided

1 teaspoon table salt

½ teaspoon pepper

¼ teaspoon ground cinnamon

Sauce

2 tablespoons extra-virgin olive oil

½ teaspoon pepper

¼ teaspoon ground cinnamon

1 small onion, chopped coarse

2 garlic cloves, minced

2 pounds tomatoes, cored and chopped coarse

2 tablespoons tomato paste

2 teaspoons cider vinegar

1 teaspoon table salt

Zucchini

6 zucchini (6 to 7 inches long and at least 1½ inches in diameter)

2 tablespoons extra-virgin olive oil

¼ cup fresh parsley leaves

2 cups plain whole-milk yogurt

Why This Recipe Works Kousa mihshi, which translates as "stuffed squash" from Arabic, is essentially zucchini stuffed with spiced ground lamb and rice that is skillet-braised in a cinnamon-accented tomato sauce. It's a Lebanese favorite that transcends its simple ingredients with a vibrant mix of flavors, textures, and temperatures. Soaking the rice for 10 minutes before combining it with the lamb ensures that the grains cook evenly and thoroughly. Browning the stuffing, known as hashweh, and breaking it up with the back of a spatula creates small, distinct pieces that pack lightly into the squash cavities. To give the braising sauce a meaty underpinning, we sauté aromatics in the fatty juices we drained from the lamb, then combine them in a food processor with chopped fresh tomatoes, tomato paste, and vinegar. After 40 minutes of simmering the stuffed zucchini in the velvety sauce, it is tender but not mushy and the filling is cooked through. For this recipe, you'll need a zucchini corer or an apple corer, the type that removes the core only but does not slice the apple. The small end of a melon baller or a long-handled bar spoon would also work. We like ground lamb here, but you can substitute 90 percent lean ground beef. Select zucchini that are similarly sized to ensure even cooking; and to make them easier to core, choose the straightest ones. Use fresh, in-season tomatoes for the best flavor. You will need a 12-inch skillet with a tight-fitting lid for this recipe.

1 For the hashweh Place rice in fine-mesh strainer and rinse under cold running water until water runs clear. Place rice in bowl and cover with 2 cups hot water; let stand for 10 minutes. Drain rice in now-empty strainer and return to bowl (do not wash strainer). Add lamb, 1 tablespoon oil, salt, pepper, and cinnamon and mix until rice is well dispersed. Heat remaining 1 tablespoon oil in 12-inch nonstick skillet over medium-high heat until shimmering. Add lamb mixture to skillet (do not wash bowl) and, using heat-resistant spatula, mash to thin layer. Cook, stirring constantly and breaking up meat with side of spatula, until meat is almost cooked through but still slightly pink, 3 to 4 minutes. Transfer mixture to now-empty strainer set over bowl. Return juices and fat to skillet. Transfer lamb mixture to now-empty bowl and, using fork, break up mixture until meat is reduced to pieces no larger than ¼ inch.

2 For the sauce Add oil to juices and fat in skillet and heat over medium-low heat until sizzling. Stir in pepper and cinnamon and cook until just fragrant, about 30 seconds. Add onion and garlic and cook, stirring occasionally, until very soft and light golden, 7 to 9 minutes.

3 Transfer onion mixture to food processor. Add tomatoes, tomato paste, vinegar, and salt to processor and process until smooth, 1½ to 2 minutes. Transfer tomato mixture to now-empty skillet. Bring to boil over medium-high heat. Reduce heat to simmer and cook, uncovered and stirring occasionally, until sauce is thickened and heat-resistant spatula dragged across bottom of skillet leaves trail, 25 to 30 minutes. While sauce cooks, prepare zucchini.

Sizing Up Your Skillet

- **nonstick**

A 12-inch nonstick skillet provides enough space for cooking the filling and sauce and braising the stuffed zucchini. Its slick surface also ensures that the filling can be easily transferred to a strainer without sticking. Due to the acidic cooking liquid, we do not recommend using a traditional cast-iron skillet.

4 For the zucchini Remove stem end of 1 zucchini and discard. Holding zucchini with your hand, insert zucchini or apple corer into stemmed end and press and turn until cutting end of corer is about ½ inch from bottom of zucchini (or as far as corer will go), being careful not to damage walls of zucchini. (If stemmed end is too narrow to accommodate corer without damaging walls, remove additional inch of stemmed end.) Remove corer. Using melon baller or long-handled bar spoon, scoop out any remaining core in pieces until farthest part of hollow is ½ inch from bottom of zucchini. Repeat with remaining zucchini. Rinse hollows and drain zucchini on dish towel.

5 Hold 1 zucchini stemmed side up on counter. Using your hand or small spoon, drop small portions of stuffing into hollow, tapping bottom of zucchini lightly on counter to help stuffing settle, until stuffing is ½ inch from top of zucchini. Do not compact stuffing. Repeat with remaining zucchini and stuffing.

6 Remove sauce from heat. Gently arrange stuffed zucchini in single layer in skillet. Return skillet to medium-high heat and bring to boil. Adjust heat to maintain low simmer, cover, and cook for 20 minutes (small wisps of steam should escape from beneath skillet lid, but sauce should not boil). Turn zucchini over gently. Cover and continue to simmer until rice and meat are fully cooked and zucchini are tender but not mushy, 20 to 25 minutes longer. Drizzle zucchini and sauce with oil, sprinkle with parsley, and serve, passing yogurt separately.

Madras Okra Curry

Serves 4 to 6

Total Time 1 hour

6   tablespoons vegetable oil, divided

1½   pounds okra, stemmed

1   small onion, chopped fine

3   garlic cloves, minced

1   tablespoon grated fresh ginger

1   tablespoon Madras curry powder

2½   cups vegetable broth

1   cup canned coconut milk

2   teaspoons honey

1   teaspoon cornstarch

¼   teaspoon table salt

10   sprigs fresh cilantro, chopped
     coarse

     Lime wedges

Why This Recipe Works If you think of okra as a slimy vegetable best avoided, this Madras-style curry is certain to change your mind. Here we sauté whole okra pods in a large skillet until they start to soften and take on some flavorful browning. Next, we use the empty skillet to build the flavor base by sautéing onion, then blooming Madras curry powder along with garlic and ginger. Following the method for most curries and braises, we deglaze the pan with broth and simmer it until reduced a bit. Now it's time to finesse the sauce. In keeping with the Indian tradition for this dish, we add coconut milk sweetened with honey and thickened with cornstarch to the skillet with the simmering aromatic-infused broth. The okra gets another turn in the skillet, but a not a long one, because it is important to keep it crisp-tender with an appealing texture. For serving, fresh cilantro sprigs and bright lime wedges balance out the rich curry. We prefer the spicier flavor of Madras curry powder here, as it includes red chiles, but you can substitute regular curry powder. Do not use frozen okra. Serve with Pan-Grilled Flatbreads (page 299) or basmati rice.

1 Heat 2 tablespoons oil in 12-inch stainless-steel skillet over medium-high heat until just smoking. Add half of okra to skillet and cook, stirring occasionally, until crisp-tender and well browned on most sides, 5 to 7 minutes; transfer to bowl. Repeat with 2 tablespoons oil and remaining okra; transfer to bowl. Let skillet cool slightly.

2 Heat remaining 2 tablespoons oil in now-empty skillet over medium heat until shimmering. Add onion and cook until softened, about 5 minutes. Stir in garlic, ginger, and curry powder and cook until fragrant, about 1 minute. Stir in broth, scraping up any browned bits, and bring to simmer. Cook, stirring occasionally, until reduced to 1¼ cups, 15 to 20 minutes.

3 Whisk coconut milk, honey, and cornstarch in bowl to dissolve cornstarch, then whisk mixture into skillet. Bring to simmer and cook until slightly thickened, about 30 seconds. Stir in okra and any accumulated juices and salt and return to brief simmer to warm through. Season with salt and pepper to taste. Sprinkle with cilantro and serve with lime wedges.

Sizing Up Your Skillet

stainless steel • **nonstick** • **traditional cast iron** • **enameled cast iron**

A 12-inch stainless-steel skillet provides enough space for browning the okra and simmering the curry. A nonstick, traditional cast-iron, or enameled cast-iron skillet will also work for this reason. If using a cast-iron skillet, you will need to preheat the empty skillet over medium heat for 5 minutes before proceeding with step 1.

Braised Eggplant with Pomegranate and Tahini

Serves 4

Total Time 50 minutes

1   tablespoon tahini

1   tablespoon plain whole-milk yogurt

1   tablespoon lemon juice

1   teaspoon water, plus extra as needed

1   cup vegetable broth

2   tablespoons pomegranate molasses

1   teaspoon table salt

1   teaspoon cornstarch

2   (8- to 10-ounce) globe or Italian eggplants

1   tablespoon vegetable oil

2   garlic cloves, minced

2   tablespoons toasted slivered almonds

2   tablespoons minced fresh parsley

Why This Recipe Works There are many ways to cook the humble eggplant, but we are enamored of the almost custardy silkiness that it takes on in a moist-heat method like braising. And reaching for a nonstick skillet instead of a Dutch oven for this task has a few advantages: The skillet's shallow, flared sides allow for quick evaporation, so we can simmer the eggplant in a sufficient amount of liquid and then quickly reduce it to a flavorful, clingy sauce. To start, we whisk together a bracing tahini-yogurt sauce that we will use for serving. We cut the eggplant into slim wedges so that each piece has enough skin to keep it from falling apart during braising. Then we sauté garlic in oil, add the eggplant wedges, and braise them in a sweet-tart mix of vegetable broth and pomegranate molasses, with cornstarch for thickening. The key to this easy cooking process is to first cook the eggplant in the covered skillet to soften and then remove the cover so that the delicious braising liquid can reduce and coat the wedges. Giving the skillet a good shake during this time helps ensure that all the eggplant is perfectly cooked and enrobed by the sauce. Large globe and Italian eggplants disintegrate when braised, so do not substitute a single 1- to 1¼-pound eggplant here. But you can substitute 1 to 1¼ pounds of long, slim Chinese or Japanese eggplants if they are available; cut them as directed. Serve with basmati rice. You will need a 12-inch skillet with a tight-fitting lid for this recipe.

1 Stir tahini, yogurt, lemon juice, and water together in small bowl. Add extra water, 1 teaspoon at a time, as needed until mixture is thin enough to drizzle. Season with salt to taste and set aside. Whisk broth, pomegranate molasses, salt, and cornstarch together in medium bowl. Trim ½ inch from top and bottom of 1 eggplant. Halve eggplant crosswise. Cut each half lengthwise into 2 pieces. Cut each piece into ¾-inch-thick wedges. Repeat with remaining eggplant.

2 Heat oil in 12-inch nonstick skillet over medium heat until shimmering. Add garlic and cook, stirring constantly, until fragrant, about 30 seconds. Spread eggplant evenly in skillet (pieces will not form single layer). Pour broth mixture over eggplant. Increase heat to high and bring to boil. Reduce heat to maintain gentle boil. Cover and cook until eggplant is soft and has decreased in volume enough to form single layer on bottom of skillet, about 15 minutes, gently shaking skillet to settle eggplant halfway through cooking (some pieces will remain opaque).

3 Uncover and continue to cook, swirling skillet occasionally, until liquid is thickened and reduced to just a few tablespoons, 12 to 14 minutes. Off heat, season with salt and pepper to taste. Transfer to serving platter, drizzle with tahini sauce, and sprinkle with almonds and parsley. Serve.

Sizing Up Your Skillet

nonstick • **traditional cast iron** • **carbon steel**

A 12-inch nonstick skillet provides enough space for braising the eggplant. Its slick surface also ensures that the dish can be easily transferred to a serving platter without sticking. A traditional cast-iron or carbon-steel skillet will also work for these reasons. If using a traditional cast-iron skillet, you will need to preheat the empty skillet over medium heat for 3 minutes before proceeding with step 2.

Spring Vegetable Risotto with Leek and Radishes

Serves 4

Total Time 1¼ hours

5   tablespoons unsalted butter, divided

1   pound radishes, trimmed and quartered

¾   teaspoon table salt, divided

¾   teaspoon pepper, divided

1   leek, white and light green parts only, halved lengthwise, sliced 1-inch thick, and washed thoroughly

½   cup frozen peas

4   cups vegetable or chicken broth

2   cups water

1½   cups arborio rice

2   garlic cloves, minced

½   cup dry white wine

1½   ounces Parmesan cheese, grated (¾ cup), plus extra for serving

½   cup minced fresh mint

½   cup shelled pistachios, walnuts, or almonds, toasted and chopped fine

1   teaspoon grated lemon zest plus 2 tablespoons juice

Why This Recipe Works Risotto is the epitome of a slowly simmered dish, one that demands that a cook stay close to the stove. Usually, it is made in a saucepan or Dutch oven, but we found we could easily reach for a skillet to make all elements. We celebrate the abundance of spring by first building a medley of delicate vernal vegetables and flavors. Leeks and frozen peas are often a component of a classic spring risotto, but what sets this one apart is that it includes a full pound of quartered radishes that are cooked in butter for defining richness. In addition to sautéing the leek and radishes, we use the skillet to toast the nuts, to sauté the aromatics, and in classic risotto fashion, to toast the rice lightly before adding the wine and then the broth-water mixture in stages. For a colorful and delicious topping, we combine our warm spring vegetables with mint, nuts, and lemon zest and juice. To eliminate the need to keep a pan of simmering broth-water mixture on the stovetop we simply microwave it, making this recipe a true one-skillet operation. The risotto should be creamy but loose in texture.

1 Melt 2 tablespoons butter in 12-inch stainless-steel skillet over medium-high heat. Add radishes, ½ teaspoon salt, and ¼ teaspoon pepper and cook until lightly browned, 7 to 9 minutes. Add leeks and continue to cook, stirring occasionally, until leeks are softened and radishes are crisp-tender, about 5 minutes. Stir in peas and cook for 1 minute. Transfer vegetables to bowl and cover to keep warm.

2 Combine broth and water in 8-cup liquid measuring cup and microwave until steaming, about 5 minutes; set aside.

3 Melt 1 tablespoon butter in now-empty skillet over medium-high heat. Add rice and garlic and cook, stirring frequently, until grains are translucent around edges, about 3 minutes. Add wine, remaining ¼ teaspoon salt, and remaining ½ teaspoon pepper and cook, stirring frequently, until liquid is fully absorbed, about 3 minutes. Stir in 3 cups hot broth mixture and bring to simmer. Cook, stirring every 3 to 4 minutes, until liquid is absorbed and bottom of skillet is almost dry, about 15 minutes.

4 Add ½ cup broth mixture and cook, stirring constantly, until absorbed, about 3 minutes; repeat with additional broth mixture 3 or 4 times until rice is al dente. Off heat, stir in Parmesan and remaining 2 tablespoons butter. If needed, add remaining hot broth mixture, ¼ cup at a time, to loosen texture of risotto. Toss reserved vegetables with mint, pistachios, and lemon zest and juice. Top individual portions of risotto with vegetable mixture and serve, passing extra Parmesan separately.

Sizing Up Your Skillet

stainless steel • nonstick • traditional cast iron • enameled cast iron

A 12-inch stainless-steel skillet provides enough space for sautéing the vegetable topping and simmering the risotto. A nonstick, traditional cast-iron, or enameled cast-iron skillet will also work for these reasons. If using a cast-iron skillet, you will need to preheat the empty skillet over medium heat for 3 minutes before proceeding with step 1.

Sizing Up Your Skillet

stainless steel • **nonstick** • **traditional cast iron** • **enameled cast iron**

A 12-inch stainless-steel skillet provides enough space for sautéing the vegetables and simmering the paella. A nonstick, traditional cast-iron, or enameled cast-iron skillet will also work for these reasons. If using a cast-iron skillet, you will need to preheat the empty skillet over medium heat for 3 minutes before proceeding with step 1.

Cauliflower and Bean Paella

Serves 4

Total Time 1¼ hours

3 tablespoons extra-virgin olive oil, divided

12 ounces cauliflower florets, cut into 2- to 2½-inch pieces (2½ cups)

¾ teaspoon table salt, divided

6 ounces green beans, trimmed and cut into 2- to 2½-inch pieces

1 red bell pepper, stemmed, seeded, and chopped fine

1 tablespoon tomato paste

3 garlic cloves, minced

1 teaspoon smoked paprika

¼ teaspoon saffron threads, crumbled

¼ cup dry sherry

1 cup Calasparra or Bomba rice

1 (15-ounce) can butter beans, rinsed

3½ cups chicken or vegetable broth

Lemon wedges (optional)

VARIATION

Cauliflower and Bean Paella for Two

Reduce oil to 2 tablespoons and garlic to 1 large clove; halve remaining ingredients. Proceed with recipe in 10-inch skillet, using 1 tablespoon oil in steps 1 and 2.

Why This Recipe Works Most paella recipes (whether vegetarian or meat and seafood rich) are built in a skillet or Dutch oven (or paella pan) and go from stovetop to oven. This version happens all on the stovetop in a large skillet. This recipe is known as paella de verduras and is a common, versatile approach to the beloved rice dish that's prepared throughout Spain and showcases vegetables rather than merely using them to flavor the rice. This hearty version features cauliflower, green beans, and butter beans—echoing the ingredients Valencians often add to paella de verduras. In lieu of building a meaty fond in a skillet, as with paellas featuring chorizo and seafood, we retool a Spanish sofrito to make a complex flavor base. We brown bell pepper instead of just sautéing it, swap in umami-rich tomato paste for fresh tomatoes, load up on the garlic, and omit the sweet-tasting onion. Stirring and smashing the tomato paste into the skillet encourages a sort of fond. Then we mix in smoked paprika, saffron, and nutty-tasting dry sherry for brightness and depth. After adding the rice, we layer the vegetables and beans on top, add the broth, bring it all to a simmer, and then cover and simmer until the rice is perfectly tender. To ensure that the rice at the surface of the paella cooks through, we cover the pan for part of the cooking time to trap moist heat that hydrates the grains. We let the paella rest for a few minutes before serving, which helps the socarrat layer (the appealing crispy rice that forms at the bottom of the skillet) firm up so that it is even crispier and releases easily from the pan. We've included instructions for creating a socarrat, but it's optional. If neither Calasparra nor Bomba rice is available, use Arborio rice. It's worth seeking out butter beans for their large size; do not substitute small white beans. You will need a 12-inch skillet with a tight-fitting lid for this recipe.

1 Heat 1½ tablespoons oil in 12-inch stainless-steel skillet over medium heat until shimmering. Add cauliflower and ½ teaspoon salt and cook, stirring frequently, until cauliflower is spotty brown, 3 to 5 minutes. Add green beans and continue to cook, stirring frequently, until green beans are dark green, 2 to 4 minutes; transfer to bowl.

2 Heat remaining 1½ tablespoons oil in now-empty skillet over medium heat until shimmering. Add bell pepper and remaining ¼ teaspoon salt and cook, stirring occasionally, until bell pepper starts to brown, 7 to 10 minutes. Add tomato paste and cook, stirring constantly, until bell pepper pieces are coated in tomato paste, about 1 minute. Add garlic, paprika, and saffron and cook, stirring constantly, until fragrant, about 30 seconds. Add sherry and cook, stirring frequently, until excess moisture has evaporated and bell pepper mixture forms large clumps, 1 to 2 minutes.

3 Stir in rice until very well combined. Off heat, smooth into even layer. Scatter butter beans evenly over rice. Scatter cauliflower and green beans evenly over butter beans. Gently pour broth all over, making sure rice is fully submerged (it's OK if parts of vegetables aren't submerged).

4 Bring to boil over high heat. Adjust heat to maintain gentle simmer and cook until broth is just below top of rice, 10 to 15 minutes. Cover and cook until rice is cooked through, 3 to 5 minutes. Uncover and cook until rice pops and sizzles and all excess moisture has evaporated (to test, use butter knife to gently push aside some rice and vegetables), 3 to 7 minutes. (If socarrat is desired, continue to cook, rotating skillet a quarter turn every 20 seconds, until rice on bottom of skillet is well browned and slightly crusty [use butter knife to test], 2 to 5 minutes.) Let rest off heat for 5 minutes. Serve, passing lemon wedges separately, if using.

Lentilles du Puy with Spinach and Crème Fraîche

Serves 4

Total Time 1 hour

1 tablespoon extra-virgin olive oil

½ cup finely chopped onion

¼ cup finely chopped carrot

¼ cup finely chopped celery

¼ teaspoon table salt

2 cups chicken or vegetable broth

1 cup water, plus extra as needed

1 cup dried lentilles du Puy, picked over and rinsed

4 ounces (4 cups) baby spinach

2 tablespoons Dijon mustard

¼ cup crème fraîche

Why This Recipe Works This skillet-braised lentil dish, both humble and extravagant at the same time, couldn't be easier. It is made with lentilles du Puy, which are grown under strict French and European Union origin laws and often are referred to as the caviar of lentils. First, we gently cook a mirepoix (a mixture of two parts chopped onion to one part each of chopped carrots and celery) in extra-virgin olive oil with a touch of salt until just softened. Then we add the lentils and chicken broth, bring it all to a simmer, cover, and gently braise until the lentils are soft and creamy on the inside but still hold their shape, and almost all the broth is absorbed. Mineral-y spinach adds earthiness and pops of color while spoonfuls of Dijon add a pungent edge. Rich, creamy crème fraîche is the ultimate finishing touch. You can substitute other French green lentils for the lentilles du Puy, but do not substitute other types of green lentils or black, brown, or red lentils—the cooking times of the other lentil varieties can vary greatly. By the end of step 2, the lentils should have absorbed most, but not all, of the chicken broth. If the bottom of the skillet looks dry and the lentils are still somewhat firm, add hot water, ¼ cup at a time, and continue to cook until the lentils are tender. If you can't find crème fraîche, sour cream works well. You will need a 12-inch skillet with a tight-fitting lid for this recipe.

1 Heat oil in 12-inch stainless-steel skillet over medium heat until shimmering. Add onion, carrot, celery, and salt and cook until softened, about 5 minutes. Add broth, water, and lentils and bring to simmer. Reduce heat to medium-low, cover, and cook, stirring occasionally, until lentils are tender but still hold their shape, about 30 minutes. (Add hot water, ¼ cup at a time, if skillet becomes dry before lentils are cooked through.)

2 Gently fold in spinach, one handful at a time, until wilted. Off heat, stir in mustard and let sit, covered, for 5 minutes. Dollop individual portions with crème fraîche before serving.

Sizing Up Your Skillet

stainless steel • nonstick • traditional cast iron • enameled cast iron

A 12-inch stainless-steel skillet provides enough space for simmering the lentils. A nonstick, traditional cast-iron, or enameled cast-iron skillet will also work for this reason. If using a cast-iron skillet, you will need to preheat the empty skillet over medium heat for 3 minutes before proceeding with step 1.

pan-roast & bake

Pan-Roasted Chicken Breasts with Coriander, Fennel, and Lemon

Serves 4 to 6

Total Time 1½ hours, plus
1 hour salting

---

4   (12-ounce) bone-in split
     chicken breasts, trimmed

1½   teaspoons coriander seeds,
     lightly crushed

1½   teaspoons fennel seeds, lightly
     crushed

1   teaspoon grated lemon zest
     plus 1 tablespoon juice

½   teaspoon pepper

2½   teaspoons kosher salt

3   tablespoons extra-virgin olive
     oil, divided

1   tablespoon chopped
     fresh chives

VARIATIONS

Pan-Roasted Chicken Breasts with Herbes de Provence

Substitute 1 tablespoon crumbled
herbes de Provence for coriander
seeds, fennel seeds, and lemon zest.
Increase pepper to 1½ teaspoons.

Pan-Roasted Chicken Breasts with Coriander, Fennel, and Lemon for Two

Halve all ingredients. Proceed with
recipe in 10-inch skillet.

Why This Recipe Works This recipe is for those who adore chicken skin but also like white meat and can do without the bones. The magic lies in the technique: starting on the stovetop in a cold pan and then pan-roasting in the oven. First, we remove the bones from chicken breasts, season them with coriander and fennel seeds, and refrigerate for an hour (or longer) to infuse the meat with flavor. We then place the chicken in a cold skillet, turn on the heat, and cook until the fat is rendered and the skin is browned, then finish the chicken skin side up in the oven. While the chicken rests, we add additional oil to the rendered fat in the hot skillet, along with more coriander and fennel seeds, some lemon juice, and chives to deliver a big-flavored pan sauce with almost no work. This recipe was developed with Diamond Crystal Kosher Salt. (If using Morton Kosher Salt, decrease the amount to 1¾ teaspoons.) You will need a 12-inch ovensafe skillet for this recipe.

1 Place 1 chicken breast skin side down on cutting board, with ribs facing away from your knife hand. Run tip of knife between breastbone and meat, working from thick end of breast toward thin end. Angling blade slightly and following rib cage, repeat cutting motion several times to remove ribs and breastbone from breast. Find short remnant of wishbone along top edge of breast and run tip of knife along both sides of bone to separate from meat. Repeat with remaining 3 breasts.

2 Combine coriander seeds, fennel seeds, lemon zest, and pepper in small bowl. Transfer 1 teaspoon coriander seed mixture to second small bowl and set aside; add salt to remaining coriander seed mixture. Pat chicken dry with paper towels and sprinkle with salted coriander seed mixture. Transfer chicken skin side up to large plate and refrigerate, uncovered, for at least 1 hour or up to 24 hours.

3 Adjust oven rack to upper-middle position and heat oven to 325 degrees. Swirl 1 tablespoon oil evenly over surface of cold 12-inch stainless-steel skillet. Place chicken skin side down in skillet. Cook over medium-low heat until skin is deep golden brown, 18 to 20 minutes. Flip chicken skin side up, transfer skillet to oven, and cook until chicken registers 160 degrees, 7 to 9 minutes.

4 Using pot holder, remove skillet from oven and transfer chicken to clean large plate; let rest for 10 minutes. Meanwhile, being careful of hot skillet handle, add remaining 2 tablespoons oil to juices left in skillet and heat over medium heat until shimmering. Add reserved coriander seed mixture and cook until fragrant, about 1 minute. Off heat, whisk in lemon juice and chives, scraping up any browned bits. Slice chicken, transfer to serving platter, and drizzle with pan sauce. Serve.

perfecting
ROASTED CHICKEN BREASTS

Get the best of both worlds by buying bone-in skin-on breasts and removing the bones. Start in a cold skillet with oil and then turn the heat to medium-low to crisp the skin; slow cooking is the key to keeping the chicken flavorful and juicy. Then transfer the skillet to the oven to gently cook it through.

1 Keep the Skin; Lose the Bones.

2 Start the Chicken in a Cold Pan.

3 Finish in the Oven then Make a Pan Sauce.

Sizing Up Your Skillet

stainless steel • **enameled cast iron** • **nonstick** • **traditional cast iron** • **carbon steel**

A 12-inch stainless-steel skillet provides enough space for roasting four chicken breasts and develops valuable fond for building a pan sauce. An enameled cast-iron skillet will also work for these reasons. An ovensafe nonstick, traditional cast-iron, or carbon-steel skillet can also be used; however, they will not develop as much fond.

Pan-Roasted Chicken Parts

Serves 4 to 6

Total Time 45 minutes, plus
30 minutes brining

½   cup table salt for brining

3   pounds bone-in chicken
      pieces (split breasts cut in
      half, drumsticks, and/or
      thighs), trimmed

¼   teaspoon pepper

1   teaspoon vegetable oil

VARIATION

Baharat-Spiced Pan-Roasted Chicken Parts

Combine 1 teaspoon paprika, 1 teaspoon smoked paprika, 1 teaspoon
ground cumin, ½ teaspoon pepper,
½ teaspoon ground coriander, ⅛ teaspoon ground cloves,⅛ teaspoon
ground cinnamon, and ⅛ teaspoon
cayenne pepper in small bowl. Substitute spice mixture for pepper, making
sure to coat all sides of chicken.

Why This Recipe Works The restaurant technique of pan-roasting is
a great way to quickly deliver perfectly cooked bone-in chicken parts with
browned skin and plenty of fond on the bottom of the pan. To start, we give
the chicken a quick 30-minute brine, which ensures that the chicken stays
moist and tender. We then get the oil in a large stainless-steel skillet smoking
hot, add the chicken skin side down, and sear until golden. Next, we flip it
and cook until golden on the other side. Transferring the pan to a 450-degree
oven facilitates cooking and produces crispy skin without leaving burnt bits
behind in our skillet. The combination of searing and high-heat roasting
leaves plenty of caramelized drippings, or fond, in the skillet, perfect for
making a luscious and flavorful pan sauce (recipes on pages 32–33).
You will need a 12-inch ovensafe skillet for this recipe.

1 Dissolve salt in 2 quarts cold water in large container. Sub-
merge chicken in brine, cover, and refrigerate for 30 minutes.
Remove chicken from brine and pat dry with paper towels.
Sprinkle with pepper.

2 Adjust oven rack to lowest position and heat oven to
450 degrees. Heat oil in 12-inch stainless-steel skillet over
medium-high heat until just smoking. Brown chicken skin
side down until deep golden on first side, about 5 minutes.
Flip chicken and continue to cook until golden on second
side, about 3 minutes. Turn chicken skin side down, transfer
skillet to oven, and roast until breasts register 160 degrees
and drumsticks and thighs register 175 degrees, 10 to
15 minutes. Transfer chicken to serving platter and let rest
for 5 minutes. Serve.

VARIATION

Pan-Roasted Chicken Parts for Two

Halve all ingredients except for oil. Dissolve ¼ cup table salt in 1 quart
cold water in step 1. Proceed with recipe in 10- or 12-inch skillet.

Sizing Up Your Skillet

stainless steel • **enameled cast iron** • **nonstick** • **traditional cast iron** • **carbon steel**

A 12-inch stainless-steel skillet provides enough space for roasting the chicken parts
and develops valuable fond for building a pan sauce. An enameled cast-iron skillet will
also work for these reasons. An ovensafe nonstick, traditional cast-iron, or carbon-steel
skillet can also be used; however, they will not develop as much fond. If using a cast-
iron skillet, you will need to preheat the empty skillet over medium heat for 5 minutes
before proceeding with step 2.

perfecting
PAN-ROASTED CHICKEN PARTS

Brining the chicken ensures it stays moist. Searing the chicken in a stainless skillet in smoking hot oil quickly creates browning on each side. Transferring the skillet to a hot oven finishes the job perfectly and leaves behind a beautiful fond with which to make a complementary pan sauce if desired.

1 Use a Quick Brine.

2 Sear on the Stovetop in Smoking-Hot Oil.

3 Finish in a 450-Degree Oven.

Sizing Up Your Skillet

stainless steel ● **enameled cast iron** ● **nonstick** ● **traditional cast iron** ● **carbon steel**

A 12-inch stainless-steel skillet provides enough space for roasting four chicken breasts, developing flavorful fond, and creating a broccoli side dish. An enameled cast-iron skillet will also work for these reasons. An ovensafe nonstick, traditional cast-iron, or carbon-steel skillet can also be used; however, they will not develop as much fond.

Skillet-Roasted Chicken Breasts with Garlic-Ginger Broccoli

Serves 4 to 6

Total Time 1¼ hours

4 (12-ounce) bone-in split chicken breasts, trimmed

2½ teaspoons kosher salt, divided

Vegetable oil spray

3 garlic cloves, sliced thin

2 teaspoons grated fresh ginger

2 teaspoons toasted sesame oil

¼ teaspoon sugar

1½ pounds broccoli, florets cut into ¾-inch pieces, stalks trimmed, peeled, and sliced on bias ¼ inch thick

½ cup water

Why This Recipe Works The savory elixir left behind after roasting chicken is always pure gold. Here, instead of making a pan sauce, we make the most of the chicken juices by adding broccoli to the skillet to cook on the stovetop while the chicken rests, delivering a twofer from one skillet. First, we season bone-in, skin-on chicken breasts under the skin with salt. We place them skin side down in a cold skillet and then turn on the heat to slowly render the fat and brown the skin without overcooking the delicate flesh just beneath. Once the skin is well browned, we flip the breasts and place them in a 325-degree oven for about 30 minutes to cook through. While the cooked chicken breasts rest, we add garlic, ginger, sesame oil, salt, and sugar to the skillet and cook until the chicken juices have reduced and the aromatics begin to sizzle in the chicken fat and release flavor. We then add broccoli to the pan along with a little water, cover the pan, and let the broccoli cook through. With the skillet uncovered, the savory, chicken-y liquid thickens to coat the broccoli. This recipe was developed with Diamond Crystal Kosher Salt. (If using Morton Kosher Salt, which is denser, decrease the amount for the chicken to 1⅛ teaspoons and the amount for the broccoli to ¾ teaspoon.) You will need a 12-inch ovensafe skillet with a tight-fitting lid for this recipe.

1 Adjust oven rack to lower-middle position and heat oven to 325 degrees. Working with 1 breast at a time, use your fingers to carefully separate skin from meat. Peel back skin, leaving skin attached at top and bottom of breast and at ribs. Sprinkle 1½ teaspoons salt evenly over chicken (⅜ teaspoon per breast). Lay skin back in place. Using metal skewer or tip of paring knife, poke 6 to 8 holes in fat deposits in skin of each breast. Spray skin with oil spray.

2 Place chicken skin side down in cold 12-inch stainless-steel skillet and set over medium-high heat. Cook, moving chicken as infrequently as possible, until skin is well browned, 7 to 9 minutes. Carefully flip chicken and transfer skillet to oven. Roast until chicken registers 160 degrees, 25 to 30 minutes.

3 Using potholders, remove skillet from oven. Being careful of hot skillet handle, transfer chicken to plate. Add garlic, ginger, oil, sugar, and remaining 1 teaspoon salt to liquid left in skillet and cook over medium-high heat, stirring occasionally and scraping up any browned bits, until moisture has evaporated and mixture begins to sizzle, 2 to 4 minutes. Add broccoli and water and bring to simmer. Cover skillet, reduce heat to medium, and cook until broccoli is crisp-tender, 5 minutes, stirring halfway through cooking. Uncover and continue to cook, stirring frequently, until broccoli is fully tender and sauce coats broccoli, 2 to 4 minutes. Add any accumulated chicken juices to skillet and toss to combine. Season with salt to taste. Serve chicken with broccoli.

VARIATION

Skillet-Roasted Chicken Breasts with Garlic-Ginger Broccoli for Two

Reduce garlic to 1 large clove. Halve remaining ingredients. Proceed with recipe in 10-inch ovensafe skillet.

Harissa-Rubbed Chicken Thighs with Charred Cucumber and Carrot Salad

Serves 4 to 6

Total Time 1 hour

2 tablespoons white wine vinegar

1 small shallot, minced

1 teaspoon caraway seeds, toasted and cracked

1 teaspoon Dijon mustard

1 teaspoon table salt, divided

5 tablespoons extra-virgin olive oil, divided

1 pound carrots, peeled and shaved into ribbons using vegetable peeler

1 English cucumber, halved lengthwise and sliced 1 inch thick on bias

8 (5- to 7-ounce) bone-in chicken thighs, trimmed

1 tablespoon harissa

½ cup pitted kalamata olives, chopped coarse

¼ cup walnuts, toasted and chopped

2 tablespoons chopped fresh dill

Why This Recipe Works There is perhaps nothing more delicious than pan-seared and then roasted chicken thighs burnished a deep mahogany brown with crispy skin. Here, a skillet pulls double duty: creating an unusual side dish of deeply charred yet still tender cucumber chunks and also taking the chicken thighs from stovetop to oven in a classic pan-roasting technique. We brush the chicken skin with a little harissa, the spiced North African chili paste, but only after the initial sear, so the skin darkens beautifully in the oven and it also prevents the harissa from burning. To transform the humble cucumber, we cut it on the bias into large pieces and cook it in the hot, dry preheated pan, preserving its essential interior freshness while adding a layer of complex, smoky char—something a cast-iron skillet does exceptionally well. We transform carrots by shaving them into thin ribbons whose raw crunch is softened by marinating in a concentrated, caraway-laced dressing. The acidity of the vinegar and the sweetness of the carrots and cucumber in the salad balance the spicy richness of the chicken. Some briny olives, crunchy walnuts, and fresh dill add a variety of textures and flavors to complete this one-pan, weeknight-friendly meal. If your chicken thighs are larger than 5 to 7 ounces each, use fewer of them to maintain a total weight of 2½ to 3½ pounds; adjust cooking time as needed. You will need a 12-inch ovensafe skillet for this recipe.

1 Adjust oven rack to middle position and heat oven to 400 degrees. Whisk vinegar, shallot, caraway seeds, mustard, and ¼ teaspoon salt together in large bowl. Whisking constantly, slowly drizzle in ¼ cup oil. Add carrots and toss until well coated; set aside.

2 Heat 12-inch cast-iron skillet over medium heat for 3 minutes. Increase heat to medium-high and arrange cucumber cut side down in skillet (skillet will be full). Cook, moving cucumber as little as possible, until charred on first side, 5 to 7 minutes. Flip cucumber and continue to cook until charred on second side, 3 to 5 minutes. Transfer to bowl with carrots and set aside.

3 Pat chicken dry with paper towels and sprinkle flesh side with remaining ¾ teaspoon salt. Heat remaining 1 tablespoon oil in now-empty skillet over medium-high heat until just smoking. Add chicken skin side down and cook until well browned, 6 to 8 minutes. Off heat, flip chicken and brush harissa evenly over skin. Transfer skillet to oven and roast until chicken registers 175 degrees, 10 to 15 minutes.

4 Transfer chicken to serving platter and let rest while finishing salad. Add olives, walnuts, and dill to bowl with carrots and cucumber and toss to combine. Season with salt and pepper to taste. Serve chicken with salad.

Sizing Up Your Skillet

traditional cast iron ● **enameled cast iron** ● **stainless steel**

The superior heat retention of a 12-inch traditional cast-iron skillet is key to achieving plenty of char on the cucumber, and the size allows for plenty of space to roast eight chicken thighs. An enameled cast-iron skillet can also be used for these reasons; add 1 teaspoon olive oil to skillet and heat until smoking before charring the cucumber. A stainless-steel skillet can also be used; before charring the cucumber, heat 1 teaspoon olive oil in the skillet over medium-high heat until just smoking.

Couscous-Stuffed Chicken Thighs with Roasted Cherry Tomatoes and Shallots

Serves 4 to 6

Total Time 1½ hours

¾ teaspoon ground cumin

¾ teaspoon pepper

½ teaspoon ground sumac

1¾ teaspoons table salt, divided

3 tablespoons extra-virgin olive oil, divided

3 garlic cloves, minced

⅓ cup couscous

1⅓ cups chicken broth, divided

½ preserved lemon, pulp and white pith removed, rind rinsed and minced (3 tablespoons), divided

3 tablespoons chopped fresh parsley, divided

1½ tablespoons tahini

8 (3- to 5-ounce) boneless chicken thighs, trimmed

10 ounces cherry tomatoes, halved

4 shallots, quartered

Why This Recipe Works With a bit of strategy and an abundance of Mediterranean flavors, this chicken meal is a welcome addition to the dinnertime table. Like many of our other pan-roasted chicken dishes, this one travels from stovetop to oven and back to the stovetop to finish the sauce. An easy couscous stuffing flavored with citrusy preserved lemon and warm spices makes it a one-dish meal. A pungent tahini holds the stuffing together and ensures that it stays tightly packed in the rolled-up boneless thigh bundles. Pounding the thighs before stuffing them is key to the success of this dish. After browning both sides of the rolled chicken thighs on the stovetop, we scatter halved cherry tomatoes and quartered shallots into the skillet before transferring it to the oven. We remove the skillet from the oven after 30 minutes, transfer the thighs to a plate, and put the skillet back on the stovetop. Then we turn the luscious roasted and caramelized tomato-shallot mixture into a lively sauce by simply adding broth, scraping up the browned bits, and letting everything meld and reduce for a just a few minutes. Additional chopped preserved lemon and parsley complete the bright and beautiful sauce. If sumac is unavailable, substitute an equal amount of dried thyme. You will need a 12-inch ovensafe skillet with a tight-fitting lid for this recipe.

1 Combine cumin, pepper, and sumac in small bowl. Measure out and reserve ½ teaspoon spice mixture. Stir 1½ teaspoons salt into remaining spice mixture; set aside.

2 Cook 1 tablespoon oil, garlic, and reserved unsalted spice mixture in 12-inch stainless-steel skillet over medium-high heat until fragrant, about 1 minute. Stir in couscous, ⅓ cup broth, and remaining ¼ teaspoon salt. Off heat, cover and let sit until all liquid has been absorbed and couscous is tender, about 5 minutes. Transfer couscous mixture to a large bowl and add 1 tablespoon preserved lemon, 1 tablespoon parsley, and tahini and fluff mixture with fork until evenly combined. Wipe skillet clean with paper towels.

3 Adjust oven rack to middle position and heat oven to 400 degrees. Cut kitchen twine into sixteen 10-inch lengths. Arrange chicken thighs on large cutting board skinned side down with narrow sides facing you. Cover with plastic wrap and pound to even ¼-inch thickness. Sprinkle chicken with remaining salted spice mixture. Divide filling among thighs and spread evenly over surface, pressing gently to adhere. Starting with edge closest to you, roll chicken away from you into compact cylinder and secure with 2 evenly spaced pieces of twine.

4 Toss tomatoes and shallots with 1 tablespoon oil. Heat remaining 1 tablespoon oil in now-empty skillet over medium-high heat until just smoking. Add thighs seam side up and cook until well browned on first side, about 5 minutes. Flip thighs and scatter tomato mixture around chicken. Transfer skillet to oven and roast until thickest part of filling registers 185 degrees, 30 to 35 minutes.

5 Using pot holders, remove skillet from oven. Transfer thighs to cutting board, tent with aluminum foil, and let rest while finishing sauce. Being careful of hot skillet handle, add remaining 1 cup broth to skillet, scraping up any browned bits, and cook over medium-high heat until flavors meld and sauce thickens slightly, 5 to 7 minutes. Off heat, stir in remaining 2 tablespoons preserved lemon and remaining 2 tablespoons parsley. Remove twine and serve chicken with tomato and shallot sauce.

Sizing Up Your Skillet

stainless steel ● **enameled cast iron** ● **nonstick** ● **traditional cast iron**

A 12-inch stainless-steel skillet provides enough space for roasting eight stuffed chicken thighs and develops valuable fond for building a pan sauce. An enameled cast-iron skillet will also work for these reasons. An ovensafe nonstick or traditional cast-iron skillet can also be used; however, they will not develop as much fond.

Weeknight Roast Chicken

Serves 4 to 6

Total Time 1½ hours

1   tablespoon kosher salt

½   teaspoon pepper

1   (3½- to 4-pound) whole chicken, giblets discarded

1   tablespoon extra-virgin olive oil

VARIATION

Weeknight Roast Chicken with Sage and Fenugreek

Instead of the salt, pepper, and olive oil in the recipe, process 1 cup chopped fresh parsley, 2 tablespoons minced fresh sage, 2 tablespoons olive oil, 1½ tablespoons ground fenugreek, 1 tablespoon salt, 2 teaspoons garlic powder, and ½ teaspoon pepper in food processor until finely ground, about 30 seconds, scraping down sides of bowl as necessary. Rub herb paste evenly over surface and under skin of chicken before tying legs together.

Why This Recipe Works When you want a hands-off, absolutely foolproof way to roast a chicken, this is the recipe to use. In fact, we think everyone should memorize it—it's that good. Rather than fussing with a V-rack or flipping the chicken, we simply preheat a skillet in the oven. Direct contact with the superhot pan jump-starts the thighs' cooking. Roasting the chicken for 30 minutes in a 450-degree oven and then turning the oven off allows the more delicate white meat to remain moist and tender as the bird finishes cooking in the oven's residual heat. This recipe was developed with Diamond Crystal Kosher Salt. (If using Morton Kosher Salt, which is denser, decrease the amount to 2¼ teaspoons.) We prefer to use a 3½- to 4-pound chicken for this recipe. If roasting a larger bird, increase the time the oven is on in step 2 to 35 to 40 minutes. While the chicken rests, consider utilizing the leftover fond to create a pan sauce (pages 32–33). You will need a 12-inch ovensafe skillet for this recipe.

1 Adjust oven rack to middle position, place 12-inch stainless-steel skillet on rack, and heat oven to 450 degrees. Combine salt and pepper in bowl. Pat chicken dry with paper towels. Using your fingers, gently loosen skin covering breast and thighs. Rub entire surface with oil. Sprinkle salt mixture evenly over surface and under skin of chicken. Rub in mixture with your hands to coat evenly. Tie legs together with twine and tuck wing tips behind back.

2 Transfer chicken breast side up to preheated skillet in oven. Roast chicken until breast registers 120 degrees and thighs register 135 degrees, 25 to 35 minutes. Turn off oven and leave chicken in oven until breast registers 160 degrees and thighs register 175 degrees, 25 to 35 minutes.

3 Transfer chicken to carving board and let rest for 20 minutes. Carve chicken and serve.

VARIATION

Weeknight Roast Jerk Chicken

Instead of the salt and pepper in recipe, combine 4 teaspoons packed brown sugar, 1 tablespoon ground allspice, 1 tablespoon salt, 1½ teaspoons dry mustard, 1 teaspoon garlic powder, 1 teaspoon dried thyme, ¾ teaspoon cayenne, and ½ teaspoon pepper in bowl. Sprinkle spice mixture evenly over surface and under skin of chicken before tying legs together.

Sizing Up Your Skillet

stainless steel • nonstick • traditional cast iron • enameled cast iron • carbon steel

A 12-inch stainless-steel skillet provides enough space for roasting a whole chicken. An ovensafe nonstick, traditional cast-iron, enameled cast-iron, or carbon-steel skillet will also work well for this reason.

perfecting
ROAST CHICKEN

This method for roasting a whole chicken in a skillet ensures that both the dark and white meat are perfectly cooked and juicy. We preheat the skillet in the oven and then add the chicken breast side up so the thighs are exposed to the hot skillet. Turning off the heat when the breasts register 120 degrees and the thighs 135 degrees allows the chicken to finish cooking gently in the oven's residual heat.

1   Preheat the Skillet in the Oven.

2   Tie the Legs Together and Tuck the Wingtips.

3   Turn Off the Oven and Let Carryover Cooking Do the Work.

Sizing Up Your Skillet

stainless steel • **nonstick** • **traditional cast iron** • **enameled cast iron** • **carbon steel**

A 12-inch stainless-steel skillet provides enough space for roasting a whole chicken and root vegetables. An ovensafe nonstick, traditional cast-iron, enameled cast-iron, or carbon-steel skillet will also work well for this reason.

Honey-Rosemary Roast Chicken and Root Vegetables

Serves 4 to 6

Total Time 2½ hours

3 tablespoons extra-virgin olive oil, divided

1 tablespoon minced fresh rosemary, divided

2 teaspoons table salt, divided

1 (3½- to 4-pound) whole chicken, giblets discarded

1 pound celery root, peeled and cut into 1-inch pieces

1 pound carrots, peeled and cut into 2½-inch lengths, thick pieces halved or quartered lengthwise if necessary ½ to 1 inch in diameter

3 large shallots, halved lengthwise

2 tablespoons honey, divided

1 pound radishes, trimmed and halved if larger than 2 inches

1 tablespoon white wine vinegar

Why This Recipe Works It is tricky to roast a whole chicken with vegetables without ending up with an overcooked chicken or undercooked vegetables. You can't just put everything into the oven at once. The key is browning the vegetables first on the stovetop, which ensures that they have a deeply caramelized crust; we use an appealing mix of earthy celery root and carrots and sweet shallots. Then we simply place the chicken right on top of the vegetables where it bastes them with flavorful juices during roasting. For a fresh and different twist, we add whole radishes to the mix partway through roasting, so they retain a bit of appealing crispness. While the chicken rests, we return the vegetables to the oven to finish softening. Finally, for a traditional but not boring spin on a classic, we flavor our bird with fresh rosemary and honey. And not wanting to waste the valuable juices in our skillet, we create a quick sauce by whisking together the pan juices, extra rosemary and honey, and a splash of white wine vinegar. You will need a 12-inch ovensafe skillet for this recipe.

1 Adjust oven rack to lower-middle position and heat oven to 400 degrees. Combine 2 tablespoons oil, 2 teaspoons rosemary, and 1 teaspoon salt in bowl. Pat chicken dry with paper towels and use your fingers or handle of wooden spoon to carefully separate skin from breast. Rub oil mixture all over chicken and underneath skin of breast. Tie legs together with kitchen twine and tuck wingtips behind back.

2 Toss celery root, carrots, and shallots with remaining 1 tablespoon oil and remaining 1 teaspoon salt. Arrange vegetables in single layer in 12-inch stainless-steel skillet. Place skillet over medium heat and cook vegetables, without moving them, until brown on bottom, 10 minutes (do not flip).

3 Place chicken breast side up on top of vegetables and transfer skillet to oven. Roast chicken until breast registers 125 degrees, 40 to 50 minutes. Using potholders, remove skillet from oven. Being careful of hot skillet handle, gently brush chicken evenly with 1 tablespoon honey.

4 Arrange radishes around chicken and return to oven. Roast until breast registers 160 degrees and thighs register 175 degrees, 40 to 50 minutes. Transfer chicken to carving board, tent with aluminum foil, and let rest while finishing vegetables.

5 Increase oven temperature to 450 degrees. Pour pan juices into liquid measuring cup (use slotted spoon to hold vegetables in skillet), let settle for 5 minutes, then skim off excess fat from surface; set aside. Meanwhile, stir vegetables to combine, return to oven, and roast until tender, about 20 minutes. Using slotted spoon, transfer vegetables to serving platter. To skillet, add reserved pan juices, accumulated chicken juices, remaining 1 teaspoon rosemary, remaining 1 tablespoon honey, and vinegar and whisk, scraping up any browned bits. Bring to simmer over medium-high heat and season with salt and pepper to taste. Carve chicken and serve with vegetables and pan sauce.

Roasted Herb Chicken Under a Brick with Potatoes

Serves 4 to 6

Total Time 1½ hours

1 (3½- to 4-pound) whole chicken, giblets discarded

1 tablespoon plus ¼ teaspoon kosher salt, divided

¾ teaspoon pepper, divided

1 teaspoon plus 2 tablespoons vegetable oil, divided

2 tablespoons lemon juice, plus 1 lemon, cut into wedges

3 cloves garlic, minced

1 tablespoon minced fresh thyme, divided

⅛ teaspoon red pepper flakes

1½ pounds red potatoes, unpeeled, halved if small or quartered if large

1 tablespoon minced fresh parsley leaves

Why This Recipe Works Cooking a butterflied chicken under a brick in a skillet not only looks cool but also produces amazingly crisp skin. The "brick" helps to keep the chicken flat as it cooks, forcing all of the skin to make contact with the pan, thus creating a beautiful golden-brown and crisp exterior. After trying a few methods, we found that placing several cans in a Dutch oven offered a better distribution of weight on the chicken than bricks. Plus, few people have loose bricks hanging about their kitchen. This recipe uses the pan-roasting method: We brown the chicken first, flip it over, and transfer the skillet to a hot oven. The hot, dry air of the oven ensures that the skin remains crisp and intact as the meat finishes cooking. For a flavorful and easy side dish of roasted potatoes, we simply add potatoes to the pan underneath the browned and seasoned oil–brushed chicken before it goes into the oven. While the chicken is resting, the potatoes go back into the oven to finish cooking and pick up some gorgeous color. This recipe was developed with Diamond Crystal Kosher Salt. (If using Morton Kosher Salt, which is denser, decrease the amount for the chicken to 2¼ teaspoons and the amount for the potatoes to ⅛ teaspoon.) Look for red potatoes that are 1 to 2 inches in diameter. You will need a 12-inch ovensafe skillet for this recipe.

1 Adjust oven rack to lowest position and heat oven to 450 degrees. With chicken breast side down, use kitchen shears to cut through bones on either side of backbone; discard backbone. Flip chicken over and press on breastbone to flatten. Tuck wingtips behind back. Pat chicken dry with paper towels and sprinkle with 1 tablespoon salt and ½ teaspoon pepper.

2 Wrap bottom and sides of Dutch oven with large sheet of aluminum foil, anchoring foil on rim; set aside. Heat 1 teaspoon oil in 12-inch stainless-steel skillet over medium-high heat until just smoking. Add chicken skin side down and reduce heat to medium. Place Dutch oven loaded with 2 heavy cans on top of chicken and cook until evenly browned, about 25 minutes. After 20 minutes, chicken should be golden brown; if it is not, increase heat to medium-high and continue to cook until well browned.

3 Meanwhile, mix remaining 2 tablespoons oil, lemon juice, garlic, 1½ teaspoons thyme, and pepper flakes in small bowl; set aside.

4 Using tongs, carefully transfer chicken, skin side up, to plate and pour off any accumulated fat from skillet. Add potatoes to skillet and sprinkle with remaining ¼ teaspoon salt, remaining ¼ teaspoon pepper, and remaining 1½ teaspoons thyme. Place chicken skin side up on potatoes and brush skin with reserved lemon juice–thyme mixture. Transfer skillet to oven and roast until breast registers 160 degrees, about 10 minutes.

5 Using potholders, remove skillet from oven. Being careful of hot skillet handle, transfer chicken to carving board and let rest while finishing potatoes. Return skillet with potatoes to oven and roast until browned and cooked through, about 15 minutes. Using slotted spoon, transfer potatoes to large bowl, leaving fat behind. Toss potatoes with parsley. Carve chicken and serve with potatoes and lemon wedges.

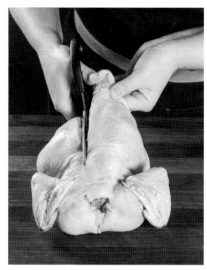

Sizing Up Your Skillet

stainless steel • nonstick • traditional cast iron • enameled cast iron • carbon steel

A 12-inch stainless-steel skillet provides enough space for roasting a whole chicken and potatoes. An ovensafe nonstick, traditional cast-iron, enameled cast-iron, or carbon-steel skillet will also work well for this reason. If using a cast-iron skillet, you will need to preheat the empty skillet over medium heat for 5 minutes before proceeding with step 2.

Sizing Up Your Skillet

traditional cast iron • **enameled cast iron** • **stainless steel** • **carbon steel**

The superior heat retention of a 12-inch traditional cast-iron skillet is key to achieving plenty of char on the tomatillos and provides enough space for the filled enchiladas. An enameled cast-iron skillet can also be used for these reasons; add 1 teaspoon oil to skillet and heat until smoking before charring the tomatillos. A stainless-steel or carbon-steel skillet can also be used; before charring the tomatillos, heat 1 teaspoon vegetable oil in the skillet over medium-high heat until just smoking.

Enchiladas Verdes

Serves 4

Total Time 1¾ hours

1	pound tomatillos, husks and stems removed, rinsed well and dried, halved
3	tablespoons vegetable oil, divided
1	onion, chopped
2	poblano chiles, stemmed, seeded, and chopped
1	teaspoon table salt, divided
3	garlic cloves, minced
1	teaspoon dried oregano
½	teaspoon ground cumin
¾	cup chicken broth
1½	teaspoons sugar
1	pound boneless, skinless chicken breasts, trimmed
½	cup coarsely chopped fresh cilantro
6	ounces Monterey Jack or pepper Jack cheese, grated (1½ cups), divided
8	(6-inch) corn tortillas
2	scallions, sliced thin
	Sour cream
	Lime wedges

VARIATION

Enchiladas Verdes for Two

Reduce garlic to 1 large clove; halve remaining ingredients. Proceed with recipe in 10-inch skillet. Spread ½ cup of sauce over bottom of skillet in step 5.

Why This Recipe Works We love the bright taste of enchiladas verdes, and it is really appealing to make the whole dish right in a skillet. We wanted moist, tender chicken and fresh, citrusy flavors wrapped in soft corn tortillas and topped with just the right amount of melted cheese. To get the characteristic smoky taste, we char fresh tomatillos right in a dry, preheated cast-iron skillet, which blisters them perfectly. We skip the step of painstakingly scraping off their blackened skins; in a smooth puree, the skins are not at all bothersome. The chicken is easy: We poach boneless breasts in chicken broth we enhanced with sautéed onion, poblanos, garlic, and cumin. Once the chicken is done, we transfer that savory broth, with its backbone of aromatics, to the food processor with the tomatillos and puree it all for a smooth, fresh sauce for the enchiladas. To keep the tortillas from tearing while rolling, we first brush both sides with oil and heat them briefly in the oven, again using our skillet. This also helps them firm up, so they don't turn to mush once covered in sauce. We bake the enchiladas right in that same skillet for an easy and streamlined cleanup. Just for fun and presentation, you can bring the skillet full of bright green, cheesy enchiladas right to the table for serving. You will need a 12-inch ovensafe skillet with tight-fitting lid for this recipe.

1 Adjust oven rack to middle position and heat to 450 degrees. Heat 12-inch cast-iron skillet over medium heat for 3 minutes. Increase heat to medium-high, add tomatillos cut side down and cook until blackened 3 to 5 minutes. Flip and continue to cook until skins have blistered, about 3 minutes; transfer to food processor.

2 Heat 1 tablespoon oil in now-empty skillet over medium-high heat until shimmering. Add onion, poblanos, and ½ teaspoon salt and cook until softened and well browned, 7 to 9 minutes. Stir in garlic, oregano, and cumin and cook until fragrant, about 30 seconds. Stir in broth, sugar, and remaining ½ teaspoon salt, scraping up any browned bits. Nestle chicken into skillet and bring to simmer. Reduce heat to medium-low, cover, and cook until chicken registers 160 degrees, 15 to 20 minutes, flipping halfway through cooking.

3 Transfer chicken to cutting board and let cool slightly. Transfer cooking liquid to food processor with tomatillos. Process until sauce is mostly smooth, about 45 seconds, scraping down sides of bowl as needed. Season with salt and pepper to taste; set aside. Wipe skillet clean with paper towels.

4 Shred chicken into bite-sized pieces using 2 forks. Combine chicken, cilantro, 1 cup Monterey Jack, and ½ cup sauce in bowl.

5 Brush both sides of tortillas with remaining 2 tablespoons oil. Shingle tortillas in even layer in now-empty skillet and bake until warm and pliable, about 5 minutes; transfer tortillas to plate. Spread ¾ cup sauce over bottom of again-empty skillet. Spread ⅓ cup filling down center of each tortilla. Roll each tortilla tightly around filling and place seam side down in skillet. Spread remaining sauce evenly over top and sprinkle with remaining ½ cup Monterey Jack.

6 Cover skillet and transfer to oven. Bake until enchiladas are heated through and cheese is melted, 15 to 20 minutes. Let cool for 10 minutes. Sprinkle with scallions. Serve, passing sour cream and lime wedges separately.

Maple-Glazed Pork Tenderloins

Serves 4 to 6
Total Time 50 minutes

6   tablespoons maple syrup

¼   cup whole-grain mustard

2   tablespoons molasses

2   teaspoons cider vinegar

1½   teaspoons table salt, divided

     Pinch cayenne pepper

2   tablespoons cornstarch

2   (12- to 16-ounce) pork
     tenderloins, trimmed and
     halved crosswise

¼   teaspoon pepper

1   tablespoon vegetable oil

VARIATION

Pomegranate-Glazed Pork Tenderloins

Omit mustard, molasses, vinegar, and cayenne from the glaze and add ⅓ cup pomegranate molasses, 1 teaspoon ground allspice, and 1 teaspoon minced fresh thyme.

Why This Recipe Works The stovetop-to-oven technique is the perfect method for delivering lean yet tender meat coated with subtle spice and inviting sweetness with a gorgeously burnished crust. Rubbing the tenderloins with cornstarch ensures that the glaze will adhere. After shaking off the excess cornstarch, we add the tenderloins (halved) to the skillet when the oil is smoking hot and sear them until well browned. Then we add the glaze ingredients to the skillet so it can reduce and thicken while also absorbing some of the fond from searing the pork. While maple syrup is a natural pairing with pork, we mix the syrup with molasses, mustard, cider vinegar, and a pinch of cayenne to balance out its sweetness and add viscosity. Choose tenderloins that are equal in size to ensure that the pork cooks at the same rate. We prefer natural pork in this recipe. If using enhanced pork (injected with a salt solution), reduce the salt in step 2 to ½ teaspoon. We prefer grade B maple syrup in this recipe. Shake off the cornstarch mixture thoroughly, as any excess will leave gummy spots. You will need a 12-inch ovensafe skillet for this recipe.

1 Adjust oven rack to middle position and heat oven to 350 degrees. Combine maple syrup, mustard, molasses, vinegar, ½ teaspoon salt, and cayenne in bowl.

2 Add cornstarch to shallow dish. Pat tenderloins dry with paper towels and sprinkle with remaining 1 teaspoon salt and pepper. Coat tenderloins in cornstarch, shaking off excess.

3 Heat oil in 12-inch stainless-steel skillet over medium-high heat until just smoking. Brown tenderloins well on all sides, 6 to 8 minutes. Off heat, add syrup mixture to skillet and turn tenderloins to coat with glaze. Transfer skillet to oven and roast until pork registers 135 to 140 degrees, turning tenderloins halfway through roasting, 5 to 10 minutes.

4 Using potholder, remove skillet from oven. Being careful of hot skillet handle, turn tenderloins to coat with glaze. Transfer to cutting board, tent with aluminum foil, and let rest for 10 minutes. Slice tenderloin ¼ inch thick. Serve, passing glaze separately.

Sizing Up Your Skillet

stainless steel • **enameled cast iron** • **nonstick** • **traditional cast iron** • **carbon steel**

A 12-inch stainless-steel skillet provides enough space for roasting two tenderloins and develops valuable fond for building a glaze. An enameled cast-iron skillet will also work for these reasons. An ovensafe nonstick, traditional cast-iron, or carbon-steel skillet can also be used; however, they will not develop as much fond. If using a cast-iron skillet, you will need to preheat the empty skillet over medium heat for 5 minutes before proceeding with step 3.

perfecting
MAPLE-GLAZED PORK TENDERLOINS

This easy recipe shows how the stovetop-to-oven method can really shine. To ensure that the tenderloins fit in the skillet, we cut them in half crosswise, and then rub them with a little cornstarch to help the glaze adhere. For a maple glaze that doesn't veer into too-sweet territory, we temper it with molasses, mustard, cider vinegar, and a hit of cayenne.

1   A Bit of Butchery Is Necessary.

2   Coat Tenderloins with Cornstarch.

3   Make a Sweet-Tart Glaze.

Pan-Roasted Pork Tenderloins with Endive, Cherries, and Hazelnut Brittle

Serves 4 to 6

Total Time 1 hour

½ cup hazelnuts, toasted, skinned, and chopped

1 tablespoon honey or maple syrup

1 teaspoon plus pinch table salt, divided

½ teaspoon minced fresh rosemary

4 tablespoons unsalted butter, cut into 4 pieces and chilled, divided

4 (4-ounce) heads Belgian endive, trimmed and halved lengthwise

2 (12- to 16-ounce) pork tenderloins, trimmed and halved crosswise

2 teaspoons ground fennel

1 cup chicken broth

2 teaspoons cornstarch

10 ounces fresh sweet cherries, pitted and halved

VARIATION

Pan-Roasted Pork Tenderloin with Endive, Cherries, and Hazelnut Brittle for Two

Halve all ingredients. Proceed with recipe in 10- or 12-inch ovensafe skillet. Reduce roasting time to 5 to 10 minutes.

Why This Recipe Works Pork tenderloin has a lot going for it—it's widely available, relatively inexpensive, quick to cook, and can be meltingly tender. However, it's also prone to drying out from overcooking and can be bland. In this company-worthy and beautiful recipe, we put our skillet to work in multiple ways: to brown the delicate endive, to sear the pork tenderloins and then pan-roast in the oven, and finally, to build a pan sauce, making the most of the fond left behind. Searing the halved Belgian endives on just one side tames its natural bitterness while maintaining its crunch for a satisfying side. To amp up the mild flavor of the pork, we rub it with fennel—the ultimate pork spice. We then brown it in butter on just one side. This minimizes the time the pork is exposed to high heat while still getting flavorful browning from the butter. While the pork rests after pan-roasting in the oven, all the flavorful fond from the skillet is used to make a glossy, rich pan sauce from chicken broth, with cornstarch adding body and butter adding the requisite richness. We add fresh cherries and the endive to the sauce until just warmed through; they add a touch of welcome sweetness and acidity. To really play up the savory-sharp-sweet-bitter notes, we make a brittle in the microwave, binding honey with crunchy hazelnuts and fresh, piney rosemary. Choose tenderloins that are equal in size to ensure that the pork cooks evenly. We prefer natural pork in this recipe. If using enhanced pork (injected with a salt solution), reduce the salt in step 3 to ½ teaspoon. You can substitute 8 ounces thawed frozen cherries for fresh cherries. You will need a 12-inch ovensafe skillet for this recipe.

1 Adjust oven rack to middle position and heat oven to 350 degrees. Line large plate with sheet of parchment paper. Combine hazelnuts, honey, and pinch salt in bowl. Microwave until hazelnuts darken slightly, 2 to 3 minutes, stirring every 45 seconds. Stir in rosemary, then quickly spread mixture evenly over prepared plate; set aside for serving.

2 Melt 1 tablespoon butter in 12-inch stainless-steel skillet over medium-high heat. Add endive cut side down and cook, gently pressing down with spatula occasionally, until deep golden brown on first side, 3 to 5 minutes; transfer to plate.

3 Pat pork dry with paper towels and sprinkle with fennel and remaining 1 teaspoon salt. Melt 1 tablespoon butter in now-empty skillet over medium-high heat. Add pork and cook until well browned on 1 side, about 5 minutes. Flip pork, transfer skillet to oven, and roast until pork registers 135 to 140 degrees, 10 to 15 minutes.

4 Using potholder, remove skillet from oven. Being careful of hot skillet handle, transfer pork to carving board, tent with aluminum foil, and let rest while finishing endive.

5 Whisk broth and cornstarch together in small bowl. Add mixture to now-empty skillet, scraping up any browned bits. Bring to simmer over medium heat and cook until thickened, about 2 minutes. Off heat, whisk in remaining 2 tablespoons butter, 1 piece at a time, until melted and sauce is thickened and glossy. Whisk in any accumulated meat juices. Add endive and cherries and cook over low heat, tossing gently to coat with sauce, until heated through, about 2 minutes. Season with salt and pepper to taste. Slice pork ½ inch thick and serve with endive-cherry mixture, topping individual portions with hazelnut brittle.

Sizing Up Your Skillet

stainless steel • **enameled cast iron** • **nonstick** • **traditional cast iron** • **carbon steel**

A 12-inch ovensafe stainless-steel skillet provides enough space for browning two tenderloins and develops valuable fond for building a sauce. An enameled cast-iron skillet will also work for these reasons. An ovensafe nonstick, traditional cast-iron, or carbon-steel skillet can also be used; however, they will not develop as much fond. If using a cast-iron skillet, you will need to preheat the empty skillet over medium heat for 3 minutes before proceeding with step 2.

Sizing Up Your Skillet

stainless steel • **nonstick** • **traditional cast iron** • **enameled cast iron** • **carbon steel**

A 12-inch stainless-steel skillet provides enough space for roasting a large pork loin and browning a generous portion of asparagus. An ovensafe nonstick, traditional cast-iron, enameled cast-iron, or carbon-steel skillet are also appropriate for these reasons. If using a cast-iron skillet, you will need to preheat the empty skillet over medium heat for 5 minutes before proceeding with step 2.

Herbed Roast Pork Loin with Asparagus

Serves 6

Total Time 1¼ hours, plus 1 hour 20 minutes salting and resting

1 (2½- to 3-pound) boneless center-cut pork loin roast, trimmed

4 teaspoons kosher salt, divided

1 tablespoon minced fresh thyme or 1 teaspoon dried

2 teaspoons ground coriander

½ teaspoon pepper

2 tablespoons vegetable oil

1 teaspoon grated lemon zest, plus 2 lemons, halved

10 garlic cloves, peeled

8 tablespoons unsalted butter, softened

½ cup minced fresh parsley, mint, dill, and/or tarragon

2 pounds thick asparagus, trimmed

Why This Recipe Works Pork loin is a fabulously easy cut to serve at a gathering, but it does need to be treated right, as it has a pretty mild flavor and can easily dry out. Salting our roast for an hour seasons the meat and helps keep it juicy and then rubbing our roast in advance with a thyme and coriander mixture ensures that the exterior is well flavored. Browning the whole roast in a skillet develops a flavorful crust and toasts the spice mix too. We then move the pork to a low oven to allow for a more even and gentle cook–the exterior does not overcook by the time the center reaches the right temperature. We throw some whole garlic cloves in to roast with the pork, then mash the flesh to make a vibrant garlic-herb butter. The butter pairs equally well with the pork and some asparagus, which we pan-roast in the flavorful meat juices left behind in the skillet while the meat rests. Look for a pork loin that is 7 to 8 inches long and 3 to 3½ inches in diameter. We prefer natural pork in this recipe. If using enhanced pork (injected with a salt solution), skip step 1. Look for asparagus spears that are at least ¾ inch thick. This recipe was developed with Diamond Crystal Kosher Salt. (If using Morton Kosher Salt, which is denser, decrease the amount for the pork to 2¼ teaspoons, the amount for the herb butter to ¼ teaspoon, and the amount for the asparagus to ¼ teaspoon.) You will need a 12-inch ovensafe skillet with a tight-fitting lid for this recipe.

1 Pat pork dry with paper towels and sprinkle evenly with 1 tablespoon salt. Wrap pork in plastic wrap and refrigerate for at least 1 hour or up to 24 hours.

2 Adjust oven rack to middle position and heat oven to 300 degrees. Combine thyme, coriander, and pepper in bowl. Unwrap pork and pat dry with paper towels. Sprinkle with spice mixture. Heat oil in 12-inch stainless-steel skillet over medium-high heat until just smoking. Add lemon halves cut sides down and cook until lightly charred, about 5 minutes; set aside for serving. Brown pork on all sides in now-empty skillet over medium-high heat, about 7 minutes. Flip pork fat side down and scatter garlic around perimeter.

3 Transfer skillet to oven and roast until pork registers 130 to 135 degrees, 40 to 60 minutes, flipping pork halfway through roasting. Using potholder, remove skillet from oven. Being careful of hot skillet handle, transfer pork to carving board, tent with aluminum foil, and let rest for 20 minutes.

4 Meanwhile, mash roasted garlic cloves to paste in small bowl and let cool slightly. Stir in butter, parsley, lemon zest, and ½ teaspoon salt until combined; set aside.

5 Add half of asparagus to fat left in skillet with tips pointed in one direction; add remaining spears with tips pointed in opposite direction. Using tongs, distribute spears in even layer (spears will not quite fit into single layer). Cover and cook over medium-high heat until asparagus is bright green and still crisp, about 5 minutes.

6 Uncover, sprinkle with remaining ½ teaspoon salt, increase heat to high, and continue to cook until spears are tender and well browned along one side, 5 to 7 minutes, using tongs to occasionally move spears from center of skillet to edge to ensure that all are browned. Season with salt and pepper to taste. Slice pork ¼ inch thick and dollop with half of herb butter. Serve with asparagus and charred lemon wedges, passing remaining herb butter separately.

Pan-Roasted Fish Fillets

Serves 4

Total Time 30 minutes

4   (6- to 8-ounce) skinless cod fillets, 1 inch thick

½   teaspoon table salt

¼   teaspoon pepper

½   teaspoon sugar

1   tablespoon vegetable oil

Why This Recipe Works This method of pan-roasting fish is superior to many other techniques because the flavor contributed by browning the fish is outstanding and the fish turns tender and succulent with little effort. So what do we do exactly? We sear the fillets in a hot nonstick skillet, flip, then transfer to the oven to continue cooking rather than finishing on the stove. To brown the fish quickly before the hot pan has a chance to dry out the fish's exterior, we turn to a sprinkling of sugar, which accelerates browning for supersavory—not sweet—flavor. A well-browned crust appears after about a minute, giving the interior time to turn succulent in the oven. We love this technique for almost any white fish. Black sea bass, haddock, hake, and pollock are good substitutes for the cod. Serve the cod with a herb sauce, relish, or chutney (pages 150–151). You will need a 12-inch ovensafe nonstick skillet for this recipe

1 Adjust oven rack to middle position and heat oven to 425 degrees. Pat cod dry with paper towels, sprinkle with salt and pepper, and sprinkle sugar lightly over 1 side of each fillet.

2 Heat oil in 12-inch ovensafe nonstick skillet over medium-high heat until just smoking. Lay fillets sugared side down in skillet and, using spatula, lightly press fillets for 20 to 30 seconds to ensure even contact with skillet. Cook until browned on first side, 1 to 2 minutes.

3 Using 2 spatulas, flip fillets, then transfer skillet to oven. Roast until fish flakes apart when gently prodded with paring knife and registers 135 degrees, 7 to 10 minutes. Serve.

VARIATIONS

Miso-Marinated Pan-Roasted Fish Fillets

Omit salt and pepper. Increase sugar to ⅓ cup and whisk together with ½ cup white miso, ¼ cup mirin, 2 tablespoons sake, 1½ tablespoons soy sauce, and 1 tablespoon sesame oil in bowl. Gently place cod in 1-gallon zipper-lock bag and pour miso mixture over cod. Press out air, seal bag, and turn to coat cod in marinade. Refrigerate for at least 8 hours or up to 24 hours, turning occasionally. Remove cod from marinade and pat dry with paper towels. Proceed with step 2.

Pan-Roasted Fish Fillets for Two

Halve all ingredients except for oil. Proceed with recipe in 10- or 12-inch ovensafe nonstick skillet.

PAN-ROASTED FISH FILLETS

This stovetop-to-oven method delivers beautifully browned fillets that are tender and moist. A little sugar enhances browning and then browning on just one side keeps the fish from overcooking. Flip the fish carefully before transferring the skillet to the oven.

1 Look for Thick Fillets.

2 Pat Fish Dry.

3 Sprinkle with Sugar.

4 Use a Nonstick Skillet.

5 Sear, then Roast.

Sizing Up Your Skillet

nonstick • traditional cast iron • carbon steel

The slick surface of a 12-inch ovensafe nonstick skillet ensures that the savory browning sticks to the fish, not the pan. A traditional cast-iron or carbon-steel skillet will also work well for this reason. If using a cast-iron skillet, you will need to preheat the empty skillet over medium heat for 5 minutes before proceeding with step 2.

HERB SAUCES, RELISHES, AND CHUTNEYS

With their fresh flavors and vivid colors, herb sauces, relishes, and chutneys bring vibrancy and beauty to just about anything. A basic salsa verde, an all-purpose green sauce usually made with chopped parsley, olive oil, garlic, and vinegar, is an excellent base from which you can make substitutions for ingredients (cilantro for parsley, vinegar for lemon juice) or add additional aromatics to make your own. And while relishes and chutneys are something of a catch-all condiment term, encompassing a range of fruit and vegetable combinations that can be cooked, pickled, or fresh, one thing they all have in common is bold, assertive flavors that help balance richness in a dish. All these condiments can be refrigerated for up to 2 days; bring to room temperature before serving and give them a stir, if necessary, to recombine.

Salsa Verde

Makes about 1½ cups

This vibrant and tangy sauce pairs well with poultry, meat, fish, and vegetables. It is also great drizzled over eggs, used in quesadillas, or dolloped over tacos or pulled pork.

4   cups fresh parsley leaves
2   slices hearty white sandwich bread, lightly toasted and cut into ½-inch pieces (1½ cups)
¼   cup capers, rinsed
4   anchovy fillets, rinsed
1   garlic clove, minced
¼   teaspoon table salt
¼   cup lemon juice (2 lemons)
¾   cup extra-virgin olive oil

Pulse parsley, bread, capers, anchovies, garlic, and salt in food processor until finely chopped, about 5 pulses. Add lemon juice and pulse briefly to combine. Transfer mixture to medium bowl and slowly whisk in oil until incorporated. Cover and let sit at room temperature for at least 1 hour to allow flavors to meld. Season with salt and pepper to taste.

Chermoula

Makes about 1½ cups

This Mediterranean sauce pairs well with poultry, meat, fish, and vegetables. It's particularly good with grilled shrimp and lamb as well as roasted hearty vegetables like cauliflower and winter squash.

2¼   cups fresh cilantro leaves
8   garlic cloves, minced
1½   teaspoons ground cumin
1½   teaspoons paprika
½   teaspoon cayenne pepper
½   teaspoon table salt
6   tablespoons lemon juice (2 lemons)
¾   cup extra-virgin olive oil

Pulse cilantro, garlic, cumin, paprika, cayenne, and salt in food processor until coarsely chopped, about 10 pulses. Add lemon juice and pulse briefly to combine. Transfer mixture to medium bowl and slowly whisk in oil until incorporated. Cover and let sit at room temperature for at least 1 hour to allow flavors to meld. Season with salt and pepper to taste

Green Olive, Almond, and Orange Relish

Makes about 1 cup

This relish pairs well with poultry, meat, and fish. It is also great tossed with pasta. If the olives are marinated, rinse and drain them before chopping.

½ cup slivered almonds, toasted

½ cup green olives, pitted and chopped coarse

1 garlic clove, minced

1 teaspoon grated orange zest plus ¼ cup juice

¼ cup extra-virgin olive oil

¼ cup minced fresh mint

2 teaspoons white wine vinegar

   Cayenne pepper

Pulse almonds, olives, garlic, and orange zest in food processor until nuts and olives are finely chopped, 10 to 12 pulses. Transfer to bowl and stir in orange juice, oil, mint, and vinegar. Season with salt and cayenne to taste.

Sun-Dried Tomato and Basil Relish

Makes about 1 cup

This relish pairs well with scallops, fish, and chicken. It is also nice served with flatbread or crackers or tossed with pasta.

¼ cup oil-packed sun-dried tomatoes, rinsed and chopped fine

¼ cup chopped fresh basil

¼ cup chopped fresh parsley

¼ cup extra-virgin olive oil

2 tablespoons balsamic vinegar

1 small shallot, minced

Combine all ingredients in bowl and season with salt and pepper to taste.

Tangerine-Ginger Relish

Makes about 1 cup

This relish pairs especially well with salmon, pork, or chicken.

4 tangerines

1½ teaspoons grated fresh ginger

1 scallion, sliced thin

2 teaspoons unseasoned rice vinegar

2 teaspoons toasted sesame oil

Cut away peel and pith from tangerines. Cut tangerines into 4 wedges, then slice crosswise into ½-inch-thick pieces. Place tangerines in strainer set over bowl and let drain for 15 minutes; measure out and reserve 1 tablespoon drained juice. Combine reserved juice, ginger, scallion, vinegar, and oil in bowl. Stir in tangerines and let sit for 15 minutes. Season with salt, pepper, and sugar to taste.

Mango-Mint Salsa

Makes about 1 cup

This sauce pairs well with poultry, pork, and fish. You can also serve it as a dip with tortilla chips or as an accompaniment to tacos. Raise the salsa's heat level by adding the jalapeño seeds, if desired.

1 mango, peeled, pitted, and cut into ¼-inch pieces

1 shallot, minced

3 tablespoons lime juice (2 limes)

2 tablespoons chopped fresh mint

1 jalapeño chile, stemmed, seeded, and minced

1 tablespoon extra-virgin olive oil

1 garlic clove, minced

Combine all ingredients in bowl and season with salt and pepper to taste.

Pistachio-Crusted Salmon with Beet, Orange, and Avocado Salad

Serves 4

Total Time 1 hour

1	pound beets, trimmed, peeled, and cut into ½-inch wedges
2	teaspoons kosher salt, divided
1½	tablespoons shelled pistachios
2½	teaspoons sesame seeds
¾	teaspoon fennel seeds
¾	teaspoon coriander seeds
2	oranges, plus 2 teaspoons grated orange zest, divided
4	(6- to 8-ounce) skin-on salmon fillets, 1 to 1½ inches thick
2	tablespoons extra-virgin olive oil, divided
2	avocados, halved, pitted, and cut into ½-inch pieces
1	small shallot, minced
¼	cup fresh mint leaves, torn
5	teaspoons white wine vinegar

Why This Recipe Works If you're looking to impress dinner guests, this easy recipe is one to have in your back pocket. You'll often hear that you should sear the skin of salmon to get a bit of crunch, but here we get it by coating the flesh side of the salmon with a dukkah-inspired spice mix (featuring orange zest with ground pistachios, sesame, fennel, and coriander seeds), searing it in a ripping-hot nonstick skillet flesh side down, and finishing it in the oven until medium-rare. This is a case where the pan-roasting technique really shines, delivering a beautiful crust with a multitude of seeds and perfectly tender fish thanks to the even heat of a low oven. The salad stars beet wedges that we microwave until soft and tender enough to be pierced with a knife. Then it's just a quick toss with oranges, their zest and juice, creamy avocado, minced shallot, mint, vinegar, and oil for a salad so gorgeous that it nearly upstages the salmon. Look for small- to medium-sized beets that are 2 to 3 inches in diameter. To ensure uniform cooking, buy a 1½- to 2-pound center-cut salmon fillet and cut it into four pieces. If using wild salmon, cook it until it registers 120 degrees. This recipe was developed with Diamond Crystal Kosher Salt. (If using Morton Kosher Salt, which is denser, decrease the amount for the beets to ¼ teaspoon, the amount for the salmon to ¾ teaspoon, and the amount for the salad to ¼ teaspoon.) A mortar and pestle can be used in place of the spice grinder. If you don't want to serve the fish with the skin, we recommend peeling it off the fish after it is cooked. You will need a 12-inch ovensafe skillet for this recipe.

1 Microwave beets, ¼ cup water, and ½ teaspoon salt in covered bowl until beets are tender and can be easily pierced with a paring knife, 15 to 20 minutes, stirring halfway through microwaving. Drain beets and set aside.

2 Adjust oven rack to middle position and heat oven to 325 degrees. Pulse pistachios, sesame seeds, fennel seeds, and coriander seeds in spice grinder until coarsely ground, about 3 pulses. Empty spice grinder into shallow dish and stir in 1 teaspoon orange zest and 1 teaspoon salt. Brush flesh sides of salmon with 2 teaspoons oil, then dredge oiled sides in spice mixture, pressing gently to adhere.

3 Heat 1 teaspoon oil in 12-inch ovensafe nonstick skillet over medium-high heat until just smoking. Place salmon skin side up in skillet and cook until golden brown on first side, about 1 minute. Using two fish spatulas, carefully flip salmon. Transfer skillet to oven and roast salmon until center is still translucent when checked with tip of paring knife and registers 125 degrees (for medium-rare), 12 to 16 minutes.

4 Meanwhile, cut away peel and pith from oranges. Cut oranges into 8 wedges each, then slice crosswise into ½-inch-thick pieces. Gently toss oranges and any released juices with beets, avocados, shallot, mint, vinegar, remaining 1 teaspoon orange zest, remaining 1 tablespoon of oil, and remaining ½ teaspoon salt in bowl. Season with salt and pepper to taste. Serve salmon with salad.

Sizing Up Your Skillet

nonstick • **traditional cast iron** • **carbon steel**

The slick surface of a 12-inch ovensafe nonstick skillet ensures that the pistachio crust sticks to the fish, not the pan. A traditional cast-iron or carbon-steel skillet will also work well for this reason. If using a cast-iron skillet, you will need to preheat the empty skillet over medium heat for 5 minutes before proceeding with step 3.

Sizing Up Your Skillet

nonstick • traditional cast iron • carbon steel

The slick surface of a 12-inch ovensafe nonstick skillet ensures that the prosciutto stays on the cod, not the pan. A traditional cast-iron or carbon-steel skillet will also work well for this reason. If using a cast-iron skillet, you will need to preheat the empty skillet over medium heat for 3 minutes before proceeding with step 1.

Prosciutto-Wrapped Cod with Crispy Polenta and Roasted Red Pepper Relish

Serves 4

Total Time 1 hour

4   (6- to 8-ounce) skinless cod fillets, 1 inch thick

¼   teaspoon pepper, divided

8   thin slices prosciutto (4 ounces)

¼   cup extra virgin olive oil, divided

1   (18-ounce) tube cooked polenta, sliced ¾ inch thick

3   red bell peppers, stemmed, seeded, and cut into ½-inch-wide strips

1   shallot, sliced thin

4   teaspoons sherry vinegar

1   tablespoon capers, rinsed

⅛   teaspoon table salt

½   cup fresh parsley leaves

Why This Recipe Works There are several moving parts to this elegant meal, one that looks way more complicated to make than it really is, thanks to the way we press our non-stick skillet into service and the use of a convenient supermarket tube of cooked polenta. We heat the oil in the skillet until smoking hot and then quickly sear the polenta slices, creating crunchy golden disks with a creamy interior—no need to make polenta ourselves. Then we char red bell pepper slices so that they're softened into a complex smoky-sweet relish component and add a kick with sherry vinegar, briny capers, and parsley leaves. Now we are ready to tackle cooking the cod, and here we use the classic pan-roasting method, which takes the fish from stovetop to oven. We have wrapped the fillets in prosciutto to sear in the hot skillet, which not only infuses the fish with the prosciutto's salty pork flavor but makes the fillets appealingly crisp while insulating the fish from overcooking, keeping it supermoist. We arrange the polenta slices around the edge of the skillet walls so that they can rewarm in the oven while the cod roasts to moist perfection. Do not season the cod with salt before wrapping with the prosciutto; the briny capers and salty prosciutto add plenty of salt to the dish. Black sea bass, haddock, hake, and pollock make good substitutions for the cod. You will need a 12-inch ovensafe nonstick skillet for this recipe.

1 Adjust oven rack to upper-middle position and heat oven to 450 degrees. Pat cod dry with paper towels and sprinkle with ⅛ teaspoon pepper. For each fillet, shingle 2 slices prosciutto on cutting board, overlapping edges slightly. Lay fillet in center, then wrap prosciutto around cod; set aside.

2 Line large plate with paper towels. Heat 1 tablespoon oil in 12-inch ovensafe nonstick skillet over medium-high heat until shimmering. Add polenta and cook until golden brown, 3 to 5 minutes per side. Transfer to prepared plate.

3 Heat 1 tablespoon oil in now-empty skillet over medium-high heat until just smoking. Add peppers and cook, without moving, until charred on first side, 3 to 4 minutes. Toss peppers and continue to cook until softened, about 2 minutes. Transfer peppers to bowl; add shallot, vinegar, capers, salt, and remaining ⅛ teaspoon pepper and toss to combine; set aside. Wipe skillet clean with paper towels.

4 Heat 1 tablespoon oil in again-empty skillet over medium-high heat until just smoking. Add prosciutto-wrapped cod and cook until lightly browned, about 2 minutes per side. Arrange polenta slices around cod so they rest against skillet walls. Transfer skillet to oven and roast until cod registers 135 degrees, 6 to 9 minutes. Add parsley and remaining 1 tablespoon oil to pepper mixture and toss to combine. Season with salt and pepper to taste. Serve cod with polenta and pepper relish.

VARIATION

Prosciutto-Wrapped Cod with Crispy Polenta and Roasted Red Pepper Relish for Two

Reduce bell peppers to two small peppers; halve remaining ingredients. Proceed with recipe in 10-inch skillet.

French Onion White Bean Bake

Serves 4 to 6

Total Time 1½ hours

8	ounces baguette, cut into 1-inch pieces
5	tablespoons extra-virgin olive oil, plus extra as needed
4	ounces pancetta, cut into ¼-inch pieces
1	large onion, halved through root end and sliced ¼ inch thick
1	fennel bulb, 2 tablespoons minced fronds, stalks discarded, bulbs halved, cored, and sliced thin
3	garlic cloves, minced
2	teaspoons minced fresh thyme or ¾ teaspoon dried
½	teaspoon pepper
½	cup dry sherry
2	(15-ounce) cans cannellini beans, undrained
1	cup beef broth
1	bay leaf
4	ounces Gruyère cheese, shredded (1 cup)
2	ounces Parmesan cheese, grated (⅔ cup)

Why This Recipe Works This humble but comforting casserole in a skillet combines canned white beans with the flavors of French onion soup, mimicking even the crusty, cheesy topping. We start by caramelizing onion and fennel—for faintly sweet, licorice background notes—in the rendered fat of crisped pancetta. Sherry, beef broth, and canned cannellini beans and their liquid give the mixture sauciness and body. After a short simmer to allow the flavors to meld, we top our skillet dinner with a layer of crisp croutons and handfuls of Gruyère and Parmesan cheese, plus crispy pancetta, before placing it in a hot oven. A final sprinkle of fennel fronds makes this dish as pretty as it is satisfying. We like using a baguette for this recipe for its crust, but you will have some left over; you can use another crusty bread instead. We like cannellini's creaminess, size, and thin skins, but any canned white bean will work. Use the large holes of a box grater to shred the Gruyère and Parmesan. You will need a 12-inch ovensafe skillet with a tight-fitting lid for this recipe.

1 Adjust oven rack to middle position and heat oven to 500 degrees. Toss bread and ¼ cup water together in large bowl, squeezing bread gently until water is absorbed. Add oil and bread mixture to 12-inch stainless-steel skillet and cook over medium-high heat, stirring often, until browned and crisp, 7 to 10 minutes. Transfer to a large plate.

2 Add pancetta to now-empty skillet and cook over medium-low heat until rendered and crisp, about 10 minutes. Using slotted spoon, transfer pancetta to paper towel–lined plate; set aside.

3 Pour off all but 2 tablespoons fat from skillet. (If necessary, supplement with oil.) Add onion, sliced fennel, and ½ cup water to fat left in skillet and bring to boil over medium- high heat. Cover and cook until water has evaporated and onions start to sizzle, 8 to 10 minutes.

4 Uncover, reduce heat to medium-low, and cook until onions are softened and well browned, stirring frequently and adjusting heat as needed to prevent scorching, about 20 minutes.

5 Increase heat to medium; add garlic, thyme, and pepper; and cook until fragrant, about 30 seconds. Stir in sherry, scraping up browned bits, and cook until evaporated, 3 to 5 minutes. Stir in beans and their liquid, broth, and bay leaf and bring to simmer. Cover, reduce heat to low, and cook until thickened slightly, about 15 minutes. Season with salt and pepper to taste.

6 Discard bay leaf, then arrange reserved bread evenly over bean mixture. Sprinkle with Gruyère, Parmesan, and reserved pancetta. Transfer to oven and bake until cheese is melted and bubbly, 5 to 7 minutes. Let cool for 5 minutes, then sprinkle with minced fennel fronds and serve.

VARIATION

French Onion White Bean Bake for Two

Reduce garlic to 1 large clove; halve remaining ingredients except for bay leaf. Proceed with recipe in 10- or 12-inch skillet.

Sizing Up Your Skillet

stainless steel ● **nonstick** ● **traditional cast iron** ● **enameled cast iron**

A 12-inch stainless-steel skillet provides enough space for assembling the casserole. An ovensafe nonstick, traditional cast-iron, or enameled cast-iron skillet will also work well for this reason.

Sizing Up Your Skillet

stainless steel • **nonstick** • **enameled cast iron**

A 10-inch stainless-steel skillet provides enough space for assembling the casserole. An ovensafe nonstick or enameled cast-iron skillet will also work for this reason. If using a cast-iron skillet, you will need to preheat the empty skillet over medium heat for 3 minutes before proceeding with step 3. Due to the acidic cooking liquid, we do not recommend using a traditional cast-iron or carbon-steel skillet.

Skillet Tomato Cobbler

Serves 4 to 6

Total Time 1½ hours, plus 2 hours 20 minutes chilling and cooling

Crust

5   tablespoons unsalted butter, chilled, divided

⅔   cup (3⅓ ounces) all-purpose flour, divided

1½ teaspoons sugar

¼   teaspoon table salt

2   tablespoons ice water, divided

Filling

1   tablespoon water

2½ teaspoons cornstarch

2   tablespoons extra-virgin olive oil

3   garlic cloves, minced

1   tablespoon tomato paste

1½ teaspoons minced fresh thyme

1½ teaspoons sugar

¾   teaspoon table salt

½   teaspoon pepper

2   pounds tomatoes, cored and cut into ¾-inch pieces

1   large egg beaten with 1 tablespoon water and pinch table salt

Why This Recipe Works Cobblers are generally of the sweet variety, like peach, apple, and blueberry, but this savory version is sure to delight. It is packed full of chunky fresh tomatoes that we season with garlic and thyme and top with a buttery crust. Using a skillet instead of a pie plate is key: You can build a rich tomato filling on the stovetop, let it thicken, and then top it with wedges of the buttery homemade crust. Cooking the tomatoes for just a minute before transferring the cobbler to the oven ensures that they maintain their natural sweetness and vibrant acidity. Tomato paste brings rich depth to the filling, while a touch of cornstarch gives it body. Our undeniably rich, all-butter pie crust balances the brightness of the tomatoes. To account for the abundant juice of the filling, we cut the round of dough into six wedges and arrange them on the filling with gaps between each wedge. As the cobbler bakes, the spaces promote evaporation and concentration of the liquid, giving the filling a scoopable texture. The end result is a luscious, tomato-forward treat that looks so enticing with its beautifully browned and fragrant pastry wedges and a bright filling that bubbles up around them. Everyone will want to dig in immediately. For the best results, we recommend weighing the flour. Use in-season tomatoes that are ripe but firm; do not use plum tomatoes. Serve the cobbler as a light meal with a green salad or a side dish. We like to dollop servings with sour cream, ricotta, or mascarpone. You will need a 10-inch ovensafe skillet for this recipe.

1 For the crust Grate 1 tablespoon butter on large holes of box grater and place in freezer. Cut remaining 4 tablespoons butter into ½-inch cubes. Pulse ⅓ cup flour, sugar, and salt in food processor until combined, 2 pulses. Add cubed butter and process until homogeneous paste forms, 20 to 30 seconds. Using your hands, carefully break paste into 1-inch chunks and redistribute around processor blade. Add remaining ⅓ cup flour and pulse until mixture is broken into pieces no larger than ½ inch (most pieces will be much smaller), about 3 pulses. Transfer mixture to bowl. Add grated butter and toss until butter pieces are separated and coated with flour.

2 Sprinkle 1 tablespoon ice water over mixture. Toss with rubber spatula until evenly moistened. Sprinkle remaining 1 tablespoon ice water over mixture and toss to combine. Press with spatula until dough sticks together. Wrap dough in plastic wrap and press to form compact, fissure-free 4-inch disk. Refrigerate for at least 2 hours or up to 2 days. Let dough soften on counter for 10 minutes before rolling.

3 For the filling Adjust oven rack to middle position and heat oven to 400 degrees. Whisk water and cornstarch together in small bowl. Heat oil in 10-inch stainless-steel skillet over medium heat until shimmering. Add garlic and cook until fragrant, about 30 seconds. Add tomato paste and cook, stirring constantly, until oil is tinted red, about 30 seconds. Add thyme, sugar, salt, and pepper and stir to combine. Add tomatoes and stir until coated. Whisk cornstarch mixture to recombine. Stir into tomato mixture and cook, stirring occasionally, until juice is slightly thickened, 1 to 2 minutes. Remove from heat.

4 Roll dough into 8-inch round on lightly floured counter. Cut into 6 equal wedges. Brush wedges with egg wash. Using bench scraper or spatula, place wedges on filling, spacing rounded edges ½ inch from edge of skillet and leaving gaps between wedges. Bake until crust is deep golden brown, 40 to 45 minutes. Let cool for 20 minutes before serving.

Skillet Spanakopita

Serves 4

Total Time 1¼ hours

1   tablespoon unsalted butter

20   ounces frozen chopped spinach,
     thawed and squeezed dry

¼   teaspoon table salt

¼   teaspoon pepper

3   garlic cloves, minced

⅛   teaspoon ground nutmeg

⅛   teaspoon cayenne pepper

8   ounces feta cheese, crumbled
     (2 cups)

6   ounces (¾ cup) whole-milk ricotta
     cheese

4   scallions, sliced thin

2   large eggs, lightly beaten

¼   cup minced fresh mint

2   tablespoons minced fresh dill

20   (14 by 9-inch) phyllo sheets, thawed

     Olive oil spray

Why This Recipe Works This beautiful one-skillet spanakopita features a crackly phyllo crust atop a cheesy, scallion-y spinach mixture, with no soggy bottoms and no lengthy process of layering endless phyllo dough sheets. For the filling, we cook convenient thawed frozen spinach in a 10-inch stainless steel skillet to evaporate excess moisture. A mix of feta and ricotta cheeses adds lots of creamy texture and briny flavor, while mint and dill deliver a fresh herbal backbone. For the festive pastry top, we spray sheets of phyllo with flavorful olive oil spray, crumple each into a ball, and arrange them right on top of the filling in the skillet. This creates plenty of surface area for a supremely crisp pastry topping—and it doesn't matter if any of the sheets tear. Just 25 minutes in the oven produces a perfectly crispy crust that resembles a bouquet of golden rosettes. Phyllo dough is also available in larger 18 by 14-inch sheets; if using, cut them in half to make 14 by 9-inch sheets. Don't thaw the phyllo in the microwave; let it sit in the refrigerator overnight or on the counter for 4 to 5 hours. You will need a 10-inch ovensafe skillet for this recipe.

1 Adjust oven rack to lower-middle position and heat oven to 375 degrees. Melt butter in 10-inch stainless-steel skillet over medium heat. Add spinach, salt, and pepper and cook until mixture is dry, about 4 minutes. Stir in garlic, nutmeg, and cayenne and cook until fragrant, about 30 seconds. Transfer mixture to large bowl and let cool slightly, about 5 minutes.

2 Stir feta, ricotta, scallions, eggs, mint, and dill into cooled spinach mixture until well combined. Spread mixture evenly into now-empty skillet.

3 Lay one sheet of phyllo on clean counter and spray liberally with oil spray. Crumple oiled phyllo into 2-inch ball and place on top of spinach mixture in skillet. Repeat with remaining phyllo.

4 Transfer skillet to oven and bake until phyllo is golden brown and crisp, about 25 minutes, rotating skillet halfway through baking. Let spanakopita cool for 10 minutes before serving.

Sizing Up Your Skillet

stainless steel • nonstick • traditional cast iron

A 10-inch stainless-steel skillet provides enough space for assembling the casserole. An ovensafe nonstick or traditional cast-iron skillet will also work well for this reason. If using a cast-iron skillet, you will need to preheat the empty skillet over medium heat for 3 minutes before proceeding with step 1.

Savory Dutch Baby with Burrata, Prosciutto, and Arugula

Serves 4

Total Time 45 minutes

Dutch Baby

¼ cup extra-virgin olive oil, divided

1¼ cups (6¼ ounces) all-purpose flour

½ teaspoon table salt

4 large eggs

1 cup skim milk

2 tablespoons chopped fresh basil, oregano, thyme, parsley, and/or tarragon, plus extra for sprinkling

Topping

4 ounces burrata cheese, room temperature

¾ cup baby arugula

½ teaspoon extra-virgin olive oil, plus extra for drizzling

½ teaspoon balsamic vinegar, plus extra for drizzling

1 ounce thinly sliced prosciutto, torn into bite-size pieces

Why This Recipe Works Dutch babies, traditionally made in sweet versions as a homey dessert or brunch dish, have been enjoying a welcome renaissance, and this has led to all kinds of fun with modern savory renditions such as this dramatic and impressive skillet-size pancake. It's a delicious study in contrasts: The edge of the batter cake puffs dramatically in the hot cast-iron skillet to form a tall, crispy rim with a texture similar to that of a popover, while the base remains flat, custardy, and tender, similar to a thick crepe. Dutch babies are much easier to prepare than their pomp and circumstance would suggest. Pour a simple batter of flour, egg, and milk into a hot skillet and bake, and then add your toppings of choice for serving. Here, a tangle of peppery arugula is overlaid with salty prosciutto and burrata cheese, itself a study in contrasting textures. You can use whole or low-fat milk instead of skim, but the Dutch baby won't be as crisp. You can substitute fresh mozzarella for the burrata. For a dramatic presentation, garnish and slice the Dutch baby right in the skillet in step 5. You will need a 12-inch ovensafe skillet for this recipe.

1 For the Dutch baby Adjust oven rack to middle position and heat oven to 450 degrees. Add 2 tablespoons oil to 12-inch stainless-steel skillet, place skillet in oven, and heat until oil is shimmering, about 10 minutes.

2 Meanwhile, whisk flour and salt together in large bowl. In separate bowl, whisk eggs until frothy, then whisk in milk, basil, and remaining 2 tablespoons oil until incorporated. Whisk one-third of milk mixture into flour mixture until no lumps remain. Slowly whisk in remaining milk mixture until smooth.

3 Being careful of hot skillet handle, quickly pour batter into skillet and bake until Dutch baby puffs and turns golden brown (edges will be dark brown), about 20 minutes, rotating skillet halfway through baking.

4 For the topping While Dutch baby bakes, tear burrata into bite-size pieces over plate, collecting creamy liquid. Toss arugula with oil and vinegar and season with salt and pepper to taste.

5 Using pot holders, remove skillet from oven. Being careful of hot skillet handle, transfer Dutch baby to cutting board using spatula. Top Dutch baby with arugula mixture, followed by prosciutto and burrata and any accumulated liquid. Sprinkle with extra basil, drizzle with extra oil and vinegar, and season with pepper to taste. Slice into wedges and serve immediately.

Sizing Up Your Skillet

stainless steel • **nonstick** • **traditional cast iron** • **enameled cast iron** • **carbon steel**

A 12-inch stainless-steel skillet provides enough space for the Dutch baby as it expands in the oven. An ovensafe nonstick, traditional cast-iron, enameled cast-iron, or carbon-steel skillet will also work well for this reason.

Cast-Iron Pan Pizza

Serves 4

Total Time 1¼ hours, plus 14 hours resting

Dough

2   cups (11 ounces) bread flour

1   teaspoon table salt

1   teaspoon instant or rapid-rise yeast

1   cup (8 ounces) warm water (105 to 110 degrees)

Vegetable oil spray

Sauce

1   (14.5-ounce) can whole peeled tomatoes

1   teaspoon extra-virgin olive oil

1   garlic clove, minced

¼   teaspoon sugar

¼   teaspoon table salt

¼   teaspoon dried oregano

Pinch red pepper flakes

Pizza

3   tablespoons extra-virgin olive oil

4   ounces Monterey Jack cheese, shredded (1 cup)

7   ounces whole-milk mozzarella cheese, shredded (1¾ cups)

Why This Recipe Works This recipe showcases the perks of using a traditional cast-iron skillet, which makes pizza easier, cheesier, and crispier than a baking stone ever could. We start with a simple stir-together dough of bread flour, salt, yeast, and warm water; the warm water jump-starts yeast activity so that the crumb is open and light. Instead of kneading the dough, we let it rest overnight in the refrigerator. During this rest, the dough's gluten strengthens enough for the crust to support the toppings but still have a tender crumb. Baking the pie in a generously oiled cast-iron skillet "fries" the outside of the crust. We also move the skillet to the stove for the last few minutes of cooking to crisp up the underside of the crust. For the crispy cheese edge known as frico, we press shredded Monterey Jack cheese around the edge of the dough and up the sides of the skillet. For the sauce, we crush canned whole tomatoes (which are less processed and therefore fresher-tasting than commercial crushed tomatoes) by hand, which allows some of their juice to drain so that the sauce is thick enough to stay put on the pie, and then puree them in the food processor with classic seasonings—no cooking required. For the best results, we recommend weighing the flour and water. Use a block cheese, not fresh mozzarella, for this recipe. Avoid pre-shredded cheese; it contains added starch, which gives the melted cheese a drier, chewier texture. Additional toppings make this pizza even better; aim for a maximum of 1½ cups and scatter them between even layers of the mozzarella.

1 For the dough Using wooden spoon or spatula, stir flour, salt, and yeast together in bowl. Add warm water and mix until most of flour is moistened. Using your hands, knead dough in bowl until dough forms sticky ball, about 1 minute. Spray 9-inch pie plate or cake pan with oil spray. Transfer dough to prepared plate and press into 7- to 8-inch disk. Spray top of dough with oil spray. Cover tightly with plastic wrap and refrigerate for 12 to 24 hours.

2 For the sauce Place tomatoes in fine-mesh strainer and crush with your hands. Drain well, then transfer to food processor. Add oil, garlic, sugar, salt, oregano, and pepper flakes and process until smooth, about 30 seconds. (Sauce can be refrigerated for up to 3 days.)

3 For the pizza Two hours before baking, remove dough from refrigerator and let sit at room temperature for 30 minutes.

4 Coat bottom of 12-inch traditional cast-iron skillet with oil. Transfer dough to prepared skillet and use your fingertips to flatten dough until it is ⅛ inch from edge of skillet. Cover tightly with plastic and let rest until slightly puffy, about 1½ hours.

5 Thirty minutes before baking, adjust oven rack to lowest position and heat oven to 400 degrees. Spread ½ cup sauce evenly over top of dough, leaving ½-inch border (save remaining sauce for another use). Sprinkle Monterey Jack evenly over border. Press Monterey Jack into side of skillet, forming ½- to ¾-inch-tall wall. (Not all cheese will stick to side of skillet.) Evenly sprinkle mozzarella over sauce. Bake until cheese at edge of skillet is well browned, 25 to 30 minutes.

6 Using potholder, transfer skillet to stovetop and let sit until sizzling stops, about 3 minutes. Being careful of hot skillet handle, run butter knife around rim of skillet to loosen pizza. Using thin metal spatula, gently lift edge of pizza and peek at underside to assess browning. Cook pizza over medium heat until bottom crust is well browned, 2 to 5 minutes (skillet handle will be hot). Using 2 spatulas, transfer pizza to wire rack and let cool for 10 minutes. Slice and serve.

VARIATIONS

Cast-Iron Pan Pizza with Taleggio, Mushrooms, and Scallion

Substitute Taleggio cheese, rind removed, broken into rough ½-inch pieces, for mozzarella. Heat 1 tablespoon extra-virgin olive oil in traditional 12-inch cast-iron skillet over medium-high heat until shimmering. Add 12 ounces cremini, shiitake, and/or oyster mushrooms, trimmed and sliced thin, and ¼ teaspoon salt and cook until softened and lightly browned, about 10 minutes. Transfer mushrooms to bowl and wipe skillet clean with paper towels. Let skillet cool slightly before proceeding with step 4. Sprinkle half of Taleggio over sauce in step 5, followed by mushrooms and remaining Taleggio. Sprinkle pizza with 1 thinly sliced scallion before serving.

Cast-Iron Pan Pizza with Pepperoni, Pickled Peppers, and Honey

Sprinkle half of mozzarella over sauce in step 5, followed by 1 ounce thinly sliced pepperoni, ¼ cup thinly sliced jarred hot cherry peppers, and remaining mozzarella. Drizzle pizza with 2 teaspoons honey before serving.

Sizing Up Your Skillet

- **traditional cast iron**

The superior heat retention of a 12-inch traditional cast-iron skillet aids in the development of a golden brown crust. Its tall sides also support the "cheese wall" that turns into browned, crispy frico. We do not recommend using an alternative skillet in this recipe.

CHAPTER FOUR

griddle
& fry

Cheddar-Crusted Grilled Cheese

Serves 2

Total Time 35 minutes

- 2 teaspoons mayonnaise
- 4 slices hearty white sandwich bread
- 2 slices deli American cheese (1½ ounces)
- 4 ounces white sharp cheddar cheese, shredded (1 cup), divided
- 2 tablespoons unsalted butter, divided

VARIATIONS

Cheddar-Crusted Grilled Cheese with Tomato

Shingle 2 thin tomato slices on top of American cheese in each sandwich. Sprinkle tomato slices with 1 tablespoon grated Parmesan and pinch each of table salt, pepper, red pepper flakes, dried oregano, and garlic powder. Sprinkle cheddar over tomato layer.

Cheddar-Crusted Grilled Cheese with Bacon and Pepper Jelly

Substitute ¼ cup pepper jelly for mayonnaise and yellow sharp cheddar for white sharp cheddar. Place 4 half slices of cooked bacon between cheese layers in each sandwich.

Why This Recipe Works Grilled cheese sandwiches are an American institution, but do you really need a recipe to make one? Our answer is a definitive yes. With a nonstick skillet and a few easy techniques, a grilled cheese sandwich can go from good to spectacular. First, for richness, we spread a little mayonnaise on one side of the bread. As for the cheese, sliced American cheese from the deli is key, as it clings to the bread and melts like a dream. We also add shredded sharp cheddar for its distinctive richness and flavor. Rather than buttering the sandwiches, we simply melt butter in the skillet over medium heat, add the sandwiches, and cover the skillet; this traps the heat, which helps the cheese melt as the bread slowly browns. Once the first side is nicely browned, we flip the sandwiches, add more butter, and repeat the browning process. But wait, there's more. We push the limits by making a crispy frico—a thin, crisp cheese crust—in the empty skillet by arranging more shredded cheddar in two rectangles (in the shape of the bread) and then add the sandwiches directly over the cheese. Cooking over medium heat allows the cheese to fuse to the sandwiches, making for a delectable cheesy crust. A 5-minute rest on a wire rack helps the sandwiches cool to a comfortable eating temperature and allows the crust to continue to crisp. When sprinkling the cheese in the skillet for the crust, be sure to leave enough room between the portions so that the cheese doesn't run together. And while crisping the cheese crust, avoid flipping the sandwiches too early. At first, the cheese will be soft and melty, but it will crisp as it cooks. For the best flavor, buy the American cheese at the deli counter, not the individual cheese slices that come wrapped in cellophane. To serve four, double the ingredients; once the first two grilled cheese are cooked, transfer them to a wire rack set in a rimmed baking sheet and keep warm in a 200-degree oven. You will need a 12-inch skillet with a tight-fitting lid for this recipe.

1 Spread mayonnaise evenly on 1 side of each slice of bread. Layer 1 slice American cheese and ¼ cup cheddar on mayonnaise side of each of 2 slices bread. Top with remaining 2 slices bread, mayonnaise side down.

2 Melt 1 tablespoon butter in 12-inch nonstick skillet over medium heat. Place sandwiches in skillet. Cover and cook until deep golden brown on bottom, 4 to 7 minutes.

3 Using spatula, carefully flip sandwiches. Add remaining 1 tablespoon butter to center of skillet between sandwiches and tilt to distribute butter as it melts. Cover and continue to cook until second side is deep golden brown and cheese is visibly melted around edges of sandwiches, 2 to 5 minutes. Transfer sandwiches to wire rack.

4 Remove skillet from heat and wipe clean with paper towels. Sprinkle two ¼-cup portions of remaining cheddar into rectangles just larger than slices of bread, about 6 by 4 inches, on opposite sides of now-empty skillet. Place sandwiches directly on top of cheddar.

5 Return skillet to medium heat and cook until edges of cheddar beneath sandwiches are well browned and crisp, 2 to 4 minutes. (Do not slide spatula under sandwiches before cheddar is crisp; it will pull cheddar and ruin crust.) When cheddar is browned along edges, slide spatula underneath sandwiches and transfer, cheddar crust side up, to rack. (For decorative purposes, you can upturn edges of cheddar crust, if desired.) Let sandwiches sit for 5 minutes to allow cheese to set. Transfer sandwiches to cutting board and cut diagonally. Serve.

Sizing Up Your Skillet

nonstick • **traditional cast iron** • **carbon steel**

A 12-inch nonstick skillet provides enough space to griddle two assembled sandwiches and can produce steady, even heat to create a uniform golden-brown crust. The slick surface of the skillet also ensures that the cheese crust sticks to the sandwiches and not the skillet. A traditional cast-iron or carbon-steel skillet will also work for these reasons. If using a traditional cast-iron skillet, you will need to preheat the empty skillet over medium heat for 3 minutes before proceeding with step 2.

Roast Beef Panini with Tangy Coleslaw

Serves 4

Total Time 40 minutes

Coleslaw

¼	cup mayonnaise
1	tablespoon spicy brown mustard
1	tablespoon prepared horseradish, drained
¼	teaspoon table salt
¼	teaspoon pepper
2	cups shredded green coleslaw mix
½	small red onion, sliced thin

Sandwiches

4	teaspoons mayonnaise, divided
8	slices hearty pumpernickel rye sandwich bread
8	thin slices deli smoked gouda cheese (4 ounces)
12	ounces thinly sliced deli roast beef

Why This Recipe Works Italians have it right when it comes to sandwiches: They load meat, cheese, and flavorful condiments between slices of hearty bread and then compact the sandwich in a heated, ridged press. We wanted a roast beef panini recipe that we could make without a fancy press, so we turned to our trusty nonstick skillet, which can produce steady, even heat just like that specialized appliance. To build the sandwiches, we create a quick, zesty coleslaw flavored with spicy brown mustard and horseradish that perfectly complements the roast beef and smoky gouda. We also brush some of the mayonnaise mixture on the bread to help create a crisp, golden exterior and eliminate the need to add oil to the skillet. Starting the sandwiches in a cold skillet allows the crust to form without burning the sandwiches. Pressing the sandwiches in the skillet underneath a heavy Dutch oven as they cook creates a perfectly pressed panini. Buy refrigerated prepared horseradish, not the shelf-stable kind, which contains preservatives and additives. Other hearty sandwich breads that are roughly ½ inch thick can be used in place of the pumpernickel. Swiss, Muenster, or sharp cheddar can be used in place of the gouda.

1 For the coleslaw Combine mayonnaise, mustard, horseradish, salt, and pepper in large bowl. Add coleslaw mix and onion and toss to combine.

2 For the sandwiches Adjust oven rack to middle position and heat oven to 200 degrees. Set wire rack in rimmed baking sheet. Spread mayonnaise evenly on 1 side of each slice of bread and arrange, mayonnaise side down, on cutting board. Divide gouda, roast beef, and coleslaw among 4 slices of bread. Top with remaining bread, mayonnaise side up.

3 Wrap bottom and sides of Dutch oven with large sheet of aluminum foil, anchoring foil on rim. Place 2 sandwiches in cold 12-inch nonstick skillet and weigh down with prepared Dutch oven. Cook over medium heat until golden brown on first side, about 3 minutes. Remove Dutch oven, flip panini, replace Dutch oven, and continue to cook until golden brown on second side and cheese is melted, about 2 minutes. Transfer sandwiches to prepared rack and keep warm in oven. Wipe skillet clean with paper towels and repeat with remaining 2 sandwiches. Serve.

VARIATIONS

Turkey Panini with Pickled Fennel and Apple

Microwave ½ cup apple cider vinegar, ½ cup water, and ¼ teaspoon salt in medium bowl until steaming, about 3 minutes. Add ½ thinly sliced fennel bulb and ½ thinly sliced Granny Smith apple and stir until submerged. Let sit for 10 minutes. Drain fennel and apple, return to bowl, and stir in 2 tablespoons fig jam until evenly coated; set aside. Substitute fennel and apple mixture for coleslaw, hearty whole wheat sandwich bread for pumpernickel rye, deli cheddar cheese for smoked gouda, and oven-roasted deli turkey for roast beef.

Ham Antipasto Panini

Combine 2 cups baby arugula, ½ cup sliced pepperoncini peppers, and ¼ cup olive tapenade in bowl. Substitute baby arugula mixture for coleslaw, rustic Italian bread for pumpernickel rye sandwich bread, 6 ounces salami and 6 ounces deli ham for roast beef, and deli provolone cheese for smoked gouda.

Sizing Up Your Skillet

nonstick • **traditional cast iron** • **carbon steel**

A 12-inch nonstick skillet provides enough space to press two assembled sandwiches and can produce steady, even heat to create a uniform golden-brown crust. A traditional cast-iron or carbon-steel skillet will also work for these reasons.

Shaved Steak Sandwiches

Serves 4

Total Time 50 minutes

3 tablespoons vegetable oil, divided

2 onions, chopped

¾ teaspoon table salt, divided

2 pounds shaved steak

⅛ teaspoon pepper

¼ cup grated Parmesan cheese

8 slices white American cheese (8 ounces)

4 (8-inch) Italian sub rolls, split lengthwise, toasted, if desired

Why This Recipe Works Shaved steak sandwiches are a mainstay of delis, food trucks, and diners everywhere, and no wonder. Who doesn't love thinly shaved beef quickly cooked on a griddle and then layered into rolls with thinly sliced cheese? But how do you make them at home without a griddle at the ready? To adapt this recipe for the home kitchen and a skillet, we had to make a few adjustments. We skip the tedious step of shaving the meat by hand and use preshredded steak from the meat counter instead. To best approximate the spacious griddle typically used in sandwich shops, we cook the meat in two batches in a nonstick skillet and drain off any excess moisture before giving it a final sear. Finally, to bind it all together, we let slices of American cheese melt into the meat, along with a bit of grated Parmesan to boost its flavor. For the best results, look for fresh shaved rib-eye or sirloin steak; avoid frozen shaved steak. An equal weight of sirloin steak tips, trimmed, cut into 1½-inch pieces and pounded very thin can be substituted. Top these sandwiches with chopped pickled hot peppers, sweet relish, or hot sauce.

1 Heat 1 tablespoon oil in 12-inch nonstick skillet over medium-high heat until shimmering. Add onions and ¼ teaspoon salt and cook, stirring frequently, until well browned and softened, 6 to 12 minutes; transfer to bowl.

2 Heat 1 tablespoon oil in now-empty skillet over high heat until just smoking. Add half of meat in even layer and cook, without stirring, until well browned on first side, about 5 minutes. Stir and continue to cook until meat is no longer pink, about 2 minutes. Transfer meat to colander set in large bowl. Wipe skillet clean with paper towels. Repeat with remaining 1 tablespoon oil and remaining sliced meat.

3 Drain excess moisture from meat, discarding any liquid in bowl. Return meat to again-empty skillet and add onions, remaining ½ teaspoon salt, and pepper. Cook over medium heat, stirring constantly, until mixture is heated through, about 2 minutes. Reduce heat to low, sprinkle with Parmesan, and shingle slices of American cheese over meat. Allow cheeses to melt, about 2 minutes. Divide mixture evenly among rolls. Serve.

VARIATION

Shaved Steak Sandwiches for Two

Reduce pepper to pinch; halve remaining ingredients. Proceed with recipe in 10- or 12-inch nonstick skillet.

Sizing Up Your Skillet

nonstick • **traditional cast iron** • **carbon steel**

The slick surface of a 12-inch nonstick skillet ensures that the savory browning sticks to the meat, not the pan. A traditional cast-iron or carbon-steel skillet will also work for this reason. If using a traditional cast-iron skillet, you will need to preheat the empty skillet over medium heat for 3 minutes before proceeding with step 1.

Smashed Burgers

Serves 2

Total Time 40 minutes

Sauce

2   tablespoons mayonnaise

1   tablespoon minced shallot

1½ teaspoons finely chopped dill pickles plus ½ teaspoon brine

1½ teaspoons ketchup

⅛   teaspoon sugar

⅛   teaspoon pepper

Burgers

2   hamburger buns, toasted, if desired

8   ounces 80 percent lean ground beef

¼   teaspoon vegetable oil

¼   teaspoon kosher salt, divided

2   slices American cheese (2 ounces)

    Bibb lettuce leaves

    Thinly sliced tomato

Why This Recipe Works This diner icon shares the same thin, verging-on-well-done profile and array of condiments as a typical fast-food burger, but the big selling point is an ultrabrown, crispy crust. The key to success here is to use a traditional cast-iron skillet, which allows for supercrispy browning of the thin burgers without overcooking them. We use commercial ground beef instead of grinding our own because the former is ground finer and thus exposes more myosin, a sticky meat protein that helps the patties hold together when they are smashed. Using a small saucepan to press straight down on the meat ensures that it spreads and sticks uniformly to the skillet (instead of shrinking as it cooks), which helps guarantee deep browning. We make two smaller patties at a time instead of one larger one because they fit nicely inside a burger bun. Sandwiching an ultramelty slice of Kraft American cheese between the two patties helps the cheese melt thoroughly and seep into the meat almost like a rich, salty cheese sauce would. Our creamy, tangy burger sauce adds more richness and moisture, lettuce and thinly sliced tomato provide freshness and acidity, and the soft bun offers tenderness. You can use 85 percent lean ground beef instead of 80 percent, but 90 percent lean will produce a dry burger. Open a window or turn on your exhaust fan before cooking. Be assertive when pressing the patties. We strongly prefer Kraft Singles here for their meltability. To make four burgers, double the ingredients for the sauce and burgers, but use the same amount of oil. Cook the patties in four batches. Once each batch is cooked, transfer the patties to a wire rack set in a rimmed baking sheet, adding cheese to the first four, and keep warm in a 200-degree oven. Place on buns right before serving.

1 For the sauce Stir all ingredients together in bowl.

2 For the burgers Spread 1 tablespoon sauce on cut side of each bun top. Divide beef into 4 equal pieces (2 ounces each) and form into loose, rough balls (do not compress). Using paper towel, rub oil into bottom of 12-inch traditional cast-iron skillet (reserve paper towel). Heat over medium-low heat for 5 minutes. While skillet heats, wrap bottom and sides of small saucepan with large sheet of aluminum foil, anchoring foil on rim, and place large plate next to cooktop.

3 Increase heat to high. When skillet begins to smoke, place 2 balls about 3 inches apart in skillet. Use bottom of prepared saucepan to firmly smash each ball until 4 to 4½ inches in diameter. Place saucepan on plate next to cooktop. Sprinkle patties with ⅛ teaspoon salt and season with pepper. Cook until at least three-quarters of each patty is no longer pink on top, about 2 minutes (patties will stick to skillet). Use thin metal spatula to loosen patties from skillet. Flip patties and cook for 15 seconds. Slide skillet off heat. Transfer 1 burger to each bun bottom and top each with 1 slice American cheese. Gently scrape any browned bits from skillet, use tongs to wipe with reserved paper towel, and return skillet to heat. Repeat with remaining 2 balls and remaining salt and place patties on top of cheese. Top with lettuce and tomato. Cap with prepared bun tops. Serve immediately.

Sizing Up Your Skillet

traditional cast iron • carbon steel

The superior heat retention of a 12-inch traditional cast-iron skillet allows you to quickly achieve plenty of browning on the patties without overcooking them. A carbon-steel skillet will also work for this reason.

Crispy California Turkey Burgers

Serves 4

Total Time 45 minutes

½ cup mayonnaise, divided

1 teaspoon grated lemon zest plus 1 teaspoon juice

¾ teaspoon table salt, divided

½ teaspoon pepper, divided

1 pound 93 percent lean ground turkey

1 cup panko bread crumbs

2 ounces Monterey Jack cheese, shredded (½ cup)

2 teaspoons vegetable oil

4 hamburger buns, toasted, if desired

4 leaves Bibb or Boston lettuce

1 ripe avocado, halved, pitted, and sliced ¼ inch thick

¼ cup alfalfa sprouts

½ red onion, sliced thin

Why This Recipe Works If you're looking for a delicious burger inspired by the ubiquitous West Coast patty topped with sprouts and avocado, this one more than fits the bill. These burgers have stayed in vogue for years and years and no wonder. Packed with flavorful shredded Monterey Jack cheese, they deliver a wallop of rich flavor in every bite, not to mention a juicy interior and crispy cheese around the edges, courtesy of the pan frying in our trusty nonstick skillet. We also add panko and a little mayonnaise to the turkey mixture to keep the burgers just firm enough so that they don't fall apart in the skillet. Once cooked, we load up the burgers with creamy avocado and tender alfalfa sprouts, and we include crisp red onion and lettuce for even more freshness. For the crowning touch, we slather a sweet-savory classic burger sauce over the buns before topping off the burgers.

1 Combine ¼ cup mayonnaise, lemon zest and juice, ¼ teaspoon salt, and ¼ teaspoon pepper in bowl; set aside.

2 Break ground turkey into small pieces in large bowl. Add panko, Monterey Jack, remaining ¼ cup mayonnaise, and remaining ¼ teaspoon pepper and gently knead with hands until well combined. Divide turkey mixture into 4 equal portions, then gently shape each portion into ¾-inch-thick patty. Using your fingertips, press center of each patty down until about ½ inch thick, creating slight divot.

3 Sprinkle patties with remaining ½ teaspoon salt. Heat oil in 12-inch nonstick skillet over medium heat until just smoking. Transfer patties to skillet, divot side up, and cook until well browned on first side, 4 to 6 minutes. Flip patties, reduce heat to medium-low, and continue to cook until browned on second side and meat registers 160 degrees, 5 to 7 minutes. Transfer burgers to plate and let rest for 5 minutes.

4 Spread 1 tablespoon sauce on cut side of each bun top and arrange lettuce on bun bottoms. Serve burgers on buns, topped with avocado, alfalfa sprouts, and onion.

VARIATION

Crispy California Turkey Burgers for Two

Halve ingredients. Proceed with recipe in 10- or 12-inch nonstick skillet.

Sizing Up Your Skillet

nonstick • traditional cast iron • carbon steel

A 12-inch nonstick skillet provides enough space to griddle four patties and produces steady, even heat to create a uniform golden-brown crust. The slick surface of the skillet also ensures that the patties don't stick to the pan. A traditional cast-iron or carbon-steel skillet will also work for these reasons. If using a traditional cast-iron skillet, you will need to preheat the empty skillet over medium heat for 5 minutes before proceeding with step 3.

Hearty Quesadillas with Chicken, Mushrooms, and Poblanos

Serves 4

Total Time 50 minutes

8   ounces cremini or white mushrooms, trimmed and sliced thin

2   poblano chiles, stemmed, seeded, and chopped fine

¼   cup water

¼   cup plus ½ teaspoon vegetable oil, divided

½   teaspoon table salt

2¼   cups shredded rotisserie chicken

4   ounces Monterey Jack cheese, shredded (1 cup)

4   ounces sharp cheddar cheese, shredded (1 cup)

1   tablespoon minced canned chipotle chile in adobo sauce

¾   teaspoon ground cumin

4   (10-inch) flour tortillas

Why This Recipe Works A gooey on the inside, crisp and golden on the outside cheese quesadilla is a go-to snack for good reason. The treat requires only a few ingredients and can be prepared in minutes. Making a quesadilla with a complex filling, rather than just cheese, however, poses a few challenges for the cook that can lead to undercooked, bland, or limp and soggy results. We address these issues by using precooked rotisserie chicken along with mushrooms and poblano peppers that we cook quickly in a large nonstick skillet so that they don't sog out the quesadillas. Chipotle chiles in adobo deliver superconvenient yet bold flavor. Monterey Jack cheese melts easily without breaking, and cheddar adds distinctive sharpness. Finally, using 2 tablespoons of oil to cook the quesadillas, rather than in a dry skillet, promotes enhanced browning for flavor and a crispness that stands up to the heavier filling.

1 Cook mushrooms, poblanos, and water in 12-inch nonstick skillet over high heat, stirring occasionally, until skillet is almost dry and mushrooms begin to sizzle, about 3 minutes. Reduce heat to medium-high. Add ½ teaspoon oil and salt and toss until vegetables are evenly coated. Continue to cook, stirring occasionally, until mushrooms are well browned, 4 to 6 minutes. Transfer vegetables to large bowl; add chicken, cheeses, chipotle chile, and cumin; and stir to combine. Wipe skillet clean with paper towels.

2 Spread one-quarter of filling over half of each tortilla, leaving ½-inch border at edge. Fold tortillas over filling and press firmly to seal. Set wire rack in rimmed baking sheet and line half of rack with triple layer of paper towels.

3 Heat 2 tablespoons oil in now-empty 12-inch nonstick skillet over medium heat until shimmering. Place 2 quesadillas in skillet, pressing into pan with thin spatula, and cook until browned on both sides and cheese has melted, about 2 minutes per side. Transfer to paper towel-lined side of prepared rack to drain for about 15 seconds per side, then move to unlined side of rack. Repeat with remaining 2 tablespoons oil and remaining 2 quesadillas. Let cool for at least 3 minutes. Cut into wedges and serve.

VARIATIONS

Hearty Quesadillas with Shrimp, Roasted Red Peppers, and Cilantro

Combine 8 ounces peeled and deveined shrimp, cut into ½-inch pieces, and 1½ teaspoons Old Bay seasoning in bowl. Heat 1 teaspoon vegetable oil in 12-inch nonstick skillet over medium-high heat until shimmering. Add 4 thinly sliced scallion greens and cook, stirring occasionally, for 1 minute. Add shrimp and cook, stirring constantly, until shrimp are opaque throughout, about 2 minutes. Transfer shrimp mixture to large bowl. Add 1¼ cups finely chopped jarred roasted red peppers, 2 cups shredded Monterey Jack cheese, 1 cup chopped fresh cilantro, 1 teaspoon grated lime zest plus 2 tablespoons juice, ½ teaspoon table salt, and ½ teaspoon pepper and stir to combine. Substitute shrimp filling for chicken filling.

Hearty Quesadillas with Chicken, Mushrooms, and Poblanos for Two

Reduce chicken to 1¼ cups; halve remaining ingredients. Proceed with recipe in 12-inch nonstick skillet, still using ¼ cup water in step 1.

Sizing Up Your Skillet

nonstick • **traditional cast iron**

A 12-inch nonstick skillet provides enough space to griddle two quesadilla without sticking and can produce steady, even heat to create a uniform golden-brown crust. A traditional cast-iron skillet will also work for these reasons. If using a traditional cast-iron skillet, you will need to preheat the empty skillet over medium heat for 5 minutes before proceeding with step 1.

Cheese Pupusas

Serves 4

Total Time 1 hour, plus 1½ hours refrigerating and resting

Curtido

1   cup cider vinegar

½   cup water

1   tablespoon sugar

1½   teaspoons table salt

½   head green cabbage, cored and sliced thin (6 cups)

1   onion, sliced thin

1   carrot, peeled and shredded

1   jalapeño chile, stemmed, seeded, and minced

1   teaspoon dried oregano

1   cup chopped fresh cilantro

Pupusas

2   cups (8 ounces) masa harina

½   teaspoon table salt

2   cups boiling water, plus warm tap water as needed

2   teaspoons vegetable oil, divided

10   ounces quesillo, cut into 10 pieces

Why This Recipe Works   The national dish of El Salvador, these griddle cakes are made by stuffing cheese, beans, and braised meat (or a combination thereof) into a ball of masa harina dough. The ball is flattened into a disk and traditionally cooked on a cast-iron griddle (called a comal) until the tender cake forms a crisp, spotty-brown shell. Here we use a large nonstick skillet to keep the pupusas from sticking and create the trademark crusty exterior. Served with curtido (a pickled cabbage slaw), the result is irresistible. Quesillo is a firm, low-fat white Mexican cheese; if unavailable, you can substitute a combination of 2 ounces cotija or feta cheese and 8 ounces Monterey Jack cheese. For an accurate measurement of boiling water, bring a full kettle of water to a boil and then measure out the desired amount. Properly hydrated masa dough should be tacky, requiring damp hands to keep it from sticking to your palms. If the dough feels the slightest bit dry at any time, knead in warm tap water, 1 teaspoon at a time, until the dough is tacky. An occasional leak while cooking the pupusas is to be expected, and the browned cheese is delicious. For a spicier curtido, add the jalapeño seeds. In addition to the curtido, serve with a simple tomato salsa, if desired.

1 For the curtido   Whisk vinegar, water, sugar, and salt in large bowl until sugar has dissolved. Add cabbage, onion, carrot, jalapeño, oregano, and cilantro and toss to combine. Cover and refrigerate for at least 1 hour or up to 24 hours.

2 For the pupusas   Mix masa harina and salt together in medium bowl. Add boiling water and 1 teaspoon oil and mix with rubber spatula until soft dough forms. Cover dough and let rest for 20 minutes.

3   While dough rests, draw 4-inch circle in center of 1 side of 1-quart or 1-gallon zipper-lock bag with marker. Cut open seams along both sides of bag, but leave bottom seam intact so that bag opens completely. Line rimmed baking sheet with parchment paper. Process quesillo in food processor until it resembles wet oatmeal, about 30 seconds (it will not form cohesive mass). Remove processor blade. Form cheese into 8 balls, weighing about 1¼ ounces each, and place balls on 1 half of prepared sheet.

4   Knead dough in bowl for 15 to 20 seconds. Test dough's hydration by flattening golf ball-size piece. If cracks larger than ¼ inch form around edges, add warm tap water, 2 teaspoons at a time, until dough is soft and slightly tacky. Transfer dough to counter, shape into large ball, and divide into 8 equal pieces. Using your damp hands, roll 1 dough piece into ball and place on empty half of prepared sheet. Cover with damp dish towel. Repeat with remaining dough pieces.

5   Place open cut bag marked side down on counter. Place 1 dough ball in center of circle. Fold other side of bag over ball. Using glass pie plate or 8-inch square baking dish, gently press dough to 4-inch diameter, using circle drawn on bag as guide. Turn out disk into your palm and place 1 ball cheese filling in center. Bring sides of dough up around filling and pinch top to seal. Remoisten your hands and roll ball until smooth, smoothing any cracks with your damp fingertip. Return ball to bag and slowly press to 4-inch diameter. Pinch closed any small cracks that form at edges. Return pupusa to sheet and cover with damp dish towel. Repeat with remaining dough and filling.

6   Heat remaining 1 teaspoon oil in 12-inch nonstick skillet over medium-high heat until shimmering. Wipe skillet clean with paper towels. Carefully lay 4 pupusas in skillet and cook until spotty brown on both sides, 2 to 4 minutes per side. Transfer to serving platter and repeat with remaining 4 pupusas. Toss curtido, then drain. Return slaw to bowl and stir in cilantro. Serve pupusas warm with curtido.

Sizing Up Your Skillet

nonstick ● **traditional cast iron**

A 12-inch nonstick skillet provides enough space to griddle four pupusas without sticking and can produce steady, even heat to create a uniform golden-brown crust. A traditional cast-iron skillet will also work for these reasons; you will need to preheat the empty skillet over medium heat for 3 minutes before proceeding with step 6.

Sizing Up Your Skillet

traditional cast iron • **carbon steel** • **nonstick**

A 12-inch traditional cast-iron skillet provides adequate space to griddle the pancake without sticking and can produce steady, even heat to create a uniform golden-brown crust. A carbon-steel skillet will also work well for these reasons. A 12-inch nonstick skillet can also be used; add oil to skillet in step 3 before heating and do not reduce heat.

Okonomiyaki

Serves 4

Total Time 1 hour

Okonomiyaki Sauce

2   tablespoons ketchup

1   tablespoon Worcestershire sauce

1   tablespoon soy sauce

1   tablespoon sugar

Okonomiyaki

¾   cup boiling water

¾   teaspoon instant dashi powder, such as Hondashi

1   cup (5 ounces) all-purpose flour

2   large eggs

3   tablespoons finely grated yamaimo

¾   teaspoon table salt

2½ cups ½-inch-pieces green cabbage

6   ounces thinly sliced pork belly, cut into 1-inch pieces

2   scallions, sliced thin

2   tablespoons beni-shoga (red pickled ginger), drained, plus extra for serving

1   tablespoon vegetable oil

    Kewpie mayonnaise

    Katsuobushi

    Aonori

VARIATION

Shrimp Okonomiyaki

Substitute 8 ounces peeled and deveined shrimp, cut into ½-inch pieces, for pork belly.

Why This Recipe Works Okonomiyaki is a savory filled pancake popularized in Japan as an inexpensive yet filling dish beginning in the early 1900s, when earthquakes and war left many in Japan with a short supply of food. It has evolved to become a common Japanese street food as well as a staple in Japanese home kitchens with many delectable variations, and it is easy to re-create in an American kitchen. It almost always features flour, eggs, cabbage, and pork for the griddled base, but the translation of okonomiyaki, "grilled as you'd like," means that it can certainly change based on personal taste and availability of ingredients. Our recipe aims to represent the popular Osaka-style okonomiyaki, in which ingredients are mixed into the batter, as opposed to Hiroshima-style, in which the ingredients and batter are cooked in distinct layers. Traditionally prepared on a teppan, a Japanese iron griddle, okonomiyaki lends itself perfectly to cooking in a traditional cast-iron skillet, which we preheat so that it is superhot when we add the batter. A defining characteristic of okonomiyaki is its soft yet slightly custardy interior texture, which it gets from adding grated yamaimo, Japanese mountain yam; as you grate the yam, it forms a viscous, slippery paste to mix into the batter to provide creaminess. Delicious as it is, the pancake is only complete with the traditional toppings: Homemade okonomiyaki sauce provides tanginess and sweetness; a drizzle of Kewpie mayo adds a savory richness; and katsuobushi (smoked bonito flakes) and aonori (dried and powdered green seaweed) bring umami and slight saltiness to the okonomiyaki. Yamaimo can also be labeled nagaimo, or Chinese yam. When peeling and grating, use disposable kitchen gloves, as the yamaimo will produce a slippery, liquid-y paste that may cause skin irritation when handled raw. If unavailable, substitute 3 tablespoons potato starch. Thinly sliced uncured pork belly can often be found in the freezer section of a Japanese or Chinese grocery store; if using frozen pork belly, be sure to thaw it completely before using. Thinly sliced hickory bacon is a suitable alternative. Okonomiyaki is typically served whole on a communal platter; provide a thin spatula or pie server to help separate portions. You will need a 12-inch skillet with a tight-fitting lid for this recipe.

1 For the okonomiyaki sauce Combine all ingredients in bowl; set aside for serving.

2 For the okonomiyaki Combine boiling water and instant dashi powder in small bowl; let cool slightly. Whisk dashi, flour, eggs, yamaimo, and salt in large bowl until combined. Gently fold in cabbage, pork belly, scallions, and beni-shoga until just combined.

3 Heat 12-inch cast-iron skillet over medium heat for 3 minutes. Reduce heat to medium-low. Add oil to skillet, swirling to coat bottom, and heat until shimmering. Add cabbage mixture and spread into even 10-inch round, about 1 inch thick. Cover and cook until okonomiyaki is lightly golden on bottom, 10 to 12 minutes, rotating skillet halfway through cooking and adjusting heat if bottom begins to brown too quickly.

4 Slide okonomiyaki onto large plate, then invert onto second large plate. Slide okonomiyaki back into skillet browned side up and cook, uncovered, until golden brown on bottom, about 10 minutes, rotating skillet halfway through cooking and adjusting heat if bottom begins to brown too quickly.

5 Off heat, spread sauce evenly over top of okonomiyaki. Drizzle generously with Kewpie mayonnaise, sprinkle with katsuobushi and aonori, and top with extra beni-shoga. Serve.

Kimchi Jeon

Serves 2

Total Time 40 minutes

Dipping Sauce

5   tablespoons plus 1 teaspoon sugar

5   tablespoons plus 1 teaspoon
     soy sauce

5   tablespoons plus 1 teaspoon water

1½   teaspoons unseasoned rice vinegar

1   garlic clove, minced

Pancake

¼   cup (1¼ ounces) all-purpose flour

1   large egg white

1   cup cabbage kimchi, drained with
     2 tablespoons juice reserved,
     chopped coarse

4   scallions, white parts sliced thin,
     green parts cut into 1-inch lengths

3   tablespoons vegetable oil, divided

Why This Recipe Works Kimchi is a ubiquitous condiment on the Korean table, adding spice and tang to soups, rice, and noodles and even flavoring this savory pancake. It has been said that when Korean farmers couldn't tend to their crops due to inclement weather, making kimchi pancakes was a comforting way to pass the time. Today these delicious pancakes are popular in both restaurants and homes, and the key to making them successfully is to prevent the kimchi, with its relatively high moisture content, from turning them soggy. You achieve this by draining the pickled cabbage but reserving a measured 2 tablespoons of liquid for the batter. Binding the kimchi with just this liquid, one egg white, and a little flour encourages the kimchi to shine. Scallions add more flavor and a pop of color. It can be challenging to flip the delicate pancake to cook on the second side without it breaking and the kimchi falling out; instead, gently slide the pancake onto a plate and invert it onto another plate. This makes for a flawless flip, and you'll be able to easily slide the pancake, browned side up, back into the skillet to brown the second side. The salty-sweet dipping sauce counterbalances the kimchi's spiciness. This recipe can easily be doubled; make the pancake batter in two separate bowls and cook the pancakes in two batches.

1 For the dipping sauce Simmer all ingredients in small saucepan over medium heat, stirring occasionally, until thickened and reduced to about ¾ cup, about 5 minutes. Let cool completely before serving.

2 For the pancake Whisk flour, egg white, and reserved kimchi juice together in large bowl. Stir in scallions and kimchi until well combined.

3 Heat 2 tablespoons oil in 10-inch nonstick skillet over medium-high heat until shimmering. Add pancake batter and spread into even layer with rubber spatula. Cook until well browned around edges, about 4 minutes. Run spatula around edge of pancake and shake skillet to loosen. Slide pancake onto large plate.

4 Heat remaining 1 tablespoon oil in now-empty skillet over medium heat until shimmering. Invert pancake onto second large plate, then slide it, browned side up, back into skillet. Cook until pancake is well browned on second side, about 4 minutes. Slide pancake onto cutting board, cut into wedges, and serve with dipping sauce.

Sizing Up Your Skillet

nonstick • **traditional cast iron** • **carbon steel**

A 10-inch nonstick skillet provides enough space to griddle the pancake without sticking. A traditional cast-iron or carbon-steel skillet will also work for this reason. If using a traditional cast-iron skillet, you will need to preheat the empty skillet over medium heat for 3 minutes before proceeding with step 3.

Crispy Pan-Fried Chicken Cutlets

Serves 4 to 6
Total Time 30 minutes

- 2 cups panko bread crumbs
- 2 large eggs
- 1 teaspoon table salt
- 4 (6- to 8-ounce) boneless, skinless chicken breasts, trimmed
- ½ cup vegetable oil for frying, divided

VARIATIONS

Crispy Pan-Fried Chicken Milanese Cutlets

Stir ¼ cup finely grated Parmesan cheese into panko.

Crispy Pan-Fried Chicken Cutlets for Two

Halve all ingredients. Proceed with recipe in 10-inch skillet.

Why This Recipe Works Crispy, golden-brown chicken cutlets are a very appealing dinner option, and while they seem like they should be easy to execute well, results are often a mixed bag of issues like a soggy and greasy coating and uneven browning. For our first step, we replace the often-used homemade bread crumbs with drier, crunchier panko, which we break down into smaller crumbs by pounding in a zipper-lock bag. To streamline the traditional multi-step bound-breading process, we ditch the flour. The result, with just beaten egg and the panko, is a more delicate crust that crisps up perfectly in a nonstick skillet. Whisking salt right into the egg allows us to avoid seasoning each cutlet separately, and there is no need to pat the chicken dry before starting since there is no flour in the mix. If your chicken breasts are larger than 6 to 8 ounces each, use fewer of them to maintain a total weight of 1½ to 2 pounds. To make slicing the chicken easier, freeze it for 15 minutes. This recipe also works well using 4 (3- to 4-ounce) boneless pork or veal cutlets in place of the chicken cutlets.

1 Adjust oven rack to middle position and heat oven to 200 degrees. Place panko in large zipper-lock bag and lightly crush with rolling pin; transfer to shallow dish. Whisk eggs and salt in second shallow dish until well combined.

2 Starting at thick end, cut each chicken breast in half horizontally. Cover chicken breast cutlets with plastic wrap. Using meat pounder, gently pound chicken to uniform ¼-inch thickness. Working with 1 cutlet at a time, dip cutlets in egg mixture, allowing excess to drip off, then coat all sides with panko, pressing gently so crumbs adhere. Transfer cutlets to rimmed baking sheet and let sit for 5 minutes.

3 Set wire rack in second rimmed baking sheet and line half of rack with triple layer of paper towels. Heat ¼ cup oil in 12-inch nonstick skillet over medium-high heat until shimmering. Place 4 cutlets in skillet and cook until deep golden brown on both sides, 4 to 6 minutes. Transfer cutlets to paper towel–lined side of prepared rack to drain for about 15 seconds per side, then move to unlined side of rack and season with salt to taste; keep chicken warm in oven. Wipe skillet clean with paper towels. Repeat with remaining ¼ cup oil and remaining 4 cutlets. Serve immediately.

Sizing Up Your Skillet

nonstick ● **traditional cast iron**

A 12-inch nonstick skillet provides enough space to fry cutlets and can produce steady, even heat to create a uniform golden-brown crust. The slick surface of the skillet also ensures that the panko crust sticks to the cutlets and not the skillet. A traditional cast-iron skillet will also work for these reasons; you will need to preheat the empty skillet over medium heat for 5 minutes before proceeding with step 3.

perfecting

CRISPY PAN-FRIED CHICKEN CUTLETS

One of the keys to making perfectly crisp and browned chicken cutlets is to forgo the traditional bound-breading method, ditch the flour coating, and rely on crushed panko and beaten egg seasoned with salt and pepper.

1 Freeze Chicken Briefly to Make Slicing Easier.

2 Pound the Cutlets to Uniform Thickness.

3 Coat in Egg Mixture and then Panko.

Sizing Up Your Skillet

● **traditional cast iron**

The superior heat retention of a 12-inch traditional cast-iron skillet allows you to oven-fry 3 pounds of bone-in chicken pieces simultaneously and still achieve a crunchy, deeply seasoned exterior. We do not recommend using an alternative skillet in this recipe.

Cast-Iron Oven-Fried Chicken

Serves 4 to 6

Total Time 1¼ hours

3   pounds bone-in chicken pieces (split breasts cut in half crosswise, drumsticks, and/or thighs), trimmed

4   teaspoons table salt, divided

3½   teaspoons pepper, divided

4   large eggs

2   cups all-purpose flour

1   tablespoon paprika

2   teaspoons baking powder

2   teaspoons garlic powder

¼   teaspoon cayenne pepper

3   tablespoons water

½   cup vegetable oil

Why This Recipe Works Fried chicken has a cultural and emotional resonance few foods can match. But while many of us crave fried chicken, it falls out of our rotation because of the time and effort it takes to make, not to mention dealing with all the oil and the splatter of deep frying. We wanted to find an easier way to get that crunchy, deeply seasoned exterior and juicy meat we all love—without deep frying. This means using the oven instead of the stovetop. And the key to this method is a traditional cast-iron skillet, which we preheat in a 450-degree oven. While the oven preheats and the skillet gets superhot, we coat the chicken pieces in egg and dredge it in a well-seasoned flour mixture. Then we add just ½ cup vegetable oil to the hot skillet, add the chicken skin side down, and return the skillet to the oven to "fry" the chicken. The chicken crackles when added to the hot oil, just as it does when deep fried on the stovetop. We flip the chicken halfway through cooking, which helps crisp both sides of each piece. One 4½- to 5-pound whole chicken will yield the 3 pounds of parts called for in this recipe.

1 Adjust oven rack to middle position, place 12-inch traditional cast-iron skillet on rack, and heat oven to 450 degrees. Set wire rack in rimmed baking sheet and line half of rack with triple layer of paper towels. Sprinkle chicken with 1 teaspoon salt and ½ teaspoon pepper.

2 Lightly beat eggs and 1 teaspoon salt together in medium bowl. Whisk flour, paprika, baking powder, garlic powder, cayenne, remaining 2 teaspoons salt, and remaining 1 tablespoon pepper together in second medium bowl. Add water to flour mixture. Using your fingers, rub flour mixture and water until water is evenly incorporated and shaggy pieces of dough form.

3 Working with 1 piece of chicken at a time, dip in egg mixture, allowing excess to drip off, then dredge in flour mixture, pressing firmly to adhere. Transfer coated chicken to large plate, skin side up.

4 When oven reaches 450 degrees, remove skillet from oven using potholders. Being careful of hot skillet handle, add oil to skillet and immediately place chicken skin side down in skillet. Return skillet to oven and bake for 15 minutes.

5 Remove skillet from oven and flip chicken. Return skillet to oven and continue to bake until breasts register 160 degrees and drumsticks/thighs register 175 degrees, 10 to 15 minutes.

6 Transfer chicken skin side up to paper towel-lined side of prepared wire rack to blot grease from underside of chicken, then move chicken to unlined side of rack. Let chicken cool for about 10 minutes. Serve.

VARIATION

Cast-Iron Oven-Fried Chicken For Two

Halve all ingredients. Proceed with recipe in traditional 10-inch cast-iron skillet.

Crispy Salmon Cakes with Frisée and Celery Salad

Serves 4

Total Time 45 minutes

2   tablespoons lemon juice, divided

1   small shallot, minced

2   tablespoons plus ½ teaspoon mayonnaise, divided

1½   teaspoons Dijon mustard, divided

3   tablespoons vegetable oil

3   tablespoons plus ¾ cup panko bread crumbs

½   teaspoon table salt

¼   teaspoon pepper

1¼   pounds skinless salmon fillet, cut into 1-inch pieces

½   cup vegetable oil for frying

1   head (6 ounces) frisée, torn into bite-size pieces

2   celery ribs, sliced thin on bias

¼   cup fresh parsley leaves

VARIATION

Crispy Salmon Cakes with Frisée and Celery Salad for Two

Reduce shallot to 1 tablespoon minced; halve remaining ingredients. Proceed with recipe in 12-inch nonstick skillet, pulsing salmon in 2 batches.

Why This Recipe Works Salmon cakes can often disappoint, whether you make them at home or order them in a restaurant. Why? They are often mushy in the center or have so much binder that you don't even taste the fish. A great salmon cake should have a crisp exterior, a moist interior, and a supersimple cooking technique. Oven-fried salmon cakes disappointed us every time: pale, dry, and with a "fishy" flavor. It turns out that the longer you cook salmon cakes, the stronger the fishy aroma and flavor. So we tried quick pan-frying the cakes in a nonstick skillet and were happy to discover that it easily beat out oven frying. Fresh salmon is clearly better than canned or even precooked salmon, and for a binder, we use mayonnaise and bread crumbs. For cakes that hold together without turning pasty, we pulse chunks of fresh salmon in the food processor in three batches. Coating the cakes in panko bread crumbs ensures the right crisped exterior. A few additions (mayonnaise, Dijon mustard, and lemon juice) take these salmon cakes to the next level without adding much more work. A fresh and easy-to-make frisée and celery salad tossed with an assertive dressing makes a lovely accompaniment. When processing the salmon, it is OK to have some pieces that are larger than ¼ inch. It is important to avoid overprocessing the fish. If buying a skin-on salmon fillet, purchase 1⅓ pounds; this will yield 1¼ pounds fish after skinning.

1 Whisk 1 tablespoon lemon juice, shallot, ½ teaspoon mayonnaise, and ½ teaspoon mustard in medium bowl until thoroughly combined. Whisking constantly, slowly drizzle in oil until glossy and lightly thickened, with no pools of oil visible. (If pools of oil are visible on surface as you whisk, stop adding oil and whisk until mixture is well combined, then resume whisking in oil in slow stream.) Season with salt and pepper to taste; set aside.

2 Combine 3 tablespoons panko, salt, pepper, remaining 1 tablespoon lemon juice, remaining 2 tablespoons mayonnaise, and remaining 1 teaspoon mustard in bowl. Working in 3 batches, pulse salmon in food processor until coarsely chopped into ¼-inch pieces, about 2 pulses, transferring each batch to bowl with panko mixture. Gently mix until uniformly combined.

3 Place remaining ¾ cup panko in shallow baking dish or pie plate. Using ⅓-cup measure, scoop level amount of salmon mixture and transfer to baking sheet; repeat to make 8 cakes. Carefully coat each cake in panko, gently patting cake into disk measuring 2¾ inches in diameter and 1 inch high. Return coated cakes to baking sheet.

4 Set wire rack in second rimmed baking sheet and line with triple layer of paper towels. Heat ½ cup oil in 12-inch skillet over medium-high heat until shimmering. Place cakes in skillet and cook, without moving, until golden brown on first side, about 2 minutes. Carefully flip cakes and cook until second side is golden brown, 2 to 3 minutes. Transfer cakes to paper towel–lined side of prepared rack to drain for about 15 seconds per side, then move to unlined side of rack.

5 Whisk dressing to recombine. Add frisée, celery, and parsley and toss gently until evenly coated. Serve salmon cakes with salad.

Sizing Up Your Skillet

nonstick • traditional cast iron

A 12-inch nonstick skillet provides enough space to griddle eight salmon cakes and can produce steady, even heat to create a uniform golden-brown crust. The slick surface of the skillet also ensures that the panko crust sticks to the cakes and not the skillet. A traditional cast-iron skillet will also work for these reasons; you will need to preheat the empty skillet over medium heat for 5 minutes before proceeding with step 4.

Sizing Up Your Skillet

nonstick ● **traditional cast iron**

A 12-inch nonstick skillet provides enough space to fry six tacos without sticking and can produce steady, even heat to create a uniform golden-brown crust. A traditional cast-iron skillet will also work for these reasons; you will need to preheat the empty skillet over medium heat for 5 minutes before proceeding with step 2.

Tacos Dorados

Serves 4

Total Time 1¼ hours

1   tablespoon water

¼   teaspoon baking soda

12   ounces 90 percent lean ground beef

3   tablespoons vegetable oil, divided

1   onion, chopped fine

1½   tablespoons chili powder

1½   tablespoons paprika

1½   teaspoons ground cumin

1½   teaspoons garlic powder

1   teaspoon table salt

2   tablespoons tomato paste

2   ounces cheddar cheese, shredded (½ cup), plus extra for serving

12   (6-inch) corn tortillas

¼   cup vegetable oil for frying

VARIATION

Tacos Dorados for Two

Halve all ingredients except oil for frying. Proceed with recipe in 12-inch nonstick skillet, frying all filled tacos in 1 batch.

Why This Recipe Works Crispy-shell tacos have long existed in Mexico with the name tacos dorados. The way they are prepared is pure genius: Soft corn tortillas are filled, folded in half and then fried. At the table, the tacos are opened like a book and stuffed with garnishes. We first toss ground beef with a bit of baking soda to help it stay juicy before adding it to a savory base of sautéed onion, spices, and tomato paste. Next, we stir in some shredded cheese to make the filling more cohesive. To build the tacos, we brush corn tortillas with oil, warm them in the oven to make them pliable, and stuff them with the filling. Finally, we pan-fry the tacos in a large nonstick skillet in two batches until they are super-crispy and golden. Arrange the tacos so that they face the same direction in the skillet to make them easy to fit and flip. To ensure crispy tacos, cook the tortillas until they are deeply browned. For garnishes, we like to include shredded iceberg lettuce, chopped tomato, sour cream, and pickled jalapeño slices.

1 Adjust oven rack to middle position and heat oven to 400 degrees. Combine water and baking soda in large bowl. Add beef and mix until thoroughly combined; set aside.

2 Heat 1 tablespoon oil in 12-inch nonstick skillet over medium heat until shimmering. Add onion and cook until softened, about 5 minutes. Stir in chili powder, paprika, cumin, garlic powder, and salt and cook until fragrant, about 1 minute. Stir in tomato paste and cook until paste is rust-colored, about 2 minutes. Add beef mixture and cook, using wooden spoon to break meat into pieces no larger than ¼ inch, until beef is no longer pink, 5 to 7 minutes. Transfer beef mixture to bowl and stir in cheddar until cheese has melted and mixture is homogeneous. Wipe skillet clean with paper towels.

3 Thoroughly brush both sides of tortillas with remaining 2 tablespoons oil. Arrange tortillas, overlapping, on rimmed baking sheet in 2 rows (6 tortillas each). Bake until tortillas are warm and pliable, about 5 minutes. Remove tortillas from oven and reduce oven temperature to 200 degrees.

4 Place 2 tablespoons filling on 1 side of 1 tortilla. Fold and press to close tortilla (edges will be open, but tortilla will remain folded). Repeat with remaining tortillas and remaining filling. (Filled tortillas can be covered and refrigerated for up to 12 hours.)

5 Set wire rack in second rimmed baking sheet and line half of rack with triple layer of paper towels. Heat ¼ cup oil in now-empty skillet over medium-high heat until shimmering. Arrange 6 tacos in skillet with open sides facing away from you. Cook, adjusting heat so oil actively sizzles and bubbles appear around edges of tacos, until tacos are crispy and deeply browned on 1 side, about 3 minutes. Using tongs and thin spatula, carefully flip tacos. Cook until deeply browned on second side, about 3 minutes, adjusting heat as necessary.

6 Remove skillet from heat and transfer tacos to paper towel-lined side of prepared rack. Blot tops of tacos with additional paper towels, then move to unlined side of rack. Transfer tacos to oven to keep warm. Return skillet to medium-high heat and cook remaining tacos. Serve immediately.

Tofu Katsu Sandwiches

Serves 4

Total Time 45 minutes

¼ cup ketchup

4 teaspoons Worcestershire sauce

2 teaspoons soy sauce

1 teaspoon garlic powder

1 teaspoon sugar, divided

2 large eggs

2 tablespoons all-purpose flour

1½ cups panko bread crumbs

1 (14-ounce) block extra-firm or firm tofu

½ teaspoon table salt

¾ cup vegetable oil for frying

2½ teaspoons unseasoned rice vinegar

1½ teaspoons toasted sesame oil

3 cups shredded red or green cabbage

8 slices soft white sandwich bread

Why This Recipe Works Japanese katsu involves frying up a thin, panko-breaded cutlet and serving it up with a sweet and savory tonkatsu sauce. The sandwiches of the same name take things a step further, layering the cutlets and sauce with shredded cabbage between slices of fluffy Japanese milk bread. Using tofu "cutlets" is the first step to re-creating a mouthwatering version sans the meat. To help the panko crust adhere to the tofu, we dredge slices in a mixture of flour and beaten egg, creating a glue-like paste that locks the panko in place and then we sear them in a large nonstick skillet until appealingly browned. Ketchup, Worcestershire, soy sauce, garlic powder, and a pinch of sugar make up the tonkatsu sauce. Last but not least is the crunchy cabbage, which needs nothing more than a quick toss with some rice vinegar, toasty sesame oil, and a pinch of sugar for seasoning before it, too, is ready to be piled atop the bread (soft white sandwich bread in lieu of milk bread) and drizzled with sauce.

1 Whisk ketchup, Worcestershire, soy sauce, garlic powder, and ½ teaspoon sugar together in small bowl; set aside.

2 Whisk egg and flour together in shallow dish. Place panko in large zipper-lock bag and lightly crush with rolling pin; transfer to second shallow dish. Slice tofu crosswise into 8 (½-inch-thick) slabs, pat dry with paper towels, and sprinkle with salt. Working with 1 slab at a time, dip tofu in egg mixture, allowing excess to drip off, then coat all sides with panko, pressing gently to adhere; transfer to large plate.

3 Place wire rack in rimmed baking sheet and line half of rack with triple layer of paper towels. Heat vegetable oil in 12-inch nonstick skillet over medium-high heat until shimmering. Add tofu slabs and cook until deep golden brown, 2 to 3 minutes per side. Transfer tofu to paper towel-lined side of prepared rack to drain for about 15 seconds per side, then move to unlined side of rack.

4 Combine vinegar, sesame oil, and remaining ½ teaspoon sugar in large bowl. Add cabbage and toss to coat. Arrange cabbage and tofu on four slices of bread. Drizzle with sauce and top with remaining bread slices. Serve.

VARIATION

Tofu Katsu Sandwiches for Two

Halve all ingredients except vegetable oil. Proceed with recipe in 10- or 12-inch nonstick skillet.

Sizing Up Your Skillet

nonstick • **traditional cast iron**

A 12-inch nonstick skillet provides enough space to fry the tofu and can produce steady, even heat to create a uniform golden-brown crust. The slick surface of the skillet also ensures that the panko crust sticks to the tofu and not the skillet. A traditional cast-iron skillet will also work for these reasons; you will need to preheat the empty skillet over medium heat for 5 minutes before proceeding with step 3.

Ta'ameya with Tahini-Yogurt Sauce

Serves 4

Total Time 1 hour

¾ cup torn pita, plus 2 (8-inch) pitas, halved

½ teaspoon fennel seeds, toasted and cracked

21 ounces frozen shucked fava beans, thawed and outer casings removed

¼ cup chopped fresh cilantro and/or parsley

1 large egg

2 scallions, sliced thin

2 garlic cloves, minced

½ teaspoon baking powder

½ teaspoon ground coriander

½ teaspoon ground cumin

½ teaspoon table salt

¼ teaspoon pepper

2 teaspoons sesame seeds

½ cup extra-virgin olive oil for frying

1 tomato, cored and chopped

2 Persian cucumbers, halved lengthwise and sliced thin

½ red onion, sliced thin (½ cup)

½ cup Yogurt-Tahini Sauce (page 102)

1 teaspoon nigella seeds (optional)

Why This Recipe Works Falafel (balls or patties) nestled into pita bread and adorned with vegetables and tahini sauce is a delectable street-cart food across the Mediterranean. While a lot of falafel is made from ground chickpeas, falafel in Egypt, known as ta'ameya, uses sweet, nutty fava beans. The fried patties boast a gorgeous green hue amplified by plentiful fresh herbs and scallions. To make them, we first process torn pita pieces and fennel seeds in a food processor and then add the fava beans, cilantro, egg, scallions, and warm spices, plus a little baking powder for fluffiness. The ground pitas and an egg ensure that these falafel hold together when browned in a nonstick skillet. After forming the mixture into patties, we sprinkle them with sesame seeds, which increase the crispness that encases their luscious, creamy interiors. No falafel is complete without toppings, and a creamy yogurt-tahini sauce, plus juicy tomatoes, crisp cucumbers, and onions all add richness and freshness. To remove the outer casing of the fava beans, use a paring knife to make a small incision and then squeeze to remove the bean. You can use ¼ of an English cucumber in place of the Persian cucumbers.

1 Process torn pita pieces and fennel seeds in food processor until finely ground, about 15 seconds. Add fava beans, cilantro, egg, scallions, garlic, baking powder, coriander, cumin, salt, and pepper and pulse until fava beans are coarsely chopped and mixture is cohesive, about 15 pulses, scraping down sides of bowl as needed. Working with 2 tablespoons mixture at a time, shape into 2-inch-wide patties and transfer to large plate (you should have 16 patties). Sprinkle sesame seeds evenly over falafel patties; press lightly to adhere.

2 Set wire rack in rimmed baking sheet and line half of rack with triple layer of paper towels. Heat oil in 12-inch nonstick skillet over medium heat until shimmering. Add 8 patties and cook until deep golden brown, about 3 minutes per side, using 2 spatulas to carefully flip patties. Transfer falafel to paper towel–lined side of prepared rack to drain for about 30 seconds, then move to unlined side of rack. Repeat with remaining falafel, adjusting heat as needed if falafel begins to brown too quickly.

3 Stuff each pita half with falafel, tomato, cucumbers, and onion. Top with yogurt sauce and nigella seeds, if using. Serve.

Sizing Up Your Skillet

nonstick ● **traditional cast iron**

A 12-inch nonstick skillet provides enough space to fry the falafel in 2 batches and can produce steady, even heat to create a uniform golden-brown crust. The slick surface of the skillet also ensures that the pita crust sticks to the falafel and not the skillet. A traditional cast-iron skillet will also work for these reasons; you will need to preheat the empty skillet over medium heat for 5 minutes before proceeding with step 2.

CHAPTER FIVE

pasta & noodles

Pasta with Simple Tomato Sauce

Serves 4

Total Time 45 minutes

- 3 tablespoons extra-virgin olive oil
- 3 garlic cloves, minced
- 1 (28-ounce) can crushed tomatoes
- ½ teaspoon table salt
- ¼ teaspoon sugar
- 3 cups water
- 12 ounces (3¾ cups) penne, fusilli, or other short, tubular pasta
- ¼ cup chopped fresh basil

  Grated Parmesan or Pecorino Romano cheese (optional)

VARIATIONS

Pasta with Creamy Tomato Sauce

Reduce oil to 1 tablespoon. Add ¼ teaspoon red pepper flakes to skillet with garlic. Stir ¾ cup heavy cream into pasta after uncovering skillet. Add ½ cup grated Parmesan to sauce with basil.

Pasta with Simple Tomato Sauce for Two

Reduce crushed tomatoes to 1 (14.5-ounce) can or 1½ cups and reduce water to 2 cups; halve remaining ingredients. Proceed with recipe in 10- or 12-inch skillet.

Why This Recipe Works Consider this recipe a blueprint for making an incredibly easy one-pan skillet pasta with no need to boil water separately to cook the pasta. Simply add the ingredients to your skillet in stages and in 45 minutes you'll have a delicious meal with just one pan to clean up. When cooking pasta directly in sauce, the key to getting it al dente, with a well-textured sauce, starts with the right ratio of liquid to pasta. We achieve this by using 3 cups of water and a large can of crushed tomatoes for 12 ounces of penne—the greatest amount of pasta and sauce we found could comfortably be accommodated by most skillets. We especially like the tubular shape of penne, which traps the sauce inside. We cover the skillet to start so that the sauce doesn't dry out and our pasta remains fully submerged, ensuring that it cooks and hydrates evenly. Then we finish it uncovered to let the sauce reduce to the right consistency. Starch released from the pasta thickens the sauce and helps create a silky emulsion that clings to the pasta. Cooking garlic and other aromatics like chile flakes before adding tomatoes builds a deeper flavor base. You will need a 12-inch skillet with a 2-quart capacity and a tight-fitting lid for this recipe. If you have a skillet or straight-sided sauté pan with a larger capacity, you can increase the penne to 1 pound and the water to 3½ cups, leaving remaining ingredients unchanged.

1 Cook oil and garlic in 12-inch stainless-steel skillet over medium heat until fragrant but not brown, about 2 minutes. Stir in tomatoes, salt, and sugar. Bring to gentle simmer and cook, stirring occasionally, for 10 minutes.

2 Stir in water and penne, increase heat to medium-high, and bring to vigorous simmer. Reduce heat to medium, cover, and cook, stirring occasionally, until pasta is nearly al dente, about 8 minutes. Uncover and continue to cook, stirring gently, until pasta is al dente and sauce is thickened, 4 to 7 minutes; if sauce becomes too thick, add extra water as needed. Off heat, stir in basil and season with salt and pepper to taste. Serve, passing Parmesan, if using, separately.

VARIATION

Pasta with Meaty Tomato Sauce

Reduce oil to 1 tablespoon and increase garlic to 4 cloves. Add 8 ounces hot or sweet Italian sausage meat to skillet after garlic is fragrant and cook, breaking up meat with wooden spoon, until no longer pink, 3 to 5 minutes.

PASTA WITH SIMPLE TOMATO SAUCE

This method of cooking pasta right in a simple pantry-based sauce is a weeknight workhorse that makes the most of a skillet. It is also easy to vary using different aromatics and incorporating cream for richness or Italian sausage for a heartier meal.

1 Tubular Penne Are Ideal with This Method.

2 Build Sauce, Then Add Water and Pasta.

3 Cook Covered and Uncovered to Get the Right Saucy Consistency.

Sizing Up Your Skillet

stainless steel • **nonstick** • **enameled cast iron**

A 12-inch stainless-steel skillet provides enough space for simmering the pasta and sauce. A nonstick or enameled cast-iron skillet will also work for this reason. Due to the acidic cooking liquid, we do not recommend using a traditional cast-iron or carbon-steel skillet.

Sizing Up Your Skillet

- nonstick

A 12-inch nonstick skillet provides enough space for simmering the spaghetti and ensures that the pasta doesn't stick to the pan while crisping. Due to the acidic cooking liquid, we do not recommend using a traditional cast-iron or carbon-steel skillet.

Spaghetti all'Assassina

Serves 4

Total Time 1¼ hours

6   cups boiling water

¼   cup tomato paste

1   teaspoon sugar

⅓   cup plus 2 tablespoons extra-virgin
     olive oil, divided

2   garlic cloves, minced

½   teaspoon red pepper flakes

1   cup tomato passata

1¾   teaspoons table salt

12   ounces spaghetti

Why This Recipe Works This is another dish where the pasta cooks right in the sauce, but it probably is unlike any spaghetti you've ever had—unless you've dined out in Bari, the bustling port city on Italy's Adriatic cost (or taken a deep dive into books on classic Italian cooking). The defining aspects of this dish are spaghetti strands with textures that run from soft to al dente to crisp (even within a single strand) and a spicy, concentrated tomato sauce that clings tightly to the pasta. To achieve these hallmarks, we start by making a sauce with a generous amount of extra-virgin olive oil, garlic, red pepper flakes, and passata di pomodoro (uncooked tomato puree) in a nonstick skillet. We then add raw spaghetti, followed periodically by cupfuls of a simple tomato broth (tomato paste diluted with water). Each time the pan threatens to dry out, we add more broth. We make sure not to stir the pasta too much as it turns tender and starts to crisp in spots. To finish this delicious, deeply satisfying dish, we turn the heat to full blast so that some of the strands develop a smoky char. This recipe was developed with our winning spaghetti, De Cecco Spaghetti no. 12. Other brands of spaghetti may vary in thickness, which will affect the cooking time and the amount of broth required. Fish spatulas work well for flipping the pasta in step 4. We use the Pomì brand of passata; if you cannot find it, tomato puree can be used. For a spicier dish, use ¾ teaspoon red pepper flakes. The sauce will splatter as it cooks, which is why we call for using a long-handled spatula in step 2; a splatter screen helps contain the splattering.

1 Whisk boiling water, tomato paste, and sugar together in bowl; cover to keep warm. Heat ⅓ cup oil, garlic, and pepper flakes in 12-inch nonstick skillet over medium heat. Cook, stirring frequently with long-handled rubber spatula, until garlic is golden brown, about 2 minutes. Stir in passata and salt. Cook, stirring frequently, until sauce thickens and oil around edges of skillet begins to sizzle, about 4 minutes.

2 Add pasta in even layer and increase heat to medium-high. Add 1 cup tomato broth and cook, pushing between pasta strands frequently with edge of spatula to prevent clumping, until broth has been mostly absorbed by pasta and sauce around edges of skillet begins to sizzle, 4 to 5 minutes. Add 1 cup broth and cook, shaking skillet occasionally and continuing to prod pasta strands with spatula, until broth has been mostly absorbed and sauce begins to sizzle, 5 to 7 minutes.

3 Using 2 thin spatulas, gently flip half of pasta so bottom is on top and spread into even layer. Repeat with remaining half of pasta. Add 1 cup broth and cook, continuing to shake skillet and prod pasta, until broth has been mostly absorbed and sauce begins to sizzle, 5 to 7 minutes. Add 1 cup broth and repeat cooking until sauce begins to sizzle, 5 to 7 minutes. Repeat dividing and flipping pasta.

4 Add 1 cup broth and repeat cooking until sauce begins to sizzle, 5 to 7 minutes. Pasta should be firm but cooked through. If not, add remaining 1 cup broth, ½ cup at a time, and continue to cook, checking frequently, until pasta is cooked through.

5 Increase heat to high and cook pasta, without moving it, until underside is deeply browned and crisp and some strands are beginning to char, 3 to 5 minutes. Remove skillet from heat, drizzle with remaining 2 tablespoons oil, and serve immediately.

Shrimp Scampi with Campanelle

Serves 4

Total Time 1 hour

1½ pounds extra-large shrimp (21 to 25 per pound), peeled, deveined, and tails removed, shells reserved

¾ teaspoon table salt, divided

¼ teaspoon pepper

2 tablespoons extra-virgin olive oil, divided

1 cup dry white wine

3 cups water, plus extra as needed

8 garlic cloves, minced

¼ teaspoon red pepper flakes

8 ounces (2½ cups) campanelle

2 tablespoons unsalted butter

2 tablespoons minced fresh parsley

½ teaspoon grated lemon zest plus 1 tablespoon juice, plus lemon wedges for serving

Why This Recipe Works Sautéed shrimp and a bright lemon-garlic sauce come together seamlessly in this one-pot interpretation of the Italian classic shrimp scampi. The key to making this pasta dish more than the sum of its parts is to coax maximum flavor out of each ingredient. To that end, we save the shrimp shells and make a quick shrimp broth by simmering them in our skillet with white wine and water. We use this flavorful liquid to cook our pasta, which becomes infused with the shrimp's briny flavor as the liquid reduces. Finally, we finish the dish with fresh parsley, bright lemon zest and juice, and a little butter for good measure. We prefer untreated shrimp, but if your shrimp are treated with sodium or preservatives like sodium tripolyphosphate, skip the salting in step 1. You can substitute penne, ziti, medium shells, or farfalle for the campanelle; however, the cup measurements will vary. See page 339 for more information on pasta sizes and volume amounts. You will need a 12-inch skillet with a tight-fitting lid for this recipe.

1 Toss shrimp with ¼ teaspoon salt and pepper; set aside. Heat 1 tablespoon oil in 12-inch stainless-steel skillet over medium-high heat until shimmering. Add shrimp shells and cook, stirring frequently, until they turn bright pink, 2 to 4 minutes. Stir in wine and simmer for 2 minutes. Stir in water, bring to simmer, and cook for 5 minutes. Strain shrimp stock through fine-mesh strainer into large bowl, pressing on solids to extract as much liquid as possible; discard shells. (You should have about 3 cups liquid; if necessary, supplement with extra water.) Wipe skillet clean with paper towels.

2 Cook remaining 1 tablespoon oil, garlic, and pepper flakes in now-empty skillet over medium-low heat, stirring occasionally, until garlic is fragrant and just beginning to brown, about 3 minutes. Stir in shrimp stock, campanelle, and remaining ½ teaspoon salt. Increase heat to medium-high and bring to vigorous simmer. Reduce heat to medium, cover, and cook, stirring occasionally, until pasta is nearly al dente, about 8 minutes.

3 Stir in shrimp, return to simmer, and cook, uncovered, stirring often, until shrimp are opaque throughout, pasta is al dente, and sauce has thickened, 3 to 5 minutes; if sauce becomes too thick, add extra water as needed. Off heat, stir in butter, parsley, and lemon zest and juice until butter has melted. Season with salt and pepper to taste. Serve with lemon wedges.

Sizing Up Your Skillet

stainless steel • nonstick • traditional cast iron • enameled cast iron

A 12-inch stainless-steel skillet provides enough space for simmering the pasta and sauce. A nonstick, traditional cast-iron, or enameled cast-iron skillet will also work for this reason. If using a traditional cast-iron skillet, you will need to preheat the empty skillet over medium heat for 3 minutes before proceeding with step 1.

Pearl Couscous with Chorizo and Chickpeas

Serves 4 to 6

Total Time 45 minutes

8   ounces Spanish-style chorizo, cut into ½-inch pieces

2   cups pearl couscous

2   teaspoons smoked paprika

2   teaspoons ground cumin

2⅔ cups chicken or vegetable broth

4   carrots, peeled and chopped

2   (15-ounce) cans chickpeas, rinsed and patted dry

½   cup chopped fresh parsley

½   cup raisins

2   tablespoons extra-virgin olive oil

2   tablespoons lemon juice, plus lemon wedges for serving

Why This Recipe Works This warm pasta salad is flavored aggressively with chunks of chorizo and smoked paprika and is so delicious you will want to eat it right out of the skillet, not to mention save some for the next day's lunch. As a bonus, it comes together very quickly once the couscous is cooked since you simply need to add the remaining ingredients. First, we toast pearl couscous in a skillet with chorizo and carrots and then stir in broth with some smoked paprika and cumin and let the couscous cook through absorption in the covered skillet. Creamy canned chickpeas contrast with the chewy pasta and add heft, while parsley freshens up this warm, spicy dish. Raisins provide even more textural contrast as well as sweetness, and a squeeze of lemon juice brightens all these beautiful flavors. Pearl couscous is sometimes labeled Israeli couscous. You will need a 12-inch skillet with a tight-fitting lid for this recipe.

1 Cook chorizo in 12-inch stainless-steel skillet over medium heat until fat begins to render, about 5 minutes. Stir in couscous, paprika, and cumin and cook until fragrant, about 3 minutes. Stir in broth and carrots, scraping up any browned bits, and bring to simmer. Cover, reduce heat to low, and simmer, stirring occasionally, until broth is absorbed, 10 to 15 minutes. Let sit off heat, covered, for 3 minutes.

2 Stir in chickpeas, parsley, raisins, oil, and lemon juice. Season with salt and pepper to taste. Serve with lemon wedges.

Sizing Up Your Skillet

stainless steel • **nonstick** • **traditional cast iron** • **enameled cast iron**

A 12-inch stainless-steel skillet provides enough space for simmering the couscous and folding in the chickpeas and aromatics. A nonstick, traditional cast-iron, or enameled cast-iron skillet will also work for these reasons.

Tortellini with Fennel, Peas, and Spinach

Serves 4

Total Time 45 minutes

2 ounces thinly sliced prosciutto, cut into ¼-inch pieces

1 tablespoon unsalted butter

1 fennel bulb, stalks discarded, bulb halved, cored, and cut into ½-inch pieces

2 garlic cloves, minced

2¾ cups chicken broth

2 (9-ounce) packages fresh cheese tortellini

½ cup heavy cream

5 ounces (5 cups) baby spinach

1 cup frozen peas

1 ounce Parmesan cheese, grated (½ cup), plus extra for serving

1 tablespoon lemon juice

Why This Recipe Works For most people, grabbing a few packages of fresh tortellini is a desperation move to get dinner on the table. But this recipe shows how to make tortellini into a special and elegant meal in short order. It's not as fast as boiling it and adding jarred sauce, but it is ever so much more satisfying. Tender tortellini, spring vegetables, and a luxurious (but not overly rich) sauce utilize just one pan and cook in under an hour. Fennel, peas, and spinach are the perfect trio of vegetables, providing sweetness, freshness, and texture. Browning the fennel in butter in a skillet deepens its flavor before adding the cooking liquid (chicken broth works well here) and pasta. Once the tortellini are tender and the sauce is nicely thickened, we add quick-cooking spinach and peas, along with some cream for richness and body. Parmesan helps thicken the sauce and contributes nutty flavor, while a splash of lemon juice adds brightness. To top it all off, we add a garnish of crisped prosciutto, which we cooked first and set aside—this enables us to incorporate its rendered fat into the dish, adding another layer of flavor. For the best flavor and texture, be sure to buy fresh tortellini sold in the refrigerator case at the supermarket. Do not substitute frozen or dried tortellini, as they require different liquid amounts and will not work in this recipe. You will need a 12-inch skillet with a tight-fitting lid for this recipe.

1 Cook prosciutto in 12-inch stainless-steel skillet oven over medium heat, stirring often, until browned and crisp, 5 to 7 minutes. Using slotted spoon, transfer prosciutto to paper towel–lined plate.

2 Add butter to fat left in skillet and cook fennel until softened and lightly browned, 6 to 9 minutes. Stir in garlic and cook until fragrant, about 30 seconds. Stir in broth and tortellini, increase heat to medium-high, and bring to vigorous simmer. Reduce heat to medium, cover, and cook, stirring occasionally, until tortellini is tender and sauce is thickened, 6 to 9 minutes.

3 Uncover; reduce heat to low; and stir in cream, spinach, and peas. Cook, stirring gently, until spinach is wilted and tortellini is coated in sauce, 2 to 3 minutes. Off heat, stir in Parmesan and lemon juice and season with salt and pepper to taste. Adjust consistency with water as needed. Serve, sprinkling individual portions with prosciutto and extra Parmesan.

VARIATION

Tortellini with Fennel, Peas, and Spinach for Two

Reduce broth to 1½ cups; halve remaining ingredients except for butter. Proceed with recipe in 10- or 12-inch skillet.

Sizing Up Your Skillet

stainless steel • **nonstick** • **traditional cast iron** • **enameled cast iron**

A 12-inch stainless-steel skillet provides enough space for simmering the tortellini and folding in the vegetables. A nonstick, traditional cast-iron, or enameled cast-iron skillet will also work for these reasons.

Crispy Gnocchi with Shredded Brussels Sprouts and Gorgonzola

Serves 4

Total Time 40 minutes

3 tablespoons extra-virgin olive oil, divided

1 pound vacuum-packed gnocchi

1 red onion, halved and sliced thin

1 pound brussels sprouts, trimmed, halved, and sliced thin

½ teaspoon table salt

3 ounces Gorgonzola cheese, crumbled (¾ cup), divided

1 tablespoon white wine vinegar

2 teaspoons minced fresh sage

1 tablespoon honey, plus extra for drizzling

3 tablespoons chopped toasted walnuts

Why This Recipe Works Making your own gnocchi is certainly something to strive for, as its ethereal texture lends itself to the simplest of preparations. But what could one do with the ubiquitous vacuum-packed bags of gnocchi that are in every grocery store? Our answer: Forget about boiling them and sear them first. In a hot nonstick skillet, with a glug of oil and a handful of minutes, store-bought gnocchi transforms into crispy little hot nuggets with lacy edges and satisfyingly chewy interiors. To complete the meal, we build a dry "sauce" in the pan by softening sweet red onions and sautéing brussels sprouts. Off the heat we add an abundant amount of creamy Gorgonzola to bind everything together and then white wine vinegar to cut its richness. A little sage pairs beautifully with the shaved brussels sprouts and cheese. For a crowning touch, we drizzle the final dish with honey and sprinkle on more cheese and some toasted walnuts. Suddenly grocery store gnocchi feels like something you might be served in a fine restaurant. The partially cooked, vacuum-packed gnocchi found in the pasta aisle work best here. Refrigerated gnocchi can also be used; avoid frozen gnocchi. A food processor's slicing blade can be used to slice the brussels sprouts; do not halve them before processing.

1 Heat 2 tablespoons oil in 12-inch nonstick skillet over medium-high heat until shimmering. Add gnocchi, separating pieces with wooden spoon. Cook, without moving gnocchi, until well browned on first side, 5 to 7 minutes. Stir gnocchi and continue to cook until heated through, about 2 minutes; transfer to bowl.

2 Heat remaining 1 tablespoon oil in now-empty skillet over medium-high heat until shimmering. Add onion and cook until starting to soften, about 3 minutes. Stir in brussels sprouts and salt and spread into even layer. Cook, stirring occasionally, until sprouts are spotty brown and just tender, 5 to 7 minutes.

3 Off heat, stir in gnocchi, ½ cup Gorgonzola, vinegar, and sage until Gorgonzola is melted and coats gnocchi. Season with salt and pepper to taste. Drizzle with honey and sprinkle with walnuts and remaining ¼ cup Gorgonzola. Serve, passing extra honey for drizzling.

VARIATION

Crispy Gnocchi with Shredded Brussels Sprouts and Gorgonzola for Two

Halve all ingredients. Proceed with recipe in 10- or 12-inch nonstick skillet.

Sizing Up Your Skillet

nonstick • traditional cast iron

A 12-inch nonstick skillet provides enough space to brown the gnocchi and sauté the brussels sprouts. The slick surface of the skillet also ensures that the golden-brown crust sticks to the gnocchi and not the skillet. A traditional cast-iron skillet will also work for these reasons; you will need to preheat the empty skillet over medium heat for 3 minutes before proceeding with step 1.

Cheesy Stuffed Shells

Serves 6 to 8

Total Time 2 hours

2 tablespoons extra-virgin olive oil

1 onion, chopped

¾ teaspoon table salt, divided

6 garlic cloves, minced, divided

¼ teaspoon red pepper flakes

1 (28-ounce) can tomato puree

2 cups water

1 teaspoon sugar

½ teaspoon pepper

10 ounces (1¼ cups) whole-milk ricotta cheese

8 ounces fontina cheese, shredded (2 cups), divided

2 ounces Pecorino Romano cheese, grated (1 cup)

2 large eggs

¼ cup chopped fresh basil, divided

4 teaspoons cornstarch

1 teaspoon dried oregano

24 jumbo pasta shells

Why This Recipe Works Unless you have a lazy Sunday afternoon (or an Italian grandmother), making stuffed shells is a once-in-a-while occurrence, as they can be a lot of work. For an easier version, we aimed to press a skillet into service and, like many of our skillet pasta recipes, we wanted to avoid boiling the shells separately. We found that the quickest and easiest way to fill the raw pasta shells was to choose jumbo shells with wide openings and pipe in the filling using a pastry bag. For a supercheesy filling, we mix creamy ricotta, shredded fontina, and grated Pecorino Romano cheeses with savory minced garlic, fragrant chopped fresh basil, and dried oregano. A little cornstarch keeps the ricotta from becoming grainy once it is baked. We also stir in two eggs to make the filling pipable and to keep it from oozing out of the shells during baking. Covering the filled shells with a thin tomato sauce, which we create in our skillet, allows the raw pasta to cook through properly during baking, absorbing liquid while still leaving behind a full-bodied—not chunky or dehydrated—sauce. Plus, it means that this family favorite is a one-pan meal! We first bake the shells covered to trap in as much moisture as possible to cook the pasta and then uncover the skillet to brown the cheese sprinkled over the top and reduce the sauce. Shred the fontina on the large holes of a box grater. Be sure to use only open, unbroken shells. We developed this recipe using Barilla Jumbo Shells and were able to easily find at least 24 open shells in each 1-pound box we used. You will need a 12-inch ovensafe skillet with a tight-fitting lid for this recipe.

1 Adjust oven rack to middle position and heat oven to 400 degrees. Heat oil in 12-inch ovensafe stainless-steel skillet over medium heat until shimmering. Add onion and ½ teaspoon salt and cook until softened and lightly browned, 5 to 7 minutes. Stir in two-thirds of garlic and pepper flakes and cook until fragrant, about 30 seconds. Stir in tomato puree, water, sugar, and pepper and bring to simmer. Reduce heat to medium-low and cook until flavors have melded, about 5 minutes. Off heat, measure out and reserve 2 cups sauce; leave remaining sauce in skillet.

2 Stir ricotta, 1 cup fontina, Pecorino, eggs, 3 tablespoons basil, cornstarch, oregano, remaining ¼ teaspoon salt, and remaining garlic in bowl until thoroughly combined. Transfer filling to pastry bag or large zipper-lock bag (if using zipper-lock bag, cut 1 inch off 1 corner of bag). Place shells open side up on counter. Pipe filling into shells until each is about three-quarters full. Divide remaining filling evenly among shells.

3 Arrange shells open side up in skillet and spoon reserved sauce evenly over tops. Cover and bake until shells are tender, about 45 minutes.

4 Using pot holders, remove skillet from oven. Being careful of hot skillet handle, sprinkle shells with remaining 1 cup fontina. Return skillet to oven and bake, uncovered, until fontina is spotty brown, about 15 minutes. Let shells cool for 10 minutes. Sprinkle with remaining 1 tablespoon basil before serving.

Sizing Up Your Skillet

stainless steel • nonstick • enameled cast iron

A 12-inch stainless-steel skillet provides enough space for creating the sauce and simmering the stuffed shells. An ovensafe nonstick or enameled cast-iron skillet will also work for these reasons. If using an enameled cast-iron skillet, you will need to preheat the empty skillet over medium heat for 3 minutes before proceeding with step 1. Due to the acidic cooking liquid, we do not recommend using a traditional cast-iron or carbon-steel skillet.

Simple Stovetop Macaroni and Cheese

Serves 4

Total Time 45 minutes

½ cup panko bread crumbs

2 tablespoons extra-virgin olive oil

⅛ teaspoon table salt

⅛ teaspoon pepper

2 tablespoons grated Parmesan cheese

1¾ cups water

1 cup milk

8 ounces elbow macaroni or small shells

4 ounces American cheese, shredded (1 cup)

½ teaspoon Dijon mustard

4 ounces extra-sharp cheddar cheese, shredded (1 cup)

Why This Recipe Works This is a fast and fuss-free macaroni and cheese to make in a skillet without the bother of a béchamel or custard (and the need to dirty multiple pots). Inspired by an innovative macaroni and cheese recipe that calls for adding sodium citrate, an emulsifying salt, to cheese to keep it smooth when heated (instead of adding flour to make a béchamel), we base our sauce on American cheese, which contains a similar ingredient. Because American cheese has plenty of emulsifiers but not a lot of flavor, we combine it with more-flavorful extra-sharp cheddar. A bit of mustard and cayenne pepper add piquancy. We cook the macaroni in a smaller-than-usual amount of water (along with some milk) so that we don't have to drain it; the liquid left after the elbows are hydrated is just enough to form the base of the sauce. Rather than bake the mac and cheese, we sprinkle crunchy, cheesy toasted panko bread crumbs on top. Because the macaroni is cooked in a measured amount of liquid, we don't recommend using different shapes or sizes of pasta. Use a 4-ounce block of American cheese from the deli counter rather than presliced cheese. You will need a 12-inch skillet with a tight-fitting lid for this recipe.

1 Combine panko, oil, salt, and pepper in 12-inch stainless-steel skillet until panko is evenly moistened. Cook over medium heat, stirring frequently, until evenly browned, about 5 minutes. Transfer panko mixture to small bowl and stir in Parmesan; set aside for serving. Wipe skillet clean with paper towels.

2 Bring water and milk to boil in now-empty skillet over high heat. Stir in macaroni and reduce to vigorous simmer. Cook, stirring frequently, until macaroni is soft (slightly past al dente), 6 to 8 minutes. Add American cheese and mustard and cook, stirring constantly, until cheese is completely melted, about 1 minute. Off heat, stir in cheddar until evenly distributed but not necessarily melted. Cover skillet and let sit for 5 minutes.

3 Stir macaroni until sauce is smooth (sauce may look loose but will thicken as it cools). Season with salt and pepper to taste. Sprinkle panko mixture over top and serve immediately.

VARIATION

Simple Stovetop Macaroni and Cheese for Two

Reduce both salt and pepper to pinch and water to 1 cup; halve remaining ingredients. Proceed with recipe in 10- or 12-inch skillet.

Sizing Up Your Skillet

stainless steel • **nonstick** • **traditional cast iron** • **enameled cast iron**

A 12-inch stainless-steel skillet provides enough space for simmering the pasta and sauce. A 12-inch nonstick, traditional cast-iron, or enameled cast-iron skillet will also work for this reason.

Ground Beef Stroganoff

Serves 4

Total Time 50 minutes

2 tablespoons vegetable oil, divided

8 ounces white mushrooms, trimmed and sliced thin

1 teaspoon table salt, divided

1 onion, chopped fine

2 garlic cloves, minced

¾ teaspoon pepper, divided

1 pound 85 percent lean ground beef

3 tablespoons all-purpose flour

4 cups chicken broth

¼ cup dry white wine

8 ounces (4 cups) egg noodles

½ cup sour cream, plus extra for serving

2 tablespoons minced fresh parsley or chives

Why This Recipe Works Stroganoff, the hearty blend of beef and mushrooms in a sour cream–enriched gravy served over egg noodles, has countless iterations, from the fanciest versions using pricey beef tenderloin to recipes that prize convenience over all else, relying on canned cream of mushroom soup. This recipe comes together fast enough to make anytime but skips the canned soup in favor of fresh mushrooms, good-quality store-bought broth, and white wine. It also uses 85 percent lean ground beef for both speed and big beefy flavor. Increasing the typical amounts of liquid to cook the noodles right in the sauce makes it a one-pot meal to boot. After sautéing sliced mushrooms until browned, transfer them to a bowl, soften some onion and garlic, and then add the ground beef. A bit of flour thickens the juices, and then the noodles simmer in the liquid. Ten minutes later, the noodles will be tender and the flavors melded. Stir in some tangy sour cream to finish your stroganoff in style.

1 Heat 1 tablespoon oil in 12-inch stainless-steel skillet over medium-high heat until shimmering. Add mushrooms and ¼ teaspoon salt and cook until liquid has evaporated and mushrooms begin to brown, 5 to 7 minutes; transfer to bowl.

2 Heat remaining 1 tablespoon oil in now-empty skillet over medium-high heat until shimmering. Add onion, garlic, ½ teaspoon salt, and ½ teaspoon pepper and cook until softened, about 5 minutes. Add beef, remaining ¼ teaspoon salt, and remaining ¼ teaspoon pepper and cook, breaking up meat with wooden spoon, until no longer pink, 5 to 7 minutes.

3 Stir in flour until beef is well coated and cook for 1 minute. Stir in broth and wine and bring to simmer, scraping up any browned bits. Cook until mixture is slightly thickened, about 3 minutes. Stir in noodles, reduce heat to medium, and cook, uncovered, until noodles are tender, 10 to 12 minutes, stirring occasionally.

4 Off heat, stir in sour cream and mushrooms until fully combined. Season with salt and pepper to taste. Serve, sprinkling individual bowls with parsley and passing extra sour cream.

Sizing Up Your Skillet

stainless steel ● **nonstick** ● **traditional cast iron** ● **enameled cast iron**

A 12-inch stainless-steel skillet provides enough space for simmering the noodles and sauce. A nonstick, traditional cast-iron, or enameled cast-iron skillet will also work for this reason. If using a cast-iron skillet, you will need to preheat the empty skillet over medium heat for 3 minutes before proceeding with step 1.

Tuna Noodle Casserole

Serves 4 to 6

Total Time 40 minutes

2 tablespoons unsalted butter

10 ounces cremini or white mushrooms, trimmed and sliced thin

1 onion, chopped fine

½ teaspoon table salt

8 ounces egg noodles (3 cups)

2 cups chicken broth

1 cup heavy cream

3 (5-ounce) cans solid white tuna in water, drained and flaked

1 cup frozen peas

2 tablespoons minced fresh parsley

1 cup crushed kettle-style potato chips or Ritz or saltine crackers

Lemon wedges

Why This Recipe Works It has long been considered a dowdy budget dish, but this unabashedly old-school casserole, when made with fresh ingredients and just a little care, earns its justified place in the modern comfort-food pantheon. Here we trade in a casserole dish for a large skillet and begin by sautéing mushrooms and onions in butter until they are lightly browned; the mushrooms add a deep savory note and a little bit of upscale elegance to this delightfully creamy dish. Next, we simply simmer the noodles in a rich mixture of broth and cream until tender. Now it's time to add the mix-ins: the mushroom mixture, along with tuna, peas, and fresh parsley. For the crispiest topping, sprinkle crushed potato chips or crackers over the casserole or over individual bowls before serving. You will need a 12-inch skillet with tight-fitting lid for this recipe.

1 Melt butter in 12-inch stainless-steel skillet over medium heat. Add mushrooms, onion, and salt. Cook until vegetables are softened and lightly browned, about 15 minutes; transfer to bowl.

2 Combine noodles, broth, and cream in now-empty skillet and bring to simmer over medium-high heat. Reduce heat to medium-low, cover, and cook, stirring occasionally, until noodles are tender, about 10 minutes.

3 Stir in mushroom mixture, tuna, peas, and parsley and allow to heat through, about 1 minute. Season with salt and pepper to taste. Top with crushed potato chips and serve, passing lemon wedges separately.

Sizing Up Your Skillet

stainless steel • **nonstick** • **traditional cast iron** • **enameled cast iron**

A 12-inch stainless-steel skillet provides enough space for simmering the casserole. A 12-inch nonstick, traditional cast-iron, or enameled cast-iron skillet will also work for this reason. If using a cast-iron skillet, you will need to preheat the empty skillet over medium heat for 3 minutes before proceeding with step 1.

Scallion Oil Noodles

Serves 4

Total Time 30 minutes

¼	cup light soy sauce
2	tablespoons dark soy sauce
5	teaspoons sugar
15–18	scallions (6 ounces), white and green parts separated
1	(1-inch) piece ginger, peeled
4	(3-ounce) packages ramen noodles, seasoning packets discarded
½	cup plus 2 teaspoons vegetable oil, divided
4	large eggs
½	English cucumber, cut into 2-inch matchsticks
1	carrot, peeled and cut into 2-inch matchsticks

Why This Recipe Works Scallion oil noodles, a popular Shanghainese dish, features springy noodles liberally dressed with scallion-infused oil, savory soy sauce, and sugar for balance. Traditionally, fresh wheat noodles are used, but they need to be boiled in plenty of water to help remove their excess starch. For convenience, we simply hydrate ramen noodles with boiling water to serve as the vehicle for our intensely flavored sauce. We slowly simmer scallions and strips of ginger (for freshness) in peanut oil to draw out their flavors. Dark soy sauce, light soy sauce, and sugar are added to form a glossy, savory-sweet sauce. A sprinkling of fresh cucumber and carrot helps cut through the richness, and a final topping of a soft-cooked fried egg completes the meal. Folding the runny yolk into the finished noodles adds a roundness to the complex, salty-sweet soy sauce. We prefer to use a combination of Chinese light and dark soy sauces here. If dark soy sauce is unavailable, omit it and increase the light soy sauce to 6 tablespoons; however, the flavor will not be as nuanced. Feel free to personalize these noodles further by topping them with pea shoots, bean sprouts, sliced radish, and/or cilantro leaves.

1 Combine light soy sauce, dark soy sauce, and sugar in small bowl; set aside. Halve scallion whites lengthwise, then slice into 1½-inch segments. Slice green parts into 1½-inch segments. Slice ginger crosswise into thin rounds. Stack rounds and slice into thin matchsticks.

2 Place noodles in large bowl and cover with 2 quarts boiling water. Let sit until just tender, about 5 minutes, stirring once halfway through soaking. Drain noodles and set aside.

3 Meanwhile, heat ½ cup oil in 12-inch nonstick skillet over medium heat until shimmering. Add scallions and ginger and cook, stirring often, until golden and wilted, 6 to 9 minutes.

4 Stir soy sauce mixture to recombine and add to scallion mixture in skillet. Cook, stirring often, until sugar is dissolved and sauce is rapidly bubbling, 1 to 2 minutes. Add noodles and toss until evenly coated in sauce and heated through, 2 to 3 minutes. Transfer noodles to serving bowls. Wipe skillet clean with paper towels.

5 Crack 2 eggs into small bowl. Repeat with remaining 2 eggs in second small bowl. Heat remaining 2 teaspoons oil in now-empty skillet over medium-high heat until shimmering. Working quickly, pour 1 bowl of eggs into 1 side of pan and second bowl of eggs into other side. Cover and cook for 1 minute. Remove skillet from burner and let stand, covered, for 15 to 45 seconds for runny yolks (white around edge of yolk will be barely opaque), 45 to 60 seconds for soft but set yolks, or about 2 minutes for medium-set yolks. Separate eggs and slide onto noodles, then top with cucumber and carrot. Serve.

Sizing Up Your Skillet

nonstick • traditional cast iron • carbon steel

A 12-inch nonstick skillet provides enough space to prepare the noodles and fry the eggs without concern for sticking. A traditional cast-iron or carbon-steel skillet will also work for these reasons. If using a traditional cast-iron skillet, you will need to preheat the empty skillet over medium heat for 3 minutes before proceeding with step 3.

Sizing Up Your Skillet

carbon steel • nonstick

A traditional 12-inch carbon-steel skillet is a good alternative to the traditional 14-inch flat-bottomed wok used for stir-frying because its relative light weight allows for ease while tossing, and its superior heat retention provides for rapid high-heat cooking. While a 12-inch nonstick skillet does not have the same heat retention, it can also be used.

Singapore Noodles

Serves 4 to 6

Total Time 1 hour

6 ounces mei fun (dried rice vermicelli)

12 ounces large shrimp (26 to 30 per pound), peeled, deveined, and tails removed

½ teaspoon table salt, divided

6 tablespoons vegetable oil, divided

6 ounces char siu (Chinese barbecue pork), sliced thin (optional)

4 large eggs

2 large shallots, halved and sliced thin

1 red or green bell pepper, stemmed, seeded, and sliced thin

3 garlic cloves, minced

1 teaspoon grated fresh ginger

2 tablespoons curry powder

⅛ teaspoon cayenne pepper

¼ cup water

2 tablespoons soy sauce

1 teaspoon sugar

4 ounces (2 cups) bean sprouts

4 scallions, sliced thin

VARIATION

Singapore Noodles for Two

Reduce oil to ¼ cup; use 2 teaspoons oil in step 2, 2 teaspoons oil in step 3, 2 teaspoons oil in step 4, and 2 tablespoons oil in step 5. Halve remaining ingredients, but do not reduce volume of boiling water in step 1. Proceed with recipe in 12-inch carbon-steel skillet.

Why This Recipe Works Thin, resilient rice noodles, Chinese seasonings—garlic, ginger, soy sauce—and fragrant curry powder come together in this stir-fry which, despite its name, is native to Hong Kong. The curry powder (likely a British influence) lends a distinctive aroma balanced by a little sugar for sweetness and bright lime juice. Overall, the typical ingredient list is simple—dried noodles, eggs, shrimp, vegetables, and a handful of seasonings. Some versions add char siu or ham. Some go heavier on veggies such as bean sprouts or cabbage; others focus on the noodles. Regardless of add-ins, this stir-fry isn't saucy; instead it's light, almost fluffy. To distribute the seasonings evenly and avoid grittiness, we bloom the curry powder and aromatics in oil, releasing fat-soluble flavor compounds while also keeping the dish from tasting too lean. We cook our ingredients in the pan in stages, adding a bit more oil with each to assure browning and avoid sticking. Finally, we add our softened noodles to the skillet and toss with the curry, cayenne, and soy sauce mixture to heat through. Mei fun are often labeled rice vermicelli. When shopping, make sure to buy a Chinese brand. Other kinds of rice vermicelli may be too thin and stick together after soaking. This dish progresses quickly; it's important that your ingredients are ready to go when you start stir-frying. We prefer untreated shrimp, but if your shrimp are treated with sodium or preservatives like sodium tripolyphosphate, skip the salting in step 2.

1 Place noodles in large bowl and cover with 2 quarts boiling water. Let sit until just tender, about 3 minutes, stirring once halfway through soaking. Drain noodles and transfer to greased wire rack set in rimmed baking sheet; set aside.

2 Cut shrimp in half lengthwise, pat dry with paper towels, and sprinkle with ¼ teaspoon salt. Heat 1 tablespoon oil in 12-inch carbon-steel skillet over high heat until just beginning to smoke. Add shrimp and cook, tossing slowly but constantly, until opaque throughout, about 2 minutes. Add char siu, if using, and cook, stirring frequently, until heated through, about 1 minute; transfer to bowl.

3 Beat eggs and remaining ¼ teaspoon salt in separate bowl until well combined. Heat 2 teaspoons oil in now-empty skillet over high heat until just smoking. Add eggs and cook, stirring constantly, until very little liquid egg remains, 30 to 60 seconds; transfer to bowl with shrimp mixture.

4 Heat 1 tablespoon oil in again-empty skillet over medium-high heat until just smoking. Add shallots and bell pepper and cook, tossing slowly but constantly, until crisp-tender, about 2 minutes. Push vegetables to 1 side of skillet and add 1 teaspoon oil, garlic, and ginger to clearing. Cook, mashing mixture into skillet, until fragrant, about 30 seconds. Stir garlic-ginger mixture into vegetables, then transfer to bowl with shrimp, char siu, and eggs.

5 Add remaining 3 tablespoons oil to again-empty skillet and heat over medium heat until just smoking. Off heat, add curry powder and cayenne. Cook, stirring constantly, until fragrant and darkened in color, about 2 minutes. Stir in water, soy sauce, and sugar until sugar has dissolved.

6 Return skillet to medium heat, add noodles, and toss gently until well coated. Add shrimp mixture and bean sprouts and cook, tossing gently, until heated through, about 1 minute. Sprinkle with scallions and serve.

Bún Chả

Serves 4 to 6

Total Time 1 hour

Noodles and Salad

8   ounces bún (dried rice vermicelli)

1   head Boston or Bibb lettuce (8 ounces), leaves separated and torn into bite-size pieces

1   English cucumber, peeled, quartered lengthwise, seeded, and sliced thin on bias

1   cup fresh cilantro leaves and tender stems

1   cup fresh mint or Thai basil leaves, torn if large

Nước Chấm

1   small Thai chile, stemmed and minced

3   tablespoons sugar, divided

1   garlic clove, minced

⅔   cup hot water

5   tablespoons fish sauce

¼   cup lime juice (2 limes)

Pork Patties

1   large shallot, minced

1   tablespoon fish sauce

1½   teaspoons sugar

½   teaspoon baking soda

½   teaspoon pepper

1   pound ground pork

2   teaspoons vegetable oil

VARIATION

Bún Chả for Two

Halve all ingredients, but do not reduce volume of boiling water in step 1. Proceed with recipe in 10- or 12-inch cast-iron skillet.

Why This Recipe Works Vietnamese bún chả—a vibrant mix of pork patties, crisp cucumber and lettuce, and bún (dried rice vermicelli), all united by a light yet potent sauce—makes a flavorful composed salad that diners assemble themselves and wrap in lettuce leaves. We soak rice vermicelli in hot water, rinse the noodles well, and spread them on a platter to dry. Then we mix up the bold and zesty sauce known as nước chấm using lime juice, sugar, and fish sauce. To ensure that every drop of the sauce is flavored with garlic and chile, we use a portion of the sugar to help grind the pungent ingredients into a fine paste. For juicy pork patties, we mix baking soda into ground pork because it raises the meat's pH, which helps the meat retain moisture and brown during the cooking time. We also season the pork with shallot, fish sauce, sugar, and pepper; we then briefly soak the patties in the nước chấm, a step that further imbues them with flavor. While the traditional version of this dish features grilled pork patties, here we swap the grill for a preheated cast-iron skillet to achieve the requisite charred exterior. Pressing the patties into ½-inch-thick disks ensures that they have plenty of contact with the skillet. We plate the components separately to allow diners to combine them according to taste. Bún are often labeled rice vermicelli. When shopping, look for Vietnamese or Taiwanese brands, which are thinner than Chinese brands. We prefer the more delicate springiness of bún made from 100 percent rice flour to those that include a secondary starch such as cornstarch. If you can find only the latter, just soak them longer—up to 12 minutes. For a less spicy sauce, use only half the Thai chile. To serve, place platters of noodles, salad, sauce, and pork patties on the table and allow diners to combine components to their taste. The sauce is potent, so use it sparingly.

1 For the noodles and salad Place noodles in large bowl and cover with 2 quarts boiling water. Let sit until just tender, about 3 minutes, stirring once halfway through soaking. Drain noodles and rinse under cold running water until chilled. Drain well, spread on large plate, and let sit at room temperature to dry. Arrange lettuce, cucumber, cilantro, and mint separately on serving platter and refrigerate until needed.

2 For the Nước Chấm Using mortar and pestle (or on cutting board using flat side of chef's knife), mash Thai chile, 1 tablespoon sugar, and garlic to fine paste. Transfer to medium bowl and add hot water and remaining 2 tablespoons sugar. Stir until sugar has dissolved. Stir in fish sauce and lime juice; set aside.

3 For the pork patties Combine shallot, fish sauce, sugar, baking soda, and pepper in medium bowl. Add pork and mix until well combined. Shape pork mixture into 12 patties, each about 2½ inches wide and ½ inch thick.

4 Heat empty cast-iron skillet over medium heat for 3 minutes. Add oil, increase heat to medium-high, and heat until oil just smoking. Transfer patties to skillet and cook until well browned on first side, about 3 minutes. Flip patties and continue to cook until browned on second side and meat registers 130 to 135 degrees, about 2 minutes. Transfer patties to bowl with sauce and toss gently to coat. Let sit for 5 minutes.

5 Transfer patties to serving plate, reserving sauce. Serve noodles, salad, nước chấm, and pork patties separately.

Sizing Up Your Skillet

traditional cast iron ● **enameled cast iron** ● **stainless steel**

The superior heat retention of a traditional 12-inch cast-iron skillet allows you to quickly achieve plenty of char on the patties without overcooking them. An enameled cast-iron skillet will also work for this reason. A stainless-steel skillet can also be used; add the oil to the skillet and heat over medium-high heat until just smoking before adding the patties.

Sizing Up Your Skillet

stainless steel • nonstick • enameled cast iron

A 12-inch stainless-steel skillet provides enough space for simmering the pasta and sauce. A nonstick or enameled cast-iron skillet will also work for this reason. Due to the acidic cooking liquid, we do not recommend using a traditional cast-iron or carbon-steel skillet.

Sopa Seca

Serves 4

Total Time 1 hour

8	ounces fideos (2 cups)
¼	cup vegetable oil, divided
1	pound plum tomatoes, cored and quartered (4 to 6 tomatoes)
1	onion, chopped
2	garlic cloves, smashed and peeled
2	cups water, plus extra as needed
2	tablespoons chicken bouillon powder
½–1	tablespoon minced canned chipotle chile in adobo sauce
1	teaspoon dried oregano
½	teaspoon table salt
½	teaspoon pepper
1	avocado, halved, pitted, and sliced thin
1½	ounces queso fresco, crumbled (⅓ cup)
½	cup Mexican crema
¼	cup chopped fresh cilantro
½	cup crushed chicharrones (optional)

VARIATION

Sopa Seca for Two

Halve all ingredients. Proceed with recipe in 10-inch skillet. In step 2, heat oil over medium-low heat. In step 3, transfer mixture to 4-cup liquid measuring cup and add extra water as needed to reach 2½ cups.

Why This Recipe Works Sopa seca, which translates as "dry soup" and is a staple in Mexican and Mexican American cuisine, takes one-pan noodles to the next level. This weeknight-friendly skillet dish features fideos, which are short, golden noodles with an angel hair–like thinness. We start by toasting the noodles to bring out their nutty flavors, then finish cooking them in a savory, tomato-based simmering liquid. To build the liquid, we cook down tomatoes, onion, and garlic to eliminate any harsh, raw flavors; this extra step also yields a creamier, more velvety consistency from the tomatoes. We then blend the mixture with chipotle chiles, which add a subtle heat and smoky flavor. A combination of water and chicken bouillon thins out the cooking liquid while infusing it with savory flavor. The noodles and liquid simmer together in the skillet until the sauce is absorbed and coats each noodle with a luxurious finish. Topping the sopa seca with cooling crema and queso fresco, along with fresh and bright cilantro and avocado, balances the spice. Look for short, "broken" fideos pasta, about 1 inch in length, and not coiled noodles, which are also known as fideos. If you can't find short fideos, substitute 8 ounces thin spaghetti or angel hair and break into 1- to 2-inch lengths: Loosely wrap pasta in dish towel and then press the bundle against the corner of the counter to break into short pieces. Knorr brand chicken bouillon is traditional; if you can't find the loose powder, you can crush two to three bouillon cubes and then measure out 2 tablespoons. For a spicier dish, use the greater amount of chipotle chile.

1 Heat fideos and 3 tablespoons oil in 12-inch stainless-steel skillet over medium-high heat, stirring constantly, until fideos are deep golden brown but not burnt, 4 to 5 minutes. Transfer fideos to large bowl; set aside. Wipe skillet clean with paper towels.

2 Heat remaining 1 tablespoon oil in now-empty skillet over medium heat until shimmering. Add tomatoes, onion, and garlic and cook until tomatoes are very soft and have released some of their juices, 8 to 10 minutes.

3 Process tomato mixture, water, bouillon powder, chipotle, oregano, salt, and pepper in blender until smooth, about 1 minute, scraping down sides of blender jar as needed. Transfer mixture to 8-cup liquid measuring cup; add extra water as needed to reach 5 cups.

4 Transfer tomato mixture to again-empty skillet. Using rubber spatula or wooden spoon, gently stir in fideos until fully submerged in tomato mixture. Spread fideos into even layer and bring to simmer over medium-high heat. Reduce heat to low, cover, and simmer, stirring every 5 minutes, until fideos are tender and sauce is fully absorbed, 20 to 25 minutes, adjusting heat as needed to maintain very gentle simmer. Season with salt and pepper to taste.

5 Transfer sopa seca to serving bowls. Divide avocado, queso fresco, crema, and cilantro evenly over fideos. Sprinkle with chicharrones, if using, and serve.

CHAPTER SIX

eggs &
breakfast

Perfect Fried Eggs

Serves 2

Total Time 20 minutes

- 2 teaspoons vegetable oil
- 4 large eggs, divided
- ¼ teaspoon table salt, divided
- ¼ teaspoon pepper, divided
- 2 teaspoons unsalted butter, cut into 4 pieces and chilled

VARIATIONS

Chili-Garlic Fried Eggs

Add 2 thinly sliced garlic cloves and ⅛ teaspoon red pepper flakes to skillet with butter.

Cumin-Caraway Fried Eggs

Add ½ teaspoon cumin seeds and ½ teaspoon caraway seeds to skillet with butter.

Why This Recipe Works There are two common problems when it comes to fried eggs: undercooked whites and overcooked yolks. This method produces diner-style fried eggs with crisp edges and runny yolks. The first thing you need is a nonstick skillet. Next, don't skip preheating the pan: It ensures that the pan's surface will be evenly hot, which is extra-important for quick-cooking foods such as eggs. We use vegetable oil, with its high smoke point, while preheating the pan, and then add butter just before the eggs to impart richness. Covering the skillet with a lid traps heat and steam so that the eggs cook from above as well as below, firming up the whites before the yolks overcook. When checking the eggs for doneness, lift the lid just a crack to prevent loss of steam should they need further cooking. To fry just two eggs, use an 8-inch nonstick skillet and halve the amounts of oil and butter. You can use this method with extra-large or jumbo eggs without altering the timing. You will need a 12-inch skillet with a tight-fitting lid for this recipe.

1 Heat oil in 12-inch nonstick skillet over low heat for 5 minutes. Meanwhile, crack 2 eggs into small bowl and sprinkle with ⅛ teaspoon salt and ⅛ teaspoon pepper. Repeat with remaining 2 eggs, remaining ⅛ teaspoon salt, and remaining ⅛ teaspoon pepper in second small bowl.

2 Increase heat to medium-high and heat until oil is shimmering. Add butter to skillet and quickly swirl to coat skillet. Working quickly, pour 1 bowl of eggs in 1 side of skillet and second bowl of eggs in other side. Cover and cook for 1 minute. Let skillet stand off heat, covered, 15 to 45 seconds for runny yolks (white around edge of yolk will be barely opaque), 45 to 60 seconds for soft but set yolks, and about 2 minutes for medium-set yolks. Slide eggs onto plates and serve.

Sizing Up Your Skillet

nonstick • **traditional cast iron** • **carbon steel**

A 12-inch nonstick skillet provides enough space to fry 4 eggs without concern for sticking. A traditional cast-iron or carbon-steel skillet will also work for this reason.

perfecting
FRIED EGGS

The seeming simplicity of making fried eggs belies the fact that technique really matters for great results. Using oil first, and then adding butter adds flavor. Preheating the skillet is key and will ensure that the quick-cooking eggs are evenly done. From there, a lid and timing are essential.

1   Preheat the Pan for 5 Minutes.

2   Use Two Fats.

3   Add Eggs All at Once.

4   Cover it Up.

5   Finish Off the Heat.

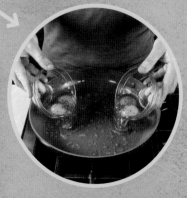

Creamy French-Style Scrambled Eggs

Serves 4

Total Time 25 minutes

---

8   large eggs

½   teaspoon table salt

3   tablespoons water, divided

1   teaspoon minced fresh parsley, chives, or tarragon

Why This Recipe Works The rich, velvety texture of traditional French-style scrambled eggs is believed to be the combined result of slow cooking and the addition of plenty of cream and butter, but we found a way to make them without all the added fat. We use steaming water rather than melted butter to indicate when our nonstick skillet is hot enough to begin cooking the eggs very slowly over low heat. Stirring constantly controls the coagulation of the proteins so that some form delicate curds while the rest thicken into a saucy consistency. Adding another tablespoon of water at the end of cooking dilutes the proteins, giving our eggs the perfect texture. For the creamiest, richest-tasting result, be sure to cook these eggs slowly, following the visual cues provided. It should take 12 to 14 minutes total. Though the eggs will be rather loose, their extended cooking time ensures that they reach a safe temperature.

1 Using fork, beat eggs and salt in bowl until few streaks of white remain. Heat 2 tablespoons water in 10-inch nonstick skillet over low heat until steaming. Add egg mixture and immediately stir with rubber spatula. Cook, stirring slowly and constantly, scraping edges and bottom of skillet, for 4 minutes. (If egg mixture is not steaming after 4 minutes, increase heat slightly.)

2 Continue to stir slowly until eggs begin to thicken and small curds begin to form, about 4 minutes longer (if curds have not begun to form, increase heat slightly). If any large curds form, mash with spatula. As curds start to form, stir vigorously, scraping edges and bottom of skillet, until eggs are thick enough to hold their shape when pushed to 1 side of skillet, 4 to 6 minutes. Remove skillet from heat. Add remaining 1 tablespoon water and parsley and stir vigorously until incorporated, about 30 seconds. Serve.

VARIATION

Creamy French-Style Scrambled Eggs for Two

Reduce water to 5 teaspoons; halve remaining ingredients except for parsley. Proceed with recipe in 8-inch nonstick skillet. Heat 1 tablespoon water in skillet in step 1 and add remaining 2 teaspoons water to eggs in step 2.

Sizing Up Your Skillet

nonstick • **traditional cast iron** • **carbon steel**

A 10-inch nonstick skillet provides enough space to scramble 8 eggs without concern for sticking. A traditional cast-iron or carbon-steel skillet will also work for this reason.

Menemen

Serves 4

Total Time 45 minutes

---

5   tablespoons extra-virgin olive oil, divided

1   small onion, chopped fine

2   Anaheim chiles, stemmed, seeded, and cut into ½-inch pieces

1   teaspoon pul biber, divided

¾   teaspoon dried oregano

¾   teaspoon table salt, divided

¼   teaspoon pepper, divided

2   large tomatoes, cored and cut into ½-inch pieces (2½ cups)

6   large eggs

2   ounces tulum cheese, crumbled (½ cup) (optional)

1   tablespoon minced fresh parsley

    Crusty bread, flatbread, or pita

VARIATION

Menemen for Two

Reduce oregano and salt to ½ teaspoon and parsley to 2 teaspoons; halve remaining ingredients. Proceed with recipe in 8-inch nonstick skillet.

Why This Recipe Works   Menemen, the creamy-dreamy, spicy-savory eggs that are central to Turkish foodways, is a traditional breakfast dish but can be enjoyed for lunch or dinner as well. The most popular style features scrambled eggs that are tender and soft along with onion, chiles, cheese, and herbs. But there are a few tricks to achieving the lush consistency. First, the vegetables in the dish need to be cooked long enough to soften and evaporate excess moisture. Removing the skillet from the heat after sautéing the vegetables allows the skillet to cool slightly before the eggs are added, preventing them from setting too quickly. The second key is to cook the eggs very slowly over low heat (as we do with Creamy French-Style Scrambled Eggs, page 232) while constantly stirring so that the eggs heat gently and evenly, turning deliciously creamy. To finish the dish, we sprinkle on chopped fresh parsley, tulum cheese, and pul biber chile flakes for mild heat and a smoky essence. Cubanelle peppers can be used in place of the Anaheim chiles. Tulum, a crumbly Turkish sheep or goat's milk cheese, can be found online and at specialty cheese shops; feta can be substituted. If not using cheese, season the menemen with salt to taste before serving. We strongly recommend seeking out the mild Turkish red pepper flakes pul biber; Aleppo pepper may be substituted. Though the eggs will be loose, the extended cooking time ensures that they reach a safe temperature. You will need a 10-inch skillet with a tight-fitting lid for this recipe.

1   Heat 3 tablespoons oil in 10-inch nonstick skillet over medium-low heat until shimmering. Add onion, Anaheims, ½ teaspoon pul biber, oregano, ¼ teaspoon salt, and ⅛ teaspoon pepper and stir to combine. Cover and cook until vegetables are soft, 8 to 10 minutes, stirring once halfway through cooking. Add tomatoes. Increase heat to medium and cook, uncovered, until tomatoes are soft and excess moisture has evaporated, 4 to 8 minutes.

2   Move skillet off heat for 2 minutes to cool slightly. While skillet is cooling, use fork to beat eggs, remaining ½ teaspoon salt, and remaining ⅛ teaspoon pepper in bowl until few streaks of white remain.

3   Return skillet to heat and adjust heat to low. Add eggs. Cook, stirring slowly and constantly, scraping edges and bottom of skillet with rubber spatula, for 4 minutes. (If egg mixture is not steaming after 4 minutes, increase heat slightly.)

4   Continue to stir slowly until eggs thicken and are just set (spatula drawn across bottom of skillet should leave clean trail), 5 to 6 minutes. Remove skillet from heat. Drizzle remaining 2 tablespoons oil over top and sprinkle with cheese (if using), parsley, and remaining ½ teaspoon pul biber. Serve immediately, passing bread separately.

Sizing Up Your Skillet

nonstick • **traditional cast iron** • **carbon steel**

A 10-inch nonstick skillet provides enough space to scramble eggs with the vegetables without concern for sticking. A traditional cast-iron or carbon-steel skillet will also work for this reason. If using a traditional cast-iron skillet, you will need to preheat the empty skillet over medium heat for 3 minutes before proceeding with step 1.

Cheddar and Chive Omelet

Makes 1 omelet

Total Time 10 minutes

3   large eggs

Pinch table salt

1   ounce extra-sharp cheddar cheese, shredded (¼ cup)

1½   teaspoons unsalted butter

1½   teaspoons chopped fresh chives

VARIATIONS

Kale, Feta, and Sun-Dried Tomato Omelet

Omit chives. Melt 1½ teaspoons butter in 10-inch nonstick skillet over medium heat. Add 1 minced garlic clove and ¼ teaspoon cumin and cook, stirring constantly, until fragrant, about 30 seconds. Add 1½ cups thinly sliced lacinato kale, 2 tablespoons thinly sliced oil-packed sun-dried tomatoes, and pinch table salt and cook, stirring occasionally, until wilted and no liquid remains, about 3 minutes. Off heat, push kale mixture to side of skillet opposite handle and top with 2 tablespoons crumbled feta. Proceed with recipe, substituting kale mixture for cheddar.

Ham, Pear, and Brie Omelet

Omit chives. Melt 1½ teaspoons butter in 10-inch nonstick skillet over medium heat. Add ¼ cup chopped ripe pear and pinch table salt and cook, stirring occasionally, until pear begins to brown, 1 to 2 minutes. Add ¼ cup chopped thinly sliced deli ham and cook, stirring constantly, until ham is warmed through, about 1 minute. Off heat, push pear-ham mixture to side of skillet opposite handle and top with 1 ounce slice Brie cheese. Proceed with recipe substituting pear mixture for cheddar.

Why This Recipe Works Rolling sunny, tender eggs around a tidy filling doesn't require much more skill or time than a hearty scramble, but the result is much more polished and satisfying. To make this elegant cheese omelet, we start by cooking three beaten eggs in an 8-inch nonstick skillet; this yields an omelet that is delicate but strong enough to support the cheese filling. Stirring constantly as the eggs cook breaks up the curds so that the texture of the finished omelet is even and fine. Once a small amount (about 10 percent) of liquid egg remains, it helps to cut the heat and smooth this "glue" over the curds so that the whole thing holds together in a cohesive round. The filling must be at serving temperature before rolling it into the omelet; briefly microwaving shredded cheddar cheese on a plate melts it just enough. Shaping the cheese filling into a 2-inch-wide strip and centering it in the omelet perpendicular to the handle makes it easy to roll the egg around the filling and out of the skillet. Briefly covering the skillet off the heat after adding the filling traps steam that helps the bottom of the eggs set enough to withstand rolling. (It also keeps the filling warm.) Using a rubber spatula to slide the eggs to the far side of the skillet and folding them partway over the filling starts the rolling process. Switching our grip so that we can tilt the skillet forward allows us to fully invert the omelet onto a plate below. To serve two, make two three-egg omelets instead of a single six-egg omelet. Omelets can be held for 10 minutes in an oven set to the lowest temperature. You will need an 8-inch skillet with a tight-fitting lid for this recipe.

1   Using fork, beat eggs and salt in bowl until few streaks of white remain.

2   Sprinkle cheese in even layer on small plate. Microwave at 50 percent power until cheese is just melted, 30 to 60 seconds. Set aside.

3   Melt butter in 8-inch nonstick skillet over medium heat, swirling skillet to distribute butter across skillet bottom. When butter sizzles evenly across skillet bottom, add eggs. Cook, stirring constantly with rubber spatula and breaking up large curds, until eggs are mass of small to medium curds surrounded by small amount of liquid egg. Immediately remove skillet from heat.

4   Working quickly, scrape eggs from sides of skillet, then smooth into even layer. Using fork, fold cheese into 2-inch-wide strip and transfer to center of eggs perpendicular to handle. Cover for 1 minute. Remove lid and run spatula underneath perimeter of eggs to loosen omelet. Gently ease spatula under eggs and slide omelet toward edge of skillet opposite handle until edge of omelet is even with lip of skillet. Using spatula, fold egg on handle side of skillet over filling. With your nondominant hand, grasp handle with underhand grip and hold skillet at 45-degree angle over top half of plate. Slowly tilt skillet toward yourself while using spatula to gently roll omelet onto plate. Sprinkle chives over omelet and serve.

Sizing Up Your Skillet

nonstick • **carbon steel**

An 8-inch nonstick skillet provides enough space to form a sturdy omelet; its small size and slick surface also make it easy to maneuver the omelet when it comes time to flip it onto the plate. A carbon-steel skillet will also work for these reasons.

Broccoli and Feta Frittata

Serves 4 to 6

Total Time 40 minutes

12	large eggs
⅓	cup whole milk
¾	teaspoon table salt, divided
1	tablespoon extra-virgin olive oil
12	ounces broccoli florets, cut into ½-inch pieces (4 cups)
	Pinch red pepper flakes
3	tablespoons water
½	teaspoon grated lemon zest plus ½ teaspoon juice
4	ounces feta cheese, crumbled into ½-inch pieces (1 cup)

VARIATIONS

Shiitake Mushroom and Pecorino Frittata

Substitute 1 pound shiitake mushrooms, stemmed and cut into ½-inch pieces, for broccoli, and ¼ teaspoon pepper for pepper flakes. Reduce water to 2 tablespoons and substitute 2 minced scallion whites, 1 tablespoon sherry vinegar, and 1½ teaspoons minced fresh thyme for lemon zest and juice. Substitute ¾ cup shredded Pecorino Romano for feta and add 2 thinly sliced scallion greens to eggs with cheese.

Broccoli and Feta Frittata for Two

Halve all ingredients. Proceed with recipe in 8-inch ovensafe nonstick skillet.

Why This Recipe Works The frittata is sometimes called a lazy cook's omelet. After all, it contains the same ingredients but doesn't require folding the eggs around a filling, a skill that takes practice to master. But even the practical frittata requires a little know-how, lest the bottom turn rubbery or the center end up loose and wet. We wanted to uncover the keys to a tender, evenly cooked, cohesive frittata, and we wanted it to be big and hearty enough to serve at least four for dinner. We started with well-seasoned add-ins made with bold ingredients and then combined them with a dozen eggs to make a substantial dinner. To ensure that the frittata is cohesive, we chop the add-in ingredients small so that they are surrounded and held in place by the eggs. To help the eggs stay tender even when cooked to a relatively high temperature, we add milk and salt. The liquid dilutes the proteins, making it harder for them to coagulate and turn the eggs rubbery, and the salt weakens the interactions between proteins, producing a softer curd. Finally, for eggs that are cooked fully and evenly, we start the frittata on the stovetop, stirring until a spatula leaves a trail in the curds, and then transfer the skillet to the oven to gently finish. This frittata can be served warm or at room temperature. Pair with a salad to serve as a meal. You will need a 12-inch ovensafe skillet for this recipe.

1 Adjust oven rack to middle position and heat oven to 350 degrees. Using fork, beat eggs, milk, and ½ teaspoon salt in bowl until well combined.

2 Heat oil in 12-inch ovensafe nonstick skillet over medium-high heat until shimmering. Add broccoli, pepper flakes, and remaining ¼ teaspoon salt and cook, stirring frequently, until broccoli is crisp-tender and spotty brown, 7 to 9 minutes. Add water and lemon zest and juice and continue to cook, stirring constantly, until broccoli is just tender and no water remains in skillet, about 1 minute.

3 Add feta and egg mixture and cook, using rubber spatula to stir and scrape bottom of skillet until large curds form and spatula leaves trail through eggs but eggs are still very wet, about 30 seconds. Smooth curds into even layer and cook, without stirring, for 30 seconds. Transfer skillet to oven and bake until frittata is slightly puffy and surface bounces back when lightly pressed, 6 to 9 minutes. Using rubber spatula, loosen frittata from skillet and transfer to cutting board. Let stand for 5 minutes before slicing and serving.

perfecting
FRITTATA

This easy-to-make frittata requires a few tricks to ensure a tender and cohesive result. Bold ingredients are key, as is chopping them small. Milk keeps the eggs from coagulating, and salt produces a softer curd.

1 **Break Out Your Best Nonstick Skillet.**

2 **Add Milk and Salt to Keep Eggs Tender.**

3 **Start on the Stove; Finish in the Oven.**

Sizing Up Your Skillet

nonstick • carbon steel

A 12-inch nonstick skillet provides enough space to assemble the frittata; its slick surface and shallow sides also make it easy to maneuver the frittata when it comes time to slide it onto the cutting board. A carbon-steel skillet will also work for these reasons.

Huevos Rancheros

Serves 2 to 4

Total Time 1 hour

3   tablespoons vegetable oil, divided

1½ pounds cherry tomatoes

2¼ teaspoons table salt, divided

2   jalapeño chiles, stemmed, seeded, halved, and ribs removed

½   onion, cut into 1-inch pieces

1   tablespoon tomato paste

2   garlic cloves, lightly crushed and peeled

½   teaspoon ground cumin

3   tablespoons minced fresh cilantro, divided

1   tablespoon lime juice, plus lime wedges for serving

4   large eggs

¼   teaspoon pepper

4   (6-inch) corn tortillas, warmed

Why This Recipe Works This spicy dish of eggs, salsa, and tortillas makes for an eye-opening breakfast or a lazy dinner. We use a nonstick skillet to char the vegetables that make up the flavorful salsa base: cherry tomatoes (which are quick and easy to char), jalapeño chiles, and chunks of onion. After a quick sauté in a smoking-hot skillet, our charred vegetables are chopped in a food processor to the perfect consistency before simmering in the skillet to develop even more flavor. We then crack our eggs into small wells in the simmering salsa and cover the skillet to allow the eggs to gently poach and absorb flavor from the zesty vegetables. For more heat, add the jalapeño ribs and seeds in step 3. Serve with refried beans, diced avocados, and chopped scallions.

1 Heat 1 tablespoon oil in 12-inch nonstick skillet until just smoking. Add tomatoes and 1 teaspoon salt and cook, stirring occasionally, until lightly charred and blistered, about 10 minutes; transfer to bowl.

2 Heat remaining 2 tablespoons oil in now-empty skillet over medium heat until shimmering. Add jalapeños and onion and cook until lightly charred, about 8 minutes. Stir in tomato paste, garlic, cumin, and 1 teaspoon salt and cook until fragrant, about 30 seconds.

3 Process jalapeño-onion mixture in food processor until finely ground, about 15 seconds, scraping down sides of bowl as needed. Add tomatoes and pulse until coarsely chopped, about 10 pulses. (Salsa can be refrigerated for up to 24 hours.)

4 Bring salsa to simmer in now-empty skillet over medium heat. Cook, stirring occasionally, until thickened slightly, about 10 minutes. Off heat, stir in 2 tablespoons cilantro and lime juice and season with salt and pepper to taste.

5 Using back of large spoon, make 4 shallow indentations (about 3 inches wide) in salsa. Crack 1 egg into each indentation and sprinkle with remaining ¼ teaspoon salt and pepper. Cover and cook over medium-low heat, 4 to 5 minutes for runny yolks (white around edge of yolk will be barely opaque), 5 to 6 minutes for soft but set yolks, or 6 to 7 minutes for medium-set yolks. Sprinkle with remaining 1 tablespoon cilantro. Serve immediately with warm tortillas and lime wedges.

Sizing Up Your Skillet

● **nonstick**

A 12-inch nonstick skillet provides enough space for simmering the salsa and poaching 4 eggs without concern for sticking. Due to the acidic salsa, we do not recommend using a traditional cast-iron or carbon-steel skillet.

All-American Breakfast Sandwiches

Serves 4

Total Time 40 minutes

---

4   English muffins, split

3   tablespoons unsalted butter, softened

¼   cup mayonnaise

1   tablespoon ketchup

4   large eggs

8   ounces bulk breakfast sausage

4   slices deli American cheese (4 ounces)

1½   ounces (1½ cups) baby spinach

4   thin tomato slices

1   avocado, halved, pitted, and sliced thin (optional)

VARIATIONS

All-American Bacon and Cheddar Breakfast Sandwiches

Substitute 1 teaspoon hot sauce for ketchup. Substitute 6 slices bacon for sausage and cook over medium heat until crispy, 7 to 9 minutes; transfer to paper towel–lined plate. When cool enough to handle, break each slice in half. Substitute 1 cup shredded sharp cheddar cheese for American cheese.

All-American Breakfast Sandwiches for Two

Halve all ingredients. Proceed with recipe in 10- or 12-inch nonstick skillet.

Sizing Up Your Skillet

nonstick • traditional cast iron • carbon steel

A 12-inch nonstick skillet provides enough space to brown the sausage patties and fry 4 eggs without concern for sticking. A traditional cast-iron or carbon-steel skillet will also work for these reasons. If using a traditional cast-iron skillet, you will need to preheat the empty skillet over medium heat for 3 minutes before proceeding with step 2.

Why This Recipe Works To bring this sausage, egg, and cheese favorite home and make enough for a family of four, a nonstick skillet and the broiler are key. We start by using the broiler to toast buttered English muffins. After forming patties from bulk breakfast sausage and cooking them in the skillet, we set them aside and use the flavorful drippings to cook four eggs. After a minute over the heat, we top the eggs with the sausage and American cheese and cover the pan to allow the eggs to cook through and the cheese to melt perfectly. We then assemble the sandwich in the butter-broiled English muffins, combining the egg and sausage with tomato and baby spinach to add freshness. A simple mixture of mayonnaise and ketchup contributes richness and tang. The result is crispy, buttery, gooey sandwiches that beat deli versions hands down and, despite the name, are irresistible 24-7. You will need a nonstick skillet with a tight-fitting lid for this recipe.

1 Adjust oven rack 5 inches from broiler element and heat broiler. Spread insides of muffins evenly with butter and arrange split side up on rimmed baking sheet. Combine mayonnaise and ketchup in bowl; set aside. Crack 2 eggs into small bowl and season with salt and pepper. Repeat with remaining 2 eggs and second small bowl.

2 Working with wet hands, form sausage into four 4-inch-diameter patties. Cook sausage patties in 12-inch nonstick skillet over medium heat until well browned and cooked through, 3 to 5 minutes per side; transfer to paper towel–lined plate. Broil muffins until golden brown, 2 to 4 minutes, rotating sheet halfway through broiling. Flip muffins and broil until just crisp on second side, 1 to 2 minutes; set aside while cooking eggs.

3 Pour off all but 1 tablespoon fat from skillet and heat over medium-high heat until shimmering. (If necessary, add oil to skillet to equal 1 tablespoon.) Working quickly, pour 1 bowl of eggs in 1 side of pan and second bowl of eggs in other side. Cover and cook for 1 minute.

4 Working quickly, top each egg with 1 sausage patty and 1 slice cheese. Cover pan, remove from heat, and let stand until cheese is melted and egg whites are cooked through, about 2 minutes.

5 Spread mayonnaise mixture on muffin bottoms and place 1 sausage-and-cheese-topped egg on each. Divide spinach evenly among sandwiches, then top with tomato slices, avocado slices, if using, and muffin tops. Serve.

Sizing Up Your Skillet

nonstick • traditional cast iron

A 12-inch nonstick skillet provides enough space to assemble the scrambled egg filling and brown the filled burritos without concern for sticking. A traditional cast-iron skillet will also work for these reasons; you will need to preheat the empty skillet over medium heat for 3 minutes before proceeding with step 2.

Breakfast Burritos with Chorizo and Crispy Potatoes

Serves 4

Total Time 1 hour

Chipotle Sour Cream

¼   cup sour cream

2   tablespoons minced canned chipotle chile in adobo sauce

2   teaspoons lime juice

1   garlic clove, minced

¼   teaspoon cayenne pepper

¼   teaspoon table salt

Burritos

¼   cup vegetable oil, divided

2   cups frozen potato tots, thawed and patted dry

8   ounces Mexican-style chorizo sausage, casings removed

8   large eggs, beaten

3   ounces sharp cheddar cheese, shredded (¾ cup)

4   (10-inch) flour tortillas

Why This Recipe Works Breakfast burritos are a favorite item at delis, but are actually easy to whip up at home in a nonstick skillet. For our version, we wanted potatoes that stayed extra-crispy. Frozen potato tots, thawed and then smashed flat in the skillet, did the trick. Along with the tots, we add fluffy scrambled eggs, sharp cheddar cheese, and Mexican-style chorizo. A potent chipotle-spiked sour cream provides tang and heat. Use fresh Mexican-style chorizo here, not the dry-cured Spanish version. To thaw frozen potato tots, either let them sit in the refrigerator for 24 hours or arrange them on a paper towel-lined plate and microwave for 1½ minutes. Electric stoves can be slow to respond to a cook's commands, which can pose a problem with this recipe where you must quickly move the skillet to low heat; see page 4 for workaround strategies.

1 For the chipotle sour cream Stir all ingredients together in bowl; set aside.

2 For the burritos Heat 3 tablespoons oil in 12-inch nonstick skillet over medium-high heat until shimmering. Add potato tots to skillet and press with spatula or underside of dry measuring cup to flatten slightly. Cook until crispy and deep golden brown, about 4 minutes per side. Transfer tots to paper towel-lined plate and set aside. Wipe skillet clean with paper towels.

3 Cook chorizo in now-empty skillet over medium heat, breaking up meat with wooden spoon, until well browned, 6 to 8 minutes. Add eggs and, using rubber spatula, constantly and firmly scrape along bottom and sides of skillet until eggs begin to clump and spatula leaves trail on bottom of skillet, about 2 minutes. Reduce heat to low and add cheddar. Gently but constantly fold eggs until clumped and slightly wet, 30 to 60 seconds. Remove from heat and cover to keep warm.

4 Wrap tortillas in damp dish towel and microwave until warm and pliable, about 1 minute. Arrange tortillas on counter. Spread about 1½ tablespoons chipotle sour cream across bottom third of each tortilla, leaving 1-inch border. Divide potato tots and eggs evenly over chipotle sour cream. Working with 1 burrito at a time, fold sides of tortilla over filling, then fold up bottom of tortilla and roll tightly around filling.

5 Wipe skillet clean with paper towels. Heat remaining 1 tablespoon oil in again-empty skillet over medium heat until shimmering. Arrange burritos in skillet seam side down and cook until crisp and golden, about 1 minute per side. Serve.

VARIATIONS

Breakfast Burritos with Poblano, Beans, Corn, and Crispy Potatoes

Omit chorizo. In step 3, heat 2 tablespoons vegetable oil in now-empty skillet over medium heat until shimmering. Add 1 chopped poblano chile, ½ cup drained canned pinto beans, ½ cup frozen corn, ¼ cup chopped onion, 1 teaspoon chili powder, and ½ teaspoon table salt and cook until vegetables are softened, 6 to 8 minutes. Add eggs and proceed with recipe as directed.

Breakfast Burritos with Chorizo and Crispy Potatoes for Two

Halve all ingredients. Proceed with recipe in 10-inch nonstick skillet.

Cast-Iron Deep-Dish Cheese Quiche

Serves 8

Total Time 2¼ hours, plus 3½ hours chilling and cooling

Crust

5–7 tablespoons ice water

3 tablespoons sour cream

1¾ cups (8¾ ounces) all-purpose flour

1 teaspoon sugar

½ teaspoon table salt

12 tablespoons unsalted butter, cut into ½-inch cubes and frozen for 10 minutes

Filling

2 cups half-and-half, divided

4 teaspoons cornstarch

8 large eggs

¾ teaspoon table salt

⅛ teaspoon pepper

6 ounces sharp cheddar cheese, shredded (1½ cups)

Why This Recipe Works A traditional 10-inch cast-iron skillet might well be the ultimate vessel for baking a deep-dish quiche. Cast iron's excellent heat retention helps create a sturdy, flaky crust, with no chance of a soggy bottom. Its steep sides accommodate a decent amount of filling, more than a pie plate, and provide plenty of surface area to ensure a hearty crust to contain the filling. We did, however, hit a few roadblocks when developing this recipe. Our standard pie dough was simply too skimpy to fully line the skillet, so we had to scale up the recipe. We also found that the skillet's steep sides caused the crust to slump. To combat this, we made sure to create a thick outer edge of pastry that we could fold over the rim of the skillet. This, along with pie weights (3 to 4 cups), helped anchor the crust in place, preventing it from sagging or shrinking during blind baking. Stirring some cornstarch into the egg custard ensured a silky filling from edge to center. The cooled quiche can be served warm or at room temperature, or refrigerated for up to 3 days and reheated. To reheat the whole quiche, place skillet on the middle rack of a 325-degree oven for 20 minutes. Reheat slices on rimmed baking sheet at 375 degrees for 10 minutes.

1 For the crust Combine 5 tablespoons ice water and sour cream in small bowl. Process flour, sugar, and salt in food processor until combined, about 3 seconds. Add butter and pulse until size of large peas, about 10 pulses. Add half of sour cream mixture and pulse 3 times; scrape down sides and bottom of processor bowl. Repeat with remaining sour cream mixture. Pinch dough with fingers; if dough is floury, dry, and does not hold together, add 1 to 2 tablespoons ice water and process until dough forms large clumps and no dry flour remains, three to five 1-second pulses.

2 Transfer dough to sheet of plastic wrap. Draw edges of plastic over dough and press firmly on sides and top to form compact, fissure-free mass. Wrap in plastic and flatten to form 5-inch disk. Refrigerate dough for at least 2 hours or up to 2 days. Let chilled dough sit on counter to soften slightly, about 10 minutes, before rolling. (Wrapped dough can be frozen for up to 1 month. If frozen, let dough thaw completely on counter before rolling.)

3 Roll dough into 15-inch round on lightly floured counter. Roll dough loosely around rolling pin and unroll into 10-inch traditional cast-iron skillet. Ease dough into skillet by gently lifting and supporting edge of dough with one hand while pressing into skillet bottom and corners with your other hand. Trim any dough that extends more than 1 inch over edge of skillet. Tuck dough under itself; folded edge should overhang edge of skillet slightly. Using your fingers, crimp dough to create attractive crust that is anchored around edge of skillet. Wrap skillet loosely in plastic wrap and freeze until dough is firm, about 30 minutes.

4 Adjust oven rack to lower-middle position and heat oven to 350 degrees. Line pie crust with double layer of aluminum foil, covering edges, and fill with pie weights. Set skillet on rimmed baking sheet and bake until edges of crust are set and just beginning to turn golden, about 30 minutes. Remove foil and weights, rotate sheet, and continue to bake crust until golden brown and crisp, 20 to 25 minutes. (Crust needn't cool completely before adding filling.)

5 For the filling Reduce oven temperature to 325 degrees. Whisk ¼ cup half-and-half and cornstarch in large bowl until cornstarch has dissolved. Whisk in eggs, salt, pepper, and remaining 1¾ cups half-and-half until well combined. Sprinkle cheddar evenly over crust, then slowly pour custard over top.

6 Bake until top of quiche is set and center registers 170 degrees, 50 to 70 minutes. Transfer to wire rack and let cool for 1 hour before serving.

Cast-Iron Deep-Dish Quiche with Caramelized Onions, Porcini, and Gruyère

Bring 1 pound thinly sliced onions, ¼ cup water, 1 tablespoon extra-virgin olive oil, and ¼ teaspoon salt to boil in 10-inch traditional cast-iron skillet over medium-high heat. Cover and cook until water has evaporated and onions start to sizzle, about 5 minutes. Uncover, reduce heat to medium, and cook, stirring frequently, until onions are softened, well browned, and slightly sticky, 10 to 15 minutes. Stir in ½ ounce rinsed and minced dried porcini mushrooms and ½ cup water and cook, scraping up any browned bits, until almost dry, about 5 minutes. Transfer to bowl. (Onion mixture can be refrigerated overnight; bring to room temperature before using.) Thoroughly clean and dry skillet. Proceed with recipe, but substitute 4 ounces Gruyère cheese for cheddar and stir onion mixture into custard before adding to skillet. Sprinkle with 2 teaspoons fresh thyme leaves before baking.

Cast-Iron Deep-Dish Quiche with Smoked Trout, Potatoes, and Dill

Bring 12 ounces Yukon Gold potatoes, peeled, quartered, and thinly sliced, ¼ cup water, 1 tablespoon extra-virgin olive oil, and ¼ teaspoon table salt to boil in traditional 10-inch cast-iron skillet over high heat. Reduce heat to medium-low, cover, and cook until potatoes are just tender, 10 to 12 minutes. Uncover and continue to cook until water has evaporated, about 3 minutes. Transfer to bowl. (Potato mixture can be refrigerated overnight; bring to room temperature before using.) Thoroughly clean and dry skillet. Proceed with recipe but omit cheddar and stir cooked potatoes, 8 ounces flaked smoked trout or salmon, and 1 tablespoon grated lemon zest into custard before adding to skillet. Sprinkle with 2 teaspoons chopped fresh dill before baking.

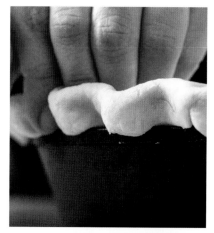

Sizing Up Your Skillet

- **traditional cast iron**

The straight sides and superior heat retention of a traditional 10-inch cast-iron skillet are key to creating a deep-dish quiche with a crisp crust and creamy custard. Its slick surface also ensures that the quiche releases easily from the pan. We do not recommend using an alternative skillet in this recipe.

Easy Pancakes

Serves 4 to 6 (makes
fifteen 4-inch pancakes)

Total Time 45 minutes

---

2   cups (10 ounces) all-purpose flour

3   tablespoons sugar

4   teaspoons baking powder

½   teaspoon baking soda

1   teaspoon table salt

2   large eggs

¼   cup plus 1 teaspoon vegetable oil,
    divided

1½ cups milk

½   teaspoon vanilla extract

Why This Recipe Works It's time to put down the box mix once and for all. You've got everything you need to make tall, fluffy pancakes right in your pantry. Everyone loves sitting down to a plate of golden, flavorful pancakes, but planning for them can be another matter. No one wants to run out for buttermilk or sour cream before the first meal of the day. Enter these easy pancakes. To make them tall and fluffy, we prepare a thick batter by using a relatively small amount of liquid and lots of baking powder and mix it minimally. Why? A lumpier batter is better able to hold on to the air bubbles formed during cooking, producing taller, more leavened pancakes: Less stirring is key. Sugar, vanilla, and baking soda provide sweetness, depth, and saline tang, respectively. Serve with salted butter and maple syrup.

1 Whisk flour, sugar, baking powder, baking soda, and salt together in large bowl. Whisk eggs and ¼ cup oil in second medium bowl until well combined. Whisk milk and vanilla into egg mixture. Add egg mixture to flour mixture and stir gently until just combined (batter should remain lumpy with few streaks of flour). Let batter sit for 10 minutes before cooking.

2 Heat ½ teaspoon oil in 12-inch nonstick skillet over medium-low heat until shimmering. Using paper towels, carefully wipe out oil, leaving thin film on bottom and sides of skillet. Drop 1 tablespoon batter in center of skillet. If pancake is pale golden brown after 1 minute, skillet is ready. If it is too light or too dark, adjust heat accordingly.

3 Using ¼-cup dry measuring cup, portion batter into skillet in 3 places, leaving 2 inches between portions. If necessary, gently spread batter into 4-inch round. Cook until edges are set, first sides are golden brown, and bubbles on surface are just beginning to break, 2 to 3 minutes. Using thin, wide spatula, flip pancakes and continue to cook until second sides are golden brown, 1 to 2 minutes. Serve. Repeat to make 4 more batches with remaining batter, using remaining ½ teaspoon oil as necessary.

VARIATION

Easy Pancakes for Two

Halve all ingredients. Proceed with recipe in 12-inch skillet.

Sizing Up Your Skillet

nonstick • **traditional cast iron**

A 12-inch nonstick skillet provides enough space to griddle 3 pancakes at a time without concern for sticking. A traditional cast-iron skillet will also work for this reason; you will need to preheat the empty skillet over medium heat for 3 minutes before proceeding with step 2.

French Toast Casserole

Serves 4 to 6

Total Time 1¼ hours

1 tablespoon unsalted butter, softened, plus 4 tablespoons melted

6 tablespoons packed (2⅔ ounces) brown sugar

1½ teaspoons ground cinnamon

¼ teaspoon ground nutmeg

Pinch table salt

10 slices potato sandwich bread, halved diagonally

1⅔ cups whole milk

4 large eggs

3 tablespoons sliced almonds, toasted

Confectioners' sugar

Why This Recipe Works French toast is a delicious, easy-to-make breakfast special, but could we make it even easier—and more crowd friendly? To meet our goal, we translated the concept of French toast into a skillet casserole. No more standing at the stove, flipping slice after slice, dripping egg wash on the counter, or serving one person at a time: Our French toast casserole is an ideal family breakfast, taking full advantage of a traditional cast-iron skillet's ability to replicate the crisp-crusted texture of conventional French toast in a simple, family-size dish. Potato bread, with its sturdy slices, is the perfect choice for the base of our casserole. To ensure that the bread fits easily in a skillet, we halve the slices and layer them in the pan with cinnamon, brown sugar, and butter. Repeating this process to create a double stack, we then pour egg custard over the top so that it can soak through the layers of bread. For a satisfying crunch, we top the casserole with sliced almonds before putting the pan in the oven and then finish the baked casserole with a light dusting of confectioners' sugar. The result? A skillet filled with layers of tender, sweet French toast, ready all at once. You will need a 12-inch ovensafe skillet for this recipe.

1 Adjust oven rack to middle position and heat oven to 350 degrees. Grease 12-inch traditional cast-iron skillet with softened butter. Mix brown sugar, cinnamon, nutmeg, and salt together in bowl.

2 Sprinkle 2 tablespoons brown sugar mixture over bottom of prepared skillet. Arrange half of bread pieces in even layer in skillet. Drizzle with 1½ tablespoons melted butter and sprinkle with 2 tablespoons brown sugar mixture. Repeat layering with remaining bread pieces, 1½ tablespoons melted butter, and 2 tablespoons brown sugar mixture.

3 Whisk milk and eggs together until well combined, then pour mixture over bread and press gently to help bread soak up egg mixture. Sprinkle with almonds and remaining brown sugar mixture.

4 Transfer skillet to oven and bake until casserole is slightly puffed and golden brown and bubbling around edges, about 30 minutes, rotating skillet halfway through baking.

5 Using potholders, transfer skillet to wire rack. Being careful of hot skillet handle, brush casserole with remaining 1 tablespoon melted butter and let cool for 15 minutes. Sprinkle with confectioners' sugar and serve.

Sizing Up Your Skillet

traditional cast iron ● **nonstick**

A 12-inch traditional cast-iron skillet provides enough space to assemble the casserole and serve without concern for sticking. Its superior heat retention also makes it an attractive serving vessel that keeps the casserole warm at the table. A nonstick skillet can also be used here, though the casserole may cool down faster.

Eggs and Breakfast 251

Better Hash Browns

Serves 4

Total Time 1¼ hours

4   teaspoons table salt for brining

2½ pounds Yukon Gold potatoes,
     peeled and shredded

¼   teaspoon pepper

¼   cup vegetable oil, divided

Why This Recipe Works Hash browns always feel like a lot of work. But here, thanks to a cake pan to form a large potato patty and then a nonstick skillet for frying, it's pretty easy to make crave-worthy wedges of crispy hash browns, the perfect addition to a lazy weekend breakfast. For better hash browns, we shred Yukon Gold potatoes and rinse them in salted water to prevent discoloration. After squeezing excess moisture from the potatoes, we parcook them in the microwave, which removes more moisture and jump-starts the gelatinization of the potato starch so that the potatoes are cohesive even before they go into the skillet. Molding the hash browns in a cake pan is easy and also makes a smoother potato cake. After a short stay in the fridge to firm up, the molded hash browns are ready to slide into a skillet with shimmering oil. Sliding the browned patty onto a plate and then inverting it onto another plate allows you to easily slide it back into the skillet, browned-side up, to cook to the ultimate crispiness on both sides. We prefer using the shredding disk of a food processor to shred the potatoes, but you can use the large holes of a box grater.

1 Spray 8-inch round cake pan with vegetable oil spray. Whisk 2 cups water and salt in large bowl until salt dissolves. Transfer potatoes to salt water and toss briefly to coat. Immediately drain in colander. Place 2½ cups potatoes in center of clean dish towel. Gather ends together and twist tightly to wring out excess moisture. Toss dried potatoes with pepper in large bowl. Microwave until very hot and slightly softened, about 5 minutes. Place remaining potatoes in towel and wring out excess moisture. Add to microwaved potatoes and toss with 2 forks until mostly combined (potatoes will not combine completely). Continue to microwave until potatoes are hot and form cohesive mass when pressed with spatula, about 6 minutes, stirring halfway through microwaving.

2 Transfer potatoes to prepared cake pan and let cool until no longer steaming, about 5 minutes. Using your lightly greased hands, press potatoes firmly into pan to form smooth disk. Refrigerate until cool, at least 20 minutes or up to 24 hours (if refrigerating longer than 30 minutes, wrap pan with plastic wrap once potatoes are cool).

3 Heat 2 tablespoons oil in 10-inch nonstick skillet over medium heat until shimmering. Invert potato cake onto plate and carefully slide cake into skillet. Cook, swirling skillet occasionally to distribute oil evenly, until bottom of cake is brown and crispy, 6 to 8 minutes. (If not browning after 3 minutes, turn heat up slightly. If browning too quickly, reduce heat.) Slide cake onto large plate. Invert onto second large plate. Heat remaining 2 tablespoons oil in skillet until shimmering. Carefully slide cake, browned side up, back into skillet. Cook, swirling skillet occasionally, until bottom of cake is brown and crispy, 5 to 6 minutes. Carefully slide cake onto plate and invert onto serving plate. Cut into wedges and serve.

Sizing Up Your Skillet

nonstick • **traditional cast iron** • **carbon steel**

A 10-inch nonstick skillet provides enough space to brown the potato cake without concern for sticking. A traditional cast-iron or carbon-steel skillet will also work for this reason. If using a traditional cast-iron skillet, you will need to preheat the empty skillet over medium heat for 3 minutes before proceeding with step 3.

Skillet Granola with Pecans

Serves 4 (makes about 3 cups)

Total Time 45 minutes

¼ cup maple syrup

1 teaspoon vanilla extract

½ teaspoon ground cinnamon

¼ teaspoon table salt

2 tablespoons vegetable oil

½ cup pecans, chopped coarse

1½ cups (4½ ounces) old-fashioned oats

Why This Recipe Works Store-bought granola is often bland and chock-full of pale oats and nuts, not to mention that it can often taste stale. Enter this skillet version, which is likely the easiest-to-make granola you have ever encountered. No need to balance a sheet pan full of ingredients in and out of the oven and then monitor things to make sure nothing burns. The solution is to do it all in a skillet where you have complete control. For a small batch of homemade granola with substantial chunks and a balanced sweet-toasty flavor, we start by toasting pecans to enhance their flavor before adding our oats. Stirring frequently after adding the oats makes for even cooking. Maple syrup holds the nuts and oats together while imparting a balanced sweetness. Salt, cinnamon, and vanilla round out the flavors. We do use a baking sheet, but only to cool the granola in a single layer, which allows us to break it into crunchy clumps. Do not substitute quick or instant oats in this recipe; old-fashioned oats provide the perfect amount of chew. It's important to stir the granola frequently in step 2 to ensure that the mixture cooks evenly.

1 Combine maple syrup, vanilla, cinnamon, and salt in bowl; set aside. Line baking sheet with parchment paper.

2 Heat oil in 12-inch nonstick skillet over medium heat until shimmering. Add pecans and cook, stirring frequently, until fragrant and just starting to darken in color, about 4 minutes. Add oats and cook, stirring frequently, until oats are golden and pecans are toasted, about 6 minutes.

3 Add maple syrup mixture to skillet and cook, stirring frequently, until absorbed and mixture turns a shade darker, about 3 minutes. Transfer granola to prepared sheet, spread into even layer, and let cool for 20 minutes. Break granola into bite-size pieces and serve.

VARIATIONS

Skillet Granola with Apricots and Walnuts

Substitute walnuts for pecans. After breaking granola into pieces, stir in ½ cup chopped dried apricots.

Skillet Granola with Coconut and Chocolate

Substitute sweetened shredded coconut for pecans. After breaking granola into pieces, stir in ½ cup semisweet chocolate chips.

Sizing Up Your Skillet

nonstick • **traditional cast iron**

A 12-inch nonstick skillet provides enough space to toss and toast the granola mixture without concern for sticking. A traditional cast-iron skillet will also work for this reason; you will need to preheat the empty skillet over medium heat for 3 minutes before proceeding with step 2.

CHAPTER SEVEN

small plates & side dishes

Warm Marinated Olives

Serves 8 to 10

Total Time 25 minutes

1 cup extra-virgin olive oil, divided

6 (2-inch) strips lemon zest plus 1 tablespoon juice

2 sprigs fresh rosemary

3 garlic cloves, sliced thin

3 bay leaves

¼ teaspoon red pepper flakes

4 cups brine-cured green or black olives with pits

Crusty bread

Why This Recipe Works Sure, you can buy pre-marinated olives at most any supermarket, but we find the flavor of most of these either too vinegar-sharp or muddy with dried herbs. For the best marinated olives, we start with good brined olives that still have their pits, which have a better texture and flavor than pitted olives. The mild olives are the perfect base for aromatic herbs and spices—rosemary, lemon, bay, and garlic—which increase the complexity of the dish. A dose of red pepper flakes makes our olives a little zestier. Briefly simmering the olives over low heat with extra-virgin olive oil and seasonings helps to expedite the marinating process. We wait until the very end to stir in any delicate fresh ingredients like citrus juice, cheese, or tender herbs to ensure that they won't lose their shape or discolor.

1 Heat oil, lemon zest, rosemary sprigs, garlic, bay leaves, and pepper flakes in 10-inch cast-iron skillet over medium heat until fragrant and starting to bubble, about 2 minutes.

2 Stir in olives, reduce heat to medium-low, and cook until flavors meld and mixture is heated through, about 10 minutes. Off heat, stir in lemon juice. Let olive mixture sit in skillet until cooled slightly, about 5 minutes. Serve (directly from skillet or in large shallow serving bowl) with crusty bread. (Marinated olives can be refrigerated for up to 4 days. Let sit at room temperature for about 10 minutes before serving or reheat in skillet over medium heat until warm, about 3 minutes.)

VARIATIONS

Warm Marinated Olives with Artichokes and Feta

Omit rosemary sprigs and pepper flakes. Reduce olives to 2 cups. Heat skillet over medium heat for 3 minutes. Add 1 tablespoon extra-virgin olive oil and heat until shimmering. Add 2 cups jarred whole baby artichoke hearts packed in water, halved and patted dry, and cook until spotty brown, about 8 minutes; transfer to bowl. Proceed with recipe as directed, adding 1 teaspoon fennel seeds with aromatics and artichokes with olives. Gently stir 4 ounces feta cheese, cut into ¾-inch pieces, into olive mixture with lemon juice. Sprinkle with 1 tablespoon chopped fresh oregano before serving.

Warm Marinated Olives with Manchego and Roasted Garlic

Reduce olives to 2 cups. Substitute 4 sprigs fresh thyme for rosemary, 12 garlic cloves, smashed and peeled, for sliced garlic, orange zest for lemon zest, and sherry vinegar for lemon juice. Combine oil and garlic in skillet and cook over medium-low heat until garlic begins to turn golden, about 10 minutes. Stir in remaining aromatics and proceed with recipe as directed. Let mixture cool for 15 minutes, then stir in 8 ounces Manchego cheese, cut into ¾-inch pieces. Sprinkle with 1 tablespoon chopped fresh parsley before serving.

Sizing Up Your Skillet

traditional cast iron • **enameled cast iron** • **stainless steel** • **carbon steel**

A 10-inch traditional cast-iron skillet provides enough space for simmering the olives. It makes an attractive serving vessel, and its superior heat retention keeps the dish warm at the table. An enameled cast-iron skillet will also work for these reasons. A stainless-steel, nonstick, or carbon-steel skillet can also be used here, though the appetizer may cool down faster.

Blistered Shishito Peppers

Serves 4 to 6

Total Time 15 minutes

2   tablespoons vegetable oil

8   ounces shishito peppers

Why This Recipe Works Little fried blistered chile peppers that you pick up by the stems and pop into your mouth whole are a bar snack that's supereasy to make at home. They require no advance prep and are ready in just a few minutes. Bright-tasting, citrusy, and mild, these green chiles are also thin-skinned, crisp-textured, and crave-worthy. Restaurants often deep-fry them, but we found that cooking shishitos in a small amount of oil in a cast-iron skillet works equally well and is much less messy. The larger granules of flake sea salt or kosher salt sprinkled on top add a wonderful crunch, but you can use regular table salt, if you prefer. Only one shishito pepper out of ten is spicy, so even guests who don't like a lot of heat can enjoy them. Serve with Herb–Yogurt Sauce (page 102) if desired.

Heat 12-inch cast-iron skillet over medium-high heat for 5 minutes. Add oil to skillet and swirl to coat. Add peppers and cook, without stirring, until skins are blistered, 3 to 5 minutes. Using tongs, flip peppers and continue to cook until blistered on second side, 3 to 5 minutes. Transfer to serving plate, season with flake sea salt or kosher salt to taste, and serve immediately.

VARIATIONS

Blistered Shishito Peppers with Mint, Poppy Seeds, and Orange

Combine 1 teaspoon ground dried mint, 1 teaspoon poppy seeds, ½ teaspoon flake sea salt, ¼ teaspoon grated orange zest in small bowl. Sprinkle blistered peppers with spice mixture before serving with orange wedges.

Smoky Shishito Peppers with Espelette and Lime

Combine 1 teaspoon ground dried Espelette pepper, 1 teaspoon smoked paprika, ½ teaspoon flake sea salt or kosher salt, and ¼ teaspoon grated lime zest in small bowl. Sprinkle blistered peppers with spice mixture before serving with lime wedges.

Sizing Up Your Skillet

traditional cast iron • **enameled cast iron** • **carbon steel** • **stainless steel**

The superior heat retention of a 12-inch traditional cast-iron skillet allows you to quickly achieve plenty of char on the peppers without overcooking them. An enameled cast-iron or carbon-steel skillet will also work for this reason. A stainless-steel skillet can also be used: Add the oil to the skillet and heat over medium-high heat until just smoking before adding the peppers.

Pork Potstickers

Makes 40 potstickers

Total Time 2 hours plus 30 minutes chilling

Pork Filling

5   cups 1-inch napa cabbage pieces

½   teaspoon table salt, plus salt for salting cabbage

12   ounces ground pork

1½   tablespoons soy sauce

1½   tablespoons toasted sesame oil

1   tablespoon vegetable oil

1   tablespoon Shaoxing wine

1   tablespoon hoisin sauce

1   tablespoon grated fresh ginger

¼   teaspoon white pepper

4   scallions, chopped fine

40   store-bought dumpling wrappers

2   tablespoons vegetable oil, divided

Why This Recipe Works Chinese potstickers can be as much fun to make as they are to eat. For our filling, we add vegetable oil and sesame oil to ground pork to mimic the richness of the fatty pork shoulder that is traditionally used. Soy sauce, ginger, Shaoxing wine, hoisin sauce, and white pepper add flavor, and cabbage and scallions contribute subtle crunch. Mixing the filling in the food processor develops myosin, a protein that keeps the filling cohesive. We use round store-bought dumpling wrappers. Both wheat and egg varieties are commonly available and both work well when using a basic half-moon fold to shape the dumplings. Look for freshly ground pork, which has a higher fat content and a coarser texture than prepackaged pork. Look for dumpling wrappers in the freezer section of supermarkets or Chinese markets. Thaw either in the refrigerator for 24 hours or on the counter for 30 minutes to 1 hour. Serve with chili oil, Chinese black or red vinegar, and/or light, dark, or sweet soy sauce. You will need a 12-inch skillet with a tight-fitting lid for this recipe.

1 For the pork filling Pulse cabbage in food processor until finely chopped, 8 to 10 pulses. Transfer cabbage to medium bowl and stir in ½ teaspoon salt; let sit for 10 minutes. Using hands, squeeze excess moisture from cabbage. Transfer cabbage to small bowl and set aside.

2 Pulse pork, soy sauce, sesame oil, vegetable oil, Shaoxing wine, hoisin, ginger, salt, and pepper in now-empty food processor until blended and slightly sticky, about 10 pulses. Scatter cabbage over pork mixture. Add scallions and pulse until vegetables are evenly distributed, about 8 pulses. Transfer pork mixture to small bowl and, using rubber spatula, smooth surface. Cover with plastic wrap and refrigerate for at least 30 minutes or up to 3 days.

3 Lightly dust 2 parchment paper–lined rimmed baking sheets with flour. Using rubber spatula, mark filling with cross to divide into 4 equal portions. Transfer 1 portion to separate bowl and refrigerate remaining filling.

4 Working with 1 wrapper at a time (keep remaining wrappers covered with damp towel), place scant 1 tablespoon filling in center of wrapper. Brush away any flour clinging to surface of wrapper and lightly moisten edge with water. Fold wrapper in half to make half-moon shape. Using index finger and thumb, pinch dumpling closed, pressing out any air pockets from filling. Lay dumpling on counter and press gently to flatten 1 side for even browning. Transfer dumpling to prepared sheet. Repeat with additional 9 wrappers and filling in bowl. Repeat dumpling-making process with remaining wrappers and remaining 3 portions filling. (Dumplings can be refrigerated for up to 24 hours or frozen on sheet until solid, then transferred to zipper-lock bag and stored in freezer for up to 1 month. Do not thaw frozen dumplings before cooking; increase water to ⅔ cup in step 5 and increase covered cook time to 8 minutes.)

5 Brush 12-inch nonstick skillet with 1 tablespoon oil. Evenly space 16 dumplings flat sides down around edge of skillet and place 4 in center. Cook over medium heat until bottoms begin to turn spotty brown, 3 to 4 minutes. Off heat, carefully add ½ cup water (water will sputter). Return skillet to medium heat and bring water to boil. Cover, reduce heat to medium-low, and cook for 6 minutes.

6 Uncover, increase heat to medium-high, and cook until water has evaporated and bottoms of pot stickers are crispy and browned, 1 to 3 minutes. Transfer pot stickers to platter. Serve immediately. (Before cooking second batch of pot stickers, let skillet cool for 10 minutes. Rinse skillet under cool water and wipe dry with paper towels. Repeat cooking process with remaining 1 tablespoon oil and ½ cup water.)

Sizing Up Your Skillet

nonstick • traditional cast iron • carbon steel

A 12-inch nonstick skillet provides sufficient space for browning 40 potstickers in only 2 batches. Its slick surface also ensures that the savory browning sticks to the potstickers, not the pan. A traditional cast-iron or carbon-steel skillet will also work for these reasons; if using carbon steel, you will need to brown the potstickers in 4 batches.

Crispy Vegetable Fritters

Makes 12 fritters

Total Time 1 hour

Sauce

⅓ cup mayonnaise

1 tablespoon prepared horseradish, drained

1 tablespoon lemon juice, plus lemon wedges for serving

Fritters

½ cup (2½ ounces) plus 1 tablespoon all-purpose flour

½ cup (2 ounces) plus 1 tablespoon cornstarch

½ teaspoon baking powder

¾ cup seltzer

1 cup thinly sliced red bell pepper

1 cup shredded zucchini

½ cup shredded carrot

½ cup thinly sliced onion

½ cup fresh cilantro leaves

2 scallions, cut into ½-inch pieces

1 garlic clove, minced

1½ cups peanut or vegetable oil for frying

½ teaspoon table salt

½ teaspoon pepper

Why This Recipe Works Vegetable fritters make an irresistible appetizer, especially when served with a pungent horseradish mayo. We tested a number of vegetable options and settled on a mix of shredded zucchini, shredded carrot, sliced red bell pepper, and thinly sliced onion. For the thick batter, we combine equal parts flour and cornstarch plus seltzer and baking powder to lighten it. We add salt to the batter just before frying so that it doesn't draw water out of the vegetables and interfere with crispiness. We carefully monitor the temperature of the shallow oil in a skillet, turning off the burner between batches to keep the oil from overheating and help ensure that each batch comes out deep golden brown, lacy, and crisp. And finally, we whip up a creamy, bright horseradish mayonnaise to complement the crunchy fritters. Buy refrigerated prepared horseradish, not the shelf-stable kind, which contains preservatives and additives.

1 For the sauce Whisk all ingredients together in bowl and season with salt and pepper to taste; refrigerate until ready to serve.

2 For the fritters Set wire rack in rimmed baking sheet and line half of rack with triple layer of paper towels. Whisk flour, cornstarch, and baking powder together in large bowl. Add seltzer and whisk until smooth, thick batter forms. Add bell pepper, zucchini, carrot, onion, cilantro, scallions, and garlic to batter and stir until vegetables are evenly coated.

3 Add oil to 12-inch traditional cast-iron skillet until it measures about ¼ inch deep and heat over medium-high heat to 350 degrees. Stir salt and pepper into vegetable batter. Using ¼-cup dry measuring cup, place 1 portion of vegetable batter in skillet and immediately spread to 4-inch diameter with spoon so top sits slightly below surface of oil. Repeat 3 times, so you have 4 fritters in skillet. Make sure vegetables do not mound in centers of fritters. Adjust burner, if necessary, to maintain oil temperature between 325 to 350 degrees.

4 Cook on first sides until deep golden brown on bottom, 2 to 4 minutes. Using 2 spatulas, flip and continue to cook until golden brown on second sides, 2 to 4 minutes, moving fritters around skillet as needed for even browning. When second sides of fritters are golden brown, turn off burner. Transfer fritters to paper towel-lined side of prepared rack to drain for about 15 seconds per side, then move to unlined side of rack and season with salt to taste.

5 Return oil to 350 degrees and repeat with remaining vegetable batter in 2 batches, stirring to recombine batter as needed. Serve with sauce and lemon wedges.

Sizing Up Your Skillet

traditional cast iron ● **stainless steel**

The superior heat retention of a 12-inch traditional cast-iron skillet allows you to easily maintain the proper oil temperature for frying. The skillet's tall sides also provide enough space for safely shallow frying the fritters. While a 12-inch straight-sided stainless-steel skillet (also known as a sauté pan) does not have the same heat retention, it can also be used.

Cast-Iron Skillet Corn Dip

Serves 6 to 8

Total Time 40 minutes

2 tablespoons vegetable oil, divided

4–6 ears corn, kernels cut from cobs (4 cups), divided

½ teaspoon table salt, divided

3 scallions, sliced thin, divided

2 garlic cloves, minced

8 ounces cream cheese, cut into 8 equal pieces and softened

8 ounces pepper Jack cheese, shredded (2 cups), divided

1 cup mayonnaise

2 serrano chiles, stemmed, seeded, and sliced thin

2 tablespoons lime juice, plus lime wedges for serving

2 teaspoons chili powder

1 ounce cotija cheese, crumbled (¼ cup)

¼ cup chopped fresh cilantro

Tortilla chips

Why This Recipe Works This recipe is inspired by esquites, a Mexican dish of grilled corn mixed with mayonnaise, cheese, chiles, and lime. We adapted these flavors into a delicious, hot, gooey dip that can be served right out of the skillet. We especially like using a cast-iron skillet here, as it is key for getting good char on the corn kernels and also keeps the dip hot during serving. The bright and vibrant cilantro and scallions, along with the dusting of salty cotija cheese, give the dip added flavor and enhance its visual appeal and wow factor. A large ear of corn should yield 1 cup of kernels, but if the ears you find are smaller, buy at least six. We prefer to use fresh corn in this recipe, but you can substitute 4 cups of thawed frozen corn; thaw corn in a single layer on a dish towel–lined platter or baking sheet and pat dry before adding to the hot oil in step 1. We like serrano chiles here, but you can substitute one jalapeño chile that has been halved lengthwise, stemmed, seeded, and sliced ⅛ inch thick crosswise. For a spicier dip, do not seed the chiles. You will need a 12-inch broiler-safe skillet for this recipe.

1 Adjust oven rack 6 inches from broiler element and heat broiler. Heat 12-inch cast-iron skillet over medium heat for 5 minutes. Increase heat to medium-high, add 1 tablespoon oil, and heat until just smoking. Add half of corn, sprinkle with ¼ teaspoon salt, and spread corn into even layer. Cover and cook without moving corn until it begins to char, 3 to 5 minutes; transfer to bowl. Repeat with remaining 1 tablespoon oil, remaining corn, and remaining ¼ teaspoon salt. Once second batch of corn begins to char, stir in half of scallions and garlic and cook for 1 minute. Remove from heat.

2 Return first batch of corn to skillet with corn-scallion mixture. Stir in cream cheese, 1½ cups pepper Jack, mayonnaise, serranos, lime juice, and chili powder until evenly combined (cheese will begin to melt). Season with salt and pepper to taste. Spread mixture into even layer and sprinkle with remaining ½ cup pepper Jack.

3 Broil until cheese is melted and spotty brown, 2 to 3 minutes. Using potholder, remove skillet from broiler and let cool for 5 minutes. Being careful of hot skillet handle, sprinkle with cotija, cilantro, and remaining scallions. Serve hot from skillet with tortilla chips and lime wedges.

Sizing Up Your Skillet

traditional cast iron • **enameled cast iron** • **stainless steel**

A 12-inch traditional cast-iron skillet provides enough space for browning the corn. It makes an attractive serving vessel, and its superior heat retention keeps the dip warm at the table. An enameled cast-iron skillet will also work for these reasons. A stainless-steel skillet can also be used here, though the dip may cool down faster; add the 1 tablespoon of oil to the skillet and heat over medium heat until shimmering before adding the first batch of corn.

Baked Goat Cheese

Serves 8 to 10

Total Time 1 hour

3   tablespoons extra-virgin olive oil, plus extra for drizzling

1   onion, chopped fine

¾   teaspoon table salt

3   garlic cloves, sliced thin

2   teaspoons smoked paprika

1   teaspoon ground cumin

¼   teaspoon red pepper flakes

¼   teaspoon pepper

1   (28-ounce) can crushed tomatoes

1   (8- to 10-ounce) log goat cheese, softened

2   tablespoons coarsely chopped fresh cilantro

1   teaspoon grated lemon zest

Why This Recipe Works   There is one thing you can count on at holiday cocktail parties: small plates featuring melted cheese. Put out a dish of cheesy buffalo dip, a bowl of queso fundido, or a wheel of baked Brie, and your guests will cluster around, spooning soft, warm morsels onto chips or bread, tucking spiderweb strands of cheese into their mouths, smiling and nodding in appreciation as they go. This warm goat cheese broiled in a skillet with a mildly spicy tomato sauce combines tangy cheese with a smoky, sweet sauce. Goat cheese logs come in different sizes. Any size from 8 to 10 ounces will work in this recipe. If you can find only small logs of goat cheese (around 4 ounces), you can press two smaller logs together. Serve with crackers or toast points.

1   Heat 12-inch enameled cast-iron skillet over medium heat for 3 minutes. Add oil and heat until shimmering. Add onion and salt and cook until softened and golden brown, about 10 minutes. Stir in garlic, paprika, cumin, pepper flakes, and pepper and cook until fragrant, about 1 minute. Stir in tomatoes and bring to boil. Reduce heat to medium-low and simmer for 15 minutes. Season with salt to taste.

2   Adjust oven rack 6 inches from broiler element and heat broiler. Place goat cheese between 2 sheets of plastic wrap. Flatten goat cheese into 1-inch-thick disk, 3 to 4 inches in diameter, cupping your hands around outside of disk as needed to make compact shape.

3   Place goat cheese in center of skillet and broil until goat cheese is well browned, about 10 minutes. Using potholder, remove skillet from oven. Being careful of hot skillet handle, sprinkle cilantro and lemon zest over sauce and drizzle with extra oil. Serve.

Sizing Up Your Skillet

enameled cast iron • stainless steel

A 12-inch enameled cast-iron skillet provides enough space for simmering the sauce and broiling the cheese. It makes an attractive serving vessel, and its superior heat retention keeps the dip warm at the table. A stainless-steel skillet can also be used here, though the dip may cool down faster; add the oil to the skillet and heat over medium heat until shimmering before adding the onion. Due to the acidic sauce, we do not recommend using a traditional cast-iron or carbon-steel skillet.

Buffalo Chicken Dip with Spicy Monkey Bread

Serves 8 to 10

Total Time 1¾ hours

- 1 (8-ounce) boneless, skinless chicken breast, trimmed
- 5 tablespoons unsalted butter, divided
- 5 tablespoons hot sauce, divided
- 1 pound pizza dough, room temperature
- 8 ounces cream cheese, cut into 8 pieces and softened
- ⅓ cup ranch dressing
- 2 ounces blue cheese, crumbled (½ cup), divided
- 1 teaspoon Worcestershire sauce
- 1 rib celery, sliced thin on bias

Why This Recipe Works There's no question that buffalo wings have their place, but if you really want to up the ante and impress your friends, give this recipe a try; it makes for a stunning presentation with tender balls of dough surrounding a creamy, tangy buffalo dip with tender shredded chicken. First, we cook a chicken breast and, once cool, shred it. Then we use the same skillet as a proofing and baking vessel for some quick dough balls made from pizza dough. Rolling them in melted butter (with a little hot sauce for spice) prevents sticking and allows them to brown evenly in the oven. Cream cheese provides a smooth base for the dip, and whisking it with hot sauce, ranch dressing, blue cheese, and a couple of teaspoons of Worcestershire sauce creates the dip's zesty tang. A little more blue cheese scattered across the top along with thinly sliced celery completes the appeal of this irresistible appetizer—what could be more fun than bringing the skillet to the table and inviting company to use the warm bread balls to scoop up the dip? Cast iron's excellent heat retention ensures that the cheese doesn't separate or become congealed but stays warm and gooey until the skillet is scraped clean. Allow the pizza dough to sit at room temperature for at least 90 minutes before starting this recipe. You will need a 10-inch ovensafe skillet with a tight-fitting lid for this recipe.

1 Adjust oven rack to middle position and heat oven to 400 degrees. Place chicken breasts on cutting board and cover with plastic wrap. Using meat pounder, gently pound chicken to even thickness. Heat 10-inch cast-iron skillet over medium heat for 5 minutes. Add 1 table-spoon butter and heat until melted. Add chicken and cook, covered, until browned on first side, about 6 minutes. Flip chicken, cover, and continue to cook until chicken registers 160 degrees, 5 to 7 minutes. Transfer chicken to cutting board and let cool. Off heat, melt remaining 4 tablespoons butter in now-empty skillet; transfer to medium bowl and stir in 1 tablespoon hot sauce. Do not clean skillet.

2 Place dough on lightly floured counter, pat into rough 8-inch square, and cut into 32 pieces (½ ounce each). Working with 1 piece of dough at a time, roll into tight ball, then coat with melted butter. Evenly space 16 balls around edge of skillet, keeping center of skillet clear. Place remaining 16 balls on top, staggering them between gaps in balls underneath. Cover loosely with greased plastic wrap and let sit until slightly puffed, about 20 minutes. Remove plastic. Transfer skillet to oven and bake until rolls are just beginning to brown, about 20 minutes, rotating skillet halfway through baking.

3 Meanwhile, shred chicken into bite-size pieces using two forks. Whisk cream cheese, ranch dressing, ¼ cup blue cheese, Worcestershire, and remaining ¼ cup hot sauce in bowl until smooth and no lumps of cream cheese remain. Fold in chicken.

4 Spoon cheese mixture into center of skillet and sprinkle with remaining ¼ cup blue cheese, return skillet to oven, and bake until dip is bubbling and rolls are golden brown, about 10 minutes. Using pot holder, remove skillet from oven. Being careful of hot skillet handle, sprinkle with celery. Serve.

Sizing Up Your Skillet

traditional cast iron • **enameled cast iron** • **nonstick**

A 10-inch traditional cast-iron skillet provides enough space for assembling the dip, and the tall sides help support the crisp, golden-brown pull-apart rolls. It makes an attractive serving vessel, and its superior heat retention keeps the dip warm at the table. An enameled cast-iron skillet will also work for these reasons. An ovensafe nonstick skillet can also be used here, though the dip may cool down faster; add the butter to the nonstick skillet and heat over medium heat until melted before adding the chicken.

Loaded Beef Nachos

Serves 6 to 8

Total Time 50 minutes

- 2 tablespoons vegetable oil
- 1 onion, chopped fine
- 8 ounces 90 percent lean ground beef
- 1 tablespoon chili powder
- 1 garlic clove, minced
- 1 teaspoon minced fresh oregano or ¼ teaspoon dried
- ½ teaspoon ground cumin
- ½ teaspoon ground coriander
- ¼ teaspoon cayenne pepper
- ⅛ teaspoon table salt
- ½ cup chicken broth
- 8 ounces Monterey Jack cheese, shredded (2 cups), divided
- 8 ounces sharp cheddar cheese, shredded (2 cups), divided
- 8 ounces tortilla chips
- ¼ cup jarred sliced jalapeño chiles, chopped, divided
- 2 scallions, sliced thin

Why This Recipe Works Who doesn't like nachos? A heaping pile of warm tortilla chips loaded with flavorful, spicy beef and gooey cheese holds undeniable appeal. But all too often, just a few minutes after emerging from the oven, the chips end up soggy, the beef is cold, and the cheese is congealed. For nachos that can hold their hot-out-of-the-oven appeal until the very last chip is snagged, we knew we'd have to move this happy-hour favorite to a cast-iron skillet. While it may not be traditional, it is the perfect vessel for nachos: Not only does it mean we could use fewer dishes (you can cook, heat, and serve the nachos in the same skillet), but cast iron holds on to heat longer than aluminum or stainless steel, so the nachos stay warmer longer after you take them out of the oven. To ensure that every bite is loaded with toppings, we layer the nachos in the skillet, so even the chips on the bottom have an ample coating of cheese and spicy beef. Don't use ground beef that's fattier than 90 percent lean or the dish will be greasy. Serve with fresh tomato salsa, guacamole, sour cream, and lime wedges. You will need a 12-inch ovensafe skillet for this recipe.

1 Adjust oven rack to middle position and heat oven to 400 degrees. Heat 12-inch cast-iron skillet over medium heat for 3 minutes. Add oil and heat until shimmering. Add onion and cook until softened, about 5 minutes. Add beef and cook, breaking up meat with wooden spoon, until no longer pink, about 5 minutes. Stir in chili powder, garlic, oregano, cumin, coriander, cayenne, and salt and cook until fragrant, about 1 minute.

2 Stir in broth, scraping up any browned bits, and cook until nearly evaporated, about 2 minutes. Transfer mixture to medium bowl and stir in 1 cup Monterey Jack and 1 cup cheddar.

3 Spread half of tortilla chips evenly in now-empty skillet. Sprinkle ½ cup Monterey Jack and ½ cup cheddar over chips, then top with half of beef mixture, followed by half the jalapeños. Repeat layering with remaining chips, ½ cup Monterey Jack, ½ cup cheddar, beef mixture, and jalapeños. Transfer skillet to oven and bake until cheese is melted and just beginning to brown, 10 to 15 minutes. Sprinkle with scallions and serve.

Sizing Up Your Skillet

traditional cast iron • **enameled cast iron** • **stainless steel** • **nonstick**

A 12-inch traditional cast-iron skillet provides enough space for cooking the ground beef topping as well as assembling and baking the nachos. It makes an attractive serving vessel, and its superior heat retention keeps the nachos warm at the table. An enameled cast-iron skillet will also work for these reasons. A stainless-steel or ovensafe nonstick skillet can also be used here, though the dip may cool down faster; add the oil to the skillet and heat over medium heat until shimmering before adding the onion.

Braised Asparagus with Lemon and Chives

Serves 4

Total Time 30 minutes

1   pound thick asparagus

1   cup water

¼   cup chicken broth

2   tablespoons extra-virgin olive oil

¼   teaspoon table salt

¼   teaspoon grated lemon zest plus 1 teaspoon juice

2   teaspoons minced fresh chives, divided

VARIATIONS

Braised Asparagus with Sherry Vinegar and Marjoram

Substitute 1 teaspoon sherry vinegar for lemon zest and juice and 1 teaspoon minced fresh marjoram for chives.

Braised Asparagus with Orange and Tarragon

Substitute orange zest and juice for lemon, but increase amount of orange juice to 1 tablespoon. Substitute minced fresh tarragon for chives.

Sizing Up Your Skillet

stainless steel • nonstick • traditional cast iron • enameled cast iron • carbon-steel

A 12-inch stainless-steel skillet provides enough space for braising the asparagus. A nonstick, traditional cast-iron, enameled cast-iron, or carbon-steel skillet will also work for this reason.

Why This Recipe Works Braising, an oft-overlooked technique, produces asparagus with a tender, silky texture and sweet, nutty flavor. It is a great way to coax the spears' gentler side into the spotlight. The crisp bite gives way to silkiness, the fresh vegetal flavor evolves into more complex nuttiness, and the braising liquid can travel into the spears to season them inside and out. To achieve consistently cooked spears, we eschew the tradition of slow cooking in a minimal amount of liquid. Instead, we vigorously simmer the vegetable in a copious amount of liquid, a mix of water, broth, and olive oil. We also allow the braising liquid to evaporate, leaving behind a light glaze that coats the asparagus. When it comes to finishing touches, a "less is more" approach is best. We add just a splash of acidity and a handsome sprinkle of fresh herbs to accentuate the vegetable's sweet flavor. Bright-green asparagus, you've finally met your match. This recipe is best with asparagus spears that are at least ¾ inch thick. You will need a 12-inch skillet with a tight-fitting lid for this recipe.

1 Trim bottom 1 inch of asparagus spears; discard trimmings. Peel bottom two-thirds of spears until white flesh is exposed. Bring water, broth, oil, and salt to simmer in 12-inch stainless-steel skillet over high heat. Add asparagus in even layer. Reduce heat to maintain vigorous simmer and cover. Cook, gently shaking skillet occasionally, until asparagus is tender and can be easily pierced with tip of paring knife, 8 to 10 minutes.

2 Remove lid and continue to cook, shaking and swirling skillet, until skillet is almost dry and asparagus is glazed, 1 to 3 minutes. Off heat, add lemon zest and juice and half of chives; toss to coat. Transfer asparagus to serving platter, sprinkle with remaining chives, and season with salt to taste. Serve.

perfecting
BRAISED ASPARAGUS

Although braising renders asparagus neither crisp-tender, browned, nor vibrant green, it delivers spears with more complex flavor. A vigorous simmer creates steam and evenly cooks asparagus.

1   Bigger Is Better for Braising.

2   Trim (of course), but Also Peel.

3   Braise in a Lot of Liquid.

4   Season Simply.

Sizing Up Your Skillet

nonstick • **traditional cast iron**

A 12-inch nonstick skillet provides adequate space for arranging the large broccoli pieces
in an even layer. Its slick surface also ensures that the savory browning sticks to the broccoli,
not the pan. A traditional cast-iron skillet will also work for these reasons.

Skillet-Roasted Broccoli with Sesame and Orange Topping

Serves 4 to 6

Total Time 35 minutes

Sesame and Orange Topping

2 tablespoons toasted sesame seeds, divided

½ teaspoon grated orange zest

¼ teaspoon kosher salt

Broccoli

1¼ pounds broccoli crowns

5 tablespoons vegetable oil

¾ teaspoon kosher salt

2 tablespoons water

Why This Recipe Works Skillet roasting turns everyday broccoli into a dynamite small plate. Deeply browning the broccoli enhances the meaty stems and delicate florets, giving them a nutty flavor and crisp texture. The crunchy, umami-rich topping, made by grinding sesame seeds with orange zest and kosher salt, is our take on the Japanese dry condiment gomasio. We cut broccoli crowns into wedges to create flat sides to sit flush with the surface of the skillet. Once the broccoli is softened, the oil fills any gaps between the broccoli and the skillet. This recipe was developed with Diamond Crystal Kosher Salt. (If using Morton Kosher Salt, which is denser, decrease the amount for the broccoli to ½ teaspoon.) You will need a 12-inch skillet with a tight-fitting lid for this recipe.

1 For the sesame and orange topping Using spice grinder or mortar and pestle, grind 1 tablespoon sesame seeds, orange zest, and salt to powder. Transfer to small bowl. Add remaining 1 tablespoon sesame seeds and toss with your fingers until sesame seeds are evenly distributed. Sprinkle one-third of topping onto platter.

2 For the broccoli Cut broccoli into 4 wedges if crowns are 3 to 4 inches in diameter or 6 wedges if 4 to 5 inches in diameter. Add oil to 12-inch nonstick skillet and tilt skillet until oil covers surface. Add broccoli, cut side down (pieces will fit snugly; if a few pieces don't fit in bottom layer, place on top). Sprinkle evenly with salt and drizzle with water. Cover and cook over high heat, without moving broccoli, until broccoli is bright green, about 4 minutes.

3 Uncover and press gently on broccoli with back of spatula. Cover and cook until undersides of broccoli are deeply charred and stems are crisp-tender, 4 to 6 minutes. Off heat, uncover and turn broccoli so second cut side is touching skillet. Move any pieces that were on top so that they are flush with skillet surface. Return skillet to high heat and cook, uncovered, pressing gently on broccoli with back of spatula, until second cut side is deeply browned, 3 to 5 minutes longer. Transfer to platter, sprinkle with remaining topping, and serve.

VARIATIONS

Skillet-Roasted Broccoli with Parmesan and Black Pepper Topping

Using your fingers, mix ½ teaspoon pepper and ½ teaspoon grated lemon zest in small bowl until evenly combined. Add ½ cup grated Parmesan cheese and toss until lemon zest and pepper are evenly distributed. Substitute for Sesame and Orange Topping.

Skillet-Roasted Broccoli with Smoky Sunflower Seed Topping

Using spice grinder or mortar and pestle, grind 2 tablespoons toasted sunflower seeds, 1 tablespoon nutritional yeast, ½ teaspoon grated lemon zest, ¼ teaspoon smoked paprika, and ¼ teaspoon kosher salt to coarse powder. Substitute for Sesame and Orange Topping.

Skillet-Roasted Brussels Sprouts with Pomegranate and Pistachios

Serves 4 to 6

Total Time 20 minutes

1   pound brussels sprouts, trimmed and halved

5   tablespoons extra-virgin olive oil

1   tablespoon pomegranate molasses

½   teaspoon ground cumin

¼   teaspoon table salt

¼   cup shelled pistachios, toasted and chopped fine

2   tablespoons pomegranate seeds

Why This Recipe Works For speedy stovetop brussels sprouts that are deeply browned on the cut sides while still bright green on the uncut sides and crisp-tender within, we start them in a cold skillet with plenty of oil and cook them covered. This gently heats the sprouts and creates a steamy environment that cooks them through without any extra moisture needed. We then remove the lid and continue to cook the sprouts cut sides down, so they develop a substantial, caramelized exterior. Using enough oil to completely coat the skillet ensures that all the sprouts make full contact with the fat to brown evenly. To elevate the flavor of the roasted sprouts, we add pomegranate molasses and cumin, with pistachios and pomegranate seeds giving them a colorful and flavorful finish. You will need a 12-inch skillet with a tight-fitting lid for this recipe.

1 Arrange brussels sprouts in single layer, cut sides down, in cold 12-inch nonstick skillet. Drizzle oil evenly over brussels sprouts. Cover skillet, place over medium-high heat, and cook until brussels sprouts are bright green and cut sides have started to brown, about 5 minutes.

2 Uncover and continue to cook until cut sides of brussels sprouts are deeply and evenly browned and paring knife meets little to no resistance, 2 to 4 minutes, adjusting heat and moving sprouts as needed to prevent them from overbrowning. While sprouts cook, combine pomegranate molasses, cumin, and salt in small bowl.

3 Off heat, add pomegranate molasses mixture to skillet and stir to evenly coat brussels sprouts. Season with salt and pepper to taste. Transfer to serving platter, sprinkle with pistachios and pomegranate seeds, and serve.

VARIATIONS

Skillet-Roasted Brussels Sprouts with Gochujang and Sesame Seeds

Substitute 1 tablespoon gochujang and 1 tablespoon rice vinegar for pomegranate molasses and cumin, and 2 teaspoons toasted sesame seeds for pistachios and pomegranate seeds.

Skillet-Roasted Brussels Sprouts with Lemon and Pecorino

Substitute 1 tablespoon lemon juice and ¼ teaspoon salt for pomegranate molasses and ¼ cup shredded Pecorino Romano cheese for pistachios and pomegranate seeds.

Sizing Up Your Skillet

nonstick • traditional cast iron

A 12-inch nonstick skillet provides adequate space for arranging the brussels sprouts in an even layer. Its slick surface also ensures that the savory browning sticks to the brussels sprouts, not the pan. A traditional cast-iron skillet will also work for these reasons.

Sizing Up Your Skillet

stainless steel • **nonstick** • **traditional cast iron** • **enameled cast iron** • **carbon-steel**

A 12-inch stainless-steel skillet provides enough space for sautéing the cabbage. A nonstick, traditional cast-iron, enameled cast-iron, or carbon-steel skillet will also work for this reason. If using a cast-iron skillet, you will need to preheat the empty skillet over medium heat for 3 minutes before proceeding with step 2.

Sautéed Cabbage with Parsley and Lemon

Serves 4 to 6

Total Time 30 minutes

1   small head green cabbage (1¼ pounds), cored and sliced thin

2   tablespoons extra-virgin olive oil, divided

1   onion, halved and sliced thin

¾   teaspoon table salt, divided

¼   teaspoon pepper

¼   cup chopped fresh parsley

1½   teaspoons lemon juice

Why This Recipe Works If you tend to walk right by the gorgeous heads of cabbage at the farmers' market or grocery store, this simple recipe will change your perception of how delicious it can be when sautéed, as opposed to just being used to make coleslaw. It's cheap and hearty, and you can find various types of seasonal cabbage in the summer and fall months. This simple preparation of humble green cabbage brings out the vegetable's natural sweetness and preserves its crisp-tender texture. It is fantastic as a side dish served with any type of roast pork or chicken. First, we soak the cabbage for just a few minutes to reduce bitterness and provide extra moisture to help it steam in the skillet. Then we pan-steam and sauté the cabbage over relatively high heat to cook it quickly, which also adds extra flavor from browning. There is something about the alchemy of cooking cabbage that gives it a richness and silkiness that is immensely appealing. Onion reinforces the cabbage's sweetness and lemon and parsley lend brightness. You will need a 12-inch skillet with a tight-fitting lid for this recipe.

1   Place cabbage in large bowl and cover with cold water. Let sit for 3 minutes; drain well.

2   Heat 1 tablespoon oil in 12-inch stainless-steel skillet over medium-high heat until shimmering. Add onion and ¼ teaspoon salt and cook until softened and lightly browned, 5 to 7 minutes; transfer to bowl.

3   Heat remaining 1 tablespoon oil in now-empty skillet over medium-high heat until shimmering. Add cabbage and sprinkle with remaining ½ teaspoon salt and pepper. Cover and cook, without stirring, until cabbage is wilted and lightly browned on bottom, about 3 minutes. Stir and continue to cook, uncovered, until cabbage is crisp-tender and lightly browned in places, about 4 minutes, stirring once halfway through cooking. Off heat, stir in onion, parsley, and lemon juice. Season with salt and pepper to taste, and serve.

VARIATIONS

Sautéed Cabbage with Chile and Peanuts

Substitute red onion for onion. Cook 1 thinly sliced jalapeño, seeded if desired, with onion in step 2. Once onion is crisp-tender, about 4 minutes, add 2 garlic cloves, minced to paste, and cook until fragrant, about 30 seconds. Substitute 4 teaspoons fish sauce and 2 teaspoons packed brown sugar for salt and pepper in step 3. When adding the onion mixture, substitute ½ cup chopped fresh cilantro for parsley and 1 tablespoon lime juice for lemon juice. Sprinkle cabbage with 2 tablespoons chopped unsalted dry-roasted peanuts before serving.

Sautéed Red Cabbage with Bacon and Caraway

Substitute red cabbage for green. Whisk 1 tablespoon cider vinegar and 2 teaspoons packed brown sugar together in medium bowl. In step 3, omit oil; instead, cook 4 slices chopped bacon in skillet over medium heat until crispy, 5 to 7 minutes. Transfer bacon to paper towel–lined plate and set aside; pour all but 1 tablespoon fat into bowl and reserve. Substitute red onion for onion and cook in fat remaining in skillet until softened, about 5 minutes. Add 1 teaspoon caraway seeds and cook for 1 minute; transfer onion to bowl with vinegar mixture. Add cabbage and 1 tablespoon reserved fat to skillet and cook as directed. Stir bacon, onion mixture, lemon, and parsley into cabbage and serve.

Skillet-Roasted Carrots with Smoky Spiced Almonds and Parsley

Serves 4

Total Time 40 minutes

¼ cup sliced almonds, chopped fine

2 teaspoons plus 2 tablespoons vegetable oil, divided

½ teaspoon smoked paprika

⅛ teaspoon plus ½ teaspoon table salt, divided

Pinch cayenne pepper

½ cup water

1½ pounds large carrots, peeled, cut crosswise into 3- to 4-inch lengths, and cut lengthwise into even pieces

1 tablespoon chopped fresh parsley

Why This Recipe Works For roasted carrots in a third of the time, we moved the process from the oven to a covered skillet on the stovetop, where we first steam the carrots for about 8 minutes before searing them. Steaming softens the carrots, which is important for two reasons: It releases the carrots' sugars, encouraging browning, and it makes the carrots more flexible so that they can be pressed flush against the skillet for optimal color. Once the lid is removed, the carrots need only 5 to 7 minutes to develop oven-worthy roasty browning. Fried almonds add a welcome crunch, while a touch of smoke from paprika and a little heat from cayenne complement the carrots' natural sweetness. Parsley adds color and freshness. We prefer large carrots from the bulk bin for this recipe. After cutting the carrots crosswise, quarter lengthwise any pieces that are larger than 1½ inches in diameter, halve lengthwise any pieces that are ¾ to 1½ inches in diameter, and leave whole carrots that are narrower than ¾ inch. You will need a 12-inch skillet with a tight-fitting lid for this recipe.

1 Combine almonds, 2 teaspoons oil, paprika, ⅛ teaspoon salt, and cayenne in 12-inch nonstick skillet. Cook over medium heat, stirring frequently, until almonds are fragrant and crisp, 3 to 4 minutes. Transfer to small bowl and let cool completely. Wipe skillet clean with paper towels.

2 Mix ½ cup water and remaining ½ teaspoon salt in now-empty skillet until salt is dissolved. Place carrots in skillet, arranging as many carrots flat side down as possible (carrots will not fit in single layer). Drizzle remaining 2 tablespoons oil over carrots. Bring to boil over medium-high heat. Cover and cook, without moving carrots, until carrots are crisp-tender and water has almost evaporated, 8 to 10 minutes.

3 Uncover and gently shake skillet until carrots settle into even layer. Continue to cook, not moving carrots but occasionally pressing them gently against skillet with spatula, until undersides of carrots are deeply browned, 3 to 5 minutes. Stir carrots and flip so that unbrowned sides face down. Cook until second sides are lightly browned, about 2 minutes. Transfer to serving dish. Stir parsley into almond mixture. Sprinkle carrots with almond mixture and serve.

VARIATIONS

Skillet-Roasted Carrots with Mustard Bread Crumbs and Chives

In step 1, substitute ¼ cup panko bread crumbs for almonds and 1 tablespoon Dijon mustard for paprika; omit cayenne. Cook panko, oil, Dijon, paprika, and salt over medium-high heat, stirring constantly, until panko is crisp, dry, and golden brown, about 5 minutes. In step 3, substitute chives for parsley and stir ⅛ teaspoon pepper into panko mixture with chives.

Skillet-Roasted Carrots with Za'atar Bread Crumbs and Cilantro

In step 1, substitute 2 tablespoons panko bread crumbs for almonds and 1 tablespoon za'atar for paprika; omit cayenne. In step 3, substitute cilantro for parsley.

Sizing Up Your Skillet

nonstick • traditional cast iron

A 12-inch nonstick skillet provides enough space for arranging carrots in a single layer. Its slick surface also ensures that the savory browning sticks to the carrots, not the pan. A traditional cast-iron skillet will also work for these reasons.

Sautéed Mushrooms with Red Wine and Rosemary

Serves 4

Total Time 40 minutes

1¼ pounds mushrooms, trimmed

¼ cup water

½ teaspoon vegetable oil

1 tablespoon unsalted butter

1 shallot, minced

1 teaspoon minced fresh rosemary

¼ teaspoon table salt

¼ teaspoon pepper

¼ cup red wine

1 tablespoon cider vinegar

½ cup chicken broth

VARIATION

Sautéed Mushrooms with Mustard and Parsley

Omit rosemary. Substitute 1 tablespoon Dijon mustard for wine and increase vinegar to 1½ tablespoons (liquid will take only 1 to 2 minutes to evaporate). Stir in 2 tablespoons chopped fresh parsley before serving.

Sizing Up Your Skillet

nonstick • traditional cast iron

A 12-inch nonstick skillet provides enough space for the bulky mushrooms before they cook down. Its slick surface also ensures that the savory glaze sticks to the mushrooms, not the pan. A traditional cast-iron skillet will also work for these reasons.

Why This Recipe Works Mushrooms always feel like an indulgent side dish, one that few of us actually make and fewer still have a technique that delivers failproof results. While mushrooms are typically cooked in oil or butter until their moisture releases, they release their moisture more quickly when first steamed in a small amount of water. The steamed mushrooms collapse and don't absorb much oil; just ½ teaspoon is needed for browning. And because we use so little fat to sauté the mushrooms, it is possible to sauce them with a butter-based reduction without making them overly rich. Use one variety of mushroom or a combination: Stem and halve portobello mushrooms and cut each half crosswise into ½-inch pieces. Trim white or cremini mushrooms; quarter them if large or medium and halve them if small. Tear trimmed oyster mushrooms into 1- to 1½-inch pieces. Stem shiitake mushrooms; quarter large caps and halve small caps. Cut trimmed maitake (hen-of-the-woods) mushrooms into 1- to 1½-inch pieces.

1 Cook mushrooms and water in 12-inch nonstick skillet over high heat, stirring occasionally, until skillet is almost dry and mushrooms begin to sizzle, 4 to 8 minutes. Reduce heat to medium-high. Add oil and toss until mushrooms are evenly coated. Continue to cook, stirring occasionally, until mushrooms are well browned, 4 to 8 minutes. Reduce heat to medium.

2 Push mushrooms to sides of skillet. Add butter to center. When butter has melted, add shallot, rosemary, salt, and pepper to center and cook, stirring constantly, until aromatic, about 30 seconds. Add wine and vinegar and stir mushrooms into mixture. Cook, stirring occasionally, until liquid has evaporated, 2 to 3 minutes. Add broth and cook, stirring occasionally, until glaze is reduced by half, about 3 minutes. Season with salt and pepper to taste, and serve.

VARIATION

Sautéed Mushrooms with Soy, Scallion, and Ginger

Substitute 1 thinly sliced scallion for shallot and grated fresh ginger for rosemary. Omit salt. Substitute 2 tablespoons soy sauce for wine and sherry vinegar for cider vinegar.

perfecting
SAUTÉED MUSHROOMS

Although mushrooms are typically sautéed in butter or oil until they give up their moisture and brown, this counterintuitive recipe starts by steaming the mushrooms in water, and only a tiny amount of fat is needed for good browning. This means you can sauce them with a butter-based reduction without tilting into overly rich territory.

1 Steam Mushrooms in Water.

2 Reduce the Heat and Drizzle with Oil.

3 Add Butter, Aromatics, Wine, Vinegar, and Broth.

4 Glaze in the Aromatic Broth Reduction.

Whole Romanesco with Berbere and Yogurt-Tahini Sauce

Serves 4

Total Time 50 minutes

- 1 head romanesco or cauliflower (2 pounds), outer leaves removed, stem trimmed flush with bottom florets
- 1 teaspoon plus 3 tablespoons extra-virgin olive oil, divided
- ¼ teaspoon table salt
- ½ teaspoon paprika
- ¼ teaspoon cayenne pepper
- ¼ teaspoon ground coriander
- ⅛ teaspoon ground allspice
- ⅛ teaspoon ground cardamom
- ⅛ teaspoon ground cumin
- ⅛ teaspoon ground black pepper
- 2 tablespoons pine nuts, toasted and chopped
- 1 tablespoon minced fresh cilantro
- 1 recipe Yogurt-Tahini Sauce (page 102)

Why This Recipe Works This dramatically beautiful, fractal-looking vegetable is a pale green relative of cauliflower and a showstopper when cooked and presented whole. Like other brassica, romanesco has plenty of earthy flavor, so strong seasoning and deep browning are valuable additional touches of drama. We use the broiler to provide the head of romanesco with a nicely charred exterior, but because this large, dense vegetable can burn under the intense heat before it's cooked through all the way, we first parcook it in the microwave. We then drizzle with olive oil and put it under the broiler to brown. We baste the broiled romanesco with a mixture of more oil and berbere, a warmly aromatic and highly flavorful Ethiopian spice blend. A bright, cooling yogurt sauce with some nutty depth from tahini pleasantly offsets the warm spices, and pine nuts provide crunch against the just-perfectly tender romanesco. You will need a 12-inch broiler-safe skillet for this recipe.

1 Adjust oven rack 6 inches from broiler element and heat broiler. Microwave romanesco in covered bowl until paring knife slips easily in and out of core, 8 to 12 minutes.

2 Transfer romanesco stem side down to 12-inch stainless-steel skillet. Drizzle romanesco evenly with 1 teaspoon oil and sprinkle with salt. Transfer skillet to oven and broil until top of romanesco is spotty brown, 8 to 10 minutes. Meanwhile, microwave paprika, cayenne, coriander, allspice, cardamom, cumin, pepper, and remaining 3 tablespoons oil in now-empty bowl, stirring occasionally, until fragrant and bubbling, 1 to 2 minutes.

3 Using potholders, remove skillet from oven and transfer to wire rack. Being careful of hot skillet handle, pour oil mixture over romanesco, then gently tilt skillet so oil pools to 1 side. Using spoon, baste romanesco until oil is absorbed, about 30 seconds.

4 Cut romanesco into wedges and sprinkle with pine nuts and cilantro. Serve with Yogurt-Tahini Sauce.

Sizing Up Your Skillet

stainless steel • traditional cast iron • enameled cast iron • carbon steel

A 12-inch stainless-steel skillet provides enough space for broiling and basting a whole romanesco head. A traditional cast-iron, enameled cast-iron, or carbon-steel skillet will also work well for this reason.

Southern-Style Baby Lima Beans

Serves 4 to 6

Total Time 1¼ hours

4 slices bacon, cut into ½-inch pieces

4 cups chicken broth

1½ pounds frozen baby lima beans

1¼ cups water

½ onion, halved

1 teaspoon pepper

¾ teaspoon table salt

Why This Recipe Works Lima beans are worth getting excited about: The frozen baby variety we call for here are sweet, petite, and tender yet still substantial. The beauty of this recipe is in its simplicity. First, we cook pieces of bacon in a large skillet until crispy; then we add the beans, chicken broth, water, and half an onion; cover; and let it all cook over low heat. After an hour the beans start to break down and the savory liquid thickens. The resulting beans and their smoky, thick, peppery broth are complex and deeply comforting. Stirring frequently as the beans cook emulsifies the bacon fat into the broth, giving it a silky texture. The flavor is so impressive that no one will suspect how easy this dish is to make. Do not thaw the baby lima beans before cooking. You will need a 12-inch skillet with a tight-fitting lid for this recipe.

Cook bacon in 12-inch stainless-steel skillet over medium heat until rendered and crispy, 5 to 7 minutes. Add broth, beans, water, onion, pepper, and salt and bring to boil. Reduce heat to medium-low, cover partially, and simmer, stirring occasionally, until beans just begin to break down and liquid is thickened, about 1 hour (liquid will continue to thicken as it sits). Discard onion. Season beans with salt and pepper to taste. Serve.

Sizing Up Your Skillet

stainless steel • **nonstick** • **traditional cast iron** • **enameled cast iron** • **carbon-steel**

A 12-inch stainless-steel skillet provides enough space for browning the bacon and simmering the beans. A nonstick, traditional cast-iron, enameled cast-iron, or carbon-steel skillet will also work for these reasons.

Black Beans and Rice

Serves 4 to 6

Total Time 1 hour

1   (15-ounce) can black beans

2¼   cups chicken broth, plus extra
     as needed

2   tablespoons vegetable oil, divided

¾   cup finely chopped onion

¾   cup finely chopped green
     bell pepper

½   teaspoon table salt

½   teaspoon pepper

3   garlic cloves, minced

1   teaspoon dried oregano

¾   teaspoon ground cumin

1½   cups long-grain white rice, rinsed

4   ounces salt pork, cut into 4 pieces

1   bay leaf

Why This Recipe Works Beans and rice are a classic pairing, but to truly make this dish appealing, you need smoky pork, aromatics, and a method. First, we brown onions and green bell peppers in a nonstick skillet alongside aromatic cumin, garlic, and dried oregano. We toast the rice in oil until the edges of the grains turn translucent so that the rice keeps its shape and doesn't turn mushy in the finished dish. Instead of using dried beans, canned beans (and their liquid) keep things easy. To add flavor to the rice, we cook it with savory salt pork, chicken broth, the reserved bean liquid, and the sautéed vegetables for just 20 minutes and then let it sit for 10 minutes before fluffing with a fork. If you can't find salt pork, you can substitute two slices of bacon, but the dish will have a smokier flavor. Rinse the rice in a fine-mesh strainer under running water until the water runs almost clear, about 1½ minutes, stirring the rice a few times with your hand. You will need a 12-inch skillet with a tight-fitting lid for this recipe.

1 Place beans in fine-mesh strainer set over 4-cup liquid measuring cup and let drain for 5 minutes; reserve bean liquid. Add enough broth to bean liquid to equal 2½ cups and stir to combine. Set aside beans and broth mixture.

2 Heat 1 tablespoon oil in 12-inch nonstick skillet over medium-high heat until shimmering. Add onion, bell pepper, salt, and pepper and cook until vegetables are softened and just beginning to brown, about 6 minutes. Stir in garlic, oregano, and cumin and cook until fragrant, about 30 seconds. Transfer vegetable mixture to bowl; set aside.

3 Heat remaining 1 tablespoon oil in now-empty skillet over medium-high heat. Add rice and cook, stirring frequently, until edges begin to turn translucent and rice is fragrant, about 2 minutes. Stir in salt pork, bay leaf, beans, broth mixture, and vegetable mixture and bring to boil (submerge salt pork as best you can). Cover, reduce heat to low, and cook, without stirring, for 20 minutes.

4 Let stand, covered, off heat for 10 minutes. Discard salt pork and bay leaf. Gently fluff rice with fork. Season with salt and pepper to taste. Serve.

Sizing Up Your Skillet

nonstick ● **traditional cast iron** ● **carbon-steel**

A 12-inch nonstick skillet provides enough space for sautéing the aromatic base and simmering the rice and beans. Its slick surface also ensures that the dish can be easily scooped out for serving without sticking. A traditional cast-iron or carbon-steel skillet will also work for these reasons. If using a cast-iron skillet, you will need to preheat the empty skillet over medium heat for 3 minutes before proceeding with step 2.

Creamy Potatoes and Leeks

Serves 6

Total Time 1 hour

4 tablespoons unsalted butter, cut into 4 pieces, divided

½ cup panko bread crumbs

1¼ teaspoons table salt, divided

2 pounds leeks, white and light-green parts only, halved lengthwise, sliced ½ inch thick, and washed thoroughly

1½ pounds yellow waxy potatoes, unpeeled, cut into ¾-inch pieces

1½ cups chicken broth

¼ cup dry white wine

¾ cup heavy cream

½ teaspoon pepper

2 ounces Gruyère cheese, shredded (⅔ cup)

2 teaspoons chopped fresh thyme or oregano

Why This Recipe Works Potatoes and leeks are made to be united in all manner of dishes—add cream, broth, wine, and cheese and you are bound to create an elegant and comforting dish. This rustic pairing is simple to execute and results in a stunning side of rich and creamy potatoes and melted leeks with a crispy panko topping, all made in a nonstick skillet. We start this side dish by toasting panko bread crumbs in butter for a crispy topping. Then, we soften leeks in more butter before adding chunks of potatoes. We cook the potatoes in chicken broth and wine, instead of water, which gives them depth and brightness. To enrich the final dish, we add some heavy cream and allow the potatoes to cook past al dente to create an even creamier consistency overall. Just as the cream reduces, we stir in a handful of nutty Gruyère cheese and top the potatoes and leeks with the buttery toasted bread crumbs and some earthy fresh thyme leaves. We prefer to use leeks measuring about 1 inch in diameter for this recipe because they're more tender than larger leeks. Larger leeks will work, but be sure to discard their more fibrous outer layers. You will need a 12-inch skillet with a tight-fitting lid for this recipe.

1 Melt 2 tablespoons butter in 12-inch nonstick skillet over medium heat. Add panko and ½ teaspoon salt and cook, stirring often, until golden brown, 3 to 6 minutes. Transfer to bowl; set aside. Wipe skillet clean with paper towels.

2 Melt remaining 2 tablespoons butter in now-empty skillet over medium heat. Add leeks and ¼ teaspoon salt and cook, covered, until softened, about 6 minutes, stirring halfway through cooking. Stir in potatoes, broth, wine, and remaining ½ teaspoon salt and spread into even layer. Cover and bring to vigorous simmer over medium-high heat. Reduce heat to medium-low and simmer, covered, until potatoes are fork-tender, 20 to 25 minutes.

3 Stir in cream and pepper and return to simmer. Continue to cook, uncovered, until spatula leaves trail when dragged through mixture, 4 to 6 minutes. Off heat, stir in Gruyère. Sprinkle evenly with panko mixture and thyme. Serve.

Sizing Up Your Skillet

nonstick • traditional cast iron

A 12-inch nonstick skillet provides enough space for simmering the leeks and potatoes. Its slick surface also ensures that the dish can be easily served. A traditional cast-iron skillet will also work for these reasons; you will need to preheat the empty skillet over medium heat for 3 minutes before proceeding with step 1.

Sizing Up Your Skillet

nonstick • **traditional cast iron** • **carbon steel**

A 10-inch ovensafe nonstick skillet provides enough space for assembling the casserole. Its slick surface also ensures that the dish can be easily scooped out for serving without sticking. A traditional cast-iron or carbon-steel skillet will also work for these reasons.

Hasselback Potato Casserole

Serves 8

Total Time 3 hours

6 slices bacon, chopped fine

2 cups finely chopped onions

1¼ cups chicken broth, divided

4 garlic cloves, minced

2 teaspoons minced fresh rosemary

4 pounds large russet potatoes, unpeeled

6 ounces Gruyère cheese, shredded (1½ cups), divided

2 ounces Parmesan cheese, grated (1 cup), divided

1 teaspoon table salt

1 teaspoon pepper

Why This Recipe Works This extra-crispy take on potato gratin, credited to chef and author J. Kenji López-Alt, an America's Test Kitchen alumnus, melds potato gratin with Hasselback potatoes (purportedly created by Leif Elisson in 1953 at the Hasselbacken Restaurant Academy in Stockholm). Stacking potato slices horizontally allows for crispier browning and better distribution of cheese and seasonings. No wonder the internet went nuts for it. Using a mandoline ensures that the potato slices are uniformly thin for an unfailingly tender interior and well-browned top. We layer in our own complementary ingredients in a nonstick skillet: crispy bacon, onion that is caramelized in the rendered bacon fat, garlic for pungent bite, and piney rosemary. Finally, we incorporate two cheeses, Gruyère plus Parmesan, to provide nuttiness and creaminess while structurally melding the potato slices together. Look for oblong russets that are 4 to 6 inches long and about 3 inches in diameter at their widest. Large potatoes are easier to peel and slice and fit well when stacked in the skillet. If you can find only small russets, you may need more than 4¼ pounds to yield enough slices to fill the pan. Do not pack the potatoes in too tightly or they may not cook through in the stated time; it's OK to have a few unused slices. We strongly recommend using a mandoline to slice the potatoes. You will need a 12-inch ovensafe skillet for this recipe.

1 Adjust oven rack to middle position and heat oven to 400 degrees. Cook bacon in 10-inch ovensafe nonstick skillet over medium heat until rendered and crispy, 5 to 7 minutes. Stir in onions and ½ cup broth. Cover and cook, stirring occasionally, until most of liquid has evaporated, 5 to 7 minutes. Uncover and continue to cook until onion is well browned, about 5 minutes. Stir in garlic and rosemary and cook until fragrant, about 1 minute; transfer to large bowl.

2 Peel potatoes. Using mandoline, slice potatoes crosswise ⅛ inch thick. Add potatoes, ¾ cup Gruyère, ½ cup Parmesan, salt, pepper, and remaining ¾ cup broth to bowl with bacon-onion mixture and toss to thoroughly combine, breaking up any stacked potatoes and making sure all slices are coated.

3 Stack 2 inches of potatoes, then lay stack horizontally against walls of now-empty skillet. Continue stacking and laying down potatoes until skillet perimeter is filled. Stack and arrange remaining potatoes in middle of skillet. (Potato slices should fit snugly without having to be squeezed in. You may not need all of them.) Pour remaining broth mixture in bowl over potatoes. Brush any pieces of bacon and onion on top of potatoes down into valleys between rows.

4 Cover skillet tightly with aluminum foil and place on foil-lined rimmed baking sheet. Bake for 1¼ hours. Uncover and continue to bake until tops of potatoes are golden brown and paring knife inserted into potatoes meets very little resistance, about 30 minutes.

5 Combine remaining ¾ cup Gruyère and remaining ½ cup Parmesan in bowl. Sprinkle potatoes with cheese mixture and bake until cheese is melted and spotty brown, about 15 minutes. Transfer skillet to wire rack and let cool for 15 minutes before serving.

Rustic Bread Stuffing

Serves 8

Total Time 1½ hours

2   baguettes (12 ounces each), bottom crust and ends trimmed and discarded

2   cups vegetable or chicken broth

6   tablespoons unsalted butter, divided

2   onions, chopped fine

3   celery ribs, minced

1   teaspoon table salt

1½ tablespoons minced fresh thyme or 1 teaspoon dried

1½ tablespoons minced fresh sage or 1 teaspoon dried

3   garlic cloves, minced

¾   teaspoon pepper

Why This Recipe Works Bread stuffing tends to appear on the table only at the holidays, but with this easy recipe in your repertoire, chances are you'll get to enjoy it throughout the year. We wanted a lighter bread stuffing, one that wouldn't upstage the main course, something loosely textured and a bit less filling than the usual fare. Eliminating eggs and cutting back on the broth offer a quick path to achieving this less heavy stuffing. Then we swap out the usual cubes of toasted white sandwich bread for torn chunks of airy baguette, which retain some crispness and chew even after combined with the rest of the ingredients. The skillet is an ideal vessel for making this stuffing, as you use it to sauté the aromatics and bake the casserole and, as a bonus, you can bring the skillet right to the table so everyone can dig in. You will need a 12-inch ovensafe skillet for this recipe.

1 Adjust oven rack to upper-middle position and heat oven to 400 degrees. Tear baguettes into rough 1-inch pieces (you should have about 12 cups) and spread into even layer in 12-inch ovensafe nonstick skillet (skillet will be very full). Bake until bread begins to brown and crisp on top, about 15 minutes.

2 Using potholders, remove skillet from oven. Being careful of hot skillet handle, transfer bread to large bowl. Drizzle with broth and toss to combine. Set aside, stirring occasionally to saturate bread.

3 Melt 2 tablespoons butter in now-empty skillet over medium heat. Add onions, celery, and salt and cook until softened and browned, 10 to 12 minutes. Stir in thyme, sage, garlic, and pepper and cook until fragrant, about 30 seconds. Stir onion mixture into bread mixture.

4 Melt remaining 4 tablespoons butter in again-empty skillet over low heat; measure out and reserve 2 tablespoons melted butter. Add stuffing to skillet, pressing firmly into even layer with spatula. Drizzle stuffing with reserved butter. Transfer skillet to oven and bake until top is deep golden brown and crisp, about 30 minutes, rotating skillet halfway through baking. Let stuffing cool for 10 minutes before serving.

VARIATIONS

Rustic Bread Stuffing with Sausage and Fennel

At the beginning of step 3, cook 8 ounces bulk pork sausage in now-empty skillet over medium heat, breaking up meat with wooden spoon, until no longer pink, 5 to 7 minutes. Proceed with step 3, but omit butter, reduce onion to 1, and substitute 1 chopped fennel bulb for celery and 1½ tablespoons minced fresh rosemary for sage. Proceed with recipe as directed.

Rustic Bread Stuffing with Apples and Cranberries

Reduce onion to 1. Add 2 apples, peeled, cored, and cut into ¼-inch pieces, to skillet with onion and celery. Add ½ cup dried cranberries and ¼ cup chopped toasted walnuts to bread with onion mixture.

Sizing Up Your Skillet

nonstick ● **traditional cast iron**

A 12-inch ovensafe nonstick skillet provides enough space for toasting the bread and cooking the aromatics as well as baking the stuffing. Its slick surface also ensures that the dish can be easily served. A traditional cast-iron skillet will also work for these reasons.

breads & desserts

Pan-Grilled Flatbreads

Makes 4 flatbreads

Total Time 1¼ hours, plus
1½ hours rising

2½ cups (13¾ ounces) bread flour

¼ cup (1⅓ ounces) whole-wheat flour

2¼ teaspoons instant or rapid-rise yeast

1½ teaspoons table salt

1 cup water, room temperature

¼ cup plain whole-milk yogurt, room temperature

2 tablespoons vegetable oil, divided

2 teaspoons sugar

4 tablespoons unsalted butter, melted

Flake sea salt

VARIATIONS

Pan-Grilled Honey-Chile Flatbreads

Add 1 tablespoon honey, 2 teaspoons minced serrano chile, and 2 teaspoons grated fresh ginger to butter before melting.

Why This Recipe Works Inspired by the soft, pillowy texture of Indian naan, we set out to make flavorful, tender-chewy all-purpose flatbreads. To give the simple flatbreads a wheat flavor without compromising the texture, we add a small amount of whole-wheat flour to bread flour. Taking a cue from naan, we enrich the dough with yogurt and oil, which tenderizes it. For the cooking vessel, we turn to a cast-iron skillet and its great heat retention to help create spotty brown flecks. To avoid a tough crust, we first mist the dough with water before cooking to moisten the flour that coats it. We cover the pan during the cooking time, trapping steam and moisture for breads that are nicely charred but still moist. Brushing the finished breads with melted butter and sprinkling them with sea salt adds a final layer of flavor. You will need a 12-inch skillet with a tight-fitting lid for this recipe.

1 Whisk bread flour, whole-wheat flour, yeast, and table salt together in bowl of stand mixer. Whisk water, yogurt, 1 tablespoon oil, and sugar in liquid measuring cup until sugar has dissolved. Using dough hook on low speed, slowly add water mixture to flour mixture and mix until cohesive dough starts to form and no dry flour remains, about 2 minutes. Increase speed to medium-low and knead until dough is smooth and elastic and clears sides of bowl but sticks to bottom, about 8 minutes. Transfer dough to lightly floured counter and knead by hand to form smooth ball, about 30 seconds.

2 Place dough seam side down in lightly greased large bowl or container, cover with plastic wrap, and let rise until doubled in volume, 1½ to 2 hours.

3 Adjust oven rack to middle position and heat oven to 200 degrees. Divide dough into quarters and cover with greased plastic. Working with 1 piece of dough at a time, form into rough ball by stretching dough around your thumbs and pinching edges together so that top is smooth. Place ball seam side down on clean counter and, using your cupped hand, drag in small circles until dough feels taut and round. Let balls rest, covered, for 10 minutes.

4 Heat 12-inch cast-iron skillet over medium heat for 5 minutes. Using wad of paper towels, grease skillet with remaining 1 tablespoon oil. Meanwhile, press and roll 1 dough ball into 9-inch round, sprinkling dough and counter with flour as needed to prevent sticking. Using fork, poke surface of dough several times, then mist top with water. Place dough moistened side down in skillet, then mist top with water. Cover and cook until flatbread is lightly puffed and bottom is spotty brown, 2 to 4 minutes. Flip flatbread, cover, and continue to cook until spotty brown on second side, 2 to 4 minutes. (If large air pockets form, gently poke with fork to deflate.)

5 Brush 1 side of flatbread with melted butter and sprinkle with sea salt. Serve immediately or transfer to ovensafe plate, cover loosely with aluminum foil, and keep warm in oven. Repeat with remaining dough balls, melted butter, and sea salt. Serve.

A cast-iron skillet delivers perfect grilled flatbreads. We incorporate a small amount of whole-wheat flour for flavor. Yogurt and oil tenderize the dough and a little sugar and salt boost flavor. Cooking covered creates steam but still allows charring.

1 Skip the Oven.

2 Enrich the Dough with Yogurt and Oil for a Pillowy Texture.

3 Lightly Mist Dough for a Tender Interior.

Sizing Up Your Skillet

traditional cast iron • **enameled cast iron** • **nonstick**

The superior heat retention of a 12-inch traditional cast-iron skillet is key to quickly creating the signature mottled brown exterior of these flatbreads; an enameled cast-iron skillet will also work for this reason. A 12-inch nonstick skillet can also be used; add 1 teaspoon vegetable to the skillet and heat over medium heat until just smoking. Wipe skillet with wad of paper towels, leaving thin film of oil on bottom and sides, then proceed with step 4.

Corn Tortillas

Makes 18 tortillas

Total Time 1½ hours

3   cups (12 ounces) masa harina

2   teaspoons table salt

2½   cups warm water, divided

2   tablespoons vegetable oil

Why This Recipe Works For fresh homemade tortillas that are light and tender and bursting with corn flavor, we begin by making a stir-together dough of masa harina (corn flour), warm water, vegetable oil, and salt. The warm water helps the dough hydrate quickly and fully, while the oil makes the dough easier to work with and tenderizes the tortillas. For easy tortilla pressing, we divide our dough into equal portions and place them, one by one, in a greased, cut-open zipper-lock bag, then press flat using a clear pie plate. We transfer the pressed tortilla to a hot nonstick skillet, flip it twice, and give it a final press with a spatula to cause it to puff, resulting in a fluffy, light texture. Finally, to ensure that our tortillas remain tender and pliable, we wrap the hot tortillas in a damp dish towel to steam them and keep them warm while we finish the batch. Using a clear pie plate to press the ball of dough into a 5½-inch circle in step 3 makes it easy to see the size of the circle as it expands. You can also use a tortilla press or a second skillet.

1 Whisk masa harina and salt together in medium bowl. Stir in 2 cups warm water and oil with rubber spatula until combined. Using your hands, knead dough in bowl until it is soft and tacky and has texture of Play-Doh. If necessary, add up to ½ cup more warm water, 1 tablespoon at a time, until proper texture is achieved. (You can test for proper hydration by gently flattening a golf ball-size piece of dough with your hands. If many large cracks form around edges, it is too dry.)

2 Divide dough into 18 equal portions, about a scant 3 tablespoons (1½ ounces) each. Roll each portion into smooth ball between your hands. Transfer dough balls to plate and keep covered with damp paper towel. Cut open seams along sides of 1-gallon zipper-lock bag, leaving bottom seam intact. Spray inside of bag lightly with vegetable oil spray; wipe excess oil spray from bag with paper towel.

3 Heat 12-inch cast-iron skillet over medium heat for 5 minutes. Meanwhile, place 1 dough ball in center of prepared bag. Fold top layer of plastic over ball. Using clear pie plate, press dough flat into thin 5½-inch circle.

4 Peel top layer of plastic away from tortilla. Using plastic to lift tortilla, place exposed side of tortilla in palm of your hand and invert tortilla. Peel away plastic. Carefully flip tortilla into skillet and cook until bottom begins to brown at edges, about 1 minute.

5 Using thin spatula, flip tortilla and cook until second side is browned at edges, about 45 seconds. Flip tortilla again and press center and edges firmly with spatula so tortilla puffs, about 15 seconds.

6 Wrap tortilla in damp dish towel. Repeat with remaining dough balls, lightly spraying bag with oil spray and wiping off excess as needed to keep tortillas from sticking. Serve. (Tortillas can be layered between sheets of parchment paper, wrapped in plastic wrap, and refrigerated for up to 5 days. Microwave tortillas, stacked in damp towel, for 2 minutes to rewarm before serving.)

Sizing Up Your Skillet

traditional cast iron • **enameled cast iron** • **nonstick**

The superior heat retention of a 12-inch traditional cast-iron skillet is key to quickly creating the signature mottled brown exterior of these tortillas; an enameled cast-iron skillet will also work for this reason. A 12-inch nonstick skillet can also be used; add 1 teaspoon vegetable to the skillet and heat over medium heat until just smoking. Wipe skillet with wad of paper towels, leaving thin film of oil on bottom and sides, then proceed with step 3.

Fluffy Dinner Rolls

Makes 12 rolls

Total Time 2 hours plus 1½ hours rising

¾ cup whole milk, room temperature

8 tablespoons unsalted butter, melted and divided, plus 1 tablespoon softened

1 large egg, room temperature

2 cups (10 ounces) all-purpose flour

2¼ teaspoons instant or rapid-rise yeast

2 tablespoons sugar

1 teaspoon table salt

1 large egg, beaten with 1 tablespoon water and pinch table salt

Why This Recipe Works Their soft, tender crumb and reflective buttery sheen are enough to make these rolls unique, but on top of these qualities, they're baked in a cast-iron skillet for a chewy, beautifully burnished crust without additional effort. The flavor of these plush rolls reminds us of pizzeria garlic knots, but they're sophisticated enough for a Sunday dinner table. Brushing them with butter just before serving makes pulling a roll from the lot an irresistible treat—there's nothing like a warm buttered roll.

1 Whisk milk, 4 tablespoons melted butter, and egg together in bowl of stand mixer. Add flour and yeast. Using dough hook on medium speed, mix until cohesive dough starts to form and no dry flour remains, about 2 minutes, scraping down bowl as needed. Cover bowl with plastic wrap and let dough rest for 15 minutes. Add sugar and salt and knead on medium speed until dough begins to pull away from sides and bottom of bowl (dough will be sticky), 8 to 12 minutes.

2 Transfer dough to lightly greased large bowl or container, cover with plastic, and let rise until doubled in volume, about 1 hour.

3 Grease 10-inch cast-iron skillet with softened butter. Press down on dough to deflate. Transfer dough to clean counter, divide into 12 equal pieces, and cover loosely with plastic. Working with 1 piece of dough at a time (keep remaining pieces covered), form each into a rough ball by stretching dough around your thumbs and pinching edges together so that top is smooth. Place balls seam side down on clean counter and, using your cupped hand, drag in small circles until dough feels taut and round.

4 Arrange dough balls seam side down in prepared skillet, placing 9 balls around edge and remaining 3 balls in center. Cover with plastic and let rise until doubled in size and dough springs back minimally when poked gently with your finger, about 30 minutes. (Rolls may be refrigerated immediately after shaping for at least 8 hours or up to 24 hours. Let rolls sit at room temperature for 30 minutes before proceeding with step 5.)

5 Adjust oven rack to middle position and heat oven to 350 degrees. Gently brush rolls with egg wash. Bake until deep golden brown, about 30 minutes, rotating skillet halfway through baking.

6 Let rolls cool in skillet on wire rack for 5 minutes. Slide rolls out of skillet onto wire rack and let cool for 15 minutes, then brush tops and sides of rolls with remaining melted butter. Serve warm.

Sizing Up Your Skillet

traditional cast iron • enameled cast iron

The superior heat retention of a 10-inch traditional cast-iron skillet makes it the ideal vessel for achieving tall rolls that develop beautiful browning on the bottom. An enameled cast-iron skillet will also work for this reason.

Southern-Style Cornbread

Serves 8 to 10

Total Time 1 hour

2¼ cups (11¼ ounces) stone-ground cornmeal

1½ cups (12 ounces) sour cream

½ cup whole milk

¼ cup vegetable oil

5 tablespoons unsalted butter, cut into 5 pieces

2 tablespoons sugar

1 teaspoon baking powder

1 teaspoon baking soda

¾ teaspoon table salt

2 large eggs

VARIATION

Fresh-Corn Cornbread

Reduce milk to ¼ cup. Process 1 cup thawed frozen corn with sour cream and milk in blender before whisking into toasted cornmeal. Stir additional 1 cup thawed frozen corn into batter before transferring to skillet.

Why This Recipe Works Cornbread means different things to different people. Northerners tend to like their cornbread sweet and light—more cake than bread. But the true, satisfying, skillet-baked cornbread that's popular in the South is a stellar savory addition to any cook's recipe arsenal. This version boasts hearty corn flavor, a sturdy moist crumb, and a golden-brown crust. Yellow stone-ground cornmeal contributes more potent corn flavor than the typical white, and toasting it in the skillet for a few minutes intensifies that flavor. We create a mush after toasting the cornmeal by softening it in a mixture of sour cream and milk. This ensures that our bread has a fine, moist crumb. The sour cream adds a pleasant tang that works well with the sweet cornmeal; plus, it reacts with the leaveners to keep this flourless bread from being too dense. You can substitute any type of fine- or medium-ground cornmeal here, but don't use coarse-ground cornmeal.

1 Adjust oven rack to middle position and heat oven to 450 degrees. Toast cornmeal in 10-inch cast-iron skillet over medium heat, stirring frequently, until fragrant, about 3 minutes. Transfer cornmeal to large bowl and whisk in sour cream and milk; set aside.

2 Wipe skillet clean with paper towels. Add oil to now-empty skillet. Place skillet in oven and heat until oil is shimmering, about 10 minutes. Using pot holders, remove skillet from oven. Being careful of hot skillet handle, carefully add butter and gently swirl skillet to melt.

3 Pour all but 1 tablespoon oil-butter mixture into cornmeal mixture and whisk to incorporate. Whisk sugar, baking powder, baking soda, and salt into cornmeal mixture until combined, then whisk in eggs.

4 Quickly transfer batter to skillet and smooth top. Transfer skillet to oven and bake until top begins to crack and sides are golden brown, 12 to 18 minutes, rotating skillet halfway through baking. Let bread cool in skillet for 15 minutes. Remove bread from skillet and transfer to wire rack. Serve warm or at room temperature.

VARIATION

Sweet-Potato Cornbread

Substitute brown sugar for granulated sugar. Prick 1 large sweet potato all over with fork. Microwave on large plate until potato is very soft and surface is slightly wet, 10 to 15 minutes, flipping every 5 minutes. Immediately slice potato in half to release steam. When potato is cool enough to handle, scoop flesh into bowl and mash until smooth (you should have about 1 cup); discard skins. Stir sour cream and milk into sweet potato before whisking into toasted cornmeal.

perfecting
SOUTHERN-STYLE CORNBREAD

Yellow stone-ground cornmeal creates potent flavor in this Southern classic. Toasting the cornmeal adds even more flavor. Softening the cornmeal in sour cream (and milk) adds a nice tang, and the sour cream reacts with the leaveners, so the bread doesn't turn out dense.

1 Toast your Cornmeal for More Intense Flavor.

2 Add Some Sour Cream for Tang.

3 Grease the Pan with Both Butter (Adds Flavor) and Vegetable Oil (Eliminates Burning).

Sizing Up Your Skillet

traditional cast iron • **enameled cast iron**

The superior heat retention of a 10-inch traditional cast-iron skillet makes it the ideal vessel for achieving a tall cornbread that develops beautiful browning on the bottom. An enameled cast-iron skillet will also work for this reason.

Sticky Buns

Makes 12 buns

Total Time 1¾ hours, plus 1½ hours rising and cooling

Dough

3   cups (16½ ounces) bread flour, divided

⅔   cup water, room temperature

⅔   cup milk, room temperature

1   large egg plus 1 large yolk, room temperature

2   teaspoons instant or rapid-rise yeast

3   tablespoons granulated sugar

1½   teaspoons table salt

6   tablespoons unsalted butter, cut into 6 pieces and softened

Topping

6   tablespoons unsalted butter

½   cup packed (3½ ounces) dark brown sugar

¼   cup (1¾ ounces) granulated sugar

¼   cup dark or light corn syrup

¼   teaspoon table salt

2   tablespoons water

1   cup pecans, toasted and chopped (optional)

Filling

¾   cup packed (5¼ ounces) dark brown sugar

1   teaspoon ground cinnamon

Why This Recipe Works Sticky buns may well be the ultimate morning treat, and here we do it all in a skillet, from making a butterscotch topping through proofing to baking. Many sticky bun recipes call for a firm, dry dough that's easy to manipulate into the requisite spiral and sturdy enough to support a generous amount of topping. But firm, dry sticky buns aren't very appealing. To make a softer, more tender, and moist sticky bun, we add tangzhong. This cooked flour-and-water paste traps water, so the dough isn't sticky or difficult to work with when spiraling into buns, and the increased hydration converts to steam during baking, which makes the buns fluffy and light. The added water also keeps the crumb moist and tender. The slight tackiness of the dough aids in flattening and stretching it in step 6, so resist the urge to use a lot of flour. Rolling the dough cylinder tightly in step 6 will result in misshapen rolls; keep the cylinder a bit slack. You will need a 12-inch ovensafe skillet for this recipe.

1 For the dough Whisk ¼ cup flour and water in small bowl until no lumps remain. Microwave, whisking every 20 seconds, until mixture thickens to stiff, smooth, pudding-like consistency that forms mound when dropped from end of whisk into bowl, 40 to 80 seconds. In bowl of stand mixer, whisk flour paste and milk until smooth. Add egg and yolk and whisk until incorporated. Add remaining 2¾ cups flour and yeast. Fit stand mixer with dough hook and mix on low speed until all flour is moistened, 1 to 2 minutes. Let rest for 15 minutes.

2 Add granulated sugar and salt to dough and mix on medium-low speed for 5 minutes. Stop mixer and add butter. Continue to mix on medium-low speed for 5 minutes, scraping down dough hook and sides of bowl halfway through mixing (dough will stick to bottom of bowl). Transfer dough to lightly floured counter and knead by hand to form smooth, round ball, about 30 seconds.

3 Place dough seam side down in lightly greased large bowl or container and lightly coat surface of dough with oil spray. Cover with plastic wrap and let rise until just doubled in volume, 40 minutes to 1 hour.

4 For the topping While dough rises, melt butter in 12-inch traditional cast-iron skillet over medium heat. Off heat, whisk in brown sugar, granulated sugar, corn syrup, and salt until smooth. Add water and whisk until incorporated. Sprinkle evenly with pecans, if using.

5 For the filling Stir brown sugar and cinnamon in small bowl until thoroughly combined; set aside.

Sizing Up Your Skillet

traditional cast iron ● nonstick

The superior heat retention of a 12-inch traditional cast-iron skillet makes it the ideal vessel for achieving tall sticky buns that develop beautiful browning on the bottom. Its slick surface also ensures that the glaze sticks to the buns, not the pan. An ovensafe nonstick skillet can also be used.

6 Press down on dough to deflate. Transfer dough to lightly floured counter. Pat and stretch dough into 18 by 15-inch rectangle with long side parallel to counter edge. Sprinkle dough evenly with filling, leaving 1-inch border on far edge, then press filling firmly into dough. Roll dough away from you into cylinder, taking care not to roll too tightly. Pinch seam to seal and roll log seam side down.

7 Mark gently with knife to create 12 equal portions. To slice, hold strand of dental floss taut and slide underneath cylinder, stopping at first mark. Cross ends of floss over each other and pull. Slice cylinder into 12 portions and arrange cut sides down over topping in skillet, placing 9 portions around edge and remaining 3 portions in center. Cover tightly with plastic and let rise until buns are puffy and touching one another, 40 minutes to 1 hour. (Buns may be refrigerated immediately after shaping for up to 14 hours. Let buns sit at room temperature until puffy and touching one another, 1 to 1½ hours, before proceeding with step 8.)

8 Adjust oven rack to lower-middle position and heat oven to 375 degrees. Bake buns until golden brown, 20 to 25 minutes. Rotate skillet, cover loosely with aluminum foil, and bake until center of dough registers at least 200 degrees, 10 to 15 minutes. Let buns cool in skillet on wire rack for 5 minutes. Place round serving platter face down over buns and invert buns onto platter. Using spoon, scoop any glaze left in skillet onto buns. Let cool for at least 10 minutes before serving.

Cast-Iron Brownie

Serves 12 to 14

Total Time 50 minutes, plus 35 minutes cooling

2	ounces marshmallows (about 8 large marshmallows)
½	cup plus 2 tablespoons warm tap water
4	tablespoons unsalted butter, cut into 4 pieces
2	ounces unsweetened chocolate, chopped fine
⅓	cup (1 ounce) Dutch-processed cocoa powder
2½	cups (17½ ounces) sugar
½	cup vegetable oil
2	large eggs plus 2 large yolks
2	teaspoons vanilla extract
1¾	cups (8¾ ounces) all-purpose flour
1	teaspoon table salt
6	ounces bittersweet chocolate, chopped

Why This Recipe Works Once you start making baked goods in a traditional cast-iron skillet, you will look at it with fresh eyes. Because of its high sides and excellent heat retention, it can turn out many breads and desserts with ease. Here we turn to it for making a big, fudgy brownie with a chewy edge and fudgy middle. A combination of Dutch-processed cocoa powder and unsweetened chocolate creates complexity, and a little vanilla adds depth. To achieve that perfect fudginess, we took inspiration from fudge. Many fudge recipes call for marshmallows or a marshmallow product. Melting some marshmallows along with the cocoa powder mixture creates a superfudgy batter. Finally, we fold in bittersweet chocolate chunks for gooey pockets of lush melted chocolate throughout the brownie. A well-greased skillet ensures that there are no issues when removing the brownie wedges from the pan. We bake the brownie on the bottom rack of a preheated 350-degree oven for about 35 minutes and then allow it to bake further on a wire rack (due to the cast iron's strong heat retention), resulting in the right soft and fudgy interior. Every wedge offers a crisp edge and fudgy middle. In step 3, you can substitute bittersweet or semisweet chocolate chips for the chopped bittersweet chocolate, if desired, but the chips won't melt as much as the chopped chocolate and the brownie will be less gooey.

1 Adjust oven rack to lowest position and heat oven to 350 degrees. Grease 12-inch traditional cast-iron skillet.

2 Combine marshmallows, warm tap water, butter, unsweetened chocolate, and cocoa in large bowl. Microwave at 50 percent power, stirring occasionally, until chocolate is fully melted and mixture is smooth, 2 to 4 minutes. Let cool for 5 minutes.

3 Whisk in sugar, oil, eggs and yolks, and vanilla until fully combined. Gently whisk in flour and salt until just incorporated. Stir in bittersweet chocolate.

4 Transfer batter to prepared skillet. Bake until toothpick inserted in center comes out with few moist crumbs and batter attached (be careful not to overbake; brownie will continue to bake as it cools), 33 to 38 minutes, rotating skillet halfway through baking. Transfer skillet to wire rack and let cool for 30 minutes (or let cool completely for neat slices). Slice into wedges and serve warm. (Cooled brownies can be stored in airtight container for up to 4 days.)

Sizing Up Your Skillet

- **traditional cast iron**

The straight sides and superior heat retention of a 12-inch traditional cast-iron skillet are key to creating a brownie that remains crisp and chewy on the edges and baked through in the middle while staying perfectly fudgy. Its slick surface also ensures that the brownie easily releases from the pan. We do not recommend using an alternative skillet in this recipe.

Cast-Iron Chocolate Chip Cookie

Serves 10

Total Time 1 hour, plus 30 minutes cooling

12 tablespoons unsalted butter, divided

¾ cup packed (5¼ ounces) dark brown sugar

½ cup (3½ ounces) granulated sugar

2 teaspoons vanilla extract

1 teaspoon table salt

1 large egg plus 1 large yolk

1¾ cups (8¾ ounces) all-purpose flour

½ teaspoon baking soda

1 cup (6 ounces) semisweet chocolate chips

Flake sea salt (optional)

VARIATIONS

Cast-Iron White Chocolate–Macadamia Cookie

Substitute ½ cup white chocolate chips plus ½ cup chopped salted dry-roasted macadamia nuts for semisweet chocolate.

Cast-Iron Peanut Butter–Bacon Cookie

Substitute ½ cup Reese's Pieces and ½ cup cooked chopped bacon for semisweet chocolate.

Why This Recipe Works A cookie in a skillet? We admit that this Internet phenomenon made us skeptical . . . until we tried it. Unlike with a traditional batch of cookies, this treatment doesn't require scooping, baking, and cooling multiple sheets of treats; the whole thing bakes at once in a single skillet. Plus, the hot bottom and tall sides of a traditional cast-iron pan create a great crust. And this treat can go straight from the oven to the table for a fun, hands-on dessert—or you can slice it and serve it like a tart for a more elegant presentation. What's not to like? We cut back on butter and chocolate chips from our usual cookie dough recipe to ensure that the skillet cookie remains crisp on the edges and bakes through in the middle while staying perfectly chewy. We also increase the baking time to accommodate the giant size, but otherwise, this recipe is simpler and faster than baking regular cookies. This is a cookie that you can have fun with by experimenting with other mix-ins because the cookie dough has a strong foundation. You can use any type of chocolate (bar or chips), incorporate other sweet stir-ins (M&M's, Reese's Pieces, butterscotch chips) in place of the chocolate, or use chopped dried fruit, nuts, or crushed cookies. Limiting the mix-ins to 6 ounces total (including the chocolate) ensures that the cookie retains its crispy exterior and chewy center.

1 Adjust oven rack to upper-middle position and heat oven to 375 degrees. Melt 9 tablespoons butter in 12-inch traditional cast-iron skillet over medium heat. Continue to cook, stirring constantly, until butter is dark golden brown and has nutty aroma and bubbling subsides, about 5 minutes longer; transfer to large bowl. Stir remaining 3 tablespoons butter into hot butter until completely melted.

2 Whisk brown sugar, granulated sugar, vanilla, and salt into melted butter until smooth. Whisk in egg and yolk until smooth, about 30 seconds. Let mixture sit for 3 minutes, then whisk for 30 seconds. Repeat process of resting and whisking 2 more times until mixture is thick, smooth, and shiny.

3 Whisk flour and baking soda together in separate bowl, then stir flour mixture into butter mixture until just combined, about 1 minute. Stir in chocolate chips, making sure no flour pockets remain.

4 Wipe skillet clean with paper towels. Transfer dough to now-empty skillet and press into even layer with spatula. Sprinkle with sea salt, if using. Transfer skillet to oven and bake until cookie is golden brown and edges are set, about 20 minutes, rotating skillet halfway through baking. Transfer skillet to wire rack and let cookie cool for 30 minutes. Slice cookie into wedges and serve warm. (Cooled cookies can be stored in airtight container for up to 4 days.)

perfecting
CAST-IRON CHOCOLATE CHIP COOKIE

A traditional cast-iron pan allows you to make a crowd-size chocolate chip cookie with a perfect crust. Using more brown sugar than granulated sugar enhances the flavor and chewiness of the cookie while the granulated sugar lends crispiness. Browning the butter adds complex flavor notes that counteract the sweetness of the cookie.

1   Use Two Types of Sugar.

2   Brown the Butter for Extra Flavor.

3   Have Fun with Mix-Ins.

Sizing Up Your Skillet

● **traditional cast iron**

The straight sides and superior heat retention of a 12-inch traditional cast-iron skillet are key in creating a cookie that remains crisp on the edges and baked through in the middle while staying perfectly chewy. Its slick surface also ensures that the cookie easily releases form the pan. We do not recommend using an alternative skillet for this recipe.

Knafeh

Serves 8 to 10

Total Time 1¼ hours, plus 1½ hours soaking

1¼ pounds Akkawi cheese, cut into rough 2-inch cubes

¼ teaspoon finely chopped mastic gum (optional)

¾ cup ghee, melted, plus 2 tablespoons softened

1 teaspoon orange gel food coloring or ½ teaspoon powdered food coloring

12 ounces kataifi, thawed

1 cup sugar

½ cup boiling water

¼ cup orange blossom water

1 tablespoon rose water

1 teaspoon lemon juice

¼ cup finely chopped pistachios

VARIATION

Extra-Gooey Knafeh

Substitute 8 ounces whole-milk block mozzarella, shredded, for 8 ounces of Akkawi cheese; you do not need to soak mozzarella with Akkawi. Toss cheeses together before spreading over kataifi in step 4.

Why This Recipe Works Across the Middle East, knafeh is a well-loved dessert composed of kataifi (a spun pastry) that is layered with Akkawi cheese (a white brined cheese named after Akka, a picturesque coastal Palestinian city), then soaked in a rose and orange blossom syrup after baking. The result is a decadent pastry featuring a crunchy, golden-brown crust paired with stringy melted cheese and a sweet floral flavor that's balanced by the mild saltiness of the cheese. ATK test cook Laila Ibrahim, who grew up in Jordan, says, "It's a source of joy for people around the Levant. Even late into the night, my mom and I would join a line of eager customers for a slice of knafeh and would eat it still piping hot in her car before the drive home." Many versions of knafeh exist, but we modeled our recipe after a version that comes from the city of Nablus, Palestine, and features the local Akkawi. It is traditionally made in large, round shallow pans because it is a dessert meant for a crowd. But the tall, straight sides of a traditional cast-iron skillet are ideal for assembling a smaller version of the pastry; the heat retention of cast iron also helps to develop an impressive golden crust. To balance out the salt level of the cheese, we let it soak as the first step in this recipe. If you cannot find Akkawi cheese, Syrian cheese or unsalted cheese curds are suitable alternatives. If using cheese curds, skip soaking in step 1 and add ¾ teaspoon salt with mastic gum (if using) before tossing. Mastic gum adds bite to the cheese and a mild pine flavor; do not grind the mastic crystals in a spice grinder or mortar and pestle, as the friction will create a sticky paste. Serve the knafeh on a platter with a raised rim to contain the syrup. Knafeh is best served warm; to reheat, bake in 375-degree oven for 10 to 15 minutes.

1 Place Akkawi in large bowl, cover with hot tap water by 1 inch, and let soak for 1½ hours, changing water once halfway through soaking. Drain Akkawi, pat dry with paper towels, and shred using largest holes of box grater. Toss Akkawi with mastic gum in bowl, if using; set aside.

2 Adjust oven rack to lower-middle position and heat oven to 400 degrees. Whisk softened ghee and food coloring in small bowl until well combined. Brush bottom of 10-inch traditional cast-iron skillet with ghee mixture; set aside.

3 Gently unfurl and loosen kataifi strands on large cutting board, then cut into rough 2-inch lengths. Toss kataifi with melted ghee in large bowl until well coated, gently pulling apart any kataifi that clumps together. Measure out and reserve 2 cups kataifi mixture.

4 Spread remaining kataifi mixture over bottom of prepared skillet and firmly press with lightly moistened hands into even layer. Spread Akkawi mixture over top, leaving ½-inch border. Sprinkle reserved kataifi mixture evenly over entire skillet and firmly press into even layer. Transfer skillet to oven and bake until top is deep golden brown, 40 to 45 minutes.

5 Meanwhile, stir sugar and boiling water in bowl until sugar has dissolved. Let cool to room temperature, about 20 minutes, then stir in orange blossom water, rose water, and lemon juice.

6 Using pot holder, remove skillet from oven. Being careful of hot skillet handle, drizzle knafeh with ½ cup syrup. Using thin spatula, slide knafeh onto 12-inch round plate. Place large round platter face down over knafeh and invert knafeh so that browned side is facing up; remove plate. Slowly drizzle knafeh with remaining syrup and sprinkle with pistachios. Slice into wedges and serve immediately, spooning extra pooled syrup on top.

Sizing Up Your Skillet

● **traditional cast iron**

The straight sides and superior heat retention of a 10-inch traditional cast-iron skillet are key to assembling the knafeh and creating a crisp golden-brown exterior. Its slick surface also ensures that the knafeh easily releases from the pan. We do not recommend using an alternative skillet in this recipe.

Peach Cornmeal Upside-Down Cake

Serves 8

Total Time 1¼ hours, plus 1¼ hours cooling

- ½ cup (2½ ounces) cornmeal
- 2 tablespoons unsalted butter, plus 6 tablespoons melted and cooled
- ⅓ cup (2⅓ ounces) sugar, plus ¾ cup (5¼ ounces), divided
- Pinch plus ½ teaspoon table salt, divided
- 1 pound peaches, peeled, halved, pitted, and cut into ¾-inch wedges
- 1 cup (5 ounces) all-purpose flour
- 1 teaspoon baking powder
- ⅛ teaspoon baking soda
- ½ cup whole milk
- 2 teaspoons grated orange zest plus ¼ cup juice
- 1 large egg plus 1 large yolk

Why This Recipe Works A skillet upside-down cake is a simple affair: Arrange the fruit atop a buttery glaze on the bottom of the skillet, top the fruit with batter, and pop the skillet in the oven. If all goes well, the cake releases from the skillet to reveal beautifully caramelized fruit perched atop a rustic, not-too-sweet cake. But too often the result is overly sweet or, worse, a soggy mess. To avoid the latter, we add toasted cornmeal to the cake batter for both flavor and texture and nestle the peaches in a sauce of sugar and butter before baking to ensure a top layer of caramelized peaches with the perfect amount of sweetness. You can substitute 12 ounces frozen sliced peaches for the fresh peaches. If using frozen peaches, be sure to thaw and drain them before using; otherwise, they will produce a mushy cake. You will need a 10-inch ovensafe skillet for this recipe.

1 Adjust oven rack to middle position and heat oven to 350 degrees. Toast cornmeal in 10-inch ovensafe nonstick skillet over medium heat until fragrant, 2 to 3 minutes, stirring frequently. Transfer to large bowl and let cool slightly.

2 Wipe skillet clean with paper towels. Melt 2 tablespoons butter in now-empty skillet over medium heat. Add ⅓ cup sugar and pinch salt and cook, whisking constantly, until sugar is melted, smooth, and deep golden brown, 3 to 5 minutes. (Mixture may look broken but will come together.) Off heat, carefully arrange peaches cut side down in tight pinwheel around edge of skillet. Arrange remaining peaches in center of skillet.

3 Whisk flour, baking powder, baking soda, and remaining ½ teaspoon salt into cornmeal. In separate bowl, whisk milk, orange zest and juice, egg and yolk, melted butter, and remaining ¾ cup sugar until smooth. Stir milk mixture into flour mixture until just combined.

4 Pour batter over peaches and spread into even layer. Bake until cake is golden brown and toothpick inserted in center comes out clean, 28 to 33 minutes, rotating skillet halfway through baking.

5 Let cake cool in skillet on wire rack for 15 minutes. Run knife around edge of skillet to loosen cake. Place large serving platter over skillet. Using pot holders and holding platter tightly, invert skillet and platter together; lift off skillet (if any peaches stick to skillet, remove and position on top of cake). Let cake cool completely, about 1 hour. Serve.

Sizing Up Your Skillet

nonstick ● **traditional cast iron** ● **carbon steel**

A 10-inch nonstick skillet provides enough space to assemble the cake; its slick surface and shallow sides also make it easy to transfer the cake to a platter without fear of sticking. A traditional cast-iron or carbon-steel skillet will also work for these reasons.

Lemon Soufflé

Serves 6

Total Time 45 minutes

5   large eggs, separated

¼   teaspoon cream of tartar

⅔   cup (4⅔ ounces) granulated sugar, divided

⅛   teaspoon table salt

1   teaspoon grated lemon zest plus ⅓ cup juice (2 lemons)

2   tablespoons all-purpose flour

1   tablespoon unsalted butter

     Confectioners' sugar, for dusting

Why This Recipe Works Soufflés are showy desserts with a bit of magic about them. But truly, they are not all that hard to execute, especially with a technique for making one in a skillet. First, we whip 5 egg whites with cream of tartar and then gradually add sugar and salt and whip some more until stiff peaks form. Adding a little flour to the simple base of whipped egg yolks keeps the soufflé creamy rather than foamy. Lemon juice and zest provide bright flavor that shines through the eggy base. We fold in the beaten egg whites and pour the mixture into a buttered skillet. After a few minutes on the stovetop, the soufflé is just set around the edges and on the bottom, so we move the skillet to the oven to finish. A few minutes later our soufflé is puffed, golden on top, and creamy in the middle. Don't open the oven door during the first 7 minutes of baking, but do check the soufflé regularly for doneness during the final few minutes in the oven. You will need a 10-inch ovensafe skillet for this recipe.

1 Adjust oven rack to middle position and heat oven to 375 degrees. Using stand mixer fitted with whisk attachment, whip egg whites and cream of tartar together on medium-low speed until foamy, about 1 minute. Gradually add ⅓ cup granulated sugar and salt, then increase mixer speed to medium-high and continue to whip until stiff peaks form, 3 to 4 minutes. Gently transfer whites to clean bowl and set aside.

2 Whip egg yolks and remaining ⅓ cup granulated sugar on medium-high speed until pale and thick, about 1 minute. Whip in lemon zest and juice and flour until incorporated, about 30 seconds. Fold one-quarter of whipped egg whites into yolk mixture until almost no white streaks remain. Gently fold in remaining egg whites until just incorporated.

3 Melt butter in 10-inch stainless-steel skillet over medium-low heat. Swirl pan to coat it evenly with melted butter, then gently scrape soufflé batter into skillet. Cook until edges begin to set and bubble slightly, about 2 minutes.

4 Transfer skillet to oven and bake soufflé until puffed, center jiggles slightly when shaken, and surface is golden, 7 to 11 minutes. Using pot holder (skillet handle will be hot), remove skillet from oven. Dust soufflé with confectioners' sugar and serve immediately.

Sizing Up Your Skillet

- **stainless steel**

The shallow sides of a 10-inch stainless steel skillet are key in getting the right texture and height in the soufflé. We do not recommend using an alternative skillet in this recipe.

Apple Pandowdy

Serves 6

Total Time 1½ hours plus 1 hour 50 minutes chilling and cooling

Pie Dough

3   tablespoons ice water

1   tablespoon sour cream

⅔   cup (3⅓ ounces) all-purpose flour

1   teaspoon granulated sugar

½   teaspoon table salt

6   tablespoons unsalted butter, cut into ¼-inch pieces and frozen for 15 minutes

Filling

2½   pounds Golden Delicious apples, peeled, cored, halved, and cut into ½-inch-thick wedges

¼   cup packed (1¾ ounces) light brown sugar

½   teaspoon ground cinnamon

¼   teaspoon table salt

3   tablespoons unsalted butter

¾   cup apple cider

1   tablespoon cornstarch

2   teaspoons lemon juice

Topping

1   tablespoon granulated sugar

¼   teaspoon ground cinnamon

1   large egg, lightly beaten

     Vanilla ice cream

Why This Recipe Works One of many old-school New England desserts with funny names, pandowdy is a skillet apple pie with an appealingly caramelized top. We toss wedges of buttery Golden Delicious apples in cinnamon and brown sugar for sweet-spiced flavor and sauté them before simmering in apple cider and lemon juice. Topping the apples with squares of dough allows steam to escape in between them during baking, preventing the apples from overcooking. "Dowdying," or pressing, the crust partway through baking creates the dessert's signature sweet finish by allowing juices from the filling to rise over the crust and caramelize. Do not use store-bought pie crust in this recipe; it yields gummy results. You will need a 10-inch ovensafe skillet with a tight-fitting lid for this recipe.

1 For the pie dough Combine ice water and sour cream in bowl. Process flour, sugar, and salt in food processor until combined, about 3 seconds. Add butter and pulse until size of large peas, 6 to 8 pulses. Add sour cream mixture and pulse until dough forms large clumps and no dry flour remains, 3 to 6 pulses, scraping down sides of bowl as needed.

2 Transfer dough to sheet of plastic wrap. Draw edges of plastic over dough and press firmly on sides and top to form compact, fissure-free mass. Wrap in plastic and flatten to form 4-inch disk. Refrigerate dough for at least 1 hour or up to 2 days. Let chilled dough sit on counter to soften slightly, about 10 minutes, before rolling. (Wrapped dough can be frozen for up to 1 month. If frozen, let dough thaw completely on counter before rolling.)

3 Adjust oven rack to middle position and heat oven to 400 degrees. Roll dough into 10-inch circle on lightly floured counter. Using pizza cutter, cut dough into four 2½-inch-wide strips, then make four 2½-inch-wide perpendicular cuts to form squares. (Pieces around edges of dough will be smaller.) Transfer dough pieces to parchment paper–lined baking sheet, cover with plastic, and refrigerate until firm, at least 30 minutes.

4 For the filling Toss apples, brown sugar, cinnamon, and salt together in large bowl. Melt butter in 10-inch stainless-steel skillet over medium heat. Add apple mixture, cover, and cook until apples become slightly pliable and release their juices, about 10 minutes, stirring occasionally.

5 Whisk cider, cornstarch, and lemon juice in bowl until no lumps remain, then stir into apple mixture. Bring to simmer and cook, uncovered, stirring occasionally, until sauce is thickened, about 2 minutes. Off heat, press lightly on apples to form even layer.

6 For the topping Combine sugar and cinnamon in small bowl. Working quickly, shingle dough pieces over filling until mostly covered, overlapping as needed. Brush dough pieces with egg and sprinkle with cinnamon sugar.

7 Bake until crust is slightly puffed and beginning to brown, about 15 minutes. Using pot holder, remove skillet from oven. Being careful of hot skillet handle, use back of large spoon to press down in center of crust until juices come up over top of crust. Repeat 4 more times around skillet. Make sure all apples are submerged and return skillet to oven. Continue to bake until crust is golden brown, about 15 minutes.

8 Transfer skillet to wire rack and let cool for at least 20 minutes. Serve with ice cream, drizzling extra sauce over top.

Sizing Up Your Skillet

stainless steel • nonstick • traditional cast iron • enameled cast iron • carbon steel

A 10-inch stainless-steel skillet provides enough space for building the pandowdy. An ovensafe nonstick, traditional cast-iron, enameled cast-iron, or carbon-steel skillet will also work for this reason.

Strawberry-Rhubarb Crisp

Serves 6

Total Time 1 hour

Topping

¾ cup (3¾ ounces) all-purpose flour

½ cup panko bread crumbs

¼ cup packed (1¾ ounces) light brown sugar

½ teaspoon table salt

¼ teaspoon ground cinnamon

6 tablespoons unsalted butter, melted

Filling

1 pound fresh rhubarb, trimmed and cut into ½-inch pieces (3½ cups)

12 ounces fresh strawberries, hulled and chopped coarse (2 cups)

1¼ cups packed (8¾ ounces) light brown sugar

2 tablespoons cornstarch

⅛ teaspoon table salt

VARIATION

Strawberry-Rhubarb Crisp for Two

Halve all ingredients. Proceed with recipe in 8-inch ovensafe skillet. Reduce cooking time in step 2 to 5 to 7 minutes.

Why This Recipe Works Do you wonder what to do with the gorgeous green and red rhubarb stalks piled up on farmers' market tables in the late spring? This easy recipe is the solution. It pairs the tart vegetable with baskets of small, sweet, juicy strawberries that appear at the same time—but then suddenly, in a seeming instant, are gone until the next year. As an added bonus, it turns out that a skillet, as opposed to a casserole dish, is a great vehicle for a crisp because you can simmer the fruit filling on the stovetop with a little cornstarch to remove excess liquid, creating the perfect jammy consistency. Then crumble the easy-to-assemble six-ingredient topping across the jewel-colored fruit and transfer the skillet to the oven to bake. The only bowl you'll need is the one to mix the topping. Frozen rhubarb and strawberries can be substituted for fresh. If using frozen strawberries, there's no need to thaw them completely; you can chop them as soon as they're soft enough. Depending on the amount of trimming required, you may need to buy more than 1 pound of rhubarb to ensure that you end up with 3½ cups. You will need a 10-inch ovensafe skillet for this recipe. Serve with ice cream, if desired.

1 For the topping Whisk flour, panko, sugar, salt, and cinnamon together in bowl. Add melted butter and stir until no dry spots of flour remain and mixture forms clumps. Refrigerate until ready to use.

2 For the filling Adjust oven rack to middle position and heat oven to 375 degrees. Toss all filling ingredients in large bowl until thoroughly combined. Transfer to 10-inch stainless-steel skillet. Cook over medium-high heat, stirring frequently, until fruit has released enough liquid to be mostly submerged, rhubarb is just beginning to break down, and juices have thickened, 8 to 12 minutes. Remove skillet from heat.

3 Squeeze topping into large clumps with your hands. Crumble topping into pea-size pieces and sprinkle evenly over filling. Bake until topping is browned and filling is bubbling around sides of skillet, 15 to 20 minutes. Let cool for 15 minutes. Serve.

Sizing Up Your Skillet

stainless steel • **nonstick** • **traditional cast iron** • **enameled cast iron** • **carbon steel**

A 10-inch stainless-steel skillet provides enough space for building the crisp. An ovensafe nonstick, traditional cast-iron, enameled cast-iron, or carbon-steel skillet will also work for this reason.

Bananas Foster

Serves 4

Total Time 20 minutes

½ cup packed (3½ ounces) dark brown sugar

¼ cup plus 2 teaspoons aged rum, divided

2 tablespoons water

1 cinnamon stick

¼ teaspoon table salt

4 ripe bananas, peeled, halved crosswise, then halved lengthwise

4 tablespoons unsalted butter, cut into 4 pieces

1 teaspoon lemon juice

Vanilla ice cream

Why This Recipe Works This iconic New Orleans dessert is usually served flambéed at tableside. To adapt this recipe for the home cook, we invert the usual order of steps and opt to skip the flambé. Most recipes start by first combining butter and sugar, sautéing the bananas, and finishing with the rum. We found that the sauce is smoother and creamier if we approach the dessert like a pan sauce: Cook the bananas in a mixture of sugar, rum, and other flavors and then whisk in butter at the end. We like the color and deep flavor of dark brown sugar in this recipe, and while any rum will do, we prefer the caramel notes of aged rum. Look for yellow bananas with very few spots; overly ripe bananas will fall apart during cooking.

1 Combine sugar, ¼ cup rum, water, cinnamon stick, and salt in 12-inch stainless-steel skillet. Cook over medium heat, whisking frequently, until sugar has dissolved, 1 to 2 minutes.

2 Add bananas cut side down to skillet and cook until glossy and golden on bottom, about 1½ minutes. Flip bananas and continue to cook until tender but not mushy, 1 to 1½ minutes. Using tongs, transfer bananas to rimmed serving dish, leaving sauce in skillet.

3 Remove skillet from heat and discard cinnamon stick. Whisk butter into sauce, 1 piece at a time, until incorporated. Whisk in lemon juice and remaining 2 teaspoons rum. Pour sauce over bananas. Serve with vanilla ice cream.

VARIATION

Bananas Foster for Two

Halve all ingredients. Proceed with recipe in 10-inch skillet.

Sizing Up Your Skillet

stainless steel • **nonstick** • **traditional cast iron** • **enameled cast iron** • **carbon steel**

A 12-inch stainless-steel skillet provides enough space for cooking the bananas in the sugar-rum mixture, and then finishing the sauce with butter. A nonstick, traditional cast-iron, enameled cast-iron, or carbon-steel skillet will also work for these reasons.

Roasted Pears with Dried Apricots and Pistachios

Serves 4 to 6

Total Time 1¼ hours

- 3 tablespoons unsalted butter, divided
- 4 ripe but firm Bosc or Bartlett pears (6 to 7 ounces each), peeled, halved, and cored
- 1¼ cups dry white wine
- ½ cup dried apricots, quartered
- ⅓ cup (2⅓ ounces) sugar
- ¼ teaspoon ground cardamom
- ⅛ teaspoon table salt
- 1 teaspoon lemon juice
- ⅓ cup shelled pistachios, toasted and chopped

VARIATION

Roasted Apples with Dried Figs and Walnuts

Substitute Gala apples for pears, red wine for white wine, dried figs for apricots, ¾ teaspoon pepper for cardamom, and walnuts for pistachios.

Sizing Up Your Skillet

stainless steel • nonstick • traditional cast iron • enameled cast iron

A 12-inch stainless-steel skillet provides enough space for browning 4 pears and creating a pan sauce. An ovensafe nonstick, traditional cast-iron, or enameled cast-iron skillet will also work for these reasons.

Why This Recipe Works Roasted fruit is an elegant dessert that most leave to restaurant chefs. But with the right ripe fruit, wine, and a handful of other ingredients, plus a skillet, you can easily roast fruit at home. Pears are an excellent fruit to roast because their shape and texture hold up well. After peeling and halving the pears, we cook them in butter on the stovetop to evaporate some of the juices and concentrate their flavor; this also jump-starts caramelization. We then move the pears to the oven to turn their flesh tender and brown. Then it's time to use the exuded juices to make a beautiful, sweet sauce in the empty skillet for drizzling over the roasted pears. First, we deglaze the pan with dry white wine and add dried apricots and cardamom; a little lemon juice adds a nice burst of citrus. A sprinkling of chopped and toasted pistachios adds crunch and a bit of earthy flavor. Select pears that yield slightly when pressed. You will need a 12-inch ovensafe skillet for this recipe.

1 Adjust oven rack to middle position and heat oven to 450 degrees. Melt 2 tablespoons butter in 12-inch stainless-steel skillet over medium-high heat. Place pear halves cut side down in skillet. Cook, without moving, until pears are just beginning to brown, 3 to 5 minutes.

2 Transfer skillet to oven and roast for 15 minutes. Flip pears and continue to roast until fork easily pierces fruit, 10 to 15 minutes.

3 Using pot holder, remove skillet from oven and transfer pears to serving dish. Being careful of hot skillet handle, return skillet to medium-high heat and add wine, apricots, sugar, cardamom, salt, and remaining 1 tablespoon butter. Bring to vigorous simmer, whisking to scrape up any browned bits. Cook until sauce is reduced and has consistency of maple syrup, 7 to 10 minutes. Off heat, stir in lemon juice. Pour sauce over pears, sprinkle with pistachios, and serve.

VARIATION

Roasted Pears with Dried Apricots and Pistachios for Two

Reduce sugar and pistachios to 3 tablespoons; halve remaining ingredients. Proceed with recipe in 10- or 12-inch ovensafe skillet.

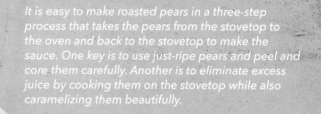

perfecting
ROASTED PEARS

It is easy to make roasted pears in a three-step process that takes the pears from the stovetop to the oven and back to the stovetop to make the sauce. One key is to use just-ripe pears and peel and core them carefully. Another is to eliminate excess juice by cooking them on the stovetop while also caramelizing them beautifully.

1 Start on the Stovetop to Evaporate Juices That Would Inhibit Caramelization.

2 Finish in the Oven, Where the Even Heat Softens the Pears Just Enough.

3 Deglaze the Empty Skillet with Wine and Aromatics to Make an Appealing Sauce.

Nutritional Information for Our Recipes

To calculate the nutritional values of our recipes per serving, we used The Food Processor SQL by ESHA research. When using this program, we entered all the ingredients, using weights wherever possible. We also used our preferred brands in these analyses. Any ingredient listed as "optional" was excluded from the analyses. If there is a range in the serving size, we used the highest number of servings to calculate nutritional values. We did not include additional salt or pepper for food that's seasoned to taste.

	Cal	Total Fat (g)	Sat Fat (g)	Chol (mg)	Sodium (mg)	Carbs (g)	Fiber (g)	Tot Sugar (g)	Added Sugar (g)	Protein (g)
Chapter One: Sauté, Sear, and Stir-Fry										
Sautéed Chicken Breasts	320	11	1.5	125	370	11	0	0	0	40
Sautéed Chicken Thighs	320	14	2.5	160	450	11	0	0	0	35
Sautéed Chicken Breasts for Two	320	11	1.5	125	370	11	0	0	0	40
Lemon-Thyme Chicken with Garlicky Greens and White Beans	520	22	4.5	135	1290	28	7	3	0	51
Lemon-Thyme Chicken with Garlicky Greens and White Beans for Two	510	22	4.5	135	1140	27	7	3	0	51
Chicken and Couscous with Fennel, Apricots, and Orange	770	33	5	125	800	69	6	18	0	48
Turkey Meatballs with Charred Zucchini and Yogurt Sauce	400	19	6	180	780	14	2	7	0	42
Pan-Seared Steaks	160	6	2	65	0	0	0	0	0	26
Spice-Crusted Pan-Seared Steaks	170	6	2	60	1	1	1	0	0	26
Pan-Seared Thick-Cut Steak for Two	240	9	3	90	95	0	0	0	0	39
Vermouth-Herb Pan Sauce	50	4	2	10	100	1	0	1	0	0
Lemon-Caper Pan Sauce	40	4	2	10	80	1	0	0	0	0
Mustard-Cream Pan Sauce	40	4	2	10	70	1	0	0	0	0
Porcini-Marsala Pan Sauce	45	3	1.5	5	100	2	0	2	0	0
Red Wine-Peppercorn Pan Sauce	50	4	2	10	35	2	0	1	1	0
Cilantro-Coconut Pan Sauce	50	5	3.5	5	15	2	0	1	0	0
Butter-Basted Rib-Eye Steak with Shallot and Thyme	740	63	27	185	260	0	0	0	0	42
with Rosemary-Orange Butter	740	63	27	185	260	0	0	0	0	42
Butter-Basted Sirloin Steaks for Four	430	28	12	130	270	0	0	0	0	40
Seared Bistro-Style Steak with Crispy Potatoes and Salsa Verde	590	41	8	80	780	28	4	2	0	29
Seared Bistro-Style Steak with Crispy Potatoes and Salsa Verde for Two	770	50	11	120	1020	38	5	3	0	42

	Cal	Total Fat (g)	Sat Fat (g)	Chol (mg)	Sodium (mg)	Carbs (g)	Fiber (g)	Tot Sugar (g)	Added Sugar (g)	Protein (g)
Chapter One: Sauté, Sear, and Stir-Fry (cont.)										
Stir-Fried Cumin Beef	350	24	5	75	700	6	1	3	2	25
Stir-Fried Cumin Beef for Two	350	24	5	75	700	6	1	3	2	25
Steak Caesar Salad	540	40	9	85	1020	16	0	4	0	28
Pan-Seared Thick-Cut Pork Chops	160	6	2	65	70	0	0	0	0	26
with Maple Agrodolce	220	6	2	65	115	14	0	12	6	26
Pan-Seared Thick-Cut Pork Chop for Two	160	6	2	65	70	0	0	0	0	26
Pan-Seared Thick-Cut Boneless Pork Chops with Apples and Spinach	360	16	2.5	85	570	19	5	11	0	33
Bacon-Wrapped Pork Tenderloin Medallions with Sweet Potatoes	390	15	3.5	90	930	24	4	10	3	31
Bacon-Wrapped Pork Tenderloin Medallions with Sweet Potatoes for Two	580	22	6	135	1260	36	5	14	4	47
Cast-Iron Pork Fajitas	340	8	3	70	1030	38	1	4	0	30
Cast-Iron Pork Fajitas for Two	520	11	4	105	1540	57	2	6	0	44
Khua Kling	210	14	4.5	40	330	7	0	2	1	11
Pan-Seared Salmon	360	23	5	95	940	0	0	0	0	35
Pan-Seared Blackened Salmon	360	23	5	95	1090	2	1	0	0	35
Pan-Seared Salmon for Two	360	23	5	95	940	0	0	0	0	35
Crispy Pan-Seared Black Sea Bass with Green Olive, Almond, and Orange Relish	480	34	4	70	850	7	2	3	1	35
Crispy Pan-Seared Black Sea Bass with Green Olive, Almond, and Orange Relish for Two	480	34	4	70	850	7	2	3	1	35
Sautéed Tilapia	200	9	1.5	70	350	0	0	0	0	28
with Chive-Lemon Miso Butter	320	21	8	100	590	3	0	2	0	29
Sautéed Tilapia for Two	200	9	1.5	70	350	0	0	0	0	28
Pan-Seared Tuna Steaks with Cucumber-Peanut Salad	340	14	2	65	930	7	2	2	1	46
Pan-Seared Shrimp with Pistachios, Cumin, and Parsley for Two	200	12	2	160	480	5	1	1	0	19
with Peanuts, Black Pepper, and Lime	210	12	2	160	480	6	1	2	1	19
Seared Scallops with Broccolini and Browned Butter–Pepper Relish	330	20	8	70	1090	12	4	2	0	25
Kimchi Bokkeumbap	310	10	1	10	690	46	2	3	0	9
Kimchi Bokkeumbap for Two	490	17	2	15	1050	69	3	4	0	14
Charred Broccoli Salad with Avocado, Grapefruit, and Ginger-Lime Dressing	530	40	4.5	0	520	43	18	20	4	10
Seared Halloumi and Vegetable Salad Bowls	380	26	10	30	880	27	6	15	8	14
Seared Halloumi and Vegetable Salad Bowls for Two	430	31	10	30	880	27	6	15	8	14
Seared Tofu with Panch Phoron, Green Beans, and Pickled Shallots	380	25	4	10	710	19	4	8	0	23

	Cal	Total Fat (g)	Sat Fat (g)	Chol (mg)	Sodium (mg)	Carbs (g)	Fiber (g)	Tot Sugar (g)	Added Sugar (g)	Protein (g)
Chapter Two: Simmer, Braise, and Poach										
Braised Chicken Thighs with Lemon, Spices, and Torn Basil	320	22	7	155	640	4	1	1	0	26
Braised Chicken Thighs with Lemon, Spices, and Torn Basil for Two	490	33	10	230	960	6	1	2	0	39
Sherry-Braised Chicken Thighs with Chorizo and Potatoes	520	32	10	170	1040	19	3	3	0	33
Braised Chicken Thighs with Fennel, Chickpeas, and Apricots	470	26	5	145	1010	26	7	8	0	31
Braised Chicken Thighs with Fennel, Chickpeas, and Apricots for Two	700	39	8	215	1510	39	10	12	0	47
Chicken Pot Pie with Leeks, Carrots, and Croissant Topping	480	27	10	130	840	29	2	7	3	29
Chicken Pot Pie with Leeks, Carrots, and Croissant Topping For Two	710	41	15	200	1260	44	3	11	4	44
Lattice-Topped Chicken Pot Pie with Spring Vegetables	450	25	11	145	840	31	3	4	0	29
Lattice-Topped Chicken Pot Pie with Spring Vegetables for Two	760	43	19	240	1040	57	5	6	0	46
Arroz con Pollo	560	27	6	120	1200	48	3	4	0	27
Arroz con Pollo for Two	280	14	3	60	650	24	1	2	0	13
Chicken Biryani	560	19	9	160	850	58	2	10	0	38
Tinga de Pollo	480	21	4.5	150	690	38	4	7	0	37
Tinga de Pollo for Two	480	21	4.5	150	710	38	4	7	0	37
Braised Steaks with Root Vegetables	460	18	5	115	680	29	6	7	0	40
Keema Aloo	460	18	5	115	680	29	6	7	0	40
Keema Aloo for Two	230	13	3.5	50	400	12	2	3	0	17
Smothered Pork Chops	350	19	5	75	550	19	4	5	0	26
with Cider and Apples	320	11	4	70	550	27	2	19	0	27
Smothered Pork Chops for Two	250	11	4	70	680	9	1	3	0	27
Mapo Tofu	270	15	2.5	25	850	9	1	2	0	19
Italian-Style Sausage and Pepper Subs	580	23	7	50	1520	62	3	14	0	37
Italian-Style Sausage and Pepper Subs for Two	570	22	7	50	1520	60	2	13	0	37
Perfect Poached Fish	380	23	5	95	390	1	0	0	0	35
Perfect Poached Salmon with Bourbon and Maple	450	26	7	100	540	10	0	9	9	35
Perfect Poached Fish for Two	380	23	5	95	390	1	0	0	0	35
Herb-Yogurt Sauce	10	0.5	0	0	5	1	0	1	0	1
Yogurt-Tahini Sauce	35	3	0.5	0	5	2	0	0	0	1
Tzatziki	20	1.5	1	0	40	0	0	0	0	1
Spicy Avocado-Sour Cream Sauce	40	3.5	2	10	30	2	0	1	0	1
Horseradish-Sour Cream Sauce	20	1.5	1	5	150	1	0	1	0	0

	Cal	Total Fat (g)	Sat Fat (g)	Chol (mg)	Sodium (mg)	Carbs (g)	Fiber (g)	Tot Sugar (g)	Added Sugar (g)	Protein (g)
Chapter Two: Simmer, Braise, and Poach (cont.)										
Rémoulade	60	7	1	5	85	1	0	0	0	0
Braised Halibut with Leeks and Mustard	370	19	11	130	740	8	1	2	0	32
Braised Halibut with Leeks and Mustard for Two	370	19	11	130	740	8	1	2	0	32
Chraime	290	12	2	90	930	14	3	6	0	31
Shrimp and Grits with Andouille	490	24	13	180	1520	38	3	8	0	30
Shrimp and Grits with Andouille for Two	490	24	13	180	1520	38	3	8	0	30
Kousa Mihshi	610	40	12	55	1320	46	7	20	0	21
Madras Okra Curry	250	22	8	0	125	13	4	4	2	3
Braised Eggplant with Pomegranate and Tahini	160	8	1	0	760	21	4	12	0	3
Spring Vegetable Risotto with Leek and Radishes	570	26	11	45	1250	68	7	6	0	19
Cauliflower and Bean Paella	380	13	1.5	0	1190	57	9	6	0	12
Cauliflower and Bean Paella for Two	420	16	2	0	1140	57	9	6	0	12
Lentilles du Puy with Spinach and Crème Fraîche	240	9	4	20	650	24	5	4	0	11
Chapter Three: Pan-Roast and Bake										
Pan-Roasted Chicken Breasts with Coriander, Fennel, and Lemon	380	24	6	115	580	1	0	0	0	38
with Herbes de Provence	380	24	6	115	580	1	0	0	0	38
Pan-Roasted Chicken Breasts with Coriander, Fennel, and Lemon for Two	570	36	9	175	870	1	1	0	0	57
Pan-Roasted Chicken Parts	320	18	5	115	310	1	1	0	0	38
Baharat-Spiced Pan-Roasted Chicken Parts	320	18	5	115	310	1	1	0	0	38
Pan-Roasted Chicken Parts for Two	490	28	7	175	460	0	0	0	0	57
Skillet-Roasted Chicken Breasts with Garlic-Ginger Broccoli	360	19	5	115	610	7	3	2	0	41
Skillet-Roasted Chicken Breasts with Garlic-Ginger Broccoli for Two	540	28	8	175	920	10	4	3	0	62
Harissa-Rubbed Chicken Thighs with Charred Cucumber and Carrot Salad	320	20	3	105	670	10	3	5	0	24
Couscous-Stuffed Chicken Thighs with Roasted Cherry Tomatoes and Shallots	390	18	3.5	185	1030	15	2	3	0	42
Weeknight Roast Chicken	400	29	8	130	680	0	0	0	0	33
with Sage and Fenugreek	430	31	8	130	690	3	1	0	0	34
Weeknight Roast Jerk Chicken	420	29	8	130	680	5	1	3	3	33
Honey-Rosemary Roast Chicken and Root Vegetables	480	25	6	110	1050	26	6	14	5	37
Roasted Herb Chicken under a Brick with Potatoes	510	32	8	130	750	19	2	2	0	35
Enchiladas Verdes	600	31	9	120	1050	42	4	12	2	42
Enchiladas Verdes for Two	600	31	9	120	1050	42	4	12	2	42

	Cal	Total Fat (g)	Sat Fat (g)	Chol (mg)	Sodium (mg)	Carbs (g)	Fiber (g)	Tot Sugar (g)	Added Sugar (g)	Protein (g)
Chapter Three: Pan-Roast and Bake (cont.)										
Maple-Glazed Pork Tenderloins	250	6	1	75	850	21	0	17	17	24
Pomegranate-Glazed Pork Tenderloins	240	5	1	75	640	24	0	18	18	24
Pan-Roasted Pork Tenderloins with Endive, Cherries, and Hazelnut Brittle	470	24	9	140	850	24	7	13	4	40
Pan-Roasted Pork Tenderloin with Endives, Cherries, and Hazelnut Brittle for Two	470	24	9	140	850	24	7	13	4	40
Herbed Roast Pork Loin with Asparagus	460	26	12	165	660	8	4	3	0	46
Pan-Roasted Fish Fillets	170	4.5	0	75	380	1	0	1	1	30
Miso-Marinated Pan-Roasted Fish Fillets	220	6	0.5	75	400	9	0	7	5	31
Pan-Roasted Fish Fillets for Two	170	4.5	0	75	380	1	0	1	1	30
Salsa Verde	100	10	1.5	0	75	2	0	0	0	1
Chermoula	70	7	1	0	0	1	0	0	0	0
Green Olive, Almond, and Orange Relish	60	6	0.5	0	60	2	0	0	0	1
Sun-Dried Tomato and Basil Relish	40	4	0.5	0	5	1	0	0	0	0
Tangerine-Ginger Relish	15	0.5	0	0	0	3	0	2	0	0
Mango-Mint Salsa	20	1	0	0	10	3	0	0	0	0
Pistachio-Crusted Salmon with Beet, Orange, and Avocado Salad	690	47	9	95	770	31	12	15	0	40
Prosciutto-Wrapped Cod with Crispy Polenta and Roasted Red Pepper Relish	480	19	2.5	95	1270	34	2	5	0	42
Prosciutto-Wrapped Cod with Crispy Polenta and Roasted Red Pepper Relish for Two	480	19	2.5	95	1270	34	2	5	0	42
French Onion White Bean Bake	550	27	9	40	1380	49	9	7	1	26
French Onion White Bean Bake for Two	550	27	9	40	1380	49	9	7	1	26
Skillet Tomato Cobbler	220	14	7	25	400	22	2	6	2	3
Skillet Spanakopita	620	29	16	175	1300	62	5	4	0	28
Savory Dutch Baby with Burrata, Prosciutto, and Arugula	460	27	8	215	660	36	0	3	0	20
Cast-Iron Pan Pizza	660	31	13	60	1460	64	2	5	0	28
with Taleggio, Mushrooms, and Scallion	770	40	16	80	1610	66	3	5	0	35
with Pepperoni, Pickled Peppers, and Honey	710	35	15	70	1740	68	2	7	3	30
Chapter Four: Griddle and Fry										
Cheddar-Crusted Grilled Cheese	550	42	23	110	890	21	1	4	0	21
with Tomato	550	42	23	110	960	22	1	4	0	21
with Bacon and Pepper Jelly	660	42	24	115	1100	47	1	30	0	24
Roast Beef Panini with Tangy Coleslaw	510	28	10	80	1690	35	1	4	2	29
Turkey Panini with Pickled Fennel and Apple	410	16	6	65	1290	38	1	14	0	28
Ham Antipasto Panini	570	28	10	85	2190	40	0	2	0	33

	Cal	Total Fat (g)	Sat Fat (g)	Chol (mg)	Sodium (mg)	Carbs (g)	Fiber (g)	Tot Sugar (g)	Added Sugar (g)	Protein (g)
Chapter Four: Griddle and Fry (cont.)										
Shaved Steak Sandwiches	930	45	18	200	1920	55	1	12	0	71
Shaved Steak Sandwiches for Two	930	45	18	200	1920	55	1	12	0	71
Smashed Burgers	700	53	14	100	830	25	0	6	0	28
Crispy California Turkey Burgers	660	38	9	70	1030	44	4	6	0	39
Crispy California Turkey Burgers for Two	660	38	9	70	1030	44	4	6	0	39
Hearty Quesadillas with Chicken, Mushrooms, and Poblanos	700	41	15	125	1360	41	1	4	0	45
with Shrimp, Roasted Red Peppers, and Cilantro	620	38	14	120	1590	42	1	5	0	28
Hearty Quesadillas with Chicken, Mushrooms, and Poblanos for Two	720	41	15	130	1370	41	1	4	0	48
Cheese Pupusas	530	27	13	65	960	56	9	7	1	24
Okonomiyaki	480	34	10	125	960	31	2	7	3	12
Shrimp Okonomiyaki	300	12	2	165	1030	32	2	7	3	15
Kimchi Jeon	360	21	1.5	0	1630	34	1	18	17	8
Crispy Pan-Fried Chicken Cutlets	300	13	12	115	390	15	0	1	0	29
Crispy Pan-Fried Chicken Milanese Cutlets	310	14	2.5	115	430	15	0	1	0	29
Crispy Pan-Fried Chicken Cutlets for Two	470	21	3.5	215	550	23	0	1	0	44
Cast-Iron Oven-Fried Chicken	490	27	6	165	1250	16	0	0	0	42
Cast-Iron Oven-Fried Chicken for Two	730	41	12	265	1780	23	0	0	0	63
Crispy Salmon Cakes with Frisée and Celery Salad	520	42	6	80	490	4	2	1	0	30
Crispy Salmon Cakes with Frisée and Celery Salad for Two	520	42	6	80	490	4	2	1	0	30
Tacos Dorados	640	41	8	65	970	49	3	7	0	26
Tacos Dorados for Two	640	41	8	65	970	49	3	7	0	26
Tofu Katsu Sandwiches	490	24	3	0	1020	50	2	11	4	17
Tofu Katsu Sandwiches for Two	490	24	3	0	1020	50	2	11	4	17
Ta'ameya with Tahini-Yogurt Sauce	390	16	3.5	50	860	48	8	10	0	18
Chapter Five: Pasta and Noodles										
Pasta with Simple Tomato Sauce	460	13	1.5	0	670	77	7	11	0	14
Pasta with Creamy Tomato Sauce	610	26	13	60	930	78	7	12	0	21
Pasta with Meaty Tomato Sauce	490	10	2.5	15	990	78	7	11	0	23
Pasta with Simple Tomato Sauce for Two	460	13	1.5	0	680	77	7	11	0	14
Spaghetti all'Assassina	580	27	3.5	0	1210	72	5	8	1	12
Shrimp Scampi with Campanelle	610	17	2.5	215	700	67	3	2	0	34
Pearl Couscous with Chorizo and Chickpeas	860	29	8	0	1620	117	9	21	0	35

	Cal	Total Fat (g)	Sat Fat (g)	Chol (mg)	Sodium (mg)	Carbs (g)	Fiber (g)	Tot Sugar (g)	Added Sugar (g)	Protein (g)
Chapter Five: Pasta and Noodles (cont.)										
Tortellini with Fennel, Peas, and Spinach	650	28	14	105	1520	68	4	9	0	31
Tortellini with Fennel, Peas, and Spinach for Two	680	31	16	115	1510	68	4	9	0	31
Crispy Gnocchi with Shredded Brussels Sprouts and Gorgonzola	430	28	11	35	940	37	5	9	4	12
Crispy Gnocchi with Shredded Brussels Sprouts and Gorgonzola for Two	430	28	11	35	940	37	5	9	4	12
Cheesy Stuffed Shells	510	21	11	105	780	57	2	9	1	25
Simple Stovetop Macaroni and Cheese	510	22	9	45	870	54	0	5	0	25
Simple Stovetop Macaroni and Cheese for Two	570	29	10	45	1150	54	0	5	0	25
Ground Beef Stroganoff	640	32	11	150	1250	52	1	6	0	33
Tuna Noodle Casserole	490	25	13	125	490	40	1	6	0	27
Scallion Oil Noodles	750	41	4	185	2300	74	7	12	6	19
Singapore Noodles	360	18	2	85	750	34	2	6	3	15
Singapore Noodles for Two	600	34	4	125	1130	50	4	10	5	23
Bún Chả	400	17	6	55	850	45	2	9	7	18
Bún Chả for Two	610	25	9	80	1280	68	2	13	11	27
Sopa Seca	550	30	7	25	1740	57	7	7	0	12
Sopa Seca for Two	550	30	7	25	1740	57	7	7	0	12
Chapter Six: Eggs and Breakfast										
Perfect Fried Eggs	220	18	6	380	430	1	0	0	0	13
Chili-Garlic Fried Eggs	220	18	6	380	430	1	0	0	0	13
Cumin-Caraway Fried Eggs	220	18	6	380	430	1	0	0	0	13
Creamy French-Style Scrambled Eggs	140	10	3	370	430	1	0	0	0	13
Creamy French-Style Scrambled Eggs for Two	140	10	3	370	430	1	0	0	0	13
Menemen	330	28	7	290	680	8	2	4	0	13
Menemen for Two	330	28	7	290	820	8	2	4	0	13
Cheddar and Chive Omelet	390	30	14	605	530	1	0	1	0	25
Kale, Feta, and Sun-Dried Tomato Omelet	440	31	15	605	760	16	3	1	0	26
Ham, Pear, and Brie Omelet	470	34	17	630	1150	8	1	5	0	31
Broccoli and Feta Frittata	240	17	7	390	530	5	1	3	0	17
Shiitake Mushroom and Pecorino Frittata	240	16	6	385	510	7	2	3	0	18
Broccoli and Feta Frittata for Two	360	25	10	585	940	9	2	4	0	26

	Cal	Total Fat (g)	Sat Fat (g)	Chol (mg)	Sodium (mg)	Carbs (g)	Fiber (g)	Tot Sugar (g)	Added Sugar (g)	Protein (g)
Chapter Six: Eggs and Breakfast (cont.)										
Huevos Rancheros	270	17	2.5	185	1470	23	3	8	0	10
All-American Breakfast Sandwiches	600	41	15	275	990	31	0	3	0	25
All-American Bacon and Cheddar Breakfast Sandwiches	660	50	20	270	870	29	0	1	0	23
All-American Breakfast Sandwiches for Two	600	41	15	275	990	31	0	3	0	25
Breakfast Burritos with Chorizo and Crispy Potatoes	940	62	20	405	2170	56	1	5	0	40
with Poblano, Beans, Corn, and Crispy Potatoes	830	51	14	405	1760	64	2	5	0	29
Breakfast Burritos with Chorizo and Crispy Potatoes for Two	940	62	20	405	2170	56	1	5	0	40
Cast-Iron Deep-Dish Cheese Quiche	500	35	21	280	540	29	0	3	1	17
with Caramelized Onions, Porcini, and Gruyère	510	35	20	270	580	31	1	5	1	17
with Smoked Trout, Potatoes, and Dill	540	33	18	285	670	36	1	4	1	22
Easy Pancakes	340	14	2.5	70	440	44	0	9	6	9
Easy Pancakes for Two	510	21	3.5	100	660	65	0	14	9	13
French Toast Casserole	360	18	9	155	340	39	1	17	12	11
Better Hash Browns	240	9	0.5	0	200	33	0	0	0	4
Skillet Granola with Pecans	320	18	1.5	0	150	37	5	14	12	5
with Apricots and Walnuts	370	19	2	0	150	48	6	22	12	7
with Coconut and Chocolate	400	20	8	0	180	54	5	29	23	5
Chapter Seven: Small Plates and Side Dishes										
Warm Marinated Olives	260	28	3	0	730	0	0	0	0	0
with Artichokes and Feta	270	28	5	10	600	3	0	1	0	2
with Manchego and Roasted Garlic	330	33	9	25	500	0	0	0	0	6
Blistered Shishito Peppers	50	4.5	0	0	0	2	1	1	0	0
with Mint, Poppy Seeds, and Orange	50	5	0	0	95	2	1	1	0	0
Smoky Shishito Peppers with Espelette and Lime	50	5	0	0	200	2	1	1	0	0
Pork Potstickers	70	3	1	5	90	7	0	0	0	3
Crispy Vegetable Fritters	180	14	1	0	120	12	1	1	0	1
Cast-Iron Skillet Corn Dip	490	44	15	80	670	13	1	4	0	11
Baked Goat Cheese	140	10	4.5	10	440	8	2	4	0	6
Buffalo Chicken Dip with Spicy Monkey Bread	330	22	10	60	720	24	0	4	0	11

	Cal	Total Fat (g)	Sat Fat (g)	Chol (mg)	Sodium (mg)	Carbs (g)	Fiber (g)	Tot Sugar (g)	Added Sugar (g)	Protein (g)
Chapter Seven: Small Plates and Side Dishes (cont.)										
Loaded Beef Nachos	450	31	14	75	640	23	2	1	0	22
Braised Asparagus with Lemon and Chives	90	7	1	0	190	5	2	2	0	3
with Sherry Vinegar and Marjoram	90	7	1	0	190	5	2	2	0	3
with Orange and Tarragon	90	7	1	0	190	5	2	2	0	3
Skillet-Roasted Broccoli with Sesame and Orange Topping	140	13	2	0	120	6	3	1	0	3
with Parmesan and Black Pepper Topping	150	14	2.5	0	190	6	2	1	0	5
with Smoky Sunflower Seed Topping	140	13	2	0	120	6	2	1	0	4
Skillet-Roasted Brussels Sprouts with Pomegranate and Pistachios	180	14	2	0	115	11	3	4	0	3
with Gochujang and Sesame Seeds	150	13	2	0	125	7	3	2	0	3
with Lemon and Pecorino	150	13	2.5	5	190	6	3	2	0	3
Sautéed Cabbage with Parsley and Lemon	70	5	0.5	0	310	8	3	4	0	2
with Chile and Peanuts	70	1.5	0	0	180	11	3	6	1	3
Sautéed Red Cabbage with Bacon and Caraway	120	8	2.5	10	440	11	3	6	2	4
Skillet-Roasted Carrots with Smoky Spiced Almonds and Parsley	180	13	1.5	0	180	16	5	7	0	3
with Mustard Bread Crumbs and Chives	160	10	1.5	0	280	18	4	7	0	2
with Za'atar Bread Crumbs and Cilantro	150	10	1.5	0	180	17	5	7	0	2
Sautéed Mushrooms with Red Wine and Rosemary	80	3.5	2	10	230	8	1	3	0	4
with Mustard and Parsley	70	3.5	2	10	320	7	1	3	0	4
with Soy, Scallion, and Ginger	80	3.5	2	10	550	10	2	4	0	5
Whole Romanesco with Berbere and Yogurt-Tahini Sauce	280	23	5	5	230	15	5	6	0	9
Southern-Style Baby Lima Beans	270	11	4.5	15	1110	30	7	1	0	15
Black Beans and Rice	410	20	6	15	1130	47	3	1	0	9
Creamy Potatoes and Leeks	410	22	13	65	780	47	5	8	0	9
Hasselback Potato Casserole	400	18	8	40	730	44	4	3	0	18
Rustic Bread Stuffing	340	10	5	25	760	52	1	3	0	9
with Sausage and Fennel	380	13	5	35	900	53	1	4	0	13
with Apples and Cranberries	390	13	6	25	760	62	2	11	0	10

	Cal	Total Fat (g)	Sat Fat (g)	Chol (mg)	Sodium (mg)	Carbs (g)	Fiber (g)	Tot Sugar (g)	Added Sugar (g)	Protein (g)
Chapter Eight: Breads and Desserts										
Pan-Grilled Flatbreads	530	16	6	20	880	81	4	3	2	15
Pan-Grilled Honey-Chile Flatbreads	550	16	6	20	880	85	4	7	6	15
Corn Tortillas	80	2.5	0	0	260	14	1	0	0	2
Fluffy Dinner Rolls	180	9	6	40	260	20	0	3	2	4
Southern-Style Cornbread	300	19	7	70	370	29	3	4	3	5
Fresh-Corn Cornbread	320	19	7	70	360	35	3	5	3	6
Sweet-Potato Cornbread	340	19	7	70	370	38	3	6	3	6
Sticky Buns	450	19	8	60	360	63	2	33	32	7
Cast-Iron Brownie	480	22	8	70	220	73	2	50	44	6
Cast-Iron Chocolate Chip Cookie	500	24	15	90	380	66	1	42	41	5
Cast-Iron White Chocolate–Macadamia Cookie	510	27	14	95	390	60	1	37	30	6
Cast-Iron Peanut Butter–Bacon Cookie	470	22	13	95	480	60	0	36	30	7
Knafeh	530	32	20	100	720	45	0	23	20	12
Extra-Gooey Knafeh	540	32	19	95	680	45	0	23	20	13
Peach Cornmeal Upside-Down Cake	350	13	8	80	200	54	2	33	27	5
Lemon Soufflé	170	6	2.5	160	110	25	0	23	22	6
Apple Pandowdy	420	23	15	90	310	51	4	32	11	3
Strawberry-Rhubarb Crisp	410	11	7	30	260	75	2	51	48	3
Strawberry-Rhubarb Crisp for Two	410	11	7	30	260	75	2	51	48	3
Bananas Foster	680	34	21	150	110	78	2	68	38	7
Bananas Foster for Two	680	34	21	150	110	78	2	68	38	7
Roasted Pears with Dried Apricots and Pistachios	270	8	3.5	15	55	40	5	29	11	2
Roasted Apples with Dried Figs and Walnuts	260	9	3.5	15	55	37	4	29	11	2
Roasted Pears with Dried Apricots and Pistachios for Two	430	14	6	25	80	62	8	46	19	3

Conversions and Equivalents

Some say cooking is a science and an art. We would say that geography has a hand in it too. Flours and sugars manufactured in the United Kingdom and elsewhere will feel and taste different from those manufactured in the United States. So we cannot promise that the loaf of bread you bake in Canada or England will taste the same as a loaf baked in the States, but we can offer guidelines for converting weights and measures. We also recommend that you rely on your instincts when making our recipes. Refer to the visual cues provided.

The recipes in this book were developed using standard U.S. measures following U.S. government guidelines. The charts below offer equivalents for U.S. and metric measures. All conversions are approximate and have been rounded up or down to the nearest whole number.

Example

1 teaspoon = 4.9292 milliliters, rounded up to 5 milliliters
1 ounce = 28.3495 grams, rounded down to 28 grams

Volume Conversions

U.S.	Metric
1 teaspoon	5 milliliters
2 teaspoons	10 milliliters
1 tablespoon	15 milliliters
2 tablespoons	30 milliliters
¼ cup	59 milliliters
⅓ cup	79 milliliters
½ cup	118 milliliters
¾ cup	177 milliliters
1 cup	237 milliliters
1¼ cups	296 milliliters
1½ cups	355 milliliters
2 cups (1 pint)	473 milliliters
2½ cups	591 milliliters
3 cups	710 milliliters
4 cups (1 quart)	0.946 liter
1.06 quarts	1 liter
4 quarts (1 gallon)	3.8 liters

Weight Conversions

Ounces	Grams
½	14
¾	21
1	28
1½	43
2	57
2½	71
3	85
3½	99
4	113
4½	128
5	142
6	170
7	198
8	227
9	255
10	283
12	340
16 (1 pound)	454

Converting Fahrenheit to Celsius

We include temperatures in some of the recipes in this book and we recommend an instant-read thermometer for the job. To convert Fahrenheit degrees to Celsius, use this simple formula:

Subtract 32 degrees from the Fahrenheit reading, then divide the result by 1.8 to find the Celsius reading. For example, to convert 160°F to Celsius:

160°F – 32 = 128°
128° ÷ 1.8 = 71.11°C
              rounded down to 71°C

Taking the Temperature of Meat

Whether cooking a burger or roasting a pork tenderloin, you should always take the temperature of the area of the meat that will be the last to finish cooking, which is the thickest part or, in some cases, the center. Bones conduct heat, so if the meat you are cooking contains bone, make sure that the thermometer is not touching it. For roasts, take more than one reading to confirm you're at the right point of doneness.

Since the temperature of meat will continue to rise as it rests, an effect called carryover cooking, meat should be removed from the pan or oven when it's 5 to 10 degrees below the desired serving temperature. Carryover cooking doesn't apply to poultry and fish (they don't retain heat as well as the dense muscle structure in meat), so they should be cooked to the desired serving temperatures. These temperatures should be used to determine when to stop the cooking process.

	Cook It Until It Registers
Beef/Lamb	
Rare	115 to 120 degrees
Medium-Rare	120 to 125 degrees
Medium	130 to 135 degrees
Medium-Well	140 to 145 degrees
Well-Done	150 to 155 degrees
Pork	
Pork Chops and Pork Loins	140 to 145 degrees
Pork Tenderloins	135 to 140 degrees

Pasta Shapes and Volume Measurements

For recipes where the pasta cooks right in the sauce, as they do in our skillet pasta recipes, the ratio of pasta to cooking liquid is critical to success. As the pasta cooks at a vigorous simmer, it absorbs the majority of the liquid and the rest reduces to a saucy consistency. Therefore, if you use more pasta than called for, there won't be enough liquid to cook it through. Conversely, if you use less, the resulting sauce will be too thin or soupy. Also, pay close attention to the shape of pasta called for in each recipe; different pasta shapes and sizes have slightly different cooking times and, therefore, not all shapes are interchangeable. The best method for measuring pasta is to weigh it using a scale. However, if you do not own a scale, we have provided the equivalent cup measurements for various shapes. Use dry measuring cups for the most accurate measurements, and pack them full.

Pasta Type	4 Ounces	6 Ounces	8 Ounces
Elbow Macaroni and Small Shells	1 cup	1½ cups	2 cups
Penne, Ziti, and Campanelle	1¼ cups	2 cups	2½ cups
Rigatoni, Rotini, Fusilli, Medium Shells, and Wide Egg Noodles	1½ cups	2⅓ cups	3 cups
Farfalle	1⅔ cups	2½ cups	3⅓ cups

*These amounts do not apply to whole-wheat pasta.

When 6, 8, or 12 ounces of uncooked strand pasta or noodles are bunched together into a tight circle, the diameter measures about 1⅛ inches, 1¼ inches, or 1¾ inches respectively.

Index

Note: Page references in *italics* indicate photographs.